306
B 397a

W9-BMC-687

ALSO BY JOHN BECKMAN

*The Winter Zoo*

# American Fun

# American Fun

### FOUR CENTURIES OF
### JOYOUS REVOLT

## John Beckman

PANTHEON BOOKS
NEW YORK

Grateful acknowledgment is made to Alfred Music
Publishing for permission to reprint an excerpt from
"Let's Misbehave" (from *Paris*), words and music by
Cole Porter, copyright © 1927 (Renewed) by WB Music
Corp. Reprinted by permission of Alfred Music Publishing.
All rights reserved.

Library of Congress Cataloging-in Publication Data
Beckman, John.
American fun : four centuries of joyous revolt /
John Beckman.
pages cm
ISBN 978-0-307-90817-9 (hardcover)
ISBN 978-0-307-90818-6 (eBook)
1. United States—Social life and customs. 2. Amusements—
United States—History. 3. Popular culture—
United States—History. I. Title.
E161.B43 2014 306.0973—dc23 2013021015

www.pantheonbooks.com

Jacket design by Pablo Delcán

Printed in the United States of America
First Edition

2 4 6 8 9 7 5 3 1

*For Marcela*

There's something wild
About you, child,
That's so contagious,
Let's be outrageous,
Let's misbehave.

—COLE PORTER,
"Let's Misbehave"

# Contents

# *Introduction*

On April 15, 1923, eight marathon dancers, aged nineteen to twenty-eight, outran the law for a chance to make history. For twenty-nine hours straight, as weaker contestants limped off the floor, they had twirled and swung each other's bodies to the fox-trot, two-step, and bunny hug. At midnight, New York police enforced a law that put a twelve-hour cap on marathon activities. They ordered the kids to cease and desist, but the dancers wanted none of it. They danced en masse out the doors of the Audubon Ballroom, across the 168th Street sidewalk, and into the back of an idling van. They danced in the van's jumpy confines all the way to the Edgewater ferry, on whose decks they danced across the choppy Hudson, before being portaged like a cage of exotic birds and released into New Jersey's Pekin dance hall.

They had been there only an hour when more cops shoved them along, and so it would go for the next two days. The venues kept changing, and the comedy mounting, as they crossed and recrossed the tri-state lines, cheerfully dancing all the while. They shed a few compatriots to squirrelly exhaustion and gave reporters a private audience in an undisclosed Harlem apartment. Back in the van, they cut fantastic steps on their way to Connecticut, where the contest would reach its strange conclusion.

The *New York Times,* filing updates as the events unfolded, struck a distinctly American tone: they touted the dancers as the pinnacle of youth—of vigor, ambition, free expression—calling them "heroes and heroines . . . alive with the spirit of civic pride." But they scorned the cops as "mean old thing[s]" who should have been ashamed of enforcing "meddlesome old laws." As tensions mounted they framed a rivalry between the upstart "West" and the noble "East." (Dancers from Cleveland had set the record only a few days before.) The upshot of all this ballyhoo, of course, was that the reporters took none of it too seriously. The *Times* just wanted to join the party and to let their readers join it too.

But their patriotism wasn't all tongue-in-cheek. Youthful antics in the 1920s were often held up as national virtues. Alma Cummings, who had set the first dance-marathon record that March, was honored with the "Star-Spangled Banner." Avon O. Foreman, a fifteen-year-old flagpole sitter, was recognized in 1929 by the mayor of Baltimore for showing "the pioneer spirit of early America." In an era when Prohibition had divided the country and the KKK had nearly five million members, the splashy high jinks of free-spirited youths were for many a welcome vision of good-natured resistance. They called to mind the Sons of Liberty—or Huck Finn lighting out to the territory.

Things got weird in the marathon's endgame. At two o'clock on Sunday morning, when the van arrived at an athletic club in East Port Chester, judges disqualified two of the last four contestants for sleeping in transit, leaving Vera Sheppard, nineteen, and Ben Solar, twenty-three, to rally for the record. At 8 a.m. Solar broke away from Sheppard and "wandered aimlessly toward the door, like a sleep-walker." Smelling salts revived him for precisely two minutes. When he collapsed, and was out, the ever-vigorous Sheppard—performing "better than at any time during the night"—galloped on with a series of relief partners. The good citizens of Connecticut, fearing for her health, or maybe her soul, had police stop the madness at 3:30 p.m. Only with special permission was she allowed to dance past four o'clock, at which point she demolished the world record. "Miss Sheppard's condition at the close," the *Times* reported, "was surprisingly good." She had also lost a cool ten pounds.

Vera Sheppard wasn't your typical rebel. An office worker from Long Island City, she lived at home with her father and two sisters and gave dance lessons most nights till twelve. She wasn't even your typical flapper. But when her sisters attributed her endurance to prayer and the fact that she didn't drink or smoke, Sheppard preferred to answer for herself. Showing all-American pride in her ethnic difference, she told reporters: "I'm Irish; do you suppose I could have stuck it out otherwise?" What kept her going for sixty-nine hours was "thinking what good fun it was."

Sheppard liked to dance, and she was willing to risk it if what she liked was against the law. More to the point, she *enjoyed* those risks. But her Jazz Age "fun" wasn't just the boon of a wealthy country at the height of its powers. It wasn't even a whirl on Coney Island's Loop-the-Loop. Her cheeky dance across three state lines, as pure and innocent as it seemed, was underwritten by centuries of studied rebellion that made it quintessentially American. Sheppard and her cheering section at the *Times* were heirs to a raffish national tradition that flaunted pleasure in the face of authority.

This book traces the lines of that tradition.

AMERICAN HISTORY GIVES US one good brawl after another. Indians fought Pilgrims; pirates bullied merchants; Patriots bloodied Redcoats' noses; slaves outwitted, sometimes butchered their masters; and hot young peppers—from Kentucky backwoodsmen to Bowery b'hoys, to greasers, break-dancers, and Riot Grrrls—declared civil war on a mincing middle class that wanted them to fall in line. "Hell, no!" Americans have always said—and such is the kernel of the national identity.

So how has such a tumultuous public, historically riven by deep social differences (class division, racial prejudice, partisan politics, culture wars) *ever* gathered in peaceable activity, let alone done it time and again? The answer is by having fun—often outrageous, even life-threatening fun. This enduring pursuit, so popular with Americans, can make even the scariest social differences exciting; it can bring even the bitterest adversaries into a state of feverous harmony. For conflict is the active ingredient in fun. Risk, transgression, mockery, rebellion—these are the revving motors of fun. True, wild fun can be downright criminal: the pirate's joy in plundering and murder, the gangster's joy in disturbing the peace—and such violent kinds of self-serving fun have sometimes put our democracy in peril. But all throughout American history the people have also proven to be radically civil—not too polite, not so clean, but practicing a rough-and-tumble respect for *other* people's fun. At even the diciest moments in history the people's rebellion has *strengthened* democracy. It has allowed the people to form close bonds in spite of prejudices, rivalries, and laws.

The scuffles and clashes depicted in this book follow a striking pattern. A group of rebels, usually much rowdier than Vera Sheppard's crew, takes joy in resisting a stern ruling class and entices the people to follow its lead. In many of these cases, inspired by the rebels' good humor and daring, the people take to reveling in the same bad behaviors (or demographic or ethnic differences) for which the group was originally repressed. Such good-natured combat gives a twofold pleasure. On the one hand, its "fun" (in the word's seventeenth-century sense) is the pleasure of mocking the ruling class for its unjust sanctions and small-minded rigidity. It's the fun of breaking the master's laws. On the other hand, in the word's eighteenth-century sense—of Samuel Johnson's "sport, high merriment, and frolicsome delight"—it's the fun of pranks, lewd dances, wild parties, and tough competitions that unites the crowd in common joy. It's the fun of eluding laws *together,* in playful, active, comical ways that often model good citizenship.


VERA SHEPPARD'S VICTORY—over ministers, over magistrates, over the American Society of Teachers of Dancing, who declared marathons "a disgrace to the art and profession of dancing"—inspired countless others to jump into the game, to push their limits in the name of silliness. Dance marathons peaked in the Great Depression (despite grim portrayals like Horace McCoy's *They Shoot Horses, Don't They?*), and they provided a vibrant public space for folks of all races, classes, and politics to duke it out on the dance floor. During this golden age of the movie theater, when audiences sat rank and file in the dark, die-hard marathons kept citizens participating.

Sheppard's little victory, harmless as it was, called up centuries of American rebels who had only wanted to unite the people, even as they stirred them up. These fun-loving troublemakers, as this book will show, reveled in defying authority's laws and limits. Obstacles only got them excited. Obstacles gave them something to work with. For beyond these obstacles, as many of them discovered, was a luscious frontier of liberty and equality.

As early as the 1620s, when the Pilgrims left free-and-easy Holland to build their fortress of cold austerity, a radical democrat named Thomas Morton, schooled in English Renaissance hedonism, founded Merry Mount thirty miles to the north and devoted himself and his band of rogues to all of the excesses outlawed at Plymouth. They drank and danced and consorted with the Massachusetts. Their May Day revels, and the showdown to follow, put New World fun in high relief: there was freedom to be found in the wilderness, but you had to be ready to fight for it.

The Pilgrims won, as we know, and their Puritan cousins swarmed in by the thousands, founding an empire on the Calvinist belief that people were fundamentally depraved. Folks were whipped, maimed, and executed just for following their carnal whims. If Puritans condoned anything close to carnival, it took the form of violent orgies like the tarring-and-featherings where the common folk did the minister's dirty work. Otherwise, throughout much of early New England, people limited their public gatherings to the stone-cold-sober meetinghouse, where they sat through often terrifying lessons in obedience, piety, and self-restraint.

Waterfront taverns were the Puritans' scourge. It was out of these taverns, where Jack Tars and dockworkers and bare-shouldered women stomped to the jigs of African-American fiddlers, that the earliest tremors of the American Revolution first rattled New England's top-down society. Radical politicians like James Otis and Samuel Adams (against the wishes of his snobbish cousin John) courted this salty counterculture and tapped their love of rebellious fun as a sensible way to bring down the British. To be sure, in the 1760s and 1770s, it wasn't musket balls and cannonballs but pranks, mockery, satire, and *snow*balls that set the tone for the early republic. Then as now, the Sons of Liberty—burning puppets, dressing as Mohawks, staging citywide practical jokes—hold high honors in the national imagination. Their antics taught disgruntled subjects how to act like citizens.

In the laid-back antebellum South, the land of mint juleps and hootenannies, public pleasure rarely caused much fuss. This aristocratically minded social system turned a kinder eye on fun. But even as members of the slave-owning élite, kicking back on their wraparound porches, reveled in the songs and marvelous dances that emanated from the slave quarters—sometimes even stepping down themselves to stamp a foot or give it a whirl—the vicious injustice that preserved their feudal lifestyles was shaping the practices of African-American fun. Intensely athletic, erotic dances struck a rough balance between old African styles and strictly enforced Methodist prohibitions. Jokes and folktales lampooned the master while teaching the people to maximize their pleasures. Even backbreaking work like cornshucking generated a repertoire of songs, games, celebrations, and jokes that asserted the slaves' humanity and freedom. Such technologies of antebellum black fun, born of resistance and the thirst for liberty, laid the infrastructure for several of America's most powerful rebel cultures: early jazz, rock 'n' roll, funk, rap, step, and so on. The will to rebel, combined with a hedonistic will to gather, made for a heady social cocktail that perennially has energized the national youth scene.

While young Vera Sheppard, of strong Irish stock, crossed state borders in the back of a van, her arm on the shoulder of an older man, the "talking machine" grinding King Oliver rolls, she didn't waste a single thought on her Puritan forebears, her revolutionary forefathers, her African-American benefactors. Of course she didn't—she was caught up in the act. Nor should she have bothered to thank her antecedents on the nineteenth-century frontier. All the same, the Wild West, with its love of the new and thirst for adventure and contempt for limits of any kind, was the great test kitchen for what Sheppard rightfully tossed off as "fun." In the half century following the Revolutionary War, as cities grew fractious, overcrowded, and dirty, the Puritans' lessons of separation and restraint came in handy when corralling a runaway U.S. population. These lessons inspired customs, codes, and laws for keeping the people, like horses, in paddocks: taverns were shuttered, theaters scrubbed up, and democracy-drunk Bowery b'hoys were eventually kept in check. At the same time, however, a rude and rugged class of argonauts chomped at the bit, bucked the saddle, and struck out for a land of fortune and danger where they could make their own civil society from scratch. Out West—from the rawest mining camps to San Francisco's Barbary Coast—Aunt Sally's starchy modes of "sivility" were ridiculed, razzed, perverted, eschewed, and supplanted with a basic love of fun. From famous humorists like Mark Twain and Dan De Quille down to anonymous jokers in disreputable saloons, these foul-mouthed rogues and seeming reprobates were in fact the innovators of a pleasure-based society where drinking, gambling, dancing, and pranks worked much better than vigilantes and religion to keep, more or less, the general peace.

The Wild West hit the mainstream in the 1920s. Average citizens packed into speakeasies, calling themselves the "Wild Wets." Reviving the memory of Thomas Morton at Merry Mount, folks flaunted a host of Puritan taboos in the face of the majority's "Dry Crusade." The spores and seeds of early black folk culture flourished, nationwide, in the so-called Harlem Renaissance. All of it emboldened even good girls like Sheppard. She didn't drink or smoke or gamble, but she didn't mind bending a few blue laws to have a bit of fun.

THERE'S A REASON WHY, until now, we haven't had a history of fun. The word itself is too easily conflated with its sorry impostors, "entertainment," "recreation," and "leisure." Look up "fun" in the *American Heritage Dictionary,* and the first two definitions involve passive "amusement." Only definition three touches the subject of this book: "playful, often noisy, activity."

"Play" is not synonymous with "fun." If "play" can be defined as sport or jest, "fun" is the pleasure one gets from this. Johan Huizinga implies this key distinction in *Homo Ludens* (1938), his seminal book on play's "civilizing function." He accepts "enjoyment" as a key incentive to play but then argues that play becomes serious, even disinterested, once the player gets caught up in the game. It is this bloodless sense of "play"—play that has been scoured of all messy pleasure—that Huizinga elevates to civic behavior in which play is no longer play as we know it but a simulacrum he calls the "play-element"—a practice as germane to business and law as it would be to running a touchdown. Examining play's rules, not its unmanageable spirit, Huizinga reasons that play "creates order, *is* order. Into an imperfect world and into the confusion of life it brings a temporary, a limited perfection. Play demands order absolute and supreme." He misses out on all the fun, however, when he exclaims that "the *fun* of playing resists all analysis, all logical interpretation" and for this reason, "as a concept, it cannot be reduced to any other mental category." As an idea, fun is fundamentally elusive. It is intractable, illogical, irreducible, but this is precisely why it is an element of "play" that remains worthy of close investigation. Huizinga adds "in passing" that "it is precisely this fun-element that characterizes the essence of play," but from here on out he treats "fun" (when at all) as play's *least* serious feature, "merely" fun, "only for fun," "make believe," and so on.

Huizinga dismisses "fun" from the start, but not before making the useful observation that "no other modern language known to [him] has the exact equivalent of the English 'fun.'" What is more, while "fun" is unique to the English language, it holds a special place in the *American* lexicon, where it is a word and concept that, for all its difficulty, has come to reflect our national values. Indeed, in late 2010, *New York Times* columnist Anand Giridharadas employed a powerful database of America's print history and determined that "achievement" and "fun" were the nation's most bountiful words, the use of "fun" increasing eightfold from the 1810s to the 2000s. Giridharadas addresses what he calls the "Fun Generation" and joins the loud chorus of American intellectuals who have long decried the value of fun, which he rightly says "comes from doing and, often, switching off the brain." He also draws a (rightful) contrast between elitist Old World pleasures and more "equitable" New World "fun" and rather seems to regret the contrast. (Couldn't Americans just relax, like Italians? And couldn't they be more reflective?) But this book contends that devalued American fun—"mere fun," "unthinking fun," the fun of what Giridharadas rejects as "doing, doing, doing"—has indeed had a "civilizing function," often a very powerful one.

Unlike the pleasures of watching and eating that have come to characterize the United States (often justifiably) as a nation of dull consumers, fun is one pleasure that can't be *felt*. Fun, like sex, must be *had*. Whether it's bantering, shooting the rapids, or playing charades, fun requires investment, engagement. It also makes you take some risks. It demands you have a bit of courage. Freud's famous "pleasure principle" refers to relaxation, vegetation, numbing away every last volt of stimulus. You can curl up lazily in the folds of such pleasure, but not so with fun. As the desire for excitement, to stir up stimulus, fun goes far "beyond the pleasure principle." To the extent that it runs a collision course, testing its velocity against total destruction, fun is closer to Freud's "death drive"—the desire to die that swerves from death. Like Charlie Chaplin in *Modern Times,* blindfolded, on roller skates, coasting backward, fun buzzes right up to the brink of destruction and glides away with a little thrill.

Fun is the active enjoyment of: stunts, pranks, hoaxes, jokes, mock trials, parties, troublemaking, dancing, protests, fights, and ad hoc games and gambling and sports. It's the discourse-disrupting thrill of slang. It's the joy of throwing your body into the mix, of raising your voice in the public sphere, and of putting your reputation at risk. In order to investigate such rowdy fun and to question how such "doing, doing, doing" has shaped American identity for the better, it is necessary to distinguish it from its impostor: the passive "fun" of entertainment.

Americans en masse confused "fun" with "entertainment" in the years right after the Civil War. In a sweeping campaign throughout the urban North, the amusement industry simulated the people's fun and marketed it for widespread entertainment—in the forms of big-top circuses, theme parks, carnivals, vaudeville, the burlesque, and Wild West shows. These shiny new products, whose avatars still abound from Disneyworld to Hollywood, from Rock Band to Wii, had the population suddenly standing in line and buying tickets to have their "fun." All at once it was a passive pursuit: performers were divided from spectators, who were increasingly divided by class and made to follow new rules of etiquette. Risk and rebellion were confined to the stage, where audiences had *vicarious* fun. Rodeos brought the frontier to the cities. Carnivals simulated low-level participation. Blackface minstrelsy, one of the industry's most popular features, twisted African-American culture into a cruel cartoon.

The best simulations of participatory fun were in Coney Island's "Fun Pavilion," where frightening rides like the "Insanitarium" automated thrills and spills. But fun's active ingredient, *liberty,* was gone.

Also in the aftermath of the Civil War, when the South was plunged into depression and chaos, average citizens of the industrializing North were going crazy for organized sports—not only for the expected baseball and football, but for croquet, lawn tennis, track and field, and many games that had been unheard-of even a decade before. Apart from the cyclists and rogue roller skaters who terrorized the sidewalks, such activity was easy to control—by parents, schools, associations, franchises, and, of course, commercial outfitters. Sports became big business. Sports also served to divide the public—by race, class, gender, and ability. Sports ranked citizens according to their talents and divided athletes from spectators in bleachers. In contrast to free-lance American fun, the marketing, organization, and regulation of sports strapped ankle weights onto the citizenry. It kept them from fending for themselves on sandlots, alleys, pickup courts, and scruffy patches of public grass.

The fun explored here originates with the people—playful, active, courageous people. When we turn over the keys to the Kool-Aid junkies, to the Barnums and Disneys who have branded "fun" since the Gilded Age, we tend to forget who invented it. We fail to see it when it's right under our noses, doing the good work of civil society. And we fail to see how powerful it can be. The Sons of Liberty weren't just amusing themselves—they were hammering out the structure of a new republic. The slaves on Congo Square weren't enjoying their "leisure"—they danced ring dances every Sunday to steal back some of their precious humanity. These would-be citizens weren't just bored, looking to be entertained. Their thirst for pleasure meant life or death. They wanted to function as full members of society, and their attempts to do so were crazy fun.

MUCH OF THE BEST AMERICAN FUN doesn't *aim* to be political. Forty-niners pulled pranks to get a laugh. Journalists staged hoaxes to get their readers' goat. Thousands swarmed into the Savoy Ballroom to mix it up with all walks of life. The friction these wags created was harmless, but friction nonetheless, challenging the people to enjoy their differences through laughter, competition, and dance. Even this story's least political funmakers are pranksters and dancers and rabble-rousers who ignited democratic feeling in the crowd and urged the people to fan its flames.

While most of the people's fun isn't meant to be political, at key points in history, like the Merry Mount colony or the early Revolution, citizens have harnessed the power of fun in an effort to lift the larger community—as in the early nineteenth century, throughout the Northeast, when African Americans held Election Day festivals that broadcast their desire to participate in society. But even when *American Fun* is telling the stories of apolitical funmakers—of dancers and jokers, of entrepreneurs and promoters—it never strays from its larger interest in the ongoing struggle for access to power, in the ongoing renovation of the public sphere: in a word, in politics.

Like Ralph Waldo Emerson scrawling "whim" on his lintel, thus giving playfulness religious import, so too have Americans long dignified fun with their other great national values—"progress," "self-reliance," and above all "democracy."

As James Madison established it in Federalist No. 10, one of the U.S. government's founding documents, a "pure democracy"—"a society consisting of a small number of citizens, who assemble and administer government in person"—can lead only to factionalism; it only indulges the body's "common passions"; and it offers "nothing to check the inducements to sacrifice the weaker party or an obnoxious individual." Since pure democracy (for the Federalists) inevitably crumbled into mob rule or tyranny, the people's power had to be contained within what Madison called a "republic"—"a government in which the scheme of representation takes place." By Madison's plan, not unlike a parliamentary monarchy, the people's passion had to be triple-distilled and bottled in the shapes of judicious politicians. That is the government Americans got, and it has functioned pretty effectively ever since. But the people didn't give up that easily. For the American people are a feisty body, just as Madison feared. Whether taking inspiration from the early revolutionaries or simply trusting in their own "demos-kratia" (people power), historically Americans have unleashed their passions without ever needing to overthrow the government. They have lived peaceably enough under the roof of one republic, and in the best cases they have *enjoyed* each other's bad behavior. More to the point, that enjoyment has made them more powerful citizens.

Radical democracy can be fun only when the citizens cut loose and get involved. In order for a society to grow and thrive, its citizens must be willing to tussle. Even in our thickly mediated culture—where experience passes through screens big and small; where communication is texted and tweeted; where play plays out on keyboards and consoles, triangulated between players on a video screen, often from points across the globe; where sex is had on pornsites and webcams; indeed, where citizenship is exercised through donation checks and in the privacy of voting booths—even in this sprawling culture of distance, classic fun remains *im*mediate: football, keggers, mosh pits, step; skateboarding, improv, political protest; hands-on, face-to-face, playful activities that require dexterity and a sense of goodwill to avoid the pitfalls of injury or shame.

In order for a society to enjoy its own power, to risk a few friendly collisions without descending into eye-gouging anarchy, it must have a radical sense of civility. Its citizens must be able to engage in rough play without losing sight of each other's pleasure. At the funnest moments in American history, citizens have done this exceptionally well. They have reveled in the law's gaps and shadows, all the while showing due respect for their neighbors' rights and happiness. They have turned social conflict into joyous upheaval and have strengthened the nation in the face of adversity. And so do we see the full measure of this subject. Fun is risky and rebellious for a reason. Fun is frivolous and silly with a purpose. The state may try to keep people apart, as it did for decades following *Plessy v. Ferguson.* Big Business may try to market thrills and get between the people and their fun, as George C. Tilyou did with Coney Island, as Nintendo ingeniously does with Wii. But the drive to get down, get dirty, *get real,* remains stronger than the rolling Mississippi.

..................

THE HISTORY OF AMERICAN FUN is in fact structured rather like the Mississippi. Its pure source water came bubbling up from a variety of early folk sources—from Merry Mount and the Revolution, from slave culture and the gold rush. These streams flowed strong during the Age of Jackson, when rowdy Americans embraced and practiced their heritage of pure folk fun—often to the horror of social reformers. Mixing and mingling in the antebellum decades, these streams combined into a national culture—of political fury, of black festivity, and of risky freedom on the wide frontier. This early American fun, born of much struggle, still flows strong in the national consciousness.

Like the Mississippi River on its southward journey, American fun's river has been strengthened and muddied by major tributaries along the way—three to be exact. Each one flows from its own cultural era; each one contributes its own political tint. The first joined the mainstream in the Gilded Age, when the people's rough and rebellious pleasures were simulated and packaged as commercial amusements; fun became spectacle and mechanized play, and the crowd was divided into actors and consumers. The second coursed in during the Jazz Age, when Sons of Liberty resistance became popular practice and the hothouse flowers of African-American folk culture inspired wide participation; disenfranchised groups—women and blacks and youth in general—made smart and creative and antic innovations to a newly energized public sphere. The third tributary flowed in the 1960s. Riding a rising tide of popular upheaval, blending an excitement for revolutionary-era rebellion with sex, drugs, rock, and pranks, a new generation of hedonistic rebels chose lacerating fun over apathy, consumerism, and violence.

These three tributaries—the commercial, playful, and radically political—keep flowing into our current Internet Age. They pour nutrients, pollutants, and sheer life-force into the great American gulf—which is to say, into the citizenry. They mix and mingle to make delightful hybrids—from commercially funded flash mobs to YouTube-fueled Rube Goldberg machines. They inspire the people to come together in marvelous ways, as in the blitzkrieg street theater of the Cacophony Society and Improv Everywhere. But so much contemporary American fun stays loyal to its heritage. To be sure, the latest innovations in popular entertainment—in 4-D movies, in millennial roller coasters, in the entire video game industry—are only perfections of the controlled participation that George C. Tilyou invented on Coney Island. By the same token, even the freshest pranks of the Occupy movement or of the ingenious pranksters, the Yes Men, hark back to the Yippies and the Diggers and, indeed, to the Sons of Liberty. In these you can taste the purest source water.

VERA SHEPPARD'S GRANDCHILDREN WERE the do-it-yourself teens of the 1970s and early 1980s. Fed up with gang violence and excluded from nightclubs, early hip-hop innovators jacked into streetlamps and reinvented pop culture on inner-city street corners. In a similar vein, hardcore punks, disgusted by Reagan-era New Traditionalism, founded a self-sufficient nation on the virtues of primitive rock 'n' roll. B-boys and B-girls fought for turf in the "cypher" with feats of acrobatic style. Hardcore punks from L.A. to Boston thrashed, bulldozed, and stage-dove in the mosh pit, unleashing their aggressions against corporate America in colliding, kicking, often bloody fury. B-boys and B-girls joined together as Zulu Nation; their motto was "Peace, Love, Unity, and Having Fun." The mosh pit had "anarchy" tattooed on its forehead. But as anarchic or criminal as it may have seemed—even to many of its young participants (not to mention the cops at the door)—the mosh pit perfected American democracy. Its raging conflict was totally consensual and held aloft by sacred rules.

In the history of American fun, B-boys and punks stand shoulder to shoulder with the earliest Patriots. For both generations freedom was more than an idea; it was a virtue to throw your whole body into. Patti Smith, a pioneer in New York's punk scene, felt the same duty to save the people's music that the Patriots felt to American liberty. Fearing it was "falling into fattened hands"—the hands of Capitol and EMI—she and her ragged CBGB crowd envisioned themselves "as the Sons of Liberty with a mission to preserve, protect and project the revolutionary spirit of rock and roll." As she remembers it, "We would call forth in our minds the image of Paul Revere, riding through the American night, petitioning the people to wake up, to take up arms. We would take up arms, the arms of our generation, the electric guitar and the microphone."

B-boys and punks, like revolutionary Patriots, exulted in their youth. Both generations strutted in primitive costumes that set their law-abiding elders' teeth on edge. Both invented do-it-yourself technologies—for publication, gathering, food, and shelter—that sidestepped corporations and the king, respectively. The Patriots had the likes of Samuel Adams and James Otis, leaders who inspired the lowliest dockworkers to believe they could form a republic of rough and active citizens. B-boys and B-girls were lightning-tongued MCs who honored the earliest black folk traditions—vocal, musical, fiercely athletic. Punks had insanely high-energy rock bands who inflamed their minds with a fierce new ethics—against commercialism, against race prejudice, against all that phony yuppie bullshit.

In past decades there's been a national explosion in bold, loud, political merriment. From anti–World Trade Organization rallies to gay pride parades to the range of ethnic holidays, identity groups from throughout the population have tapped into the nation's heritage of fun for ways to come together, be seen, and be heard. More than ever, despite a runaway entertainment industry that would keep the people warming its seats, Americans are deliberate about having their fun. For some, it's the civil way to rebel. For some—like the thousands at Burning Man or the Sturgis, South Dakota, Motorcycle Rally—rebellion is just the best reason to party.

But at a time when both the Boston Tea Party can be trademarked by drug companies and average citizens take on Wall Street, it is important to revisit the origins of rebellion. For even when the stakes were highest—for Patriots, for slaves, for forty-niners—the pioneers in American fun managed to keep the battle civil. Full of crazy punk-rock courage, they dove into the crowd with big bloody smiles and *surfed* the citizens' dangerous passion.

# American Fun

# The Forefather of American Fun

O N THE ELEVENTH DAY of the eleventh month in the year of
1620, forty-one men shuffled on the decks of a creaky cargo ship.
They had been bobbing for weeks within Cape Cod's fingertip; most of
them had not yet stepped foot on land. Despite three months of animos-
ity and sickness, they lined up to sign a binding social contract. The
signers represented less than half of the ship's passengers, and the majority were like-minded "Separatist" Pilgrims, but otherwise they were a
pretty motley crew: merchants, preachers, a physician, a tailor, a soldier
of fortune, an indentured servant, even a mutineer named Billington
who would become the first hanged man on Plymouth Plantation. The
document, of course, was the Mayflower Compact.

Some four hundred years later, many hold up this paper as the earliest vestige of American democracy. If you read it the right way, you can
almost see it: the undersigned came together in a "civill body politick"
and agreed to obey laws that would be "most meete & convenient for
the generall good of the Colonie." When you read it in its proper context, however, you see that it guarantees the authoritarian system that
the Separatists had in mind for New England. The "generall good"
was of course the Separatist good, anchored in devotion to Calvinist

law. More to the point, those who trace America's democratic tradition back to the makeshift Mayflower Compact—from framers of the Constitution to Pulitzer Prize–winning historians—prefer to see the people's power refined within government, or legally bound on a dotted line. But America's lifelong yen for democracy has much racier, messier origins.

The compact was written under serious duress. Winter was closing in. The Pilgrims had been bobbing in the harbor for weeks, and their scouts had already drawn deadly fire from indigenous people hiding in the woods. They needed to erect a "governmente" fast. William Bradford, the compact's principal author, reports that the document had two main motives. Some of the unfaithful among their number had been giving "discontented & mutinous speeches" about using "their own libertie" once they hit shore; containing these rogues was the first order of business. Indeed, without the contract, "none had the power to command them." Second, the compact, if it could get enough buy-in, would prove "to be as firme as any patent" in setting up a system that the English courts would recognize. Once a small majority had signed it, all they needed was to elect a leader. They chose the "godly" John Carver on the spot.

Carver may have been the benevolent leader that Bradford made him out to be (managing to "[quell] & overcome" uprisings with his "just & equall carrage of things"), but the following spring, after a hot day in the fields, he died of sunstroke. Bradford himself was promptly elected governor, as he would be annually for the next thirty years. Bradford's regime—much more accurately than his Mayflower Compact—tells the true story of America's character, or at least one fierce side of it. William Bradford was nobody's democrat. He crossed the Atlantic to build a fortress in the wilderness where he could wall out natural and social evils and wall in his tidy hive of "Saints." He was the first in a long line of American fortress builders—from slave owners and Klansmen to corporations and country clubs—elitists, oligarchs, and authoritarians for whom the wilderness was either weeds to be incinerated or woods to be hewn into exclusionary towns. He was also the first great American curmudgeon.

And he had his work cut out for him. Fortress builders always do.

Not only did his Pilgrims face the constant peril that they had known to expect when they left Amsterdam—sickness, starvation, Native American hostility. But, more surprisingly, they also encountered an ideological threat to their fastidious utopia: Thomas Morton, who founded a camp of free-loving bondservants within striking distance. A lover of the wilderness who consorted with Indians, a radical democrat and reckless hedonist, Morton represented an opposing side of the incipient American character, the gleefully unruly side. Cheerful, curious, horny, and lawless, he anticipated the teeming masses, the mixing millions who would exploit the New World as an open playground for freedom, equality, and saucy frolic. His experiment in insanely energized democracy at his anything-goes Merry Mount colony, thirty miles north of Plymouth's spiky fortress, made confetti of their Mayflower Compact. Bradford's coup to bring it down, in the spring of 1627, counts as the first volley on the battlefield of American fun.

BRADFORD'S CHILDHOOD WAS FILLED with misery. He was born in 1590 to a Yorkshire yeoman, and by age five he had lost both his parents and his grandparents. He suffered a prolonged and debilitating illness, and from the age of seven, his feeble health aside, he toiled in the fields, herded sheep, and probably attended some grammar school. He was twelve when he declared his independence, enraging his father's surviving brothers by abandoning the family's Anglican Church and joining a congregation of Separatist rebels in the nearby town of Babworth. Richard Clyfton, the Separatists' "grave & revered" preacher, soon became Bradford's father figure. In all likelihood, he inspired the young fellow with the Puritanical beliefs that all people are depraved, that only God elects those who will be saved, that His grace flows freely to the chosen few, and other such maxims of Calvinist philosophy that would have been meaningful, even comforting, to a boy who had been thrown into a world of unrelenting hardship.

While other children his age played quarterstaff and barleybreak, typical village sports of the period, young Bradford took Clyfton's preaching to heart and pursued intense Bible study. A boy with stern will and a spiritual zeal, he was jailed at seventeen with the rest of the Saints for trying to escape England for more religiously tolerant Holland. They emigrated successfully the following year. The Dutch tolerated Separatism, as they did other forms of aberrant behavior—drunkenness, promiscuity, festivals, free speech, and various notions of liberal government that rankled the authoritarian Saints. To be sure, as Bradford insisted, it was "not out of any newfangledness, or other such like giddie humor" that the congregation struck out for North America; it was "for sundrie weightie & solid reasons," particularly the "great licentiousness of the [Dutch] youth" and "manifold temptations of the place." Just as Eurailers flocked to Amsterdam for coffeehouses and sex tourism, so too were young Separatists hooked by Holland's "evill examples into extravagante & dangerous courses"—chief among which, in Bradford's words, was their desire to pull their "neks" from their parents' "raines." Never mind that Bradford himself had been a willful child.

All along the Saints had wanted to "separate"—from the Anglican Church, from England's monarchy, from any pollutants and social deterrents that threatened to maculate their pious cloth, hence the nickname "Separatists." Their decision to shun urban Renaissance comforts for "those vast & unpeopled" (Bradford's word) wilds of North America must have called for a deeper appreciation of the anguish that had brought them closer to God.

But separate they did. They endured their share of hardship on the crossing—from scurvy to seasickness to a narrowly avoided mutiny, but Bradford gets most exercised in his account of a "lustie" and "very profane younge" seaman whom it "plased God . . . to smite . . . with a grievous disease, of which he dyed in a desperate manner." (He was unceremoniously buried at sea.) This death is the first of many cautionary tales that brighten the pages of Bradford's *Historie*—and warn against the evils of having fun.

The Separatists themselves, with few "sadd" exceptions, liked to follow the rules. They relocated from the *Mayflower* to a Wampanoag village (whose previous tenants had died of the plague), and there they founded a highly regulated community devoted to work and constant worship. That first punishing winter on savage Cape Cod, when half of their number died, Bradford's inner circle of John Carver, William Brewster, and Myles Standish "spared no pains, night nor day" to care for each other in their hours of need—building fires, dressing meat, fetching wood, even scrubbing one another's "lothsome clothes." Meanwhile, a band of non-Separatist so-called Strangers who "had been boone companions in drinking & joylity" turned on each other when hardship set in, isolating themselves and refusing to help. One of them denied Bradford "but a small cann of beere" and in this way secured his low place in the annals of American history.

Such fun-loving, beere-cann-hoarding, fair-weather friends became a running joke for Bradford. They pitched their tents on sandy ground and looked like jerks beside the Separatists. His message was clear: a life built on frivolous pleasure, not work, spreads its infection to the surrounding community. It had best be yanked like a rotten tooth.

One year after the *Mayflower* arrived, a smaller ship, the *Fortune,* plagued Plymouth Plantation with thirty-five non-Separatist emigrants—most of them "lusty yonge men, many of them wild enough." One month later, on Christmas, a holiday that the Separatists didn't recognize, most of them refused when Bradford called them out to work. He respected their appeal to their own religious law, but when he returned from the frozen fields to find them "pitching the barr" and playing "stoole-ball, and shuch like sports"—frolicking while others toiled away—he confiscated their "implements" and officially forbade "gameing and reveling in the streets." He recounts this Christmas story as a bit of "mirth" but concludes it with a haunting boast: play was gone from Plymouth Plantation, "at least openly."

Plymouth's most severe crackdown on pleasure came in the year 1642, a year "of sundrie notorious sins," when a young servant, Thomas Granger, no older than seventeen, was spied having sexual congress with a mare. After submitting to days of interrogation, which required him to identify a parade of animals with whom he may or may not have lain, Granger confessed to committing "buggery" with: "a mare, a cowe, tow [*sic*] goats, five sheep, 2 calves, and"—a winking joke among Early American scholars—"a turkey." According to Levitican law (20:13, per Bradford), this bizarrely detailed crime of perversion (Bradford called it a "sadd accidente") required an equally ridiculous punishment. Poor Granger, whose likeness was also recognized in a certain piglet's face, had to stand by as the mare, the cow, and the "lesser catle" were slaughtered before his eyes. "Then he him selfe," Bradford writes, "was executed." The cattle were buried in a massive pit, "and no use made of any part of them." Apparently the turkey lived to sin another day.

This story warned "how one wicked person may infecte many" and showed what happens when "so many wicked persons and profane people" come pouring in from Europe to "mixe them selves amongst" the Separatists. Granger had learned to practice "such wickedness" in England (not, Bradford contended, on Plymouth Plantation), and the only way to prevent the foreign sickness from spreading throughout the God-fearing colonies was to cure it with the harshest medicine.

Granger's may have been the most perverse example in Bradford's cautionary history, but it wasn't the most menacing. That had come some fifteen years earlier, when they crushed Thomas Morton's "New English Canaan."

BRADFORD CAME TO PLYMOUTH to build a spiky fortress to fence out all things mixed and messy. His eventual enemy, Thomas Morton, crossed the same ocean two years later with an eye for natural beauty and a powerful libido. From the moment Bradford arrived in America, he put up his dukes against the "hidious & desolate wilderness, full of wild beasts & wild men," but Morton wanted to dive right in. An Anglican lawyer from England's West Country, he described the lush landscape as a light-toned virgin who "long[s] to be sped" and to "meete her lover in a Nuptiall bed." Morton belonged to a leisurely class, and an older generation. If Bradford was at the forefront of a Puritan revolution that was rattling its sabers across Northern Europe, Morton was a son of the Elizabethan Age, with its free-spirited politics and quick-witted hedonism. On his first trip over, he was taking a summer vacation.

Little is known of Morton's Devonshire youth. He was born to landed gentry around 1579. From an early age he practiced falconry and other noble sports. Yet the fact that he studied law at Clifford's Inn, on Fleet

Street, all but guarantees he had a healthy education in the "science" in the "Art of Revels." The Inns of Court and Chancery, in Morton's time, fostered a fast-paced college culture (not unlike today) that asked little more of their young gentlemen scholars than to show their faces at regular moot courts. There was just so much else to learn—especially in what King James's "Master of Revels" cheekily called the Third University of England: "To wit, London." Fencing, dancing, drinking, courting, pulling pranks, staging plays, spinning lewd verse—such rakish pursuits weren't merely diversions; they were sanctioned curriculum for a rising lawyer making his way in the halls of power. In general the revelry was licensed and orderly ("Master of Revels" and "Lord of Misrule" were ironically official titles), but even as the parades of decadent mummers fêted England's national spirit—sometimes enlisting delighted participation from the merry Stuarts themselves—there were always loose bands of free-lance rapscallions who devised sexier fun in the shadows. Morton must have belonged to this faster set, and he showed a taste for the randiest pursuits, but only decades later, among the friendly Massachusetts, would he get his honorary doctorate in the science of revelry.

He practiced law for many years in Devon, representing clients up and down the social ladder and maintaining a country lad's love of the outdoors. He was in his early fifties when he made his first crossing, arriving on the *Charity* in June 1622. Glad to take a breather from an acrimonious lawsuit raging back home with his churlish stepson, the gentleman roamed the sloping shores of Wessagusset and "did endeavour to take a survey of the Country." This hillocky region thirty miles north of Plymouth offered reedy marshes and hardwood forests and pastures cleared by previous tenants. While Andrew Weston's crew, with whom he was traveling, used the summer months to build village houses, Morton took leisurely tours of the land, fishing in streams, climbing low mountains, and exploring the tricky coast in his boat. He fell into reverie over soft breezy plains and "sweete cristall fountaines." He was lulled almost to sleep by "cleare running streames, that twine in fine meanders through the meads, making so sweete a murmuring noise to heare . . . so pleasantly doe, they glide upon the pebble stones." Something of an armchair Aristotelian, he totted great lists of flora and fauna and spotted fine differences between sycamores and oaks and among his beloved birds of prey. Indeed, when he departed in the crisp early days of September, he had already fallen in love with the country where he would die an outlaw and nobody's hero.

Returning two years later with several bondservants under the charge of Captain Wollaston, he helped to found a fur-trading colony on a tree-less hill in Passonagessit, at the site of present-day Quincy. The smooth, arable mound afforded 360-degree views of wooded mountains—and open fields—and a chain of islands in Boston Bay, but this time he hadn't come to sightsee. His new motivation, both personal and com-mercial, was to get to know the "Infidels," whom he quickly found to be "most full of humanity, and more friendly" than the local "Christians."

Morton's open love of the Massachusetts marks his sharpest differ-ence from the Separatists, whose professed mission, in Bradford's words, was to convert the "poore blinde Infidels." The Separatists had fought the Wampanoags since arriving on Cape Cod, and they maintained chilly communication through their loyal guide Squanto. Their excit-able imaginations almost seemed to relish "the continuall danger of the salvage people," whom they perceived to be not only "cruell, barbarous, & most treacherous" but downright cannibalistic—prone to flaying men alive with scallop shells, roasting their "joyntes" and "members" over coals, and savoring these "collops of their flesh in their sight whilst they live." While it remains to be proven that any northeastern tribes engaged in such acts of cannibalism, it is striking that from 1623 forward Plymouth Plantation, in a barbarous Mistah Kurtz–like warning to local Indians, kept the severed head of the Massachusett leader Witawamet on display. Operating on a rumor of aggression, and on Bradford's orders, Myles Standish and his militia had ambushed and slaughtered a band of Witawamet's men.

If Bradford's *Of Plimmoth Plantation,* the A to Z of Pilgrim his-tory, consistently reduces Native Americans to "litle more than . . . wild beasts," then Morton's *New English Canaan,* his own autobiographi-cal take on the early Bay Colony, is all the more stunning for devoting twenty chapters to admiring and praising and honoring a people who welcomed him into their midst. Railing against the Separatists' ignorant "new creede"—"that the Salvages are a dangerous people, subtill, secreat, and mischievous"—Morton testifies to the Indians' cordiality, to a decency that puts thieving Separatists to shame, and to a heightened sense of taste and civility that implicitly only a gentleman could see.

He affords the Massachusetts every last dignity. Their fastidious loincloths are signs of "modesty." They are too wise to be "cumbered" by eating utensils. Their dainty skill of drinking with their hands is the same human "feate" that made "Diogenes hurle away his dishe." He marvels at their superhuman eyesight and their ability to distinguish a Spaniard from a Frenchman simply by the smell of his hand. Even his belief that the Indians were "without Religion, Law, and King" doesn't faze him: they believed in a god, and their society was governed by a deep moral sense—hardly the cannibalism that Bradford imagined. He shows time and again how the "uncivilized" are "more just than the civilized": their commerce was sophisticated, their judgment discerning, their companionship a joy. They lived in happy and "plentifull" communities and had no need for the jails and gallows that the English built for "poore wretches" and "beggers." Plus they held elders (like himself) in high esteem.

The way Morton describes them, the Massachusetts showed a capacity for fun that harked back to his youth. He joined the "great entertainement" of their wedding ceremonies, where he seemed to see an Anglican balance between orderly "solemnities" and liberating "reveling." They invited him to join their national "Revels," where "a great company" gathered from all over the country and met "in amity with their neighbors" and where this aging alumnus of the Inns of Chancery was amazed to see their great sachem cavorting among his people. (At the Inns, the royals made only rare appearances at the masquerade parades, where it would have been unseemly for them to break the stage barrier.) Sitting among the feathered tribes, Morton watched Chief Papsiquine prove his honor by performing "feats and jugling tricks"—such as swimming underwater for what Morton suspected was an impossible length of time. Indeed, he wishfully believed the Massachusetts "worshipped *Pan* the great God of Heathens," or in any case held him "in great reverence and estimation." He drew this wild conclusion from his classicist fantasy that their language was a mix of Ancient Greek and Latin that made frequent use of the homophone "pan." More precisely, and in line with Morton's own project for a New English Canaan, he admired the Massachusetts' epicurean practicality: "According to human reason guided onely by the light of nature, these people leades the more happy and freer life, being voyde of care, which torments the mindes of so many Christians: They are not delighted in baubles, but in usefull things."

LATE IN THE WINTER of 1626, less than a year after establishing his colony, Captain Wollaston rounded up most of his bondservants and sailed to Virginia to sell them off. Morton stayed behind with the remaining seven, who were left in the charge of a Lieutenant Fitcher. The weather was bad, the granaries were low, and the rest of the crew started making noise about seeking their fortunes on surrounding plantations. According to Bradford, whose hearsay is our only source for this event, Morton, who had taken a liking to Passonagessit, prepared a feast for the hungry men, opened his personal stock of liquor, and counseled them on their legal right to rebel—before Wollaston returned and sold them too. If they took his free advice, Morton promised to join them in open society.

Bradford ventriloquizes the radical democrat: "I, having a parte in the plantation, will receive you as partners and consociats . . . and we will converse, trade, plante, & live together as equalls, & supporte & protecte one another, or to like effecte." Even as a mocking squib, his speech rings true for today's readers, who see in it the tenets of basic civility. But to its intended audience, the Separatists, it would have hissed liked the serpent in the Garden. It promised knowledge beyond man's control.

The servants took Morton's bait, ran feckless Fitcher into the forest, and quickly "fell to great licentiousness" as willing pupils in Morton's "schoole of Athisme." They also became incredibly prosperous. Even Bradford, whose own beaver trade was operating at a loss (due in no small part to his bad rapport with the Wampanoags), had to admit that this new rebel colony "gott much by trading with Indeans"—though naturally, as the antagonists in his ongoing parable, they squandered their fortunes, "10 pounds worth in a morning," on "wine & strong waters." It was thanks to this financial hardship that Plymouth Plantation itself, in the same year of 1627, was forced to take in a host of Strangers that further diluted their social purity. To be sure, in ridiculing Morton's open society, Bradford may have been, as Douglas Anderson suggests, protesting too much.

History hides the names of Morton's "worthy wights," who would have been listed among Wollaston's cargo as so much merchandise. They were the lowest of the English low. They could have been petty criminals working off sentences, or they could have been folks from the London slums who had signed away their rights in a drunken blur and ended up locked in a dockside tank. Aboard ship, confined in the airless hull, they would have suffered conditions like those of Africans making the Middle Passage: sickness, starvation, abuse, and death. Hence, to have thrown off their chains and been incorporated as traders on a thriving plantation must have given them the communal thrill that has long since been associated with coming to the New World—the land of plenty, opportunity, and freedom. Morton himself names few names in his book, but the honor he affords these new fellow colonists supports Bradford's charge that he was radically democratic:

> And pitty 't is I cannot call them Knights,
> Since they had brawne and braine and were right able,
> To be installed of prince Arthures table,
> Yet all of them were Squires of low degree,
> As did appeare by rules of heraldry.

Rules of heraldry need not apply in America, not so far as Morton was concerned. The New English Canaan need not be stratified, exclusive. For Europeans to prosper in this abundant new land, an ethic of friendship had to prevail. Traders had to mingle and deal as equals, among themselves and with the Indians. To this extent, Morton's vision of social upheaval wasn't the old European "misrule," the festive suspension of social roles that actually kept them more firmly intact. It was an explosion of Old World order, and he urged his wights to enjoy the fireworks. Though he lacked the authority to "call them Knights," on Merry Mount such titles didn't carry weight. Morton claimed the right to treat them as partners and dignify them as intellectual peers.

In his efforts to get closer to the Massachusetts, moreover, he exchanged sporting secrets and also (allegedly—he never copped to it) broke the king's ban on teaching indigenous people to shoot. Before long, his trading company was trouncing its competition up and down the New England shore. William Bradford, sounding the alarm, cited the spread of Morton's technology throughout the local tribes: "Fouling peeces, muskets, pistols & c." made the already "barbarous savages" even deadlier combatants, a point he sensationalized for European readers (though Indian archery was quicker and deadlier than heavy, clumsy early guns). But these skills also made them unbeatable hunters, for as Bradford complained, Indians were already nimbler than the English, ran faster, could see farther, and knew "the hants of all sorts of game." Compound these threats and financial costs with Morton's infectious example of democracy—"all the scume of the countrie, or any discontents, would flock to him from all places"—and one could see why, in Bradford's opinion, Morton's "nest" had to be "broken." A conspiracy of families and smaller English colonies began holding meetings at Plymouth Plantation on how to destroy this strange new menace.

IN THE SPRING OF 1627, Morton renamed Wollaston's camp "Merry Mount"—cheekily spelling it "Ma-Re Mount" as a *digitus impudicus* aimed at the Separatists. Richard Slotkin lists the name's witty abominations: its innocent homonyms with "Merry" and "Marry" call forth visions of merriment and nuptials, but it also rhymes with "Mary," a name that makes for "bawdy blasphemy" when coupled, as it is, with "mount." Worse yet, when read for its brazen spelling, "Mare Mount" flaunts the Levitican crime for which Thomas Granger (plus menagerie) was executed. But even a bawdy name like Ma-Re Mount declared the colony's permanence. Morton called it a "memorial to after ages." Bradford scoffed, "they call it Merie-mounte, as if this joylity would have lasted forever." Nathaniel Hawthorne, in his marvelous romance of the events, depicted their dispute as a battle for staying power: "Jollity and gloom were contending for an empire."

Near the end of April, to commemorate their audacious new name, Morton's wights made preparations for a May Day festival. As blossoms opened and new leaves glittered, a gentleman and seven roughnecks brewed "a barrel of excellent beare" and filled a case of bottles "with other good cheare." They fashioned green garlands to wear in their hair, disseminated word among the locals, and felled an eighty-foot-tall pine to which they would affix ribbons (after "the olde English custome") and a set of buckhorns as a New World innovation. Morton wanted the Maypole big—phallus-big, America-big—as a "faire sea marke" that would welcome visitors from all directions. The more the merrier was his position. Unlike the Separatists, who warned off visitors with tales of cannibalism, Morton advertised America's riches, inviting strangers to impregnate the land's "wombe" through "art & industry," lest it wither in "darck obscurity." He was laying plans for a thriving civilization, not an exclusive promised land.

In preparation for the festival, Morton also wrote a ribald twenty-three-line poem, overloaded with classical references. The Inns where he had studied had a thriving theater culture where biting satire had been the dominant tone, often at the expense of *pisse-froid* Puritans. Morton's legendary friendship with Ben Jonson, who was the Inns' most famous working-class interloper, will probably never be confirmed, but it is likely he counted himself among the "Sons of Ben," the cavalier writers in the younger generation who parroted Jonson's wit. He declared himself "a Satyrist" with "smarting fanges." Where Bradford preaches throughout his *Historie,* Morton cracks jokes—turning short-statured Myles Standish into "Captain Shrimpe" and the righteous John Endicott into "Captain Littleworth." And the revels themselves were soaked in satire. It has been speculated that they were inspired by a 1594 Gesta Grayorum masque, performed in front of Queen Elizabeth, featuring a Maypole and "Indeans" and even Proteus, whom Morton puts at the center of his poem and jokingly conflates with "Priapus." This may be so, but such revels were utterly changed on Merry Mount, where the instruments of monarchy became the lubricants of democracy: the "Indeans" were actual, the would-be courtiers were lowly bondservants, and their pleas for fertility weren't theatrical, but real.

For when May Day arrived, Morton's young bachelors hoped their pretty garlands would catch the eyes of local women—especially Massachusetts women. Having waited long enough for English wives, they welcomed the idea of starting households that the Separatists would have abominated. (Of course courting wasn't preliminary only to marriage.) But in a song he wrote to buoy the occasion—telling "Lasses in beaver coats," "Yee shall be welcome to us night and day"—Morton encouraged open minds among his wights, declaring Indian women far more desirable than "Scotch" or "Irish stuff," a bit of bigoted English misogyny that sent a strangely tolerant message. What is more, his harping on marriage throughout the account reinforces his interest in making Merry Mount last.

The pageant would have been a marvel to see. Local invitees filled the grassy, sun-drenched hill. Against a deep backdrop of shimmering wooded mountains, and the Shawmut hills in the distant north, a formal parade of Europeans and Indians—heralded by rifles, pistols, drums, "and other fitting instruments"—portaged an enormous, ribbon-streaming tree from the lapping beach of Boston Harbor to the crest of their village mount. They erected the thing with a communal heave, sturdily packed it deep in the ground, and tacked up the poem for the Separatists' pleasure. Cheers were raised, shots were fired, toasts of beer and spirits were drunk. Probably the poem was read aloud in honor of their germinal colony. And when the mood was right, the mummers arrayed themselves widely about the pole, joined their hands and took up ribbons, and cordially began the old pagan dance that prettily weaves a rainbow-colored braid.

One fellow was assigned to replenish "the good liquor like gammedes and Jupiter," and to lead the dancers in singing Morton's verses:

> Make greene garlons, bring bottles out;
> And fill sweet Nectar, freely about.
> Uncover they head, and feare no harme,
> For hers good liquor to keep it warme.

All the while, dancing to pipes and tabors, men ducked under the arms of women, who curtsied beneath the arms of the men, and the two traipsing rings—probably quite clumsy for lack of practice, many of them hindered for lack of English—did what they could to sing the racy chorus:

> Drinke and be merry, merry, merry boyes,
> Let all your delights be in Hymens joyes,
> So to Hymen now the day is come,
> About the merry Maypole take a Roome.

Stamping grass into mud, stumbling up a sweat, singing and shouting and entwining their ribbons, Morton's mixed company, in "harmless mirth," closed in closer and closer on the pole, soon entangling in such an erotic knot that even William Bradford, who would have been tending his fields that day, let himself go with a bit of alliteration, imagining them: "drinking and dancing aboute it many days together, inviting the Indean women, for their consorts, dancing and frisking together, (like so many fairies, or furies rather,) and worse practices." For who could resist this innovative pleasure—so youthful, vernal, innovative, and free? Naturally they wished it to continue for days. They wanted the joylity to last forever.

Morton nurtured a species of pleasure that later Americans would simply call "fun." In England, in 1755, Dr. Johnson would nail its definition: "Sport; high merriment; frolicksome delight." But Americans, following Morton's lead, would hone their fun to an even sharper edge—they would have it in spite of Puritan laws. In a land of danger and opportunity, they would often have it at high personal risk. And in an ever growing and complicated society, flooded with classes and races and cultures, where the laws were in flux, when laws applied at all, the frontier was expanding, and the competing social systems weren't held in check by legal rituals like Saturnalia, Americans learned to have fun with friends and aliens whose styles and differences revved up the pleasure. In point of fact, as this history aims to show, these necessary rebellions, these tantalizing risks, and these extraordinary prospects for open gathering are part and parcel of the fun itself. And yet, by the same token (and this is essential), it has always remained such a simple pleasure. It requires only that you get involved—throw in a joke, raise your voice in song, take up a ribbon and give it a go with one of the Maypole's merry, merry boyes. It may be illegal, dangerous, rebellious, but all of these things give tingles of freedom when you're a bondservant or gentleman or Massachusett lost in the merry, merry dance. Thomas Morton's fun, which would mature down the centuries into American fun, sprang from conflicts and dangerous differences. It was the fun of mixing, not the comfort of recoiling into a gated community. All it needed was "harmles mirth," an attitude Morton found "much distasted of the precise Separatists," who "troubl[ed] their braines more then reason would require over things that are indifferent."

It makes sense that the First Thanksgiving, and not May Day at Merry Mount, should become a national holiday, though the event doesn't rate a mention in Bradford's honored history. Thanksgiving gives the impression that even the most authoritarian system can reconcile itself with America's "savage" side, when in fact the event was a wary détente that would fall to pieces during King Philip's War. The First Thanksgiving, as such, is a wishful anodyne to rival the Mayflower Compact's "democracy." Much as laws contain the people's excesses, treaties ensure a grimace of tolerance among aggrieved and mistrustful nations. It's an American tradition worth recognizing: laws, treaties, prisons, and gallows undergird a powerful empire. They try to ensure a measure of fairness, and they keep the trains running on time. But there is also a necessary American rowdiness that is more consistent with Merry Mount. A nation that has maintained deep currents of civility throughout its rough history of Indian massacre, institutionalized slavery, and unpopular waves of immigration should also look to the successful experiments that have brought it into states of feverous harmony—dangerous intimacy—mutual enjoyment. Radical movements like Thomas Morton's launched their snowballs at cranky despots and let the people in on their joke: they posted their poems, published their books, performed their dances, whipped up the crowds. They celebrated civility *outside* the law. In centuries to follow, the ways such practices have lured people together have grown ever more daring, widespread, *sustained,* and the best ones have been an absolute blast. The best ones have become the American Way.

...................

THE WAY BRADFORD TELLS IT, the earth was still warm from all the stamping and dancing when Plymouth's militia made their ambush. In fact they waited until the following summer, June of 1628. After an unrecorded year of stormy disapproval, Standish and his men stormed in from the woods and found Morton's maskers ready for battle—doors locked, guns loaded, bullets and powder laid on the table. In Bradford's version, the wights were too "over armed with drinke" to work their guns, so they peaceably handed them over to Standish. In Morton's version, he and his men, having been warned in advance by Indians, stood the militia down at gunpoint. They shouted negotiations through the windows and brokered Morton's safe return to England, where he antici- pated getting a fair legal hearing. Only when he had secured his house and property did he offer himself up without (he boasted) "the effusion of so much noble blood." In September, with Morton on a boat home, Standish felled the Maypole with a still-ringing slam.

EARLY IN THE SUMMER of 1630, as the English *Arbella* bashed the Atlantic swells—leading ten other vessels and seven hundred passen- gers in the first strong wave of the Great Migration—John Winthrop, a wealthy Puritan whom the king had appointed governor of the Mas- sachusetts Bay Colony, stood firm on its pitching decks and regaled his congregation with the first great sermon of American exceptionalism. He was forty-three years old. He had high-arched eyebrows, a sundial nose, and a pointed shovel of a beard. His message was even nobler than the Mayflower Compact. "We must be knit together in this work as one man," he intoned. Detailing his vision of the glorious new colony, he entreated them to join in "brotherly Affection" and to rise above their "superfluities." He urged them to come together "in all meekness, gen- tleness, patience and liberality" and, best of all, to "delight in each other, make other's conditions our own, rejoice together, mourn together," et cetera. To this end, as a chosen people, in the eyes of God and all the world, they should become "as a city upon a hill."

When the fleet hit Salem on June 22, Winthrop's inspired flock got cracking. One of their first tasks, upon settling in Boston, was to burn Morton's Merry Mount to the ground. Then they paved the region under a Puritan empire that expanded and fortified with impressive speed, joining forces with the Separatists in 1648. For more than a century their City upon a Hill imposed its message throughout the Northeast. Song was silenced, dancing forbidden. The American Self was menaced from all sides—by threats of the stocks, dunking pools, whipping posts, ear-cropping, branding, banishment, public execution, and eternity in the Hands of an Angry God. Indians, of course, were the hardest to reform. During King Philip's War of 1675, for instance, when Plymouth's colonists faced shameful defeat by the martially more skillful Wampanoags, they exacted their revenge against all native peoples by burning the peaceable "praying towns" (which they had vowed to protect) and by impressing other communities' women and children as slaves.

In Boston's early years, Morton kept making his presence known—escaping from his jail cell, returning to America from his exile in England, but the dispersal of his merry, merry boyes and the spread of law throughout New England had reduced his threat to a ghostly legend. He was apprehended in Boston in 1644 for the publication of *New English Canaan,* distinguished ever since as America's first banned book. He was jailed for one year without charges or trial and eventually released for general infirmity. He was ultimately exiled from Massachusetts and died in Maine in 1647. He left more than twelve thousand acres of land to his cousins, as well as the island of Martha's Vineyard, but nobody can prove it was his to give. In any case, the cousins never claimed it.

But shining from the shadows of Winthrop's City upon a Hill came glimmers of lingering American fun. The maskers had to keep a low profile. Writing in his diary on March 10, 1687, Samuel Sewall relates a sermon by Cotton Mather, "sharply against Health-drinking, Card-playing, Drunkennes, Sabbath-breaking, &c." Two months later he shows the latest Thomas Mortons pushing back: "It seems the May-pole at Charleston [Massachusetts] was cut down last week, and now a bigger is set up, and a Garland upon it."

# Jack Tar, Unbound

O N NOVEMBER 27, 1760, something remarkable happened. Twenty-five-year-old John Adams walked into a bar. America's grand story seldom pauses for such events. Yet the arrival of this tetchy young Puritan descendant—a paunchy, bow-shouldered, overworked lawyer—at a tavern on the Braintree docks sparkles with deep historical meaning. Here was a proud scion of Massachusetts's flintiest Pilgrims lowering himself to smoke a pipe among New England's benighted souls, a drinking, dancing, frolicking class who made their lives along the wharf. What he witnessed there was nothing less than the early stirrings of the American Revolution. He didn't like what he saw.

Adams wouldn't have stooped to frequent such a place even a short six months before, when, channeling the jeremiads of his Puritan forebears, he railed in his diary against reeking taverns and their "trifling, nasty vicious Crew." Impressionable youths who squandered their time in taverns were taking a shortcut, he argued, "to Prisons and the Gallows." But this budding politician's deepest concern had been that licensed houses were fast becoming "the nurseries of our legislators." Who knew what kind of reckless republic could spring from such dens of iniquity?

Adams had not been bred for taverns. In his youth he had lived by the old Puritan values. He had berated himself daily for not studying enough, then had gotten sick from studying too much. He had gloried in the noble pleasures of the mind and forbidden himself everything else: "Let no trifling diversion, or amusement . . . ; no girl, no gun, no cards, no flutes, no violins, no dress, no tobacco, no laziness, decoy you from your books." Only years later, when the Revolution was over, did he decide his children could take up dancing—so long as they weren't at all "fond" of it.

No surprise, therefore, that the man who entered Thayer's tavern should be a wallflower. The dancing and revelry whirled all around him, but Adams only stood back and watched. It was natural to his class and professional standing to be a terrible snob. ("The Rabble," he sniffed, "filled the House.") The trimming and buttons of his fine linen coat must have glittered like jewelry amid the blouses and tattered frocks of tradesmen, dockhands, and sailors on leave. But in this environment he was treated like any man in a crowd. The smoky, fishy, ale-stinking tavern—unlike the classrooms and courtrooms where he already struck an imposing figure—pushed the pungent people together. It literally rubbed him up against the masses. Every room, even the kitchen, was packed to the walls with common people—and not the orderly types on sidewalks who doffed their hats to the upper classes, but heedless, rowdy, beer-drinking folk who spun and stamped to the music of black fiddlers. "Young fellows and Girls [danced] the Chamber as if they would kick the floor thro." One imagines Adams clutching his ears.

Rocking back in a corner with his pipe, he zeroed in on one "Fun-making animal," a popular wag named Zab Hayward whose antics kept the downstairs revelers enrapt. Indulging in a bit of armchair criticism, Adams ridiculed Hayward's dancing for lacking the grace he was used to seeing in Boston's ballrooms. But for all his mockery, he loved to watch. To be sure, Zab Hayward—cutting "absurd," "wild," "desultory, and irregular" moves—was the paragon of fun.

Hayward started out slow, catching the ladies' eyes with gentle antics, but as he picked up speed, getting looser and freer and gradually drunker, his manner turned flirty and downright cheeky. He plucked them up, one by one, radiating his pleasure throughout the crowd. He gave all the women a whirl, not just the prettiest. He took the hand of a light-haired one, notable for a "Patch on her Chin," and "tickled her Vanity" with a flattering song. He jigged with another, led her from the ring, and delighted the rest by giving her instructions: "Stand here, I call for you by and by." (Big laughs.) He charmed yet another with a bawdy joke, saying, "I must confess I am an old Man, and as father Smith says hardly capable of doing my Duty." (The crowd roared.) Clearly Adams was taking notes.

If John Adams was heir to William Bradford's respect for absolute law and order, then Zab Hayward was a Thomas Morton manqué. Not at all cowed by the lawless crowd, he was energized by it, ignited by it. And his fellow revelers responded in kind. He whipped up what the writer Elias Canetti, in his classic work *Crowds and Power,* called the "rhythmic crowd"—the most generative and powerful kind of crowd. In the rhythmic crowd, "density and equality coincide from the beginning" and "everything depends on movement." The fiddlers and dancers and cajoling Zab Hayward brought this rhythm to a rolling boil. Charming though these antics could be, however, they rankled the tightly wound John Adams, who may have recognized their force. Whether or not Adams made the connection, he was confronting a radically democratic spirit that was spreading from the docks throughout chilly Massachusetts.

Adams sat back and gaped at the show, but he knew much better than to get up and join. In his eyes, Captain Thayer's fogbound tavern was perched somewhere on the steppes of Hell, and the stomping and swearing of mixed genders and ages had all the marks of deviltry. Adams's last judgment was to plunk their fun down into the legal category of "Riot." "Fiddling and dancing, in a Chamber of young fellows and Girls, a wild Rable of both sexes, and all Ages, in the lower Room, singing dancing, fiddling, drinking flip and Toddy, and drams.—This is the Riot and Revelling of Taverns And of Thayers frolicks." Gavel cracks, case is closed.

In this visit to the pub, John Adams captured a moment in the early Revolution when the people's pleasures were threatening to collapse his trusted social order. Why he was "foolish enough to spend the whole afternoon in gazing and listening" is anybody's guess, but it seems he half understood what he saw, and it set his teeth on edge. The experience of democracy was terribly unattractive and driven by forces beyond his control. What he didn't seem to recognize in this nursery of the legislators was just how nourishing such floor-kicking fun could be to the republic in its infancy. Raucous fun was its mother's milk.

Maybe he can't be blamed for this blind spot. He was inclined by heritage, education, breeding, and possibly most strikingly by his skittish temperament to view such fun as distasteful at best, a crime against civilization at worst. But his prejudice shows how remarkable it is that his cousin Samuel, who shared the same heritage and Harvard education, may have been a connoisseur of such floor-kicking fun—and of fun far more dangerous than "Thayer's frolicks." What for John Adams could be anarchy, criminality, "Riot," for Samuel was the practice of pure democracy. The cousins, both Whigs, would divide as partisans in a war over the virtues of American fun. Often they would stand on opposite sides of the law, and the winner would set the Revolution's course. But the conflict they embodied—authoritarianism versus people power—was centuries old and destined never to be resolved.

IT WAS a sign of the times that a gentleman like Adams even stepped foot in Thayer's tavern. In previous decades such waterfront bars were exclusive to wharf rats, swabbies, and sailors—a fast crowd collectively known as "Jack Tars" after their tar-infused foul-weather gear. Typically young, uneducated, and poor, Jack Tar was a reckless agent of the seas. He strutted the docks in cheap, flashy dress. He bragged and swore about his life aboard. He danced with men and bare-shouldered women, often to the music of black musicians. On precious shore leave, he often finished the night in a brawl, or paying for sex, or being dragged home to his squalid boardinghouse. During the Great Awakening of the 1730s, while Puritans were busy punishing themselves, Jack Tar was doing the good work of Merry Mount. And before the Sons of Liberty rallied against the Stamp Act, a loudmouth society of rollicking seamen flaunted their freedom in the face of the British—calling themselves the Sons of Neptune.

According to William Bradford, and later Jonathan Edwards, young men who made their lives at sea were devil-spawned rascals hell-bent on converting impressionable Calvinists into whoring, fighting, drunken brigands. (As if the salts cared.) In fact, young mariners in the Age of Sail, if they hoped to pull their weight on ship, had to be highly skilled, industrious workers—acrobats who swung from mast to boom, crafts-men forever trimming sails. They also had to be orchestral teammates who could operate what the maritime historian Daniel Vickers calls the "eighteenth century's most complex machine." Jack Tar was no slouch. But for his maverick attitude and cavalier sociability, he was definitely seductive, and a serious cause for Puritan concern. Samuel Leech, an English seaman who would turn his coat for the United States during the War of 1812, told of his life-changing encounter with Jack Tar when he was a lad on a stagecoach headed for Bristol. He was mesmerized by "the antics of a wild, harebrained sailor" who amused the fellow passen-gers by climbing out the window, scrambling monkey-like onto the roof, and dancing a hornpipe jig up there as the speeding coach bounced its way downhill. "The more I saw of this reckless, thoughtless tar, the more enamored I became with the idea of sea life." The contagious fun of such simple-hearted tars nibbled at the edges of Puritan severity, evoking sheer liberty and easygoing camaraderie. More dangerously, their flair for serious fun got crowds engaged in their anti-British cause.

In 1747, Jack Tar's resentment against six years of impressment cul-minated in three days of waterfront rioting. On the chilly morning of November 16, a press gang under orders from Commodore Charles Knowles bullied its way along the docks, seizing random sailors and entire crews from the decks of Boston's commercial ships. The practice had been common enough in recent years, but in this case the com-modore's needs were high—he had to replace a host of deserters before sailing on to the West Indies. They had already seized forty-six civilians, many of them legally exempt from impressment, when a crowd of maybe three hundred citizens, watermen mingled with other classes, closed in on the press gang and held them hostage. One prominent witness couldn't decide if they were "a Mob, or rather body of Men"—criminals, that is, or righteous citizens—for it was his sense that these tars had a single intention: liberating "their Captivated Fr[ien]ds."

In the next three exultant days, thousands of Bostonians followed

IMPROVIDENCE OF SAILORS.

"Sailors," wrote John Sherburne Sleeper, "seemed to have no thought beyond the present moment—and they often seek for pleasure in the indulgence of the sensual appetites, at the expense of all that is moral or intellectual." (From *Tale of the Ocean and Essays for the Forecastle: Containing Matters and Incidents Humorous, Pathetic, Romantic and Sentimental*, 1847. Courtesy of Special Collections, Nimitz Library, United States Naval Academy.)

these rebels' lead, hitting the streets, banging cookery, breaking windows, dragging British officers from the doors of their homes, and beating an interfering sheriff who, according to one eyewitness, "using Rigour instead of Mildness . . . rather irritated the populace from which he was glad to get off with a Broken Head, tho' he was in danger of losing it." Another sheriff, locked in the stocks, "afforded" the rioters "diversion." Their most spectacular move was to burn a royal barge in the middle of Boston Common. Showing sober foresight, however, they chose not to torch it on Governor Shirley's lawn, for fear of burning the neighboring houses. Also, the barge itself was a hoax—belonging not to the king but to a member of the mob.

It makes sense that a historian devoted to crowd action—Paul A. Gilje, an expert on both riots *and* Jack Tars—should say that "rioting" like this "can be fun." He explains its thrills like a veteran of the crowd: "People can experience a personal sense of liberty; they can scream, shout obscenities with abandon, shatter windows, and stand entranced by the consuming flames of a bonfire. Both adrenaline and alcohol add to the excitement. Rumors spread wildly, and an electric tension fills the air that can only be released, like a bolt of lightning with a great thunderclap, as the crowd goes into action." And as Gilje puts it, nobody had more fun than Jack Tar: "the raw material for such social explosions could always be found on the waterfront. There, sailors with too little to do and a penchant for mischief were ready for fisticuffs." For this same reason, of course, such volatile action wasn't fun for everyone—certainly not for the victims and innocent bystanders at its business end.

As anarchic as the Knowles riots may have appeared, Jack Tar's knack for rousing mixed crowds—for inciting them with feelings of liberty—would fuel the early American Revolution. If they hoped to be effective, Patriots had to show restraint, but they also had to fill the sails. And Patriots hated backing down from a fight. They took great joy in the rebel throng—its energy, its conflict, its chaos, its fellowship—for there was the molten core of liberty, but they also had to steer the ship through treacherous social shoal waters. In both cases, of course, this wild work was fun. It wasn't until the 1760s, however, that Patriots took care to develop durable tactics and ethics that prevented their festivities from crumbling into violence. These measures themselves, when perfected, were among the Patriots' finest achievements.

The Knowles rioters achieved their objectives—the governor fled and the sailors were released. But the "riot" probably resembled, to the casual observer, the violent mob activities called "skimmington" or "rough music" that had plagued New England since the early 1730s, often involving sexual mutilation and shaming coats of tar and feathers. Whereas these popular carnivals of violence usually did the bidding of magistrates and preachers against outlaws, adulterers, scolds, and witches, the Knowles riots were different. They (1) flouted restraint with playful zeal, (2) turned liberty and civility into brash celebration, and (3) defied the wishes of appointed civic leaders. This kind of partying was altogether new. All the same, as effective and restrained as this upheaval was, the crucible of democracy proved too hot to handle. Boston's leadership called a town meeting, where they denounced "such Illegal Criminal Proceedings" as the work of "Foreign Seamen Servants Negroes and other Persons of Mean and Vile condition"—even though, as various historians have noted, not one of the rioters arrested by these officials was a servant or an African American.

It was a common enough canard, however. Keen to the growing fears of democracy, magistrates targeted blacks and various strangers when seeking scapegoats for white Americans' wild behavior. The practice would flourish in the decades to come, when the convenience of pinning rebellion on "primitives" mingled with the excitement of whites going native.

JOHN ADAMS'S COUSIN Samuel found his political heart in the iffy tactics of the Knowles riots. Samuel Adams had thirteen years on John, and while both men were pear-shaped Puritans with similarly piercing eyes, their temperaments could not have been more different. If John pinched his pennies, Samuel shot his wad. If John was a snob who feared the so-called rabble and put his stock in the rule of law, Samuel answered to the will of the people. And if John was a wallflower who scoffed at dancing, Samuel was more like ornery Zab Hayward: his knack was for whipping up the fun-loving crowd.

At twenty-five, the same age John was when he entered Thayer's tavern, Samuel was already writing radical tracts to legitimize the Sons of Neptune. He and his secret society of friends published their views in the *Independent Advertiser,* a pioneering weekly that got behind Boston's rebels and argued for the legality of the Knowles rioters' actions. Young Adams's many essays exclaimed the virtues of "Liberty." One famous essay decried any citizen "who despises his Neighbor's Happiness because he wears '*a worsted Cap* or a *Leathern Apron*'" or who "*struts* immeasurably above the *lower* Size of People, and pretends to adjust the rights of Men by Distinctions of Fortune." One can't help but see his cousin strutting in these lines.

Samuel lived like a radical democrat, but he was nobody's Thomas Morton. To be sure, in the words of the historian Pauline Maier, "No man was more aware than he of the legacy of his Puritan forebears, more proud of their achievements, more determined to perpetuate them into the future." What he plainly admired in these ancestors, however, was not their elitism and sectarian prejudice, nor their vicious authoritarianism—habits which he himself eschewed. Samuel Adams's trimmed-to-fit Puritan was a figure of steely purpose who rejected the aris-

tocrat's luxurious pleasures—"Folly," frippery, "Dissipation," theater—
and raised the "Cause of Liberty and Virtue" above the "self." The austerity Adams modeled for fellow Patriots dried their powder for feistier
pleasures, in particular wild thrills of mass resistance conducted with
noisy, good-humored civility. The discipline he urged, moreover, a respect
for life and property, allowed the people—or a wide swath of them—to
celebrate their freedom within generous bounds, often *too* generous for
his cousin's comfort.

John Adams, looking back on the early Revolution, recalled Samuel
as being "zealous, ardent and keen in the Cause," things one could not
always say of John himself. But while he appreciated Samuel's sympathy for colonial freedom and even his ability to penetrate the crowd, he
regretted his disregard for "the Law and Constitution" and the fact that
he put, at least in John's mind, the needs of "the Public" above himself and his family. Still, he was cautious on the topic of Samuel. John
may have held back out of Adams family loyalty, or Whig affiliation,
or deference to the rabble-rouser who did his dirty work, but Samuel's
opponents weren't nearly so polite. Governor Thomas Hutchinson called
him the "Chief Incendiary." Chief Justice Peter Oliver, a die-hard Tory,
fumed that Samuel Adams was "all serpentine cunning" and "could
transform his self into an Angel of Light with the weak Religionist"—
while even worse yet, among the "abandoned," like those godless souls
on the docks, he would "appear with his cloven Foot & in his native
Blackness of Darkness."

But Samuel Adams's greatest threat was his virtue, not his vice. He
took care to rouse the citizens' will, not to impose his own private interests. "The true patriot," he wrote, "will enquire into the causes of the
fears and jealousies of his countrymen." But unlike the cynical politician, who turns such research into campaign promises, the patriot keeps
"fellow citizens awake to their grievances" and doesn't "suffer them to
be at rest, till the causes of their just complaints are removed." Acting
thus for the nation, and not for himself, the true patriot will "stir up the
people." Adams's true patriots were risk-taking citizens who engaged the
people at the level of their passions. They acted a lot, for that matter, like
the jigging Zab Hayward. Whether rallying, dancing, joking, or sing-

ing, true patriots were citizens whose love of the crowd helped them to sustain its rhythmic power.

Samuel's bad behavior and even worse reputation (as a member of Harvard's Class of 1740, he was remembered for having "spent rather lavishly" and once was fined for "drinking prohibited Liquors") may have made him a hit among Boston's common folk. Early in his career he formed deep friendships with citizens below his station, and neighbors often tapped him to resolve civil differences. As the biographer John K. Alexander notes, "No other caucus leader rubbed shoulders with ordinary and poor Bostonians to the extent that Samuel did." Some of his popularity owes to his casual tax collecting, which he slyly attributed in 1765 to the "difficulties" and "Confusion" created by the Stamp Act. The captious Justice Oliver called Adams "a Master of Vocal Musick" and claimed he used this pernicious talent to befriend the working class: "This genius he improved, by instituting singing Societys of Mechanicks, where he presided; & embraced such Opportunities to ye inculcating Sedition, 'till it had ripened into Rebellion." Song may have been the rum in Samuel Adams's punch—indeed, his and James Otis's political festivities typically featured dozens of toasts and rousing liberty ballads—but his best social investment was the tankards he raised in the politically neglected waterfront bars. As Adams was remembered in *Sibley's Harvard Graduates*, dockworkers "had for years been complimented to have a man with a 'public education' spend his hours drinking, however abstemiously, with them."

It's uncertain how much time he spent drinking in the pubs, which, with or without his help, were becoming the Revolution's staging areas. Boston's public houses—alehouses, coffeehouses, grogshops, and taverns—had come a long way since 1681, that *annus horribilis* when the Puritan-dominated General Court shut nearly half of them down. As if invigorated by this act of proto-Prohibition, pubs had come back with a vengeance: by 1696 they had already tripled in number, by 1719 they had opened their doors to "slaves and servants," and by 1760, the year John Adams entered Thayer's tavern, they were turning into his dreaded "nurseries of our legislators." For, as gathering places of lower-class communities with booming dockside populations, pubs fast became the sites of a feisty, engaged, combative, informed, and unusually open public discourse. Throughout the northeastern cities in the mid-eighteenth century, "many Americans," as Carl Bridenbaugh puts it in his classic history, "were determined to play and play hard"—gambling, drinking, dancing, cavorting, and engaging in blood sports like cockfighting and bull-baiting, transatlantic diversions that until recent decades had been severely regulated in these colonies. In Philadelphia in particular, what Eric Foner calls a "distinct lower-class subculture" defied local regulations and crossed racial lines for all kinds of fun, including "revels, masques, street-fighting and the celebration of the May Day—on which parties of young men and women spent the day feasting and dancing in the woods outside the city and fishermen danced around maypoles." The standing institution for such sporting citizens (when they weren't lighting out for makeshift Ma-Re Mounts) was the lively tavern culture.

In Boston's taverns of the 1760s, as David W. Conroy demonstrates, the "republic of letters" reached well beyond its intended bourgeois readership, and in distinction from the eighteenth-century European public sphere famously theorized by Jürgen Habermas—a bourgeois political climate defined by print circulation—in Boston the consumption of newspapers and pamphlets mingled with "the traditional oral culture of taverns." Radical patriots like Samuel Adams and James Otis knew this environment was ripe for political action. Just as many Tory and conservative Whig politicians feared, the often raucous, nicotinean, and dipsomaniacal taverns "were where republican concepts gripped men's imaginations and unleashed new levels of participation. Here the novel but appealing republican ideal of an alert, active citizenry might be acted out in a setting that was also traditional and familiar." Familiar, naturally, to Jack Tar in particular.

From the Knowles riots up through the impressment riots of the late 1760s, it was Jack Tar who hoisted the Revolution's mainsail. Rabble-rousing played well in Jack Tar's society—especially in taverns, where races and genders mixed freely, where passions flowed like cheap malt liquor—although it took special talent to import it to the high streets, where the middle and upper ranks had behaved well for centuries. It was commonly held in the late eighteenth century that revolution came from the "body of the people," a willing majority who, in John Locke's terms, upon suffering "a long train of abuses, prevarications, and artifices . . . endeavor to put the rule into such hands which may secure to them the ends for which government was at first erected." In England the "body" comprised property-owning white males with a measure of political leverage. In America, however, as the century progressed and the public embraced notions of a more complicated citizenry (ancient notions from Roman orators like Seneca, late-breaking notions from moral-sense philosophers like Francis Hutcheson and Adam Ferguson), the body of the people itself began to change. More people came to recognize themselves as rightful citizens, and their body came to include whoever could cram into, say, Boston's Faneuil Hall or Old South Meeting House—provided they weren't female, Indian, or black. Such a body was neither legal nor illegal. In times of common crisis, it became an extralegal gathering that in the best cases justified its acts of open rebellion by practicing virtue, civility, and restraint. It helped this body's physical fitness, moreover, as Benjamin L. Carp has shown, that the colony's financial strength hinged on interdependence among the levels in Boston's waterfront community—among rich merchants and shipbuilders, middle-class shop and tavern keepers, and crowds of menial sailors and dockworkers whose "particularly strong collectivism and antiauthoritarian militancy" (resulting from their "unique culture and the close, cooperative working relationship of seamen aboard ship") kept the upper classes in check. But could the hoi polloi entice their superiors to join them in behaving badly?

The middle management of Boston's early revolution was a loose conspiracy of middle-class activists calling themselves the Sons of Liberty, 26 (out of 355) of whom had liquor licenses by the end of the 1760s. In 1765, the Sons managed a deft little dance that rallied a seeming majority against the Stamp Act without kicking off full-scale destruction. Taking cues from liberal clergymen such as Charles Chauncey and Jonathan Mayhew, the Sons ballyhooed their British loyalty, even as they directly attacked the Stamp Act as a threat to American liberty and dignity. Thus did they expand their playing field, a no-man's-land between criminality and law where citizens could riot at their own risk.

The Stamp Act stress-tested the Sons of Liberty's tactics. Widespread rage throughout the thirteen colonies could have weakened into cynicism—or exploded into violence. But starting in Boston, under the influence of Samuel Adams's "true patriots," it fostered a generation of citizens keen to risk everything for national freedom.

Following a summer of welling discontent, the Loyal Nine, a group of artisans and merchants who hid their contacts with radical assembly-men like Samuel Adams, orchestrated an open citywide rebellion against the stamp master, Andrew Oliver. To encourage participation by the North and South End gangs, two young and viciously opposing fac-tions, the Nine tapped the services of Ebenezer McIntosh, a cobbler who had led the South End to victory in the Pope's Day parades the Novem-ber before. He accepted their challenge to bury neighborhood hatchets and lead them as one against the Stamp Act.

Early on the morning of August 14, on fashionable Newbury Street, Andrew Oliver's effigy swung from what thereafter would be the Liberty Tree. It was adorned with a couplet of Thomas Morton–grade satire: "A goodlier sight who e'er did see? / A Stamp-Man hanging on a tree!" Next to Oliver was a devil puppet, crawling out of an oversize boot (a pun on the Stamp Act's Earl of Bute). "Many Gentlemen," Governor Bernard wrote to Lord Halifax, "especially some of the Council, treated it as a boyish sport," but Bernard suspected worse. Young toughs defended the dummies all day, even threatening the sheriff's deputies who tried to take them down. One-third of the city's schoolboys were given recess to witness this vision of civil disobedience. Meanwhile, as the crowds spilled over onto the Common, mock stamp stations blocked the city gates to hold up traffic in and out of Boston. By late afternoon, folks from Boston and far-flung counties—with estimates numbering up to eight thousand—had gloried in the shame of the Massachusetts colony's third-ranking official. The *Boston Newsletter* reported, "So much were they affected with a Sense of Liberty, that scarce any could attend to the Task of Day-Labour; but all seemed on the Wing of Freedom." Who could work in the midst of such fun?

Late in the day the effigies were cut down, and McIntosh paraded them, with his bumptious thousands, past the highest halls of govern-ment. They projected their message through council chamber windows, giving "three huzzas by way of defiance," then pressed on to the Kilby Street docks, gleefully dismantling Oliver's half-constructed stamp office and disporting themselves by "stamping" its bricks. This body of the people gained diversity as it went, taking on ever more respectable sorts who never would have joined a Pope's Day parade, or even raised their voices in public. Tradesmen and merchants suddenly had reason to take to the streets and cheer and wave banners and act like ruffians; even some gentlemen, disguising themselves as laborers, betrayed their class and joined the fun. Arriving after nightfall on nearby Fort Hill, the leaders built a bonfire and cremated the effigies—as "a Burnt-Offering . . . for those Sins of the People which had caused such heavy Judgements as the STAMP ACT etc. to be laid upon them." Apart from the pointed demolition of Andrew Oliver's home (and another building he had under construction), no further property was damaged, and other than the chief justice and sheriff—who received "some bruises"—not a soul was injured.

The complex prank was a roaring success. It caused Andrew Oliver's resignation, which, as Samuel Adams wrote, "gave universal Satisfaction throughout the Country." He acknowledged that the event followed a ragged discipline, but said it was "justifyd" all the same—as "legal steps" had failed.

While Samuel Adams flitted from one sphere to another, inquiring into his countrymen's "fears and jealousies," listening to all levels of his highly striated Boston, John Adams stayed committed to the Great Chain of Being. "There is," he wrote, "from the highest Species of animals upon this Globe which is generally thought to be Man, a regular and uniform Subordination of one Tribe to another down to the apparently insignificant animalcules in pepper Water." In this stratified worldview the working classes, it often seems, weren't far above the animalcules. It stands to reason that, as Richard Allen Ryerson argues, John Adams's most comfortable political position may have been, in his own fanciful terms, "republican monarchist."

Samuel didn't join his friends, the Loyal Nine, in stirring mobs against the Stamp Act. (He supported a British boycott, which would have been legal in any case.) John Adams, who disapproved of illegal crowd actions, took a subtler, even safer tack: he published "A Dissertation on the Canon and Feudal Law" in the *Boston Gazette*. This long and carefully measured screed, which only hints at the crisis of the day, "dare[s]" the people "to read, think, speak, and write." Its wildest move is to encourage deep reflection—particularly at "the pulpit" and at "the bar." As if in defiance of the noise in the streets, the "Dissertation" posits a defanged revolution that better suited his retiring nature—a thoughtful and calm revolution, apparently involving only the literate classes. In this utopian upheaval, "Colleges join their harmony in the same delightful concert," "Public disputations become researches into the . . . ends of government," and "Every sluice of knowledge [is] opened and set aflowing." His argument was praised by Boston's senior pastor, who applauded Adams for being old beyond his years ("The author is a young man, not above 33 or 34, but of incomparable sense"), but it was awkwardly out of step with his volatile, rebellious, *youthful* times.

NINE YEARS LATER, John Adams attended a plein-air dinner in a hummocky field outside Dorchester's Sign of the Liberty Tree Tavern. The event commemorated the Stamp Act repeal. Three hundred fifty Sons of Liberty were present, and the lot of them dined under a sailcloth awning hoisted to keep out the pattering rain. John looked rather twitchily around, privately concerned by his place in the crowd. It pleased him that the lawyers were seated at the "Head," but his eye was distracted by the secretary of New Jersey, who had been "cool, reserved, and guarded all day." He joined the throng in a series of toasts and noted, archly, "to the Honour of the Sons," that he "did not see one Person intoxicated, or near it."

It isn't clear how much fun John Adams had. Their host, a farmer, started the "Liberty Song," and everyone present joined in for the chorus. Adams, too, may have raised his voice, singing, to the tune of "Heart of Oak":

> Our worthy forefathers, let's give them a cheer,
> To climates unknown did courageously steer;
> Thro' oceans to deserts for Freedom they came,
> And dying, bequeath'd us their freedom and fame.

He may have been feeling it that wet summer's eve as hundreds of voices rang out to the clouds, but he kept enough distance, between huzzahs, to admire such songs for "Cultivating," as he put it, "Sensations of Freedom." For John such sensations weren't a good in themselves, not playful romps in Thayer's tavern. For him, they represented a political resource that had to be harnessed and properly packaged: "[James] Otis and [Samuel] Adams are politick in promoting these festivals, for they tinge the minds of the people, they impregnate them with sentiments of Liberty. They render people fond of their leaders in the Cause, and averse and bitter against all opposers."

Clearly he missed his cousin's point. "Politick" though Samuel Adams may have been—organizing "parades, festivals, and shows of fireworks to celebrate such happy anniversaries"—he knew that power had to rise from the people. The people had to be "fond" *of themselves,* and their leaders could only urge this along. Such sensations didn't advertise an upcoming republic. In the spirit of radical patriotism, they kept "fellow citizens awake to their grievances" while letting them experience their democracy firsthand. During this tempestuous period, patriotism itself was cause for celebration—rude, native, exuberant enjoyment—but enjoyment that still made John Adams suspicious.

The law was his refuge from the tumult of the streets. As early as 1758, returning to Boston from sleepy Braintree, he resented how his "Ears [were] ravished with every actual or imaginable sound." The country lawyer shuddered at "the Hurley burley upon Change," shrank from the "Rattling and Grumbling of Coaches and Carts," and with biting irony he drew sharp contrast between the urban "Pleasure" that "roused in [his] Imagination, scenes of still greater tumult, Discord, Deformity, and filthy" and the serene and purely intellectual "Pleasure" of listening to "the greatest Lawyers, orators, in short the greatest men, in America, haranguing at the Bar, and on the Bench." So convinced was young Adams of the law's rectitude that he challenged a friend to imagine a "higher object" or "greater character" or more superior aspiration than "to be possessed" (as Adams felt he was) "of all this [legal] knowledge."

Naturally the Tories stood firm by the law and feared the "body of the people"—whose will often ran contrary to the king's. But even cautious Whigs, those of John Adams's particular stripe, believed American liberties were best preserved within the limits of parliamentary law, certainly without provoking some rabble "body" whose every intention seemed to be to upend the system. By his own admission, he was often asked to "harangue" at town meetings, but he proudly claimed to have "constantly refused." He would only harangue at the *legitimate* bar.

The tension between Adams's faith in law, his fear of crowds, and his avowed love of American liberty came to a crisis in the spring of 1770. Having seethed for two years under the Revenue Act, which levied new British taxes to pay for colonial government and defense and which Patriots met with boycotts ("No Mobs or Tumults"), local Americans and British had been raring for a fight—particularly along the Hutchinson Street ropewalks, where in recent days a series of fistfights had broken out between working-class rebels and underpaid Redcoats. On March 5 all hell broke loose. That morning, on King Street, a British sentry, pushed to his limit by insults and snowballs, rammed the head of a mouthy wigmaker's apprentice with the butt of his flintlock rifle. Word spread fast among Bostonians, and by evening a crowd four hundred strong—ropeworkers, sailors, excited apprentices—surged around the empty sentinel box. The violence erupted when Captain Preston sent his soldiers to reclaim the post.

To judge from the dozens of sympathetic testimonies, published in a book the following week, the crowd may have adopted some of the Sons of Liberty's self-restraint—at least that is the message the pamphlet seems to send. Most of the affidavits blame the dozen or so soldiers who appeared in and around the watch house, their daggers and bayonets and cutlasses drawn. According to one William Le Baron, soldiers shouted into the crowd, "Where are the damned boogers, cowards, where are your Liberty boys," one of them pursuing him with a bare bayonet. Robert Polly testified to similar aggression: soldiers menacing the crowd with bayonets and people pressing back "without offering any insult." Fewer eyewitnesses blamed the civilians, but these less flattering testimonies were published with the rest. William Tant saw between thirty and forty roustabouts, "mostly boys and youngsters," send up three cheers and crowd around the sentry, bidding him "fire and be damned," at which point greater numbers rushed into the street, pelting the soldiers with snowballs and taunting, "Fire, fire, and be damned." Taken altogether, this fiery clash of wills—between civilians and soldiers, between patriots and loyalists, between rebellious youths and their authority figures— pushed the thrill of radical democracy to the brink, well past the point of viability. The fracas may have been buoying—exhilarating—but the fun was over when the soldiers opened fire, killing five of the taunting civilians, wounding eleven others.

Several lawyers were approached to defend Preston, who had been indicted on murder charges, but only John Adams would take on the case. "Council," he said, "ought to be the very last thing that an accused Person should want in a free country." (He declined, however, to defend the soldiers.) He supported Preston's rights at great personal risk, for he also sympathized with Preston's case. John and his wife, Abigail, fretting in bed on the night of the massacre, distrusted recent crowd actions, which had been incited, he believed, "by certain busy Characters" who wished to pit soldiers against the "Lower Classes" and "inkindle an immortal hatred between them"—much of which had been expressed by young boys wielding posters and chucking snowballs. One of them, Christopher Seider, the eleven-year-old son of German immigrants, had been killed for such actions only ten days before.

Defending Preston before a half-drunk jury, John Adams made a case against the lowest classes, whose hopeless ignobility, he argued, made them behave so brutally. He told the court:

> We have been entertained with a great variety of phrases, to avoid call-ing this sort of people a mob.—Some call them shavers, some call them genius's.—The plain English is gentlemen, most probably *a motley rab-ble of saucy boys, negroes and mulattoes, Irish teagues and out landish jack tarrs.*—And why we should scruple to call such a set of people a mob, I can't conceive, unless the name is too respectable for them.

He turned lyrical in describing this "mob's" frenzy (much as he had in describing Thayer's tavern) and actually made the events leading up to the massacre sound like crazy fun: "the multitude was shouting and huzzaing, and threatning life, the bells all ringing, the mob whistle screaming and rending like an Indian yell." He reserved special disgust for Christopher ("Crispus") Attucks, whom he tagged the "hero of the night," repeatedly referred to as "the Molatto," and painted as a brutish figure of violence: "now to have this reinforcement coming down under the command of a stout Molatto fellow, whose very looks, was enough to terrify any person, what had not the soldiers then to fear?" Exacerbating the threat—and thrill—of Attucks's race were the facts that he hailed "from *Framingham*," that his compatriot Carr hailed "from *Ireland*," and that these out-of-towners, "at the head of such a rabble of Negroes, &c. as they [could] collect together," should then "ascribe all their doings to the good people" of Boston, a city whose reputation Adams had reason to defend.

The argument worked. Preston was acquitted. But it also sent a warning. Like the city's official documents, twenty-three years before, that blamed the Knowles riots on folks of "Mean and Vile Condition," it warned of the kind of social mixing that could arise under a post-monarchical system. So long as democracy remained an abstraction (as in his vision of "the whole People rising in their Majesty"), even snobbish authoritarians like John Adams could sign their names to an American republic. But only such a thoroughgoing elitist, out of touch with his topsy-turvy times, could imagine America as a society of gentlemen. For in truth, in the New World, the "body of the people" was spilling from the halls and expanding to include a colorful majority—Indians, blacks, "out landish jack tarrs," *women*—a majority whom Adams reduced to a mob. As we know from history, when the People eventually did rise in their Majesty, it was this same mob that would lead the charge.

AS THINGS COOLED DOWN in the early 1770s (the economy was improving, impressment officers were backing off), the colonists relaxed their rallying spirit. Merchants cashed in on more peaceable trade relations with England. Townshend Act activists all but silenced their clanging pots and pans. A Puritan named Americanus, writing frequently for the *Boston Gazette,* reflected a rising movement for tavern reform: "Not one extravagance, among the numerous follies we have been guilty of, has been more destructive to our interests than tavern haunting, and gratifying our appetites with intoxicating liquors." And John Adams, now Boston's busiest lawyer, had bought his family's fifty-three-acre estate (ironically, on the site of Merry Mount) and had gotten, in the words of his wife, Abigail, "so very fat that [she herself looked] lean as a rail." This general complacency troubled Samuel Adams, whose zeal in turn troubled his Whiggish peers. His strategy in 1772, and in the years immediately following, was to rustle up radicals from the sleeping population ("Roxbury, I am told, is thoroughly awake") and, in his words, "to arouse the continent." That October, writing as Valerius Poplicola in the *Boston Gazette*, Adams concluded a plea to "Stop the Progress of Tyranny" with a piece of truly incendiary verse:

> The Country claims our active Aid.
> That let us roam; & where we find a Spark
> Of public Virtue, blow it into Flame.

During those months it may have seemed to Adams as if he were howling in the wilderness—singing "Tantarara, burn all, burn all!" with his rebel Society of Mechanicks—but in the summer of 1773 the quiet passage of Lord North's Tea Act through Parliament, combined with increased hatred of Governor Hutchinson, finally bellowed public virtue into flame.

In the fall of that year, after the East India Company had named its North American tea consignees (among them two sons of Governor Hutchinson), first the *Boston Gazette* (to which Samuel Adams was the principal contributor), and then large groups of the people themselves launched a series of pointed attacks—two of which resulted in aggressive mob action at the workplaces and homes of the consignees. By late November and early December, crowds of up to six thousand people were converging on the colony's public halls. Hutchinson, observing the November 29 meeting, was taken aback by the people's collective power, finding their "spirit" was more "determined" and "conspicuous" than in any previous gathering. What is more, members from all "ranks and orders"—the lowest of them showing in "great proportion"—were allowed to speak with "an equal voice." These meetings declared themselves the body of the people and demanded that the owners of three British tea vessels remove their cargo from Boston Harbor. Ultimately, on December 16, the custom-house deadline for seizing the *Dartmouth*'s payload, up to seven thousand citizens from as far away as Maine gathered in Boston to defend their nation.

That morning Samuel Adams's patriotic committee sent Francis Rotch, the *Dartmouth*'s twenty-three-year-old owner, on a mission to the governor's mansion in Milton: he was to ask permission, for a second time, to remove his ship without paying the tea tax. At three o'clock that afternoon, while Rotch made the twenty-mile journey on horseback, bells pealed at the corner of Cornhill and Milk streets, from the tower of the Old South Meeting House, calling the body of the people to order. Housewrights, doctors, barbers, farmers, actors, coopers, distillers, lawyers, coachmakers, glassworkers, tanners, mechanics, shipwrights, shoemakers, painters, and sailors—fathers and sons, brothers and neighbors and out-of-towners—men of all ages and social classes packed every free inch in the stately Puritan church, from the labyrinth of white wooden slip and box pews to the two lofty tiers of balustraded balconies. The mood was urgent, agitated, edgy, but the manner was regular and orderly: in the months that they had been blasting the "baleful weed," they had also been calling for disciplined resistance.

A vote was taken, declaring the use of levied tea "improper and pernicious." As the deadline approached, one rebel after another, each more famous than the last, rose to the high, white, ornamented pulpit. A scrap of Josiah Quincy Jr.'s speech is the only text that survives from the meeting. In it he calls for moderation, but he also predicts "the sharpest, the sharpest conflicts" to follow: "The exertions of this day will call forth the events which will make a very different spirit necessary for our salvation. Whoever supposes that shouts and hosannas will terminate the trials of the day, entertains a childish fancy." This very different spirit was of course mortal risk, a thrilling prospect on that do-or-die day.

Six o'clock came and went. Rain rattled the rows of high arched windows. Candles glimmered throughout the crowd. When Rotch finally arrived with Hutchinson's rebuff that "he was willing to grant anything consistent with the laws and his duty to the King," electricity passed throughout the house. An important merchant inquired from the balcony: "Who knows how tea will mingle with salt water?" Cheers rose from the gallery—as did cries for "A mob! A mob!" Once again they were called to order, and Dr. Thomas Young spoke in Rotch's defense, beseeching them to protect his person and property. But when Rotch confessed, under further questioning, that he could not risk returning his ship to England, Samuel Adams delivered the phrase that may or may not have functioned as a signal to the Sons of Liberty: "This meeting can do nothing more to save the country." To be sure, the *meeting* couldn't.

"Mohawk" war whoops shivered in from the street, causing men to rush the doors. Samuel Adams asked the crowd to stay put, suggesting that these Mohawks were their opponents' decoys, but war whoops resounded throughout the house. The leather dresser Adam Collson shouted: "Boston harbor a tea-pot to-night!" Another: "Hurrah for Griffin's wharf!" Most of the thousands poured into the streets, dropping from windows or piling through doors, but Adams and his associates stayed conspicuously behind, to distance their meeting from the illegalities to follow. Later, at their leisure, they took a stroll down by the docks.

The authors of this festive rebellion had been assembling in secret rooms all around town. The principals formed ranks at various semiofficial venues, such as the basement of the Freemasons' Green Dragon Tavern, or the "Long Room" above Benjamin Edes's *Gazette,* where grown men fashioned Indian disguises and Edes's son Peter refilled the rum punch. Countless participants, many of them young, got ready in private or not at all. Nineteen-year-old Samuel Sprague, a mason's apprentice, was on his way elsewhere—to a date—when he met a pack of boys rushing down to Griffin's Wharf. He loved what he saw, but his motive in joining them seems hardly principled: "Wishing to have my share of the fun," he said, "I looked about for some means of disguising myself." He clambered onto a roof, swiped ash from a chimney, and darkened his face like the rest of the rebels. Down among the crowd, he wasted no time in getting "busy with the tea chests." "Fun," in this case, was more than inspiration. "Fun" was political action proper.

The Tea Party *was* fun—bold, risky, lawless pleasure. Once again, it was Samuel Johnson's "Sport; high merriment; frolicksome delight." Boisterous participants wielding hatchets and tomahawks coursed toward the wharf from all directions, war-whooping, play-acting, hollering gibberish, and when they reached it, often in ranks, they worked in vigorous, disciplined silence that could have only heightened the pleasure. Eventually the moon broke through the clouds and lit a scene of outrageous proportions. Between two and three thousand wharfside supporters stood sentinel as "Mohawks" manned the tea ships. Apprentices worked with anonymous masters, hatcheting seals, hauling 360-pound crates, pitchforking such quantities of tea into the harbor that it spilled like hay back onto the decks. Several apprentices trounced a "countryman" loading tea into his canoe. Captain Connor, an Irishman, was "handled pretty roughly" for stuffing the lining of his coat. But otherwise the event was tightly focused on destroying the obnoxious tea.

The Tea Party was fun, pure American fun. Spiking the fun were the Mohawk disguises. As Philip J. Deloria has brilliantly observed, the patriots, by dressing as Native Americans, enjoyed "speak[ing] to the British from a quintessentially American position" and adding a whoop of national identity. Perhaps more important, in the gone-native spirit of Thomas Morton's Merry Mount, "[b]y being both Indian and not-Indian, repulsive savage and object of colonial desire, representation of social order and disorder, the Tea Party Indians revealed the contingency of social order itself and thus opened the door to the creation of the new." Dressing as Indians, flaunting their rude native identity in the face of colonial power (while perverting the fears of their Puritan forefathers), they reveled in the novelty of their New World democracy. In this moment they were experiencing their democracy firsthand, perhaps more purely than they ever had or would again.

The Tea Party, at bottom, was *revolutionary* fun, a pleasure unique to this New World event. Unlike the upcoming French variety, when revolution was celebrated with heads on pikes and waves of sadism consumed the people, here the reigning spirit was civility and brazen displays of participation. Josiah Quincy Jr. had warned the Tea Partiers that such rebellion was preliminary to war, and so it was, but the tone it set and the sensations it created defined the kind of nation they would give their

lives for. Its strange admixture of Puritan restraint, Enlightenment ideals, and dangerous jolts of social upheaval would resonate with Americans for centuries to come.

The enduring potency of such revolutionary fun, as opposed to
Merry Mount's fading dream, makes it all the more remarkable that our
best historians have diminished its social force. William Pencak argues
that such patriotic acts were playlike "practice" for a possible republic
to come, as though just because they spoke wittily, acted riskily, and
dressed in glittery native garb their pranks were not legitimate acts of
citizenship. Gordon S. Wood concludes that these risky acts of self-
and public assertion were just "mock ceremonies," which "were, like all
parodies, backhanded tributes to what was being ridiculed." Even Ray
Raphael, who deeply understands these nonviolent crowd actions, down-
plays their force: "In 1765 the rioters had hung effigies and conducted
mock funerals; by 1774 ordinary farmers were forcing high-ranking
government officials to resign. By intimidating real people rather than
toying with dummies, rank-and-file rebels effectively derailed all opposition." Had the "rioters" of 1765 not jubilantly mocked the Stamp Act,
but instead rebelled only violently ("by intimidating real people")—or
much worse, had they followed John Adams's wishes and only rebelled
in the safety of their minds—then a different sort of citizenry most certainly would have formed, maybe a factional one, maybe a pathetically
obedient one, maybe an untenably anarchic one that necessitated new
forms of despotic control. Precisely by "toying with dummies," however,
and by having fun at England's expense, the people of Massachusetts
sparked a national felicity that throve on democratic virtues.

Philip J. Deloria contends that the early Revolution in general,
and the "blackfaced defiance of the Tea Party" in particular, signaled
"period[s] of emptiness during which [participants] are neither one thing
or the other." By reading the Revolution in this purely structural way,
by reading it, that is, as a negative space between two ideological eras,
he overlooks the Tea Party's essential positivity—that it was not preparation for a possible republic but rather was the vivacity of democracy in
action. The participants were not "empty" of identity, of politics. On
the contrary, even as shapeshifting, masquerading youth—especially

as shapeshifting, masquerading youth, who took their rude civility to the streets—these citizens experienced a political plenitude that many Americans have yearned for ever since.

By design, Boston's crowd actions of the 1760s and 1770s were guided by the era's "moral-sense" philosophy. This school of thought (whose adherents were as varied as Adam Smith, David Hume, Lord Kames, Francis Hutcheson, and Jean-Jacques Burlamaqui) could be traced back two generations to the Earl of Shaftesbury, for whom social behavior was motivated by a *sensus communis*—an instinctual concern for one another's happiness and well-being. Just so, the Sons of Liberty's call to patriotism—in speeches, broadsides, and the actions themselves— was predicated upon the assumption that "liberty" and "happiness" were communal virtues, not just individual values. For Shaftesbury and others, political life wasn't governed by niceties and manners. It required citizens to dust it up. But in a moral-sense world, citizens fight in good faith, trusting that everyone is acting in the community's best interest.

The philosopher Adam Ferguson, a Scot, gives us the best moral-sense picture of a rowdy citizenry's fun. Writing in 1767, but sounding at times like Thomas Morton in the 1630s, Ferguson praised Spartans, Native Americans, and other "rude" nations for following "the suggestion of instinct" more "than the invention of reason." Social instinct works better than government, he asserted, because it springs from the citizens' natural inclinations: "Without police or compulsory laws, their domestic society is conducted with order, and the absence of vicious dispositions, is a better security than any public establishment for the suppression of crimes." Such "natural" citizens, he observed, take "delight" in pure action "without regard to its consequences." Speaking more generally of "mankind," he finds their affections are given freely, but they also relish risky engagement. People everywhere "embrace the occasions of mutual opposition, with alacrity and pleasure"; as members of civil society, a pervading sense of "national or party spirit" fortifies them against their enemies. Accordingly, the most "active and strenuous" citizens serve as the rude nation's "guardians," and the general tenor is boisterous and coarse. Indeed, for Ferguson, if fattened nations keep commerce and politics lubricated by maintaining a "grimace of politeness," rude, young nations enjoy "real sentiments of humanity and candour." The latter are civil in the radical sense. By extension, then, they don't view "happiness" as the "state of repose" or vicious "languor" that comes with material wealth; their happiness "arises more from the pursuit than from the attainment of any end whatever." For them, the *pursuit* of happiness—striving, grappling, thrashing, competing—is happiness itself.

As they act and fight for the common good, rude citizens enjoy what Ferguson calls "national felicity." Under such conditions, he argues, individual and communal happiness are "easily reconciled": "If the individual owe every degree of consideration to the public, he receives, in paying that very consideration, the greatest happiness of which his nature is capable." Hence, when looked at in these terms, which are largely consistent with Samuel Adams's arguments, the feistiest moment of the early Revolution—the Boston Tea Party—was also the happiest. Dressed as Mohawks, breaking British law, these rebel citizens enjoyed their position outside of any state. They throve on activity, pursued common liberty, and experienced national felicity.

JOHN ADAMS HAD SPENT the night in his office. Weeks before, true to form, he had counseled Francis Rotch to comply with the Tea Act. The next morning, however, presumably having read about the events in the *Gazette*, even he wanted to claim this triumph. He praised the Tea Party as "the most magnificent Movement of all." He recognized "a Dignity, a Majesty, a Sublimity, in this last Effort of the Patriots." But just as this wallflower judged Zab Hayward's dancing from a bench of high-cultural authority, so too did this opponent of risky crowd actions offer a bit of expert advice: "The People should never rise, without doing something to be remembered—something notable and striking." Apparently the Tea Party passed his test: "This Destruction of the Tea is so bold, so daring, so firm, intrepid and inflexible . . . that I cant but consider it as an Epocha in History." And so he praises it for posterity. Adams once scoffed at what he called the people's "genius," but only when he wasn't profiting from it.

The day after the Tea Party, Samuel Adams, by contrast, razzed Plymouth township to rise to the challenge: "The people at the Cape will behave with propriety as becomes Men resolved to save their Country." And on New Year's Eve, in private correspondence, he reveled in the event's lingering satisfaction: "You cannot imagine the height of joy that sparkles in the eyes and animates the countenances as well as the hearts of all we meet on this occasion; excepting the disappointed, disconnected Hutchinson and his tools." As Adams well knew, the "decency, unanimity, and spirit" with which this action was conducted gave it its force and potential staying power.

The Tea Party, despite its potential calamity, charmed even the wariest Whigs like John Adams with the real potential of people power. And Jack Tar, for a moment, was afforded some dignity among the "body of the people"—without having to leave his wharfside paradise.

FOLLOWING THE REVOLUTIONARY WAR, the newly minted U.S. citizenry put on events reminiscent of the parties that celebrated the Stamp Act repeal. Almanacs bulged with revolutionary holidays: honoring the Boston Massacre and the Treaty of Paris, remembering evacuations, town burnings, and battles. Sometimes the events were reenacted, as the Boston Tea Party is to this day, but most often they were honored with toasts and parades. David Waldstreicher's important book on the subject says these events "were actually a great deal of fun"—due in no small part to their "revolutionary" function of "allow[ing] both for the creation of cross-class alliances and for the partial expression of class conflict, as in the shaming of aristocratic tories." That may be so, but it is clear the people's "fun" was losing its teeth. After all, these events, so much tamer than the Boston Tea Party, "required very little sacrifice" on the participants' parts. To Samuel Adams, the original Knowles riots connoisseur, they were just decadent. Disgusted by the parties he saw in 1780, he called them "public diversions as promote Superfluity of Dress & ornament." They belied the "Christian Sparta" he once envisioned for Boston. More generally, they signaled the rampant individualism that had come to dominate the U.S. "pursuit of happiness."

No worries, however. Over the next half century, when local, state, and federal governments were scheduling parades to foster a sense of national unity, a rash of decidedly unofficial gatherings raged from the mouth of the Mississippi to grassy patches in the deep Maine woods. Whereas the former holidays were fêted with parades that modeled the tiers of a functional republic (marching ranks, waving celebrities, masses spectating from the sidelines), the latter, ostensibly chaotic gatherings, especially those driven by African-American communities, stayed focused on the kinds of bad behavior that oxygenated the nation's blood.

# Technologies of Fun

Ours is a light-hearted race. The sternest and most covetous master
cannot frighten or whip the fun out of us. . . . In those days I had
many a merry time . . . the fun and freedom were fixed facts; we had
had them and he could not help it.

—JOSIAH HENSON, former slave (1858)

FREDERICK DOUGLASS, one of the great figures of the nineteenth
century, used brains, brawn, and incredible bravura to free himself
from chattel slavery. As a field hand on Maryland's Eastern Shore, he
physically defeated a brutal white overseer and learned the difference
between being a "slave in form" and a "slave in fact." As a domestic slave
in Baltimore, he tricked white boys into teaching him to read and picked
up specialized dock-working skills that he would eventually use to make
his passage northward. Through personal grit, literary talent, and the
courage to speak for the abolitionist cause despite the heavy price on his
head, he rose to become a spokesperson for his race.

Like many American forefathers, Douglass held a hard line on fun.
In a striking passage from his classic *Narrative,* which made great strides

for the abolitionist cause, he establishes a class hierarchy among his fellow slaves that would have pleased even Cotton Mather: it divides the intelligentsia and the hunters from the hedonistic rabble. These classes came into highest relief for him during the five-day Christmas holiday, when the enslaved community was released from work. "The staid, sober, thinking and industrious ones"—presumably Douglass's own small class—went about "making corn-brooms, mats, horse-collars, and baskets" that would come in handy in the busy new year. "Another class" hunted woodland animals. "But by far the larger part engaged in such sports and merriments as playing ball, wrestling, running foot-races, fiddling, dancing, and drinking whisky." Douglass shows these fun-loving masses through the eyes of his conniving master, who provides the whiskey and enjoys the revelry because he thinks he is keeping his slaves in their place. The industrious ones are in this sense the rebels—they claim their labor back from the master and demonstrate their autonomy. The wrestlers and fiddlers are the suckers.

Douglass wanted to expose all the trickery behind slavery. Christmas holidays were his example of how masters distorted slaves' ideas of freedom. Just as the master forced slaves to drink whiskey until they were miserable, or to overeat molasses until they were vomiting, he also coerced them to party hard on the holidays, so they would gratefully go limping back to work after New Year's. This is how they were taught to confuse precious "liberty" with sickening "dissipation." Undoubtedly these were the master's intentions. Henry Bibb, another former slave turned abolitionist lecturer, made a similar argument, saying slaves who had "no moral religious instruction" absconded "to the woods in large numbers . . . to gamble, fight, get drunk, and break the Sabbath," and also to dance and sing and "pat juber"—often by the coaxing of masters, themselves looking for "sport."

Perhaps the most sympathetic account of Christmas frolics comes from former slave Solomon Northrup, an expert fiddler whose talents brought out his drunken master's best and worst—sometimes making him "buoyant, elastic, gaily 'tripping the light fantastic toe' around the piazza and all through the house," but often inspiring him to taunt exhausted slaves to dance all night for his amusement. Northrup was

"*The Sabbath among Slaves.*"

"Those who make no profession of religion resort to the woods in large numbers on that day to gamble, fight, get drunk, and break the Sabbath." (From the *Narrative of the Life and Adventures of Henry Bibb, an American Slave.* Courtesy of Manuscripts, Archives and Rare Books Division, Schomburg Center for Research in Black Culture, The New York Public Library, Astor, Lennox, and Tilden Foundations.)

also hired out to other plantations—a player in the era's larger economy of "slave minstrels," enslaved musicians, singers, and dancers who brought their masters considerable profit. On Christmas, however, when they were left to themselves, Northrup's "beloved violin" gave him the "honored seat at the yearly feasts." He taunts Southern whites (mocking the "listless and snail-like" movements of their "slow winding cotillion") "to look upon the celerity, if not the 'poetry of motion'—upon genuine happiness, rampant and unrestrained" of "slaves dancing in the starlight of a Christmas night."

Douglass describes these holidays as "safety-valves, to carry off the rebellious spirit of enslaved humanity." Without such holidays, he warns the masters, slaves would rise up in an "appalling earthquake" and possibly tear the system down. This hydraulic model of control and appeasement has a familiar ring to it. It's the same metaphor used to explain the medieval carnival: peasants were allowed a bit of Saturnalia to keep them contained for the rest of the year. Contemporary historians use it, as well, when accounting for antebellum black celebrations. Undoubtedly the masters had "safety-valves" in mind when encouraging slaves to cut loose on holiday. What all of these arguments assume, however, is that African Americans who played on holiday were putty in the masters' hands. They also underestimate the force behind fun—especially African-American fun.

Douglass gives the Puritan boilerplate on fun—it weakens the will, it's a waste of time, it turns you into the devil's plaything—and he sends this message with noble intentions. In the closing lines of *My Bondage and My Freedom*, he says he aims to liberate slaves by promoting "the moral, social, religious, and intellectual elevation of the free colored people." As a rising abolitionist—under the influence of his famous mentor, William Lloyd Garrison—Douglass was more than an opponent of slavery; he was part of the Second Great Awakening that was gathering force in the 1830s. (The "First" had seized New England a century earlier.) This national wave of revivalists and reformers targeted a range of society's evils, from slavery and domestic abuse to promiscuity and drunkenness. But in giving the reformers' party line on the profligacy of blacks, as he does in both of these books, Douglass also reinforces a common bias—that "by far the larger part" of blacks are childish folks with an incorrigibly hedonistic streak. This stereotype didn't need his help. It traveled throughout nineteenth-century America, as later chapters will show, in the wildly popular form of blackface minstrelsy. Stiff, white society oversimplified black culture as a thoughtless, oversexed free-for-all. In many circles, they loved it for that; cartoon images of hedonistic blacks provided a nice holiday from whites' own repression. Naturally Frederick Douglass hated this love, especially when it flickered in his master's eyes. He wanted fellow blacks to stop fooling around and playing into white society's hands. As a reformer, he wanted them to play by the rules. But Solomon Northrup saw it differently. For him, blacks having fun—fun of their own, not compulsory dances for their master's sadism—was a human triumph inaccessible to whites.

> It was Christmas morning—the happiest day in the whole year for the slave. That morning he need not hurry to the field, with his gourd and cotton-bag. Happiness sparkled in the eyes and overspread the coun-

tenances of all. The time of feasting and dancing had come. The cane and cotton fields were deserted. That day the clean dress was to be donned—the red ribbon displayed; there were to be re-unions, and joy and laughter, and hurrying to and fro. It was to be a day of *liberty* among the children of Slavery. Wherefore they were happy, and rejoiced.

When this reveling "class" is taken more seriously, a story of radicalism comes to light. What Douglass dismisses as foolhardy mischief—and hopefully there was a lot of that—starts to emerge as a peaceable revolution that created new strategies for staying free. Forced to survive under an authoritarian system far more forbidding than Plymouth Plantation, slaves crafted kinds of play and satire that made Merry Mount look like amateur hour. In resisting a nationwide system of tyranny protected by the U.S. Constitution, they put their fun to more strategic uses than even the Sons of Liberty did: their need was that much more severe. Their celebrations formed regional and national webs, even when much of the antebellum Union was threatening to come apart at the seams. Their jokes, stories, songs, and dances modeled sly resistance. Their wrestlers, fiddlers, dancers, jokers, whiskey drinkers, and quoits players reclaimed ownership of the people's body and soothed its lacerations with pleasure. In the process, they wrote the code for America's most *American* popular culture—and made it deeply, richly smart.

BY THE DAWN of the nineteenth century, postrevolutionary holidays—honoring the Boston Massacre and the Treaty of Paris and above all touting Independence Day—were turning into occasions for partisan conflict. All throughout the Northeast and Mid-Atlantic, Republicans and Federalists and their warring newspapers often co-opted nation-building festivities for boisterous, even violent, political advantage. The year 1803 was especially hot. In Providence that spring, when Republicans celebrated the anniversary of Congress, Federalists ran an effigy of Tom Paine through the streets, "insulting and hooting at every person not in their sect." In Trenton that July, thirty Federalists pummeled a Republican editor for depicting their festivities "as drunken and 'riotous.'" African Americans—especially those who joined in these celebrations—were deployed as scapegoats by both sides in these wars. "To Federalists," David Waldstreicher writes, "black participation in festivals and elections epitomized the low-class origins, and demagoguery, of the Jeffersonians. Yet these same Jeffersonians constructed their republican virtue atop the symbolic foundation of the underclass—a black underclass." Both groups presented blacks as civic toxins, as Newark's Republican press did that August when they charged Federalists with "'admitting black people and slaves' into the courts." By associating their opponents with blacks, they called them politically dangerous—or, worse, irrelevant.

Such partisan events provide an ironic backdrop for the "Election Day" and "Pinkster" events held by African Americans during this same time period. For while the dominant parties held now pompous, now divisive celebrations that mocked feast days of national unity, African Americans, the partisans' objects of common scorn, hosted elaborate public blowouts that, by most accounts, flaunted the joys of participatory democracy—if only for a few precious days at a stretch. These celebrations showed citizens' unguarded selves—citizens in the thrall of liberty—and whereas partisans enjoyed splitting the public sphere in half, often in sadistically violent ways, the multiracial celebrants at Election Days and Pinkster showed pride in racial and national identity, took pleasure in collective activity, made examples of amicable conflict, and throve on mutually granted freedom.

The earliest account of an African-American holiday in the Northeast was in the 1736 *New-York Weekly Journal*. Calling himself "The SPY," the reporter describes whites and blacks en masse disporting in a field outside of town; the whites were simply "crouded," but the blacks "divided into Companies," possibly "according to their different Nations, some dancing to the hollow Sound of a Drum" and other percussion instruments while "others plied the Banger," or banjo, and sang. Blacks also "exercised the Cudgel," probably a form of martial art. But everyone drank and swore and frolicked. In addition to gambling, pugilism, and cockfighting, and amid shaded booths selling unidentified merchandise (the SPY buys a beer), was a business that struck him as a "Place little better (if anything at all) than a Brothel," where the "mixt Multitude" sat with "Doxies on their Laps," or "in close Hugg," and tried to sell the disapproving SPY their services. What he clearly could not get over, however (he returns to the subject at least three times), was the festival's radically "mixt Multitude." The festivities were rude and showed "want of a better Education," but they comprised more than blacks and lower-class whites. Most dangerously, they delighted all levels of New York society: "Gentlemen, Merchants, and Mechanics of different Occupations, and even Day Labourers, of different Ages, in different Garbs." Under these free and liberal conditions, despite their highly stratified city, the motley participants "seemed to be all hail Fellow well met." The event's high spirits leveled their partiers' biases. While Shlomo Pestcoe and Greg Adams make the strong case that the event took place on Easter Monday (and that "The SPY" was the prominent New Yorker James Alexander), it remains unclear what common purpose threw this "mixt Multitude" together—apart, that is, from the chance to have fun. It does appear, in any case, that the party's instigators were black.

Since at least as early as 1741, in Salem, Massachusetts, slaves and free blacks held celebrations for the purpose of electing their "Kings" and "Governors." They took place in coastal and river-valley towns, sometimes in league with local Jack Tars, and they often followed the lead of local white elections, celebrating with parades and formal dinners and the array of toasts and liberty songs. But unlike the feasts of their white community members, which typically ended at dusk, "Negro Election Days" could last for several days of fiddling, dancing, feasting, drinking, foot-racing, gambling, and sports. The elections themselves followed a variety of practices—ballots, caucuses, viva voce, queues of supporters behind favorite candidates—but they could also involve tests of strength and agility. Sometimes the Governors held year-round authority, appointing their own courts and legislative committees, but often they served an honorary function. Sometimes Election Days dropped the elections altogether and cut straight to the games and merriment. Joseph P. Reidy notes that up through the turn of the century, in Salem and elsewhere, these predominantly African-American events were enjoyed by whites and blacks alike.

During this same period, similarly parodic celebrations went by the name Pinkster Days. Pinkster coincided with the Dutch Pentecost, or the Anglican Whitsunday, and was held every May throughout Pennsylvania, Maryland, and New York. What for the Dutch began in the early 1700s as the strictest of religious holidays evolved over the decades into a secular, multicultural rite of spring, thanks mostly to the widespread contributions of free and enslaved African Americans. Records of Pinkster's later iteration mention slaves "frolicking" together for days, eating colored eggs and dancing, sometimes joined by their reveling masters. Joyous memories of Pinkster festivals on her Dutch-American master's estate nearly provoked runaway slave Sojourner Truth to turn herself in. James Fenimore Cooper's 1845 novel *Satanstoe* relocated his turn-of-the-century memories of Albany's Pinkster festival to New York City in 1757, possibly melding it with the Easter Monday event, possibly embellishing it, though his imagery itself has the ring of truth: "Nine-tenths of the blacks of the city, and of the whole country within thirty or forty miles . . . were collected in thousands in those fields, beating banjoes, singing African songs, drinking, and worst of all, laughing in a way that seemed to set their very hearts rattling within their ribs. Everything wore the aspect of good-humour, though it was good-humour in the broadest and coarsest forms." In later years Pinkster celebrants "collected in thousands" in Manhattan's City Hall Park. By the turn of the century, especially on Albany's Pinkster Hill, the festival's fleeting experience of liberty was attracting participants from various races, classes, and national identities—and though the celebrations themselves were an evident mélange of European, African, and Caribbean traditions, they were identified with, and largely attended by, blacks.

As harmless and peaceable as the revels seemed, they preoccupied the young republic's middle class. To judge from two documents published in 1803, a contest was roiling over what Pinkster meant. One is a colorful editorial in the Albany *Centinel* that sounds an alarm against these "seasons of dissipation." The other, a pamphlet, is a long doggerel poem called *A Pinkster Ode*. Attributed to Absalom Aimwell, Esq. (a blatant nom de guerre), the *Ode* glories in Pinkster's radically democratic fun and calls out the nation's political leaders for being stingy and vicious by contrast.

New York had ruled less than four years earlier to gradually (very gradually) phase out slavery (only slaves' children could earn their freedom), and Albany had the region's largest black population. Agitating readers in this moment of transition, the *Centinel*'s reporter depicts Pinkster Days as nothing less than a military takeover. During the days of drum-beating anticipation, "negroes patrol[led] the streets more than usual" and converted the public hill into their *"theatre of action."* Throughout their vast encampment, "beastly" blacks and "beastly" whites broke into fights, cursed "in every language," danced out in the open, and did unspeakable things out of sight. Most menacing of all was the "old Guinea Negro," King Charles, "whose authority [was] absolute" and whose "will [was] law" all during the days-long celebration. The king's grand entrance through Albany's high streets, between ten and noon that Monday morning, would have reminded readers of Toussaint Louverture, the leader of Haiti's slave revolt, who had died only two months earlier. Guided through town on his high blond steed by a pair of decorated "pedestrians," preceded by his standard and a painted portrait that tallied his many years of reign, "their fictitious sovereign" commanded the crowd with "all the pomp of an eastern *nabob*"—cleaving through mobs of adoring spectators—trailing a train of "distinguished and illustrious characters."

It remains unclear whether King Charles was elected or self-appointed, but his coup wasn't what you would expect from this account. Unlike Toussaint's gory rebellion or Napoleon's intercontinental invasions (which were taking a breather that year), King Charles's putsch against stiff white Albany culminated in the wildest of parties. Pinkster Hill, an open patch of public grass, was ringed by vendors selling cheeses, fruits, breads, and liquors. Around them sprawled a massive tent city, housing visitors from the surrounding counties. In the center was the "theatre of action," where the arrival of King Charles—preceded by bands of costumed children—detonated a hootenanny of drumming, rum drinking, and unabashedly erotic dancing, "presenting the eye of the moral observer," as the reporter self-identified, "a kind of chaos of sin and folly, misery and fun." The coup may not have caused bloodshed, but it threatened to poison the cultural well.

*A Pinkster Ode*—the pamphlet—takes an opposite approach. It glories in the "graceful mien," "pleasant face," "princely air," and "Pinkster clothes" of a "slave whose soul was always free." The "Captain-General" King Charles who emerges from these lines is a fun-loving, liberating, agile lord who despises "Tyrants" everywhere and rises above the glory seekers, rioters, and slave-masters who would tear the young republic asunder. King Charles sets the tone on this Merry Mount of sorts, where courtesy reigns and "Every colour revels . . . from ebon black to lilly fair." The *Ode* has a political axe to grind. It argues that a fun-loving democracy, like the rollicking one on Pinkster Hill, could douse the wildfires encroaching on the Union: the politics, greed, competition, and slavery. The bull's-eye of its diatribe is a Republican politician, "Jo," who ballyhoos liberty and fills his pockets while abusing his constituents in the Federalist fashion—by "barter[ing their] rights away." By contrast, in the *Ode*, ethnicities and nationalities dance around the Hill, folks represented by their characteristic pleasures, "Troops . . . so gay, so delicate and sweet."

Absalom Aimwell claimed that "Peace" and "smiling" reigned in King Charles's camps—that "no rude act his glory stain[ed]"—but we should also consider the contrary opinion, expressed in the *Centinel,* that Charles and his heavies went from tent to tent, exacting dollar tributes from black families and two-dollar tributes from whites, else their shelters would be "instantly demolished." King Charles may have had a badass streak. And it is likely, in the mummers' tradition, that he demanded a tax for his troubles. It may have taken a thug with a heart of gold to keep the peace in this boisterous horde, to keep them focused on having fun, to keep them from collapsing into a mob. Whatever he was—king? slave? thug? saint?—the people, to judge from the surviving accounts, couldn't get enough of him—besides the ones who wanted to get rid of him.

In 1867, James Eights, who had grown up among the Albany celebrants, gave a child's-eye view of old "King Charley" for *Harper's Monthly*—his high-domed pate, his brigadier's redcoat and buckskin "small clothes," his silver-buckled shoes and gold-piped tricorne. But when the adult panned back to recall the "gathering multitude" that quickly absorbed the dancing king, he marveled not at lurid excess but at the harmony of a turn-of-the-century crowd representing "individuals of almost every description of feature, form and color, from the sable sons of Africa . . . to the half-clad and blanketed children of the forest." (Even the *Centinel*'s reporter is impressed to see "blacks and [a] certain class of whites, together with children of all countries and colours," but then calls on the powers of John Milton—"biographer of devils"—to describe them.) The crowd, as Eights remembered it, was civilized by their pleasure. Inspired by the children, dazzled by the horse tricks of Ricketts the Clown and the rubbery fire stunts of Monsieur Gutta Percha, emboldened by liquor and hilarity and ball games, the various pack of American strangers, some of them visiting from hundreds of miles away, broke into dancing at the sight of the king—energetic dancing that would last through the night, pick up the next day, the next and the next, and grooved until the masses had to hobble home to work.

King Charley worked hard to keep the party rolling. Even at seventy he was long and lean and "still retained all the vigor and agility of his younger years." And when he put down his drum and entered the dance, his sovereign sense of rhythm and comedy spread like medicine throughout the crowd. Pinkster Hill's most common dances were "the jug," "the double-shuffle heel-and-toe break-down," and what the *Centinel* reporter called "most lewd and indecent gesticulations," possibly some version of the ring shout. These infectious dances of African origin demanded athletic, sweat-streaming activity. But the refreshing sight of King Charley's grizzled head, smiling and bobbing above the others, kept the masses in youthful spirits:

> [T]here, enclosed within their midst, was his stately form beheld, moving along with all the simple grace and elastic action of his youthful days, now with a partner here, and then with another there, and sometimes displaying some of his many amusing antics to the delight of the crowd, and which, as frequently, kept the faces of this joyous multitude broadly expanded in boisterous mirth and jollity.

In Eights's recollection, King Charles brought the rowdiest crowd into focus. But in these volatile early years of the republic, he would have been more than a lovable wag. King Charles, though a slave, was liberty personified, and his unlikely sense of fun was contagious.

Following the lead of Melville J. Herskovits's ethnographical classic, *Myth of the Negro Past,* scholars have long read Election Days and Pinkster as acts of "cultural syncretization," as mixtures of a variety of cultural practices: Joseph P. Reidy and Shane White, who wrote groundbreaking studies of both celebrations, explored the cultural marriage of Afro-Caribbean religious and legal traditions with European Saturnalia, Whitsuntide, and May Day revels, as well as North American elections. Without question, Election Days and Pinkster arose from an array of cultural traditions, European, African, Caribbean, and North American. And it is likely that their syncretism of different rites and practices, ranging from African coronation ceremonies to various forms of medieval carnival, may itself have been a source of pleasure: the revelers' took ownership of their racial heritage while experiencing some measure of (if at the same time mockery of) national assimilation. And yet of course the international traditions that fed them had died on contact with the nineteenth-century United States. It defies reason, for instance, to describe these events, as many witnesses and scholars have done, as "safety valves" that follow the logic of carnival. On the contrary, as both the *Centinel*'s warning and the *Ode*'s rallying cry make plain, Pinkster did not preserve the social order in the manner of medieval Saturnalia, whose topsy-turvy "misrule" was a sanctioned act of parody. It wasn't a legal ritual, and all of society didn't observe it: many mocked it and looked on in horror. It was a bizarre and extralegal practice that, as Absalom Aimwell recognized, was a moral affront to a young republic that identified with virtues of liberty and equality that it refused to practice.

Like the "merry boyes" on Merry Mount and Boston's Jack Tars rioting for their civil rights, the revelers at Pinkster—black, white, young, old—did not affirm the republican system. They tested the strength of the existing civil society by needling its racism, prudery, and fear and inviting its citizens to join their wild party. They strutted their joys and forbidden freedoms in the face of a riven, slave-owning nation that made false claims to democracy. In these ways their fun was neither syncretic nor transatlantic. It was fun unique to the United States and fun proper to its moment. It was the fun of challenging a young nation that was struggling to find its footing. Nor, for that matter, were Election Days or Pinkster the return of African coronation rites. For all of their value to the community's integrity, even in the election of leaders, they did not affirm the racial community by asserting a free-standing power structure; at the end of the day, the black community remained socially and politically subordinate.

But the political thrust of their fun deserves to be taken more seriously. Paul Gilroy makes the strong case that African-American "subversive music makers" stand for "a different kind of intellectual"—in the broader sense of Antonio Gramsci's organic "intellectuals" who grow out of their immediate social conditions and find new ways to strive for power. Standing this music culture up against a verbal intellectualism associated with "bourgeois democracy," an intellectualism that "serve[d] as the ideal type for all modern political processes," Gilroy views black music as an intellectual activity that allows for, as he puts it, other political "possibilities" and other "plausible models" for advancing the people. The musical technique he lights on is "antiphony," or "call and response," and yet, as this chapter aims to demonstrate, many black-cultural displays of pleasure also supported a democratic public sphere beyond the reach of print technology, usually one grounded in bodily practice.

Pinkster affirmed the racial community by asserting its immediate virtues: active, lively, playful civility. To this extent, as an act of cultural syncretism, it marked the *obsolescence* of Old World rituals, European and African alike. As an act of vivid and playful upheaval in an otherwise hotheaded republic, it posed a threat. It was the fun expression of free-spirited community that belied the sarcasm and exclusivity of Republican and Federalist politics. The threat to which all of these documents testify is Pinkster's lurid and tantalizing spectacle of unchecked *inclusivity*, a virtue the fun-loving people craved. Pinkster should be seen, therefore, as more than another ethnological specimen—and something other than a "safety valve." It was a disruptive performance in the early republic that reflected an enslaved people's will. When African Americans refurbished their heritage to fit the volatile New World's constraints, their actions obtained new ritual purpose and seeded an important new tradition: the wild block party, to which everyone is invited.

In 1811, probably acting under middle-class pressure, Albany's Com-

mon Council passed an ordinance outlawing Pinkster Days. (The theater of action is now the site of New York State's Romanesque capitol.)
Throughout New England, however, Negro Election Days expressed
their scorching irony up until the 1850s, when black leaders themselves
began phasing them out in the interest of gaining more permanent
power. In Rockford, Illinois, they continued as late as the 1930s.

SUCH ANNUAL CELEBRATIONS often put African Americans on display, but far more common were the private gatherings when they stole
some time from their daily oppression to crack jokes, worship, and tell
their stories. These gatherings were their churches, courthouses, and
schools. "The language of the slave's speech and song," writes Leslie
Howard Owens, "was the embodiment of his community." The storytellers themselves, avatars of African griots, were often teachers and
charismatic leaders to rival the Governor or even the preacher. Their
curriculum sparkled with all kinds of mischief.

In a rustic opening in the Georgia pines, a short walk from the slaves'
quarters, a couple dozen members of a plantation community sit on logs,
lean on trees, and relax on the layers of soft pine needles that make
the floor a sumptuous mattress. Pine-knot torches trace a rough perimeter, crackling and dribbling streams of pitch. Spanish moss drips from
branches. Most of their number hail from West Africa, four or five generations back. Many arrived by way of the Caribbean or from far-flung
plantations to the north and south that are still the homes of lost families
and friends. Their wrists and ankles are scarred from shackles. Many are
branded. Many of their backs are disfigured by the lash. Some of the
wounds are still tender, or open. For all the misery that clouds their days,
tonight their attention is riveted by one stunningly energetic woman.
Her makeshift stage is a fallen tree.

They know her stories—or versions of them—and chime in with
laughter and sound effects. Many of their number could tell the tales
themselves, but she is one of the best, and the lightning-quick gestures
and pantheon of voices that spring from her strangely elastic body inten-
sify her status as a village elder. Her authority doubles, triples, explodes

when the woman vanishes into thin air—and in her place walks Brother Rabbit, a slack, easy, loping fellow. He stops in his tracks, one paw extended. He does a double take at Brother Wolf's daughter. The adults let out a knowing chuckle. The kids up front laugh and cheer. Everyone is thrilled to see Rabbit on the scene.

Little Wolf bats her eyes and turns away. She's going to make him *work* for it. Then he gets some irritating competition from oafish Brother Coon, whose heartfelt appeals hardly turn her head. Soon Brother Wolf comes trotting along and sees an opportunity. Wolf has a mountain of corn to be shucked. He tells them the one who shucks the most corn wins his daughter's hand in marriage.

The mention of corn shucking sets the crowd on fire. In one sense, it was the worst of jobs. In the autumn, all across the South, slaves would travel to neighboring plantations for the hand-splitting, back-aching shucking of corn. But it was also the biggest chance to celebrate—and to build lifelines throughout the region. Corn shuckings worked a bit like the Sons of Liberty's committees of correspondence: they were social hubs in an unofficial network that buzzed underneath a tyrannical regime. A single corn shucking could draw five hundred participants from all of the surrounding plantations. "We started shuckin' corn 'bout dinnertime and tried to finish by sundown so we could have the whole night for frolic. Some years we 'ud go to ten or twelve corn shuckin's in one year." The corn shucking itself was made bearable by fun, inspiring a marathon of circle dances, animal dances, challenge dances, jokes. The shucking itself was a rhythmic, dancelike practice, accelerated by patterns of call-and-response and peppered with improvised rewards, like the free kiss or "extra swig of liquor" (for anyone who found a red ear of corn), and it was often conducted by an elected captain, "usually the most original and amusing," a former slave recalled.

Brother Rabbit shucking corn—that would be a thing to see.

But the little trickster has no such intentions. On the day of the contest, Wolf takes them to his mountain of corn—and leaves his starry-eyed daughter to supervise. Rabbit holds back and lets Coon get busy. While the guileless beast makes his way through the heap—clawing back husks, glistening with sweat, eager to muscle his way to the prize—

Rabbit sidles up to his gorgeous foreman and gives her a taste of his native charms. He thrills her with a few of his slick dance steps. He cracks jokes that rack her little body with laughter. He woos her with sweet talk, softens her up with a fiddle serenade. He doesn't do a lick of work, of course, but when Wolf returns at the end of the day, both he and Coon claim the shucked pile as theirs. Unable to decide who's telling the truth, Wolf leaves it up to his moonstruck daughter, who naturally chooses the irresistible Rabbit. Brother Rabbit scoots on home with his prize (the storyteller hams his excited strut), but sad old Coon, broken with fatigue, can only drag himself on home.

There was a lot to be learned from Brother Rabbit, and the storyteller brought those lessons to life. If white ministers told slaves that they were beasts, soulless and doomed to serve their masters, the storyteller, especially through Brother Rabbit's example, taught them their minds were their best resources and their souls were full of irrepressible joy. In this case she teaches Frederick Douglass's frequent message: don't let anybody own your labor, certainly not if you can help it. But she also urges them to have some fun. This sybaritic little trickster takes every opportunity to cut loose and dance—to steal honey, pull pranks, generally to pursue his own happiness, and often that of his wife and his children. His sense of justice is fickle and selfish, just like the cruel old world he lives in, but the slaves claimed his triumphs as their own and winced at his occasionally brutal failures. His singular brand of daredevil fun served a serious purpose. It modeled a sane response to tyranny.

The trickster cycles of the East African Hare, the Nigerian Tortoise, and the West African Spider Anansi resurfaced in the New World in the updated forms of Brother Rabbit, Aunt Nancy, and the wily slave John. As Lawrence W. Levine demonstrates, these New World tricksters emboldened slaves to rebel. They reinforced valuable lessons in survival. The trickster's antebellum students learned to be "merciless" in reversing the cruel tactics of the powerful. They watched the weak but clever make the most of meager resources, and they laughed at the "meaningless etiquette" and "rigid hierarchies" that characterized the world of the master, who also has cameos as an inexorable trickster. Levine lists the ways slaves put these lessons to use: "slaves lied, cheated, stole, feigned illness, loafed, pretended to misunderstand orders they were given, put rocks in the bottom of their cotton baskets in order to meet their quota, broke their tools, burned their masters' property," even "mutilated themselves in order to escape work." Knowing their language and their fun mystified their masters, they turned that to their advantage as well, employing, for example, "music as a deceptive form of communication" (Randolph B. Campbell's terms) to warn other slaves of lurking bounty hunters. Fittingly, then, their hero Brother Rabbit often hid his celebrations and neatly illustrated George P. Rawick's claim that slaves "created for others from sunup to sundown," but from "sundown to sunup, and at all other times they managed to get away from work"—holidays, Saturday afternoons, and Sundays—"they created and recreated themselves." Having fun was essential to such re-creation. But it also follows that their masters, like Asa and Margaret May of Jefferson County, Florida, feared and abominated slaves' nocturnal behavior, while ignoring their role in bringing it about. "Negroes like to do everything at night in the dark, showing that their deeds are evil."

Even—especially—Frederick Douglass, despite his ostensible distaste for fun, was obviously warm to Brother Rabbit's game. Tricksters are everywhere in his autobiographies, as they are throughout African-American literature. His most memorable one may be John Covey, the mean and crafty overseer, but usually he casts himself in the role—as the picaro who slips through the hands of power. He doesn't say where he learned these lessons, but his highly animated oratorical style (getting laughs "by imitating the voices of slaveholders and southern politicians") suggested the strong influence of a well-documented storytelling culture.

Fun—not survivalism, but balls-out fun—remains Brother Rabbit's biggest attraction. The star of these tales is utterly outrageous. He wrings the pleasure out of every conquest. He double-crosses anyone (outside of his family) to satisfy his cravings and revels in the trickery as much as the prize. In a story recorded by Joel Chandler Harris, "Brother Rabbit Has Fun at the Ferry," he pulls pranks for pranks' sake: he beats Brer Bear and the Man in three battles of wits, then smiles and keeps his secrets to himself. It's more fun (he teaches) to hide your smarts than to strut them in front of the powerful. The folklorist Daryl Cumber Dance shows how Rabbit's bad behavior gave listeners no end of joy. They didn't care that he was "underhanded, unsportsmanlike," and "immoral." All that mattered was "that he bucked the system (a system which never had the slave's happiness at stake anyway)." The fact that he usually comes out on top "gave them immeasurable psychological pleasure."

But for all of his violent and selfish behavior, Brother Rabbit is terribly sociable. He smiles, he bows, he pays compliments—impeccable manners that set him apart from the boorish Native American Trickster, from whom he is at least in part derived. The barbarian Trickster—whose story cycle is remarkably consistent among most Indian tribes and nations, whether he takes the form of Hare, Coyote, Spider, or others—has two distinct sides. According to Paul Radin's classic study, he is both the "divine culture-hero," responsible for the creation of the world and culture, and the "divine buffoon," who begins his story by breaking every law and custom and lives out his days playing nature's fool—abandoning his children, killing everything in sight, carrying his insatiable penis in a box, scorching his own anus to punish it for farting. The Trickster, as such, is a *figure* of fun. His hilarity resides in his idiocy and his flagrant opposition to Indian values.

Brother Rabbit has the opposite appeal. He isn't divine (he's wonderfully human), and he takes his place at the center of society—which is nothing kinder than a battle royal of wolves, bears, foxes, and men, all of whom aim to cook him in their stewpots. He thwarts these opponents with legerdemain, and often they don't know what hit them. And unlike the Trickster's morality tales against breaking rules and indulging whims, Brother Rabbit tells you to break any law whose only intention is to break you first, which for rabbits and slaves meant all of them. But you also have to abide by customs—how-do-you-dos and RSVPs. Only by participating in civil society can you ever get ahead and ever get in on its limitless fun. The slaves' society was a deadly minefield, but Rabbit's unique ideas of civility, and his techniques for getting what he wants, taught folks to dance around those mines with the grace and agility of old King Charles.

ONE MORNING in January 1819, dashingly handsome Benjamin H. Latrobe, the architect who designed the famous White House porticoes, arrived in New Orleans by water from Baltimore. Even to a world-weary Pennsylvanian who had been wounded as a volunteer Prussian hussar, the diversity of New Orleans was overwhelming—"from round Yankees to grizzly and lean Spaniards, black negroes and negresses, filthy Indians half naked, mulattoes curly and straight-haired, quadroons of all shades, long haired and frizzled, women dressed in the most flaring yellow and scarlet gowns, the men capped and hatted." But among the mass influx of new Americans and the constant amusements of the carnival season, nothing jarred him like the "assembly of negroes" he encountered on Place Congo.

What at first he thought were "horses tramping on a wooden floor" turned out to be "a crowd of five or six hundred persons," all of them black but for "a dozen yellow faces," the mass of them moving in "circular groups" no wider than ten feet in diameter. Latrobe half admired their little orchestra—comprising an older man rapidly beating a drum, a few other drummers, and the plucker of a strange African instrument—but the singers and dancers at the centers of these rings filled him with disgust, horror. On an earlier occasion he had admired the "perfect grace" of French Creole ballroom dancing, but here he disparaged two African-American women who held crude handkerchiefs by the corners and "set to each other in a miserably dull and slow figure, hardly moving their feet or bodies." He dismissed another group of women who "walked, by way of dancing, round the music in the center," and he mocked the "women who squalled out a burden to the playing, at intervals, consisting of two notes." It appalled him to hear them singing a work song.

In antebellum New Orleans dance was nearly as regulated as race. Mixed cotillions were tolerated up through Nat Turner's 1831 rebellion, and a general racial "blending" could be found in "less respectable places like taverns." But quadroon balls, fashioned after white debutante balls, followed such rigid social codes that they were considered respectable venues for courtships between married white men and light-skinned mistresses. (The only black males in attendance were the musicians.) Far below such high social rungs, Place Congo was the bottom of the ladder.

Latrobe's snobbery followed the local fashion, but musicologists would smile at his opinion that he had "never seen anything more brutally savage and at the same time dull and stupid, than this whole exhibition." For what he had the privilege to taste was the roux that would flavor American music in the centuries to come: a pungent blend of Senegambian banjos, Congolese drums, and—according to Ned Sublette's fine analysis—early Caribbean syncopated rhythms that would inform everything from the tango to rock 'n' roll's backbeat. Spicing this stone soup over the decades were innumerable improvised ingredients: strings and skins, percussion devices, voodoo practices, and North American folk songs.

The rumbling, chanting, fiddling ensembles seemed to have inspired all kinds of dancing: "jigs, fandangos, and Virginia breakdowns," according to the music historian Henry A. Kmen, and the list was always growing: "However much of the primitive there was in Congo Square dances, it seems apparent they were borrowing rapidly from the culture around them." So some of these dances were born of black and white exchanges, as was the case up and down the coast. But the circle dances that appalled Latrobe and other observers were a different matter altogether. James Creecy, who went there some fifteen years later, better appreciated the dancers' "movements, gyrations, and attitudenizing exhibitions," noting in particular how "the most perfect time is kept, making the beats with the feet, head, or hands, or all, as correctly as a well-regulated metronome!" While it is hard to say with precision *which* circle dances dominated on Congo Square, it's a fair bet they were relatives of the basic ring shout.

The "ring shout"—believed to come from the Afro-Arabic word *saut*, which refers to the walking or running around the Kaaba—was danced by most sub-Saharan tribes, but it took on new value among American slaves, for whom it was, Sterling Stuckey argues, "a principal means by which [their] physical and spiritual, emotional and rational, needs were fulfilled." It appeared all throughout African America on Sundays, " 'praise'-nights," and whenever else possible—and not only when the master or the law decreed. For sheer numbers and diversity of participants, the circle dances on Place Congo served a grander civic function, as the whirling hub of an otherwise scattered racial community. Though there is evidence of similar Sunday gatherings in the late eighteenth century, Congo Square had been gaining force since its inception in 1803, when Napoleon's *Code Noir*—under which "any assembly of [enslaved] Negroes or Negresses, either under pretext of dancing, or of any other cause," was punishable by lashes, branding, imprisonment, even death— was eradicated under the Louisiana Purchase. Immediately thereafter the dance parties appeared, and their sound could be frightening. In 1804, a visitor from Massachusetts thought Congo Square called for civic order: "Oh, where are our select men of Salem?" But even after the German Coast Uprising of 1811, when Charles Deslondes's army of five hundred slaves was halted within fifteen miles of the city, the government let the show go on.

What Latrobe couldn't have felt from his place on the sidelines was the dance's heart-thumping sense of intimacy. Its thunderous rings— men bare-chested, women in sweat-drenched muslin work dresses— probably shuffled in a counterclockwise direction and carved a deep, dusty track over the course of many hours. Their bare feet likely tapped out small, precise motions, but their central movement—grinding, shaking, swishing, swaying—emanated from the tirelessly gyrating hips that fitted them together in a moving social organism. Their calls and responses, from deep in their throats, echoed the rumbles of the musicians. Bold new couples, one after the other, edged into the open center of the circle and executed free-form, improvised dances.

The ring shouters' undulations spread down the dancers' legs and out to the tips of their tapping, shifting toes. They also spread upward, throughout the chest, where they caused "a jerking, hitching motion which agitates the entire shoulder, and soon brings out streams of perspiration." As P. Amaury Talbot observed in southern Nigeria, this movement caused an "unceasing, wave-like ripple which runs down the muscles of the back and along the arms to the finger-tips" and made "every part of the body dance, not only the limbs." John and Alan Lomax, witnessing the dance in the twentieth century, reported that the ring shout was "'danced' with the whole body, with hands, feet, belly, and hips," all of which kept its "focus on rhythm." Its quick, propulsive action—usually involving front-and-back contact between dancers arranged by alternating gender—made it a likely cousin of King Charles's more intimate dances. It may also have been akin to what eyewitness Liliane Crété described as "sensual, even blatantly erotic dances, in which the dancers mimicked the motions of lovemaking." A white observer in the 1880s admitted "not altogether to understand" the dance but judged that it looked "more or less lascivious."

Southern blacks made major concessions for Methodist missionaries. Many dropped their fiddles, drums, and drinking. They also radically modified their dance. By agreeing not to cross their feet (an action missionaries considered sinful) they were inspired to fashion new "rhythm and excitement . . . that would satisfy and still be 'in the lord.'" What resulted was an even more intimate ring shout that pulled the dancers into tighter circles, much like the ones that troubled Latrobe. Not all missionaries were satisfied, of course. Laura Towne, a New England reformer who witnessed a Sea Islands shout, was shocked to see dancers "turning around occasionally and bending the knees, and stamping so that the whole floor swings. I never saw anything so savage. They call it a religious ceremony, but it seems more like a regular frolic to me."

The dance grounded dancers from a variety of ethnic backgrounds in a common bedrock of African experience. It also let them sidestep certain Western prohibitions. Early blacks sat through sermons that forbade their freedoms and insulted their humanity—"Obey your massa and missy, don't steal chickens and eggs and meat, but nary a word 'bout havin' a soul to save." The ring shout, however, was a religious practice that maximized eroticism, dexterity, and joy. In the cheeky spirit of Brother Rabbit, it eluded Christian prohibitions and *roused* the people's sense of soul. In the words of Richard Carruthers, a Texas slave during the 1830s: "Some gits so joyous they starts to holler loud and we has to stop up they mouth. I see niggers git so full of the Lawd and so happy they draps unconscious."

But is it accurate to call such rebellious dancing—especially properly religious dancing—fun? Christian Schultz was at Congo Square in 1808 and called what he saw both "worship" and "amusements," as if refusing to choose. Thomas Nuttall, twelve years later, judged that "the sole object of their meeting appears to be amusement." Clearly, in both cases, the word "amusement" was meant to trivialize the whole affair. "Fun," however, as this book contends, encompasses the dancers' risk and rebellion while accounting for their constant levity. The fact that they opened channels between races and classes also turned up the voltage. And the fact, moreover, that ring dancers there and elsewhere may have been practicing their chosen religion—under the noses of bewildered missionaries, under the batons of police officers—must have only heightened the fun, the exhibition of joy in risk and transgression, as their inscrutable pleasure also gave them moral and spiritual high ground. The fact that some of the dances were spiritual practices would have hardly contradicted fun, despite solemn Calvinist ideas of religion.

Where the ring shout brought dancers into shivering ecstasy, Juba, from the African "Giouba," cut them loose in wild improvisation. Juba borrowed freely from European moves—for one observer it resembled an Irish jig, for another it applied "the steps and figures of the court of Versailles with the hip movements of the Congo." Like the ring shout it was a circle dance, but it involved a more intricate call-and-response and put a premium on trickster technique. Traditional Juba told an ever-changing tale—animals and characters came and went; verses, refrains, and plot twists were decided by constant improvisation; and over the years it spawned a variety of new steps like the "Long Dog Scratch," "Yaller Cat," "Jubal Jew," "Pigeon Wing," and "Blow That Candle Out." Its most characteristic innovation was "patting." As drums were forbidden in many slave quarters, the dancers made do with their handiest resources—clapping, slapping, and thumping out rhythm on everything from their own thighs, arms, chests, and heads to the corresponding parts of their neighbors' bodies. Juba's rapid-fire comedy allowed for send-ups of the master. Even Frederick Douglass gave his reluctant approval, admitting that among Juba's "mass of nonsense and wild frolic, once in a while a sharp hit was given to the meanness of slaveholders."

Fun-loving, quick-witted "jubilee beating" also featured on Congo Square, where it injected some ego and biting satire into the circle dance's eros.

BY THE 1830S, such scenes of social harmony had grown quite rare in the overcrowded states. Andrew Jackson's 1829 inauguration kicked off the era in characteristic style. Thousands of gawkers and office seekers, angered by too little ice cream and lemonade, too few government positions to go around, and only one presidential hand to shake, mobbed the White House for their share in the feast. They pushed through doors, tumbled through windows, and smashed a fortune in cut glass and china. (Old Hickory himself skipped out the back door.) Washington socialite Margaret Bayard Smith, the most-quoted witness of this infamous scene, sounds like John Adams defending the Boston Massacre: "The Majesty of the People had disappeared, and a rabble, a mob, of boys, negros, women, children, scrambling fighting, romping. What a pity what a pity!"

Impromptu riots were common under Jackson. Despite the reformers' shrill jeremiads, loudmouth, violent, disorderly mobs went to war in the city streets—fighting to achieve political goals, fighting to oust minority religions, fighting to suppress certain racial or ethnic groups—blacks and Irish, in particular. "Hangings and public executions of any kind," the historian Edward Pessen notes, drew crowds from all levels of American society. Among all classes, personal differences were barbarously resolved through "stabbing, shooting, gouging out of eyes, biting off of nose or ears," and personal differences cropped up frequently in this testy, preadolescent nation. Michael Feldberg examines the violence during this period and distinguishes in particular between "expressive" riots (in which self-identified groups of vigilantes, neighbors, partisans, and others come out swinging to show their solidarity) and "recreational" ones (in which "election riots, volunteer firemen's riots, and street-gang battles, took on the character of organized team sports"). A popular recreation that was divisive and hateful, if not usually physically violent, was "Bobolition," Northern parades (and accompanying pamphlets, newspapers, and songs) that made public mockery of African Americans and their public bids for abolition. Such recreational violence can be considered "fun," even when it is sometimes lethal. It's rowdy, satirical, ecstatic, spontaneously communal. But when the thrill of destruction trumps the joy of the crowd, it's time to run for cover.

During this same era, however, dance became a form of peaceable defiance. For example, the fish market at New York City's Catharine Slip was a gathering place for black and Irish dancers who performed and competed on elevated wooden shingles (chosen for their percussive effect) for prizes of cakes and eels. From the 1820s through the 1840s, these competitions pushed the limits of racial and ethnic dances—blending shuffles, breakdowns, and jigs—and brought men and women and blacks and whites into what the historian April Masten calls a state of "friendly rivalry." Charmingly, "shindig," Jackson Age African-American slang for dance parties, derives from the smarting bruises and abrasions incurred from dancing Irish jigs.

In both New York and Philadelphia, each a hotbed of Jackson Age violence, the press and the courts were up in arms about a new craze in fancy-dress balls: during the winter social season, better-off African Americans, often in carriages, sometimes attended by whites in livery, would arrive by the hundreds at rented ballrooms and hold elaborate waltzes and cotillions that could carry on long into the night. Such balls were cause for alarm, and ridicule: they were frequent targets for mocking squibs and scrutinized by police for aberrant behavior. Still, the revelers didn't mute their rebellion—they wore it with style and overt pleasure. Whites sneered that the balls were juvenile imitations, and black reformers scorned them as decadent, but an event in Philadelphia in 1828, as Shane White argues, suggests that they were neither: Frank Johnson's celebrated orchestra performed, the dance floor was adorned with a map of Africa, a wall was decorated with broken shackles, and a visiting officer from Haiti's black republic was the toast of the evening. The pioneering chronicler of much antebellum black culture, White acknowledges that these fancy-dress balls involved "imitation," "parody," and "showy performance of a northern urban African-American culture" but then pointedly adds: "They must also have been something else—something that historians in their bookish dourness often omit from their renditions of human behavior—namely fun." To be sure. He includes under this category the revelers' high style, their "mingling and gossiping with friends and acquaintances," as well as their drinking and various shades of dancing, all of which point to "the way freedom was meant to be." But must this "fun" be "something else," something distinct from "parody" and "performance"? Something, it seems, lower? The fault doesn't lie with Shane White's argument but rather with our use of "fun." As it was redefined and practiced during this era by all classes of blacks, "fun" wasn't frivolous, it was a community treasure. Black "fun" gave force to a host of virtues—pride, defiance, competition, and freedom—that were fast becoming white society's vices. Without a doubt, the intimidating "sense," as White puts it, "that blacks seemed to be having more fun than were their former owners" must in itself have been good fun. It also spoke volumes about black civility.

Throughout this aggressive era—even after Nat Turner's bloody 1831 rebellion terrified the white nation—Sundays on Place Congo held on strong. Festivities began in the morning, "at a signal from a police official," and they promptly dispersed after the 9 p.m. cannon. In a world where blacks didn't own their own bodies, where their bodies were objects of industry and punishment, they seized on these parties to free themselves and build the bonds of essential community. Their parties were wild, rebellious, and sexy, but all they really threatened were Victorian sensitivities—and national feelings of white supremacy.

The novelist George Washington Cable—such a prude that Mark Twain said Cable made him "abhor & detest the Sabbath-day & hunt up new & troublesome ways to dishonor it"—as late as 1886 wrote with deep ambivalence about Jackson-era "Congo Plains." He called it a "frightful triumph of body over mind," but it is clear he also rather liked it. He trembled at its vision of wild democracy. He enjoyed the dancers' embrace of freedom and their rolling spirit of innovation, "the constant, exhilarating novelty—endless invention—in the turning, bowing, arm swinging, posturing and leaping of the dancers." He was so moved by their head-spinning diversity that he catalogued their national identities: the Senegalese, Mandingos, Foulahs, Popoes, Cotocolies, Fidas, Socoes, Agwas, Mines, Nagoes, Fonds, Awassas, Iboes, more and more—"what havoc," he cried, "the slavers did make!" At one point he lost himself completely and fell headlong into one of the rings:

Now for the frantic leaps! Now for frenzy! Another pair are in the ring! . . . What wild—what terrible delight! The ecstasy rises to madness; one—two—three of the dancers fall—*bloucoutoum! boum!*—with foam on their lips and are dragged out by arms and legs from under the tumultuous feet of crowding new-comers. The musicians know no fatigue; still the dance rages on.

At a time when so many citizens were abusing their liberties, Place Congo's congregation of slaves performed democracy at its fiercest. Free within the narrow confines of law, the people—of warringly different origins—drew from their various cultural repertoires, took from whatever was lying around, and employed their talents for the delight of the whole. Every citizen played her part, whether it was beating drums, plucking strings, rattling gourds filled with corn, or calling and dancing around the ring. Each got his fifteen minutes of glory, and the group's pervasive sense of fun managed to keep the riotous peace. And it didn't take so much as a Pinkster King to rev it up and keep it running.

The revolution in early African-American fun lacked a Samuel Adams. It also lacked a Frederick Douglass. Its most notable publicity was mockery, ridicule, sensationalism, and the distorting burlesques of blackface minstrelsy. Even today, with our full knowledge of slave culture's deep impact on America's sense of humor—and freedom, empowerment, *self*—few call it political. Indeed, many historians, following Orlando Patterson's powerful theory that people under slavery suffer a "social death," examine the soul-killing institutions themselves, lest we develop romantic ideas about these victims' utter depravity. For it is true. Slavery imposed a "social death." Even Christmas holidays were a cynical ruse to keep enslaved people contained. But nobody knew this better, of course, than antebellum blacks themselves. They recognized these weapons and stole them when they could. They hammered these weapons into tools and techniques for building a durable community. What helped their revolution endure—not for a year on Merry Mount, or a decade in Boston, but for centuries throughout the North and South—was their tireless attention to the vicious ironies that undermined the American republic. Denied the basic rights of citizens, even those of prisoners, "by far the larger part" of slaves didn't rise up in bloody resistance. They channeled their frustration into electrifying fun whose white-hot core was strategic rebellion. Not merely for amusement or recreation, these risky pleasures were the "fun and freedom" that Josiah Henson, in the epigraph to this chapter, said even "the sternest and most covetous master" could not "frighten or whip out" of slaves. As he put it, they were "fixed facts." The fun and frolic of early American blacks bred "national felicity," not social death. And their raging parties spoke for themselves.

Even when Americans aren't hurting anyone, their fun wakes up some William Bradford who promptly orders their Maypole toppled. Maybe he fears his *own* wish for fun, his own strong desire for "dancing and frisking." George Washington Cable was evidently aroused by "limbs that danced after toil, and of barbaric lovemaking," but at the end of his essay, when he noted that "all this Congo Square business was suppressed" in 1843, he added that there was "nothing to be regretted in its passing." In a moment of postcoital clarity, he concluded: "No wonder the police stopped it."

And so they did. But Place Congo, like Thomas Morton, kept coming back to life. By some reports it was kicking up dust as late as the 1870s.

WHAT'S AMAZING—and what made Place Congo and storytelling circles and street-corner sessions so *un*-American—was that with all of these liberated thousands having such an absolute lark, all day long and late into the night, and for how many decades, it didn't cost anybody (or make anybody) one red cent, one thin dime, one plug nickel.

Naturally, that was about to change.

## * 4 *

...............................

# A California Education

JOHN DAVID BORTHWICK WAS a freewheeling Scot who followed his whims into the world's dark corners, but as an artist and journalist he mostly went to watch. In March 1851, at the age of twenty-seven and recently endowed with a nice inheritance, he joined sixty argonauts taking the Panama route from New York City to San Francisco. Like the rest of them he was seeking riches, but the gold this young fellow struck—and later refined into *Three Years in California*—was a bonanza of observations regarding the emerging western character.

Borthwick's fellow travelers, having heard that weapons were like California tableware, stuffed their belts with bowie knives and never-fired revolvers. They set out down the Atlantic coast with a common spirit of adventure, spearing dolphins and musing about their fortunes, but as time wore on, and the crew got drenched by days of tropical storms, Borthwick saw a division forming in the ranks: between the few grudging travelers in rubber raingear who refused to share even a plug of chaw and the larger, more cheerful, more generous set. The stingy ones turned "quite dejected and sulky" and "oppressed with anxiety" when sheets of muggy rain wouldn't quit; the merry ones maintained "a wild state of delight at having finished a tedious passage" and at the "novelty and excitement of crossing the Isthmus." The killjoys, he reflected later, wouldn't stand a chance in the diggings, where a sense of humor was standard equipment. But the fun lovers would have the times of their lives.

He cooled his heels for a while in Panama City, where he made another important observation. There was a basic difference between the rubes heading west (who "grumbled at everything, and were rude and surly in their manners") and the comparatively "perfect gentlemen" on their way back. Both types came from the same lower social realms, but the latter had gotten their "California education." As he explained it later, once he'd been there himself, even the coarsest folks who spent time in California "received a certain degree of polish from being violently shaken up with a crowd of men of different habits and ideas from their own." Some of this violent "shaking" was lethal, of course, but the shocks that didn't kill them—the *educational* shocks—were often ungoverned, ungodly fun.

The mostly male company of diggings and boomtowns hammered out their own social tools from the crudest of materials. There was no stable government, no stable class structure, no religious authority, no strong domestic sphere. Contracts were settled by honor-bound handshakes; character was tested by games and jokes; bonds were forged at faro tables and in the sweaty throng of miners' "ballrooms." Whether it was California in the 1850s, Nevada in the 1860s, or Deadwood in the 1870s, in these cultures of excitement and cutthroat competition, citizens schooled each other in manners that allowed a spirit of freedom to prevail. Keeping it light, having fun, and toughening their hides against petty offenses, they engineered new strains of sociability that challenged, alarmed, and enthralled the young republic.

A new species of newspaper—as irreverent, disingenuous, and playful as its readership—had a strong hand in upholding such standards. Since the *New York Sun* appeared in 1833, so-called penny papers (costing one or two cents an issue) had flooded the antebellum public sphere with an entertaining and widely accessible new journalism: they deemphasized politics, sensationalized crime, and appealed to the growing urban working class with practical advice and exhilarating fraud—such as the *Sun's*

1835 Great Moon Hoax, an astronomer's report of weird plants and weirder monsters peopling the lunar surface. Out west, the penny press found fertile new ground. In gold rush California and a decade later in silver rush Nevada, "news" took its cues from coarse frontier humor and miners' rawhide attitudes. Tall tales, mad spellings, rivalries, and hoaxes inspired a journalism less concerned with facts than with spiking the social punch. A wild new permissiveness reigned in the West, and pseudonymous troublemakers like "John P. Squibob," "Ben Bolt," "Dan De Quille," and above all "Mark Twain" modeled raffish public behavior that challenged readers to live by their wits.

IT ALL BEGAN in January 1848, when James W. Marshall found an ugly yellow nugget while building Sutter's Mill in Coloma. Word leaked out. In no time some hundred thousand "forty-niners" were carving up California's hills. By September 1849, when lanky Bayard Taylor, a twenty-four-year-old world traveler, arrived on assignment from Horace Greeley's *New York Tribune,* San Francisco's fiery cosmopolitanism dazzled even his jaded eyes.

> The streets were full of people, hurrying to and fro, and of as diverse and bizarre character as the houses: Yankees of every possible variety, native Californians in sarapes [*sic*] and sombreros, Chileans, Sonorians, Kanakas from Hawaii, Chinese with long tails, Malays armed with their everlasting creeses, and others in whose embrowned and bearded visages it was impossible to recognize any especial nationality.

Just as Borthwick would two years later, Taylor abhorred the "Northern barbarians" he encountered crossing the Panamanian isthmus—clods who barged in in the middle of church services and gawked at altars with their hats on; "miserable, melancholy men" whom the majority of travelers "generally shunned." But he found Californians refreshingly sociable, especially, ironically, when the stakes were highest.

Californians gambled, fought, bought, and sold. They scurried to capitalize on the bum's rush for capital. They lived for adventure, new excitements, and prided themselves on sportsmanship. Taylor was intrigued by this orgy "for action" and "intercourse with . . . fellows," and though it wasn't easy for him to throw aside his "old instincts," he gradually warmed to the lax commercial attitudes that drove this "restless, feverish" society and to a generosity that put East Coast stinginess to shame. In particular, he saw a "disregard for the petty arts of money-making," an unusual eagerness to repay debts, and a widespread confidence "in each other's honesty" that he attributed in part to bare necessity, in part to "an honorable regard for the rights of others." This liberal attitude seemed even freer in the camps, where, for instance, he watched a mule driver refuse the "beggarly sum" of three dollars for a pistol and hand over the gun as a gift instead. When the would-be purchaser laid his money "on a log," insisting, "You must take it, for I shall never touch it again," the gift giver tossed the money in the road, scoffing, "Then I'll do what I please with it." The apparent butt of this joke for Taylor is the Irishman who "raked in the dust for some time, but only recovered about half the money."

His own ethnic slurs notwithstanding, Taylor admired Californians' civility. From booming San Francisco to deep in the diggings, he witnessed what he called the general "disposition to maintain and secure the rights of all." "In the absence of all law or available protection, the people met and adopted rules for their mutual security." And this may have been so, but it must be noted how Taylor credits this civility to the recent spike in U.S. citizens—as opposed to the "thousands of ignorant adventurers" from Mexico, Peru, Chile, and China. His 1850 runaway best seller, *El Dorado,* seldom resists such jingoism.

The gold rush was no utopia. For the thousand *natural* shocks the West was heir to—rattlers, grizzlies, sunstroke, starvation, drowning, hypothermia, food poisoning, and so on—there were just as many societal ones. Any personal dispute could erupt in gunfire, usually with an audience to cheer it along. Grifters fudged maps, made false claims, and hooked greenhorns with fake guidebooks. Forty-niners imported their native bigotries, and the whole enterprise caused immeasurable destruction for the Native American population. And though California, which was rushed into statehood, outlawed slavery in 1851, one of the legislators' most vocal concerns was that Southern miners, advantaged by slaves, would have a leg up on the rest. California featured America's inequities in microcosm. As Sucheng Chan has shown, African Americans, while well represented in the major cities as well as in largely black boomtowns like "Nigger Hill," were more disadvantaged than other races and ethnicities: "They struggled to gain freedom from slavery, the right to testify in court, the right to vote, and the right for their children to attend integrated schools." Whites privileged whites, Mexicans Mexicans, Chinese Chinese, and so on, and the rising tide of American exceptionalism, shown in miniature by Taylor's bigotry, was constantly pushing U.S. citizens up against internationals—especially against foreigners easily marked by their race or ethnicity. And of course, most starkly, it was a man's man's world where the majority of the minuscule women's population worked as prostitutes.

That same year, 1849, a wave of revolutions spreading across Europe made the forty-niners' race for lucre look pretty crass. In France, one month after the discovery at Sutter's Mill, middle-class factions teamed up with socialists to overthrow King Louis-Philippe, effectively establishing the Second Republic and declaring universal male suffrage. This upheaval inspired subjects in Germany, Italy, and Hungary to rise up against royals and demand the kind of democratic representation that Americans had enjoyed for more than half a century. Similarly, in England and the young United States, where democracy still left a lot to be desired, turmoil over human rights and social decency roiled the Victorian public sphere. In 1849 abolitionists outgrew the pulpits and achieved political viability with the Free Soil Party. That summer Gerrit Smith, the Liberty Party's presidential candidate, argued for the suffrage of women and blacks; women's rights had been brought to the national attention at the famous Seneca Falls Convention in 1848. The loudest voice in U.S. reform was the temperance movement, which combined Puritan values with revolutionary era rhetoric to urge American citizens—all of them—to emancipate themselves from "King Alcohol."

Alcohol, always a staple of the American diet, was drunk with political fervor in the early nineteenth century, when cheap, abundant, and liberating liquors were touted by many as liquid democracy—a bias, as we've seen, that dates back to the Revolution. Factory workers demanded on-the-job drams as proof of their personal freedom. Men filled taverns to shrug off the reins of an emboldened domestic sphere. But when binge drinking exploded in the 1820s—obtaining, as the historian W. J. Rorabaugh observes, "ideological overtones" of "egalitarianism"—the then-fledgling and specialized temperance movement began to achieve mainstream appeal—especially when it linked drinking to Jackson Age rioting, much of which came spilling out of taverns. As sobriety-minded Americans had been doing for two hundred years (long before John Adams entered Thayer's tavern), middle-class teetotalers now looked to temperance as a basic prerequisite of civic order; hard drinking, or so their argument went, brought out the worst in a sovereign public— theft, lying, agitation, murder. For decades this had been a minority opinion, but in 1826, an evangelical front formed the American Temperance Society (ATS) and ginned up the techniques—especially for publicity and mass organization—that persuaded America's growing, professionalized middle class during this populist era. It wasn't long before tsking over collective drinking had spread into a viable political movement.

Not content with just reforming hard drinkers, which had been the failed policy of their smaller-scale predecessors, the ATS went to the source, pillorying distillers and distributors and accusing them of corrupting American society. They also pricked the moderate drinkers' consciences—shaming them for dragging a productive young nation down. The message took. By 1833, when the Second Great Awakening was vibrating the pulpits, the ATS had expanded to six thousand societies and a million national members. In the decade to follow they promoted full-on teetotaling—total abstinence, even from small beer, which had been drunk up until then like an early American soda pop. Unlike the patrician ATS, however, the more demotic and ragtag Washingtonians— and their women's wing, the Martha Washingtonians—rose to prominence in the 1840s and represented the full sweep of the U.S. republic, drawing their numbers from all classes and persuasions and making temperance a mainstream cause. By 1851, the year J. D. Borthwick set sail for California, the concerted efforts of the American temperance groups had scored a major political goal—prohibition for Maine, the nation's original frontier.

While Europe and the United States campaigned for reform, California was going feral: whoring, drinking, gambling, swearing, shooting, killing, and going for broke. During Borthwick's three years in California, it impressed him that "the natural bad passions of men, with all the vices and depravities of civilization, were indulged with the same freedom which characterizes the life of a wild savage." But what can be, and often is, easily seen as a septic sinkhole in American social history was likewise remarkably fertile ground. When these "wild savages" nurtured their "California education," taking pains to enjoy each other's freedoms, exotic new varieties of civility took root: rude varieties, fun varieties that could flourish only in the Wild West.

Preachers and teetotalers were far outnumbered. Borthwick saw sprouts of civilization cropping up in San Francisco—a "sufficiency of schools and churches for every denomination" and "the influence of the constantly-increasing numbers of virtuous women," thanks to whom "the standard of morals was steadily improving." But there were also "gorgeous temples for the worship of the mammon," and the main currents of society congregated in bars, most profusely in Sidney Town's round-the-clock carnival of gambling halls, saloons, and factory-like brothels.

Borthwick approved of what he called the Californian's "intense rivalry in all pursuits"—particularly of the pluck required to survive it. "To keep one's place in the crowd," he said, "required an unremitted exercise of the same vigour and energy which were necessary to obtain it." Mere survival called for a leathery social hide, and success in this "hand-to-hand struggle with [one's] fellow-men" required "an excess of unscrupulous boldness and physical energy." Among such fierce competitors, "a polished education"—an Old World training like Borthwick's own—"was of little service, unless accompanied by an unwonted amount of democratic feeling." Decorousness just didn't cut it. Rivals and competitors in a lawless community needed common ground and mutual understanding, and nowhere was this "democratic feeling" stronger than in the saloons, where lonely men had the sorest need to overlook their differences.

Though Borthwick saw San Francisco's weakest competitors surrender to the "disease" of "drunkenness," he was impressed by the infrequency of alcoholism, especially "considering the enormous consumption of liquor." The way he and other gold rush chroniclers presented it, the noon-to-night guzzling of booze in saloons set the standards for polite society. It may have *looked* barbarian: "here, at all hours of the day, men are gulping down fiery mouthfuls of brandy and gin, rendered still more pungent by the addition of other ingredients." But in fact it disguised a delicate game:

> No one ever thinks of drinking at a bar alone; he looks round for some friend he can ask to join him; it is not etiquette to refuse, and it is expected that the civility will be returned: so that the system gives the idea of being a mere interchange of compliments; and many men, in submitting to it, are actuated chiefly by a desire to show a due amount of courtesy to their friends.

The game grew rowdier, though strangely daintier, the farther he drifted away from the city. While traveling among the diggings—a few days after witnessing a lynching-by-jury in the Mexican camp of San Andres (the condemned man blew "a farewell whiff of smoke through his nostrils . . . and politely took leave of the world with 'Adios, caballeros'")—Borthwick paid a visit to Angels Camp, which he considered more "civilised" than San Andres, and in the pub of a jam-packed, ramshackle hotel, he encountered a roomful of mangy fellows in the throes of a miners' ball.

Here he saw California society laid bare. All it took was a fiddler, and in this case a flute, to spring the most hardened miners to life. The fiddler shouted instructions to the crowd—"'Lady's chain,' 'Set to your partner,' with other dancing-school words of command"—and the miners faithfully took their positions, despite the small inconvenience that "none of the fair sex were present." No worries. Miners were used to making do, and in this case enough of them had volunteered to be "ladies"— marking their "inexpressibles" with distinctive canvas patches—that they could execute all the couples dances.

The dances themselves in the clapboard-walled ballroom were "very severe gymnastic exercise." "For here the men danced, as they did everything else, with all their might." Borthwick doesn't say whether he joined the dance, but clearly he examined these "long-bearded men, in heavy boots and flannel shirts" for their fragile balance of courtesy and aggression. They executed steps with "a great deal of grace," with "hearty enjoyment depicted on their dried-up sunburned faces," all the while their "revolvers and bowie-knives" kept "glancing in their belts." Just as menacing, and just as sweet, was the "crowd of the same rough-looking customers" who "stood around, cheering them on to greater efforts, and occasionally dancing a step or two quietly on their own account."

Such happenings were common among the diggings, especially in camps lacking proper gambling halls. Some folks had adopted the practice on their way to California, either dancing all-male "cotillions upon the green prairie" or aboard the ships where Jack Tars had danced hornpipes for centuries. "Dame Shirley," a doctor's wife living in Indian Bar, delighted in the details of an 1852 "Holiday Saturnalia" in which the most "generous, hospitable, intelligent, and industrious" of men rejuvenated themselves for three therapeutic weeks of nights-long dancing, continuous binge-drinking, and an "amusing" mock trial of local teetotalers—only to regret her "duty" of recording its salacious details in what she called an "unpleasant letter." But the Angels Camp event earned Borthwick's full admiration: he knew he was seeing the California schoolhouse. In his exuberant ink drawing of the same event, he shows a mixed-race crowd in loose white blouses, gaping and laughing, guzzling and smoking, while three burly couples dominating the floor put centrifugal force to the test. The focal couple is pulled in tight, their opposing arms locked, their beards up close. They smoke and hold each other's eyes with equal parts contest, defiance, and joy. If they weren't dancing, surely they'd be fighting.

What the picture doesn't show is the quaint détente, when "the 'ladies,' after their fatigues, tossed off their cocktails and lighted their pipes just as in more polished circles they eat ice-creams and sip lemonade." But which of these men plays the "lady"'s role? In Borthwick's drawing it's impossible to tell. Their easy display of this "domesticating" culture suggests that all of them do, and none.

This miners' ball, as Borthwick presents it, swirled at the vortex of a

"For here the men danced, as they did everything else, with all their might."
(J. D. Borthwick. Courtesy of the Library of Congress.)

gold rush Zeitgeist of excitement and antagonism. Men who lived lives of toil and danger, most of them thousands of miles from home, came together for orgies like this one that suited their peculiar needs. Part dance, part fight, part saucy masquerade, these mildly erotic democratic maelstroms were founded on the purest common pleasure.

IN MARCH 1849, nineteen-year-old Alfred Doten sailed from Plymouth, Massachusetts, to chronicle Merry Mount's legacy in the West. That wasn't what he set out to do, but California had a way of changing plans. His father, a sea captain, was a direct descendant of one of the Mayflower Compact's two bondservants; his mother, Rebecca Bradford, descended from the governor himself. Alfred left his job as a cod fisherman and boarded a refurbished whaler, the *Yeoman,* to get his California education. In his subsequent half century out west (he died in Nevada in 1903), this New England teetotaler became a loose bon vivant (and eventual alcoholic) living at the center of American fun. He recorded nearly every day of it, either in his cheeky newspaper dispatches or in the lively, illicit, unflinching episodes that riddle his seventy-nine leather-back journals like bullet holes.

His Puritanism clung like barnacles, at first. Two months into his rocky voyage, he was one of twenty-five stalwarts to sign an anti-tobacco pledge, declaring it "a very good move indeed." And just off Cape Horn, on July 4, a date that would soon become the annual peak of his otherwise raucous daily revels, Doten gloried in the reveille of guns, pipes, and drums, but he scoffed at the crew members who were such "slaves of King Alcohol" that they deigned to drink potato whiskey, "vile stuff." His temperance held strong up the Pacific coast—he admired sober Chileans in the streets of Concepción, in contrast to "several of the Americans drunk"—but a short while after arriving in San Francisco, which he assured his father was "the most civil country in the world" ("stealing is a rare thing, and murder is scarce, although every body goes 'armed to the teeth' at the mines"), his Plymouth morals started to loosen.

It took him a while to warm his hands on serious gold rush fun. As late as 1851, despite confessing here and there to a "fandango" or to "cards," he admired the miners who sang psalms more than the ones who spent their days "drinking and gambling." He scorned the Chileans and "howling drunk" Mexicans who held "a big spree" on the Sabbath, and he prided himself on "singing sacred music." But around 1852 his tune began to change. Holing up that September on the Calaveras River with some Chilean roughnecks (identified as "Alfaro & co"), he mused that they'd had "a hell of a spree and *some of us* got a little tight." Three days later it was "a big fandango spree," this time with "my four Mexicans from up the gulsh." After that the party was never-ending, usually with Doten and his fiddle to blame. He "astonished" crowds deep into the winter months with his "playing and singing," "broke the ice . . . with an old fiddle," and instigated parties throughout the snowy diggings. The following February, after more than a week of debauchery, he declared, "This is one of the best *'benders'* I have been on for a long time." And so would it go in the years to come, as the Plymouth boy recorded firsthand accounts of California "jollification."

Doten's daily sketches of his first six years, when he chased down rumors of lucky strikes from Spanish Gulch to Fort Grizzly, also detail the labors and daily dangers that characterized diggings life. Many folks he encountered were impoverished or killed—by fighting, mining disasters, stupidity—and a few commit suicide in his thousands of pages. But Doten was a survivor and a devoted hedonist. The industrious lad could learn to build a kiln while killing two rattlers and reading *Nicholas Nickleby,* or he could devote an evening to baking a "plum cake" after spending the day digging "30 rods." Like J. D. Borthwick and Bayard Taylor, Doten was curious about California society, but he was also more apt to join the party—or fire one up with his fiddle or banjo. In the manner of many African-American miners—who feature in countless journals and historical records for their dancing, fiddling, and banjo picking—Doten raised roof beams throughout the camps. And shaped though he was by his ingrained biases for Yankees over Southerners, Americans over Mexicans, whites over blacks and Indians, Doten moved freely throughout the populace, making friends wherever he went. He was keenly aware of racial tensions—like the near war among Chileans, Americans, and Italians that was narrowly avoided by a jury verdict; or that "Mexicans are robbing and killing the Chinese at a great rate." He railed into his diary against "thieving Mexicans," who he believed at one point were stealing his gold, and he lent a hand to hanging a Mexican convicted of murder, a somber duty he appeared to regret. And he slows now and then to mention a fistfight—or knife fight or even the occasional gun battle—but *friendly* conflict was more to his taste. His rule, if he had one, was fearless abandon, and whenever possible he kept an open guest list.

On an especially wild Christmas, in 1854, following a season of shovel-and-fiddle-breaking activity, as well as a kiln accident that nearly burned off his nose, Doten and some friends threw a housewarming party to celebrate their newly laid wooden floor. Their goal was to make "it perfectly thunder beneath"—in one of his daintier allusions—"the *tripping* of the *heavy fantastic toe.*" "The glorious old cognac flowed freely and fully entered into the *spirit* of the scene." They danced to old standards like the "Highland Fling" and invented new ones, with western flair, like the *"double-cowtird-smasher"* and several *"tird-run-variations."*

Sometime after midnight (who was keeping time?) two ruffians arrived from Spanish Gulch, one of them identified as "Cut-nosed-Bill." Doten notes that they "were not invited but were no less welcome and entered into the spirit of jollification with us." The singing and drinking doubled in volume—"the fun grew 'fast and furious'"—and before long "all felt filled with the 'milk of human kindness.'" Doten's only regret during this "most glorious frolic," which broke up after the blush of dawn, was the "two or three disgraceful little quarrels between Locke and cut-nosed Bill and others." But all was saved. The majority had "interfered," "prevented a fight," and the spirit of jollification prevailed.

Doten grew so loyal to California fun that he started to evangelize in his hometown paper, the possibly unamused *Plymouth Rock*. Writing under the nom de guerre "Ben Bolt," he had titillated his readers for years with the usual gold rush sensations: rattlers, grizzlies, vigilantes, gamblers, and the five-year explosion of San Francisco from the "little Spanish village of 'Yerba Buena'" to a booming cosmopolis. But his missives celebrating the Fourth of July, the Golden State's vaunted new holiday, provoked New England with a decidedly libertine vision of democracy. "As usual in California," he wrote in 1854—a year when activists breathed fire for prohibition throughout the northeastern states—the Fourth "was celebrated by a most unusual amount of powder burning, cracker-popping, horse racing, whiskey-drinking, patriotism, and (where the case seemed to demand it), a small 'tussle' or two." The diggings woke early when Juan Fernandez—"a native of Hindostan"—fired off a log fashioned into a bomb and initiated an all-day binge of shooting, dancing, hunting, and drinking. Things turned rather lurid after dark, when the men ("We had no ladies to grace the occasion") let themselves go in an all-out "stag dance" reminiscent of Borthwick's miners' ball. After a pause for a few cigars and songs, "all sorts of steps were taken, from polkas and waltzes, down to the 'fore and after,'" as well as giving another tip-off as to their interracial company, the "'Juba.'" Doten knew his account would raise eyebrows—and hackles. Evidently that was his aim:

Let no "old fogy," when he reads this, turn up his immaculate nose with a grim smile, at what he may term "follies." Just let him be situated precisely as we are situated here, and then see how he would act. If he has any warm blood at all about his heart, he might easily do worse than we did.

On July 4, 1855, such antics hit a boil, as "Bolt" dutifully reported to the *Rock.* Doten and his friend George rose before sunrise and roused the town of Fort John by firing their rifles "as fast as [they] could load." The miners dragged out with their "guns and pistols," held a communal reveille, breakfasted together, "marched down town with drum and fife," and went about gathering a band of "some 40—quite a force" to disport themselves throughout the day. Still feeling ornery after dinner, they marched six miles in single file with someone named "jackass at the head." Their destination was Fiddletown, where they hurled three huzzas at the various "public houses," made incendiary devices from the blacksmith's four anvils, dined and drank in its various pubs, and warmed the floor of the Spanish Dance Hall.

The locals quickly rose to the challenge, forming a band called the "Fiddletown Doughheads" and marching "in opposition" down the middle of the street—their "five fiddles" trying "in vain" to drown out Doten's band: "Our fifer, with protruding eyes and distending cheeks, blew his shrillest blast, while our ambitious drummer put in his prettiest licks. The fiddlers were nowhere; they lost their tune completely, not being able to hear their own fiddles. The 'Doughheads' gave us three cheers which we returned with earnest." They marched three rings around the dance hall and exited town, again in formation, "to the tune of Yankee Doodle." Back in Fort John, they "fired a volley in front of Vance's, took a drink and dispersed quietly to [their] beds." Faithfully reporting these events to the *Rock,* he added a poke at the temperance movement:

Whether any of the citizens of Fort John imbibed anything stronger than ginger-pop or soda water, we'll not mention in this connection, but if there was "anything stronger," "cocktails" or "sherry cobblers," for instance, taken a "corrective of the stomach," let us excuse it on the ground that the "Maine Liquor Law" has not yet extended its protecting

arm over the benighted citizens of this barbarous region. . . . Perhaps
the day may come when "Maine Liquor Riots" may become known in
these parts, when sharp-nosed policemen will invade the log cabins and
little tents of the miners, keen on the scent to discover some concealed
bottle of whiskey.

The month before, Maine's suppression of drinking through electoral
politics had indeed led to an actual, violent riot. But the Siege of Fiddletown, for all its fun and loud restraint, resembled nothing nearly so much
as the Sons of Liberty's Stamp Act parade, right down to the three improvised cheers in front of every pub. Which is to say, it was radically civil.

By 1855, at the age of twenty-five, Doten had earned his California
diploma.

MINERS HAD BEEN SCRAPING bits of gold from Nevada (then called
the Washoe Territory) as early as 1850, but in 1859 it dawned on someone why the mud in these mines was blue. The greatest silver strike
in U.S. history turned this sagebrush desert, hitherto inhabited mostly
by Mormons, into a hub of cutthroat commerce. In a matter of two
years, Virginia City, once a tent camp on the Comstock Lode, teemed
with all the luxuries of a Wild West metropolis: fire companies, hotels,
banks, brothels, gambling halls, and opium dens. The town constantly
shook from underground explosions, trickled with steam from its natural hot springs, and whizzed with volleys between its rival newspapers,
the *Union* and the *Enterprise*.

Alfred Doten quit mining in 1855, by which point the California gold
fields had been gouged, picked, sluiced, and sifted of their very last nug-
gets, slurry, and dust. He took a crack at farming and ranching for a
while, but he caught the gold bug again in 1862. He trekked his way
across the Sierras, pausing here and there, as was still his wont, for trysts,
benders, jollification, and the odd dispatch to the *Rock*. When he got to
"far famed" Virginia City on July 1, it looked to him like a step back in
time—to "San Francisco in '49." For the first time in fourteen years of
journaling, Doten was flummoxed:

No use for my pencil to try & describe this place—can't do it—big, bustling, noisy city—all process of creation—streets full of wagons, horses, omnibuses, crowd—sidewalk crowded with rushing crowd—500 houses being built . . . great circus performing here . . . lots of gambling saloons open to the public—crowded—Monte, faro, chuckerluck, rouge et noir &c—bands of music in orchestra . . . in the saloons also were dancing girls—hurdy gurdys, organs &c in the streets—lots of money flying around in this city & no mistake—

One thing is certain: it was a town mad for fun.

Three days later, on Doten's favorite holiday, the blacksmiths exploded the customary anvils, and the clubs and fire departments held parades, but there were also "considerable drunks & some fights—several men got shot in rows & two were killed." Such random violence was common in Nevada, part of the ambience, and Doten jotted it down with less ceremony than he did Martin the Wizard's "fancy tricks"—"'the vanishing coin,' swallowing my jack-knife, 'The one-armed fiddler' &c."—or the opening of a mill, two weeks later, for which three taverns spotted kegs of lager and a boisterous crowd trailed Doten's bandwagon, singing "Yankee Doodle" and "Hail Columbia." A minor riot broke out that night, leavened by gunfire and broken windows, but nobody was killed (thanks to a malfunctioning revolver), and the parties raged on for the rest of the summer. In August, he "got on a big spree, the wildest [he] ever saw, but still no fighting or anything disagreeable." Nevada was proving to be Doten's kind of place.

He set himself up in the town of Como, where he continued posting updates to the *Rock* and the odd correspondence to the *Virginia Daily Union*. That winter he kept warm with endless drinking, gambling, fiddling, and some "skylarking" that sent his friend Murphy's arm slicing through a window. And early the following March, in the midst of his cotillions-and-billiards regime, he crossed paths with a rising local celebrity: "Evening stage brought a noted correspondent of the Territorial Enterprise who writes under the 'nomme de plume' of 'Mark Twain'—his name is Samuel Clements [*sic*]." The journalists disported over the next couple of days. The minutes of this summit are unrecorded, but it is certain the conversation between these young troublemakers wasn't fit for public consumption.

AT THE TIME "Mark Twain" was barely a month old. Samuel Clemens had arrived in the Washoe in 1861. His brother Orion had come to be Governor Nye's factotum, and aimless Sam had tagged along. His résumé by then listed every last thing from printer's devil to riverboat pilot to, most recently, Confederate militia deserter; in Nevada his career was no better focused. He cast about for a year or so, picking up odd clerical jobs, failing miserably as a prospector and a placer miner, but succeeding, during a spell of unrepentant loafing, at setting several forested mountains ablaze along the banks of Lake Tahoe. He admired this "sublime" and "beautiful" sight from the safety of a rowboat: "Every feature of the spectacle was repeated in the glowing mirror of the lake!"

Clemens's follies during this fallow period—the best of them later embellished in *Roughing It*—have made deep contributions to the popular belief that even the worst of the Wild West was fun. Whether it is Sam getting bucked off an unbroken "Mexican plug" ("Oh, *don't* he buck, though!"), Sam having breakfast with the murderous "Slade" ("Here was romance, and I sitting face to face with it!"), Sam waking in a cabin filled with tarantulas ("It was dark as pitch, and one had to imagine the spectacle of those fourteen scant-clad men roosting gingerly on trunks and beds, for not a thing could be seen"), or Sam losing his rights to a million-dollar claim, Sam Clemens, neophyte argonaut, sports all the bluster and slack-jawed innocence that made America's western adventure look like a lark. Like most U.S. citizens he was out of his depth, but he was dead set on giving every ride a whirl. Blind to danger, wired for novelty, always up for an endorphin rush, Sam was his own best picaro, a character he mined for all its comic gold.

In the summer of 1862, right around the time Doten hit Nevada, Clemens was flat busted in the mountain town of Aurora. A proven flop at mining, he had been sending squibs to the *Territorial Enterprise* and signing them simply, aptly, "Josh." Writing with an ear for the region's tall tales and its special taste for the rude and absurd, he joshed his read-

ers with exaggerated mining claims, burlesques of the territory's blow-
hard chief justice, and a spoof of an Independence Day oration. Joseph
Goodman, the *Enterprise*'s armed-to-the-teeth editor, who had made his
own career provoking the locals, thought the young firebrand was what
the paper needed—for he was also suddenly understaffed: his prized
editor and staff writer, the facetious Dan De Quille (William Wright),
needed to visit his family in Iowa. When Clemens received the offer
of $25 a week (the price of a steak in flush Virginia City), he was so
elated, and so impoverished, that he closed the 130-mile distance on foot
and arrived at the *Enterprise* reeking of sweat, bristling with straw from
his makeshift beds, and bearded halfway down his chest. He cleaned
himself up right there in the offices and went about getting a *Nevada*
education: regarding the do's and do's of lying. Goodman advised
him: "Unassailable certainty," especially when the truth is *far* from certain, "is the thing that gives a newspaper the firmest and most valuable
reputation."

This was all the permission Clemens needed. Still writing as "Josh," a
name that was steadily gaining prestige, he exaggerated dull agricultural
statistics, dressed up skirmishes with handsome death tolls, and settled
into the idea that he "could take [his] pen and murder all the immigrants
on the plains if need be and the interests of the paper demanded it."
In October Josh sloughed off fact altogether and enjoyed the liberty of
an all-out hoax—a practice he may have picked up from the humorist
Artemus Ward, who had frightened readers of Cleveland's *Plain Dealer*
with his 1858 story of an escaped grave-robbing hyena. Clemens's hoax of
a "petrified man" tickled witty locals and wowed the credulous world. It
reported the discovery of a century-old cadaver "sitting" in a cave with a
curiously "pensive" bearing. Its success owed a lot to its riddling details:

> the right thumb resting against the side of the nose; the left thumb
> partially supported the chin, the fore-finger pressing the inner corner
> of the left eye and drawing it partly open; the right eye was closed, and
> the fingers of the right hand spread apart.

Close reading shows the Thinker to be thumbing his nose. Even "Judge
Sewell or Sowell," the Humboldt coroner lampooned in the piece for

holding "an inquest on the body," had to laugh at his own expense. But a medical journal, the *Lancet,* in far-off London, where they lacked the refinement of Washoe wit, cited the ridiculous marvel as fact.

In January 1863, as his stock was rising, Clemens traded "Josh" for the better brand "Mark Twain" and never looked back. He dined out for months on his *Union* rival, Clement Rice, a fellow statehouse reporter and traveling companion whom he worked up into a freeloading boor, the "Unreliable." In a series of increasingly improbable dispatches, Twain and the Unreliable crashed candy-pulls, dance parties, senators' conventions, and a wedding where the Unreliable kept requesting "the pea-nut song" and following the bride and groom "like an evil spirit." Along the way "Mark Twain" grew unassailable, skewering politicians, sending up rivals, and paying his tabs with self-mocking puff pieces for hotels as far away as San Francisco. Almost overnight, at least by the time he met Doten in Como, "Mark Twain" had become the tallest lightning rod for Washoe's firebolt sense of humor.

The capacity to tell a joke in the West, or at least to take one, was worth more than a service revolver. Jokes divided the men from the fools. One April 1 in San Francisco, Doten and friends made a day's entertainment of taking in the gags: sealed envelopes, turned down on sidewalks, were addressed to "April Fool & Co."; large crowds flocked to see a beached whale facetiously reported in the papers. "All sorts of fools traps were set and all sorts of people fell into them." Among the many pranks Dan De Quille remembered from the Comstock, most were at the expense of gormless outsiders, like the recent arrivals who watched with horror as "that most incorrigible of jokers, Bill Terry" placed a restaurant order for "baked horned toad, two broiled lizards on toast, with tarantula sauce—stewed rattlesnake and poached scorpions on the side!" He was served straightaway by conspirators in the kitchen while the onlookers "nearly twisted their necks out of joint" trying to glimpse what he was eating. Some jokes took in great masses of marks, like the California miners who poured in from all around to see William Wilson's legendary "12 pound nugget"—which turned out to be a healthy baby boy. "Each of the miners loved being had," William Bennett wrote of the prank. "As each squad came out of the cabin, every man solemnly asserted that the Wilson nugget was the 'boss,' the finest ever seen. . . .

Men came for two or three days and asked to be shown the nugget, some arriving from camps eight or ten miles distant."

One famous prank, recounted in *Roughing It* and still commemorated in Nevada, pitted a whole town against the U.S. government. The incident that started it was rather improbable: an ostensible landslide in the mountains around Carson had dropped the entirety of Tom Rust's ranch smack on top of Richard D. Sides's ranch, "exactly cover[ing] up every single vestige of his property." Apparently Rust liked the new arrangement and decided he would stay. When Sides went to fresh-off-the-coach territorial attorney general Benjamin B. Bunker, accusing Rust of "trespassing," the indignant official took up the case. He pulled together a court, complete with winking lawyers and in-the-know witnesses, and put the intruding rancher on trial. The conspiring locals were up in arms, insisting the fallen ranchland still belonged to Rust. After days of burlesque testimony, and Bunker's shrill closing statements notwithstanding, the court came back with the maddening verdict that Sides "had been deprived of his ranch by the visitation of God!" It took the attorney general a couple of months, but eventually the joke managed "to boor itself, like another Hoosac Tunnel, through the solid adamant of his understanding."

Miners took pride in telling fact from humbug, lucky strikes from "salted" mines, and they made open examples of interlopers and idiots. Writers for the *Enterprise* played to this prejudice and whipped the public into a froth. As one historian puts it, two of the paper's functions were "to provoke cascades of inextinguishable merriment" and "to give the gardaloo or raspberry to the great and saintly just for the pure, uninhibited hell of it." At a time when eastern culture, as the historian and critic Ann Douglas has shown, was being aggressively "feminized" all throughout the United States under the widespread influence of middle-class Christian journalism, western culture, with the help of the papers, was flaunting its unwashed *im*propriety. The *Enterprise* may have been the worst offender, but many of Virginia City's papers (they counted at least twelve by 1864) sent their rounders into the ring, fabricating news, talking trash in print, vilifying aspiring political candidates, and generally lowering the public tone. Hoaxes, pranks, irreverence, and slang appealed to the tastes of a mostly male *demos* who survived by grit and drank their nights away at the countless poker tables.

But in October 1863, Twain's "Empire City Massacre" hoax succeeded in turning even this case-hardened readership's iron stomach. In previous months, as the Civil War raged throughout the States and Nevadans traded blows over their constitutional convention, a rash of murders, gunfights, and hangings were keeping things interesting for Virginia City. Desensitized (or inspired) by this bellicose atmosphere, Twain dreamed up an outrageous story meant to shame the San Francisco *Bulletin* for publishing misleading investment information. Like any worthwhile hoax, however, its only real virtue was riling up readers.

The story was gruesome. Philip Hopkins, a father of six who lived in the "great pine forest which lies between Empire City and Dutch Nick's," slaughtered his family with an axe. He also slashed the throat of a witness, who galloped four miles to Carson City with Hopkins's wife's "reeking scalp" as evidence—then died. The destitute Hopkins, the story concluded, had been impoverished by "the newspapers of San Francisco." The details were ludicrous, but even the canniest readers missed Twain's tip-offs that the whole thing was a fraud: Nevada had no pines, Dutch Nick's was a tavern in Empire City, Philip Hopkins was a well-known bachelor, and no Paul Revere slashed ear to ear could weather such a nightmare ride. The next morning, over breakfast, Sam and Dan watched with interest while a hapless reader absorbed the news: "Presently his eyes spread wide open, just as his jaws swung asunder to take in a potato approaching it on a fork; the potato halted, the face lit up redly, and the whole man was on fire with excitement."

The sensation, the excitement, seized the territory, where the *Daily News* reprinted the story that afternoon. Only the *Evening Bulletin*, given time to cool off, called it "as baseless as the fabric of a dream." Twain issued a one-line response: "I take it all back." The *News* called it "a lie," to which Twain belittled their use of "small caps." But the fun, of course, was far from over, and "fun," needless to say, was the bone of contention. Among the many complaints was the *Bulletin*'s opinion that "the man who could pen such a story . . . and sen[d] a pang of terror into the hearts of many persons, as a joke, in fun, can have but a very indefinite idea of the elements of a joke." Twain replied that the writer was an "oyster-brained idiot" and that he himself felt not one "pang of remorse," as if to suggest that he in fact had a very *definite* idea "of the elements of a joke." Indeed, a gag that kept readers wringing their hands as late as January over their "shock[ed] . . . moral sense" had struck the bull's-eye of Nevada's social irony: citizens of the murderous, decadent Washoe Territory needed a bulletproof "moral sense" if they were to have any such thing at all.


DAN DE QUILLE'S *History of the Big Bonanza,* written years later in Clemens's Hartford mansion, pays keen attention to the "fun," "frolic," and "deviltry" that educated the average miner. One 1860 mining excursion, when Dan and his companions follow a sketchy rumor of "gold as large as peas," shows how reckless fun helped even quick-to-murder rogues sharpen their so-called moral sense.

Deep in the El Dorado canyon, when the men have to cross the Carson River, one miner, Tom, hires another one, Pike, to lug him on his back. Midway through the ford, sunk to his knees in mud, with Tom clinging to his hip "as closely as a young Indian," Pike starts to panic, shouting "Snake! snake!" and begging Tom to dismount. "A snake is biting me all to pieces." Tom, thinking Pike is pulling a prank, reaches around and socks him in the mouth. Their fisticuffs culminate in Tom's awkward attempt to murder Pike with his waterlogged revolver. Only when Pike explains that Tom's needle-sharp spurs were "causing him to think he [is] being bitten on all sides by water-snakes" can the men laugh it off, shake hands, and move on.

A few days later, when they have arrived in El Dorado and been thoroughly disabused of any hope of pea-sized gold, Tom is the last to rise for breakfast. Pike watches with relish as Tom pulls on his boot and lets go with a horrendous scream. "Pull off my boot, quick, somebody! There is a scorpion in it!" Pike rushes to Tom, who rolls on the ground, but insists the boot can't be removed. Tom's foot is too swollen: the boot needs to be cut. " 'Cut it off then!' roar[s] Tom, 'cut it off, I can't die this way!' " The boot is cut, the foot removed, and a prickly pear is found clinging to the heel of Tom's stocking. When the laughter subsides, everyone is surprised by Tom's calm reaction—everyone but Pike, in whose violent imagination Tom is lying low to kill him.

When they are alone in the ravines later that day, prospecting for measly specks of gold, Dan updates Tom on how frightened Pike has gotten, noting that "men are killed in this country for more trifling things." Tom's response reveals a coarse sense of civility: "I don't want to kill any man, but I do want to play even on Pike. It was mean on him to put that thing into my boot after we had shook hands down at the river." The terms were clear: a handshake was as good as a contract in the land of grizzlies and rattlesnakes, and even a joke has its time and place. Tom knows Pike is "a great coward," and his intention is to "scare the life out of him before this trip is over."

Reports in the region of eleven armed Paiutes "going eastward at a dog-trot" start bands of miners packing for Carson. Craven Pike wants to pack out, too, but Tom and Dan and the rest of the connivers argue they are safer staying put for the night, on the ruse that they have heard the Indians are lying in wait for prospectors between there and the river. The thought that they are cut off terrifies Pike, who turns jumpy and para-noid but tries to save face by boasting they would have some "fun a fightin' Injuns 'fore mornin'." (Little did he know.) Tom baits his fear by lighting a campfire and hollering a song about a yokel "from Pike." Pike himself hallucinates the rustling of predators and "lay awake a long time listening for Indians." When he finally passes out after midnight, the others sneak away into the hills, having been planning the prank all day. On cue they ambush him through the clattering shale rock, "leap-ing and making as much noise as though old Winnemucca and half the Piute tribe were coming down the mountain." They shout and curse and return imaginary fire, and a half-dead Hank staggers into camp, demanding of the panicked Pike, "Carry me off!" Pike hauls Hank about "two rods" before chucking him into some "thorny bushes" and disappearing into the night.

The next day, after fearing Pike has been drowned in the river and swearing off such "deviltry" for good, the men find him on Chinatown's main street, regaling a crowd with his tale of valor. Unable to resist one last prank, Tom's men deny every word of it and lead Pike to believe it was all a dream.

In the devilish hands of fun-loving miners, even the diggings' deadliest threats—vipers, murderers, hostile Indians—could be fashioned into marvelous playthings. The western prankster, like Brother Rabbit, did not shrink from the high-stakes game. His taste was for gunpowder, riches, and power, and his practical jokes followed suit. He also used the tricks of his trade to jostle society for its biggest laughs. Poltroons like Pike and buffoons like Attorney General "Bunscombe" went against the grain of free-spirited communities that survived by sociability, courage, and wits. Whereas vigilantes made examples of desperadoes by hanging them from the highest trees, pranksters called out hotheads and fools who threatened to drag society down, and in doing so they buoyed society up.

WHEN ARTEMUS WARD (Charles Farrar Browne), the celebrity lecturer and humorist, hit Virginia City in time for the 1863 Christmas bacchanalia, he, Sam, and Dan—Ward called them the "Three Saints"— indulged in a notorious two-week binge that found them glorified in print, entertaining packed houses, and taking a midnight tour of the rooftops that was rudely halted by Virginia City police. Ward, who was famous for crazy spellings and hedonism, soberly concluded that the town was "very wild" but "that a mining city must go through with a certain amount of unadulterated cussedness before it can settle down and behave itself in a conservative and seemly manner." These "Saints" were connoisseurs of unadulterated cussedness; they left seemly manners to the cattle train of latecomers.

By January 4 Clemens had already tapped his famous friend's connections and published a bona fide Washoe missive in the New York *Sunday Mercury*. Twain's first eastern publication, offering "'opinions and reflections' upon recent political movements," calls to mind Doten's baiting letters to *Plymouth Rock*. It aims to shock the uppity eastern states with its mockery of religion, government, and babies, but it also fires a political skyrocket, as if celebrating a New Year's Eve of territorial

THE STORY OF PIKE AND TOM.

"The Story of Pike and Tom," a tale of brinksmanship and one-upmanship. (Courtesy of Special Collections, Nimitz Library, United States Naval Academy.)

independence. "Satisfied" that Nevadans will shoot down the state constitution, on the grounds that it calls for the taxation of mines, Twain puts all the nominated officials up for sale. As advertised, some are more useful back east than out west: "One Governor, entirely new. Attended Sunday-school in his youth, and still remembers it. Never drinks. In other respects, however, his habits are good." Some, like the "second-hand" treasurer, are good to nobody but themselves: "Took excellent care of the funds—has them yet."

The freedom with which Twain skewered politicians, much like the freedom with which he needled public sympathies and roared away his nights with other drunk reporters, was enabled on some level by the permissiveness of the West, and by the viral mistrust of authority and control, but it also sprang from his fascination with community—especially reckless, chaotic community. He liked watching society run its rocky course, and he bristled when oligarchs got in the way. Twain was nobody's radical democrat. He despised Nevada juries—"composed of two desperadoes, two low beer-house politicians, three barkeepers, two ranchmen who could not read, and three dull, stupid, human donkeys!"—but he was thrilled by dance halls and theaters in uproar; delighted by Nevada's "infinitely varied and copious" slang; amused, then scared, then ultimately enlarged by the widespread sensations caused by his hoaxes, for here was humanity at its most excitable.

The *noblest* fun he witnessed along these lines—"the wildest mob Virginia had ever seen and the most determined and ungovernable"— was during his last month in Virginia City, when the citizens "rose as a man" and heaped their accumulated riches on the U.S. Sanitary Commission, a medical brigade serving both sides of the Civil War. Nevadans' "flush-times" munificence met their wartime patriotism and gave way to an extraordinary prank that evinced the territory's sterling character.

Reuel Gridley, Clemens's childhood classmate, was living in the nearby town of Austin. That March, when he lost Austin's mayoral race, Gridley also lost a bet with his Republican opponent and had to haul a fifty-pound flour sack through the streets, followed by townsfolk and a marching band. When someone suggested he auction the sack "for the benefit of the Sanitary," the crowd went wild. The first winner bought it for $250, then turned around and auctioned it off again. By the end of the day it had been bought and sold so often that it had earned a stunning $8,000. Virginia City caught wind of the gag and, not to be bested, called for the sack themselves. They were disgusted when they could raise only $5,000, and they thought they might get another chance the next morning when a parade of carriages blared its way down the high street, led by Gridley and his flour sack, "the latter splendid with bright paint and gilt lettering." But the wagons kept going out the other side of town, leaving Virginians with their wounded pride. It was a warm spring day, and the glittering procession (Clemens included) merrily rolled on over the sagebrush mountains to the mining towns of Gold Hill, Silver City, and Dayton, announcing their arrival with "drums beating and colors flying" and greeting mobs of "men, women and children, Chinamen and Indians" who had been alerted in advance by telegram.

Gridley's traveling orgy of absurd largess rolled all the way to Carson City, and eventually on to San Francisco, where its reputation preceded it. The prank held on for three months straight, and the sack was last sold at "a monster Sanitary Fair" in St. Louis, where it was displayed alongside its final purchase price, valued in bricks of Nevada silver ($150,000!), and was baked into platters of costly cakes.

WHAT J. D. BORTHWICK CALLED a "California education"—the "polish" argonauts got "from being violently shaken up with a crowd of men of different habits and ideas from their own"—conjures up lessons in plain moral sense. Borthwick's phrasing is remarkably similar to that of the third Earl of Shaftesbury, the eighteenth-century father of "moral sense" philosophy and Thomas Hobbes's fiercest philosophical rival. Unlike bitter and cynical Hobbes, who believed people entered into society out of selfish motives, Shaftesbury thought people were naturally good citizens, who, when left to their own devices, achieved their aims through brisk give-and-take. In the throes of open public discourse—as in barrooms and around campfires, where civility turns coarse and often boisterous—folks are free to rail and joke, even on occasion, in his words, to "fight." Such conflict is safe, by and large, when the majority are interested in the common good. In a society that is motivated by the generality's good, even etiquette can afford to be feisty. In fact, as Shaftesbury argued, it *has* to be. "All Politeness," he wrote, "is *owing* to Liberty. We polish one another, and rub off our Corners and rough Sides by a sort of amicable Collision. To restrain this, is inevitably to bring a Rust upon Men's Understandings. 'Tis a destroying of Civility, Good Breeding, and even Charity it-self, under pretence of maintaining it."

The argonauts Borthwick saw heading east from California showed the marks of many "collisions," "amicable" or otherwise. Californians and Nevadans were connoisseurs of collision. It toughened their hides and steeled their wills. It was also a surefire source of pleasure. The excitement and adventure that had propelled them westward—that which drove Taylor, Doten, and Twain—had also thrown them into makeshift society where cursing, pranks, gambling, song, and the capacity to hold their fiery drink were counterweights to honor and bravery. While the growing eastern middle class was minding their manners and shuttering their taverns, these emigrants and westerners pursued a radical civility that had been on the run since Merry Mount: the social bonds and personal thrills of risky, rebellious fun.

The American frontier was a woolly place, incomparable to Shaftesbury's courtly world. With its Indian wars, claims disputes, lawless justice, deadly predators, extreme weather, runaway riches, and (most often) desperate poverty, it laid the workings of society bare—often to reveal that they were badly damaged. The stakes for not getting along were high—typically isolation, mutilation, or death—and yet nobody was rewarded for acting skittish. On the contrary, as it emerges in these Sierra Nevada stories the celebrated citizens were the boldest ones—the practical jokers, rousing musicians, willing combatants, and impious journalists. These folks didn't shy away from fray; they exploited its pleasures and voiced its freedoms. In a land that demanded backbreaking participation in order simply to survive, they modeled rude and playful civility. They made a mockery of the stingy and scared and dared other citizens to join in. Their coarse behavior was delicious, infectious, and their elaborate pranks and hoaxes and parties formed spontaneous and volatile communities bound by excitement and hilarity. And when the papers and publishers spread their fame back east, this Wild West attitude riveted the nation. These creatures of slang and daring and pluck became paragons of American liberty, their fame growing into instantaneous legend.

Such boldness in the face of adversity and restraint characterized the best early American fun. Boldness in the face of Puritans, the British, slave owners, and reformers. The principals were spark plugs like Thomas Morton and Samuel Adams, charismatic figures like old King Charles, tricksters and troublemakers like Alfred Doten and Mark Twain, but in all of these cases their willing associates—sometimes numbering into the thousands—lent their fun its civic force. The crowd rose up and gave its assent, happy to join in the rebellious dance, glad to show they got the joke, ready to make wild contributions of their own. The joy of these free and lawless crowds affirmed, in flashes, the experience of democracy. It allowed citizens that would otherwise have been pushed away to feel brief thrills of liberty and equality.

IN ALL OF THESE CASES there were environmental conditions—*fundamentally American conditions*—that made the fun possible, made it necessary. Untamed wilderness. Unchecked tyranny. A world of everything and nothing to lose that benefited only the hardest characters. Whether they were adventurers tussling for ideological freedom, colonists rallying for a political identity, slaves asserting their pride and humanity, or emigrants risking life and limb to bust their fortunes out of rocks, the protagonists in these stories were attracted to conflict for all of its generative possibility. That they were advocates for group pleasure, not selfish domination, has helped to establish the coarse civility that continues to thrive in the national consciousness. The pleasure of tangling with opponents and rivals, of not backing down, of not giving up, all the while proving your style and wit, is a virtue that Sons of Liberty paraded and that Pinkster Boys reveled in. It was a survival tactic in the Wild West. Had Americans not risked such *amicable* collisions, but resorted only to violence or submission, they would have joined the low ranks of criminals and cowards who tried to keep the people apart.

Instead they were authors of a national culture that remains our greatest social resource.

# 5

# Selling It Back to the People

IN 1876, the American humorist Samuel S. Cox claimed that "Plenty,
unless gorged to dyspepsia . . . is the very father of fun." Samuel S.
Cox was a man of his age—the so-called Gilded Age. In his era of conspicuous consumption and leisure, when American calendars were suddenly abloom with weekends, vacations, and holidays, "fun" became
a catchall name for outlets that didn't require backbreaking, mind-
numbing labor—sports, spas, carnivals, circuses, vaudeville, parks, and
so on. Fun-as-plenitude prevailed during the period, and it made some
folks a lot of money.

American fun, as defined by this book, rarely *prevailed* in the early
republic. Fun, as the previous chapters show, was one of many notable
forces in the struggle between authoritarian citizens, who tried to contain
the people's freedoms, and individualistic (or communitarian) citizens,
who felt such freedoms were the life of democracy. Ambitious fun lovers
like Thomas Morton and King Charles may have made some effort to
prevail, but achieving market share wasn't their priority—or a realistic
possibility. Samuel Adams and the Sons of Liberty scored stunning vic-
tories, but a "culture of fun" wasn't their objective; their sights were set
on founding a republic. And "funmaking animals" like Zab Hayward

and Alfred Doten were happy just whipping up a crowd; for all of their spontaneous influence, they lived from one wild party to the next.

In the Gilded Age, however, it is fair to say, a culture of *entertainment* did prevail, did attract the population's broadest middle—drawing tens of thousands of upright citizens to its various, widespread, spectacular events. This revolution came about largely by the efforts of a single businessman. The progenitor of Gilded Age entertainment was the inveterate prankster P. T. Barnum. (He is also believed to be the nation's second millionaire, after fur-and-opium mogul John Jacob Astor.) Barnum's greatest humbug was to concoct a "fun" that seemed to resolve one of America's deep struggles: it pandered to Puritans while pleasing hedonists. As a bonus, it sold the novelty of the open frontier in the midst of congested urban drudgery. And for no extra cost, it captured the crowd-pleasing power of the Yankee-inflected practical joke.

It was during these same decades, from the Jackson Age to the Civil War, that the bizarre phenomenon of blackface minstrelsy turned the mockery of black folk fun into antebellum America's dominant amusement. T. D. Rice, a pioneer of this craft, reveled in the danger of black trickster figures, but in the 1840s and 1850s, when Barnum and other showmen endeavored to raise the theater to higher Victorian standards, clever crowd pleasers like Dan Emmett and Stephen Foster traded blackface's raciest content for bland sentimentality. Upbeat songs like "Camptown Races" brought plantation romance into the nation's most respectable parlors.

And it was likewise during this antebellum period that the urban subculture of b'hoys and g'hals bullied its way into the crossroads of American fun: now "fun-making animals" of the Zab Hayward school, now troublemaking stooges for radical politicians, now ardent consumers of commercial entertainment, these stylish firebrands (and volunteer firemen) were destined to become the target market of their own folk icons. What is more, their rude, unscrupulous, and often violent behavior forced the theaters to clean up their act.

During the postbellum period, then, the prosperous North feasted on commercial entertainment, much of which bore the fingerprints of these antebellum phenomena. At circuses, in vaudeville, in the Uncle

Remus tales, and in Buffalo Bill's Wild West show, all of America's weirdness and roughness was sanitized, multiplied, and packaged for mass consumption. Eventually, at the end-of-the-century theme parks, the speed and power of an industrialized nation was replicated by whirling machines. Sass and excitement were out there in the open, and everybody had some fun.

But the dirt and danger and freedom were missing.

BORN IN 1810 into a family of barkeeps and grocers, Phineas Taylor Barnum was the "pet" of his maternal grandfather, Phin, who would "go farther, wait longer, work harder and contrive deeper, to carry out a practical joke, than for anything else under heaven." Young Barnum became the target of one such joke before he could even speak. Old Phin had deeded him "the whole of 'Ivy Island,' one of the most valuable farms in the State," or so the boy was told for his first ten years. During this time his family and neighbors puffed up his pride in this legendary tract: with it came power, responsibility, and so on. When his time came to visit this bounty, however, a swampland gnarled with vines and alders rose before him with its sour "truth," that he "had been made a fool by all our neighborhood for more than half a dozen years." The boy's alleged retort to his father, that he would sell the land "pretty cheap," spoke volumes about the man he would become. For Barnum, the best punch line served the bottom line.

Barnum inherited Phin's taste for pranks—"those dangerous things"—and even if sometimes he regretted their damage, the joy was just too strong to resist. In every New England village of his childhood, he speculated, "there could be found from six to twenty social, jolly, story-telling, joke-playing wags and wits, regular originals," and staging pranks was their greatest endeavor. But this diverting pursuit played second fiddle to Barnum's most formidable trait—an "organ of acquisitiveness" (as he liked to call it) that had him pinching pennies, selling candies to soldiers, besting friends at swaps, selling lottery tickets at the age of twelve, and finessing the Yankee tradition in trickery behind his parents' grocery counter.

At age twenty-two, married, secure, and breathing the fire of Jacksonian democracy, Barnum ran a weekly called the *Herald of Freedom* that espoused his anti-Calvinist beliefs in what he called "cheerful Christianity" and that stood by his motto, cribbed from Thomas Jefferson, of "eternal hostility to every form of tyranny over the mind of man." The *Herald* was as bombastic and quirky as its editor, and it didn't shy from a public fight—typically in opposition to the killjoy blue laws that stepped on travel, amusement, and lotteries. Its most infamous potshot, against a local deacon, landed Barnum in jail for two months, during which sentence he kept publishing his paper and enjoyed an outpouring of public support: the people carpeted, papered, and furnished his jail cell, lining its walls with his personal library. They kept his story alive in the press, and they converged by the thousands on the day of his release—throwing a dinner for him in the courthouse where he'd been convicted. Cannons were fired, toasts were raised, and the ex-con was paraded home by a sparkling six-in-hand, followed by crowds and a marching band. He went on to open a grocery store, but his love affair with the public was only on hiatus, as were his plans for "cheerful Christianity."

In 1835, he seized the chance to cash in on "that insatiate want of human nature—the love of amusement." He was put in contact with an "extraordinary negro woman" who claimed not only to be 161 years old, but also to have been George Washington's childhood nurse. It wasn't your typical brand of entertainment, but the inveterate trickster knew what would fetch 'em. He bought "Joice Heth" for $1,000. She was toothless, bedridden, and "totally blind," but performing from her couch on a "tastefully" festooned stage she issued such captivating streams of lies that the press trumpeted her glory from Philadelphia to New York. Capacity crowds flooded in and gawked and gaped until they were herded toward the refreshments.

When Barnum feared the frenzy was calming down, he upped the ante with an outrageous counter-hoax, an anonymous letter to the local press claiming Joice Heth *herself* was a fake, a "curiously constructed automaton, made of whalebone, India-rubber, and numberless springs." The titillated public rushed back to the exhibit with reinvigorated excitement; Heth herself, in Barnum's words, "began to take great delight in the humbug, which was a profitable one to her." When Heth died a couple of years later, the hoax came back in a well-publicized autopsy. When her unremarkable age came to light (eighty at the oldest), Barnum staged a crowning gag in retaliation: a letter to the papers saying Joice Heth was alive and performing in Connecticut.

Barnum became a large-scale prankster in the spirit of the Sons of Liberty, but his pranks were superfluous, and his agenda was increasingly commercial. In the easily agitated Jackson era, when crowds were quick to come to blows, he emancipated their love of mischief. His 1843 "Grand Buffalo Hunt, Free of Charge" was wilder and grander than even the Joice Heth hoax. For it he bought a $700 herd of the mangiest buffalo and publicized a free safari in Hoboken. Quietly splitting profits with the ferryboat companies, who dragged twenty-four thousand Manhattanites across the Hudson, he managed to clear $3,400 without letting on that the "prince of humbugs" was behind it. The hunt itself was a blatant rip-off, "Ivy Island" for the masses—"so perfectly ludicrous," Barnum recalled, "that the spectators burst into uncontrollable uproarious laughter." The crowd, in their hilarity, spooked the buffalo, which feebly trampled through the chintzy fencing and into the surrounding marshes. "The uproar of merriment was renewed, and the multitude swinging their hats and hallooing in wild disorder." The papers got in on the fun as well, inventing injuries and buffalo deaths, but the truth was the masses had been lured from the city to enjoy some ersatz Americana. Barnum got folks to play along with his joke, even a joke on their inherent cheapness—and their yearning for a wilder world out west—and a fine June day was had by all.

But for all the mischief bred in his bones, P. T. Barnum was no Thomas Morton, and no Alfred Doten. He went to church, led carnies in prayer, and became a roaring voice for temperance. More to the point, he knew that alienating pious America was terrible for business. In 1836, when the national reform movement and his first traveling show were both just getting their sea legs, Barnum attended Sunday services "as usual" and had to endure an "abusive" preacher lambasting his "circus and all connected with it as immoral." Accosting the preacher afterwards for not allowing him a rebuttal, Barnum made a speech that won over the congregation, some of whom "apologized for their clergyman's ill-behavior." The act was such a hit that he replayed it weeks later and "addressed the audience for half an hour."

That same year Nathaniel Hawthorne published "The May-Pole of Merry Mount," his delightful romance of Morton's great showdown in which "Jollity and gloom were contending for an empire," but Barnum wasn't at war with Plymouth. Calvinist reformers weren't Barnum's enemies; they were his stiffest competition. No radical, no rebel—the original crowd pleaser—Barnum, like the reformers, set his sights on the majority. Both parties wanted the middle class to flourish, but while the Second Great Awakening demanded work over play, severity over silliness, private sobriety over public pleasure, Barnum gave the people a break. Instead of scaring them with hellfire and brimstone, he hypnotized them with Signor Vivalla's death-defying, stilts-walking, plate-spinning extravaganza.

His fun became theirs, for a nominal fee. A Yankee peddler of the wonderful and bizarre, he ensnared the public with his vision of progress. In the 1840s, when he opened his towering American Museum, he offered them the world in miniature: replicas of Niagara, Dublin, Paris, and Jerusalem; the first stateside Punch-and-Judy show; dioramas of biblical and literary dramas; "trained chickens," "industrious fleas," and a knitting machine run by a dog. With his knack for teasing the fun from diversity, he hired Chinese and Spanish jugglers, brought in war-dancing Native Americans from the Rockies and three obese Scottish brothers, "The Highland Mammoth Boys." He kept corpulent children on hand at all times (these, he found, were guaranteed to please), but the Mammoth Boys were especially versatile, practicing acts of mesmerism at their *soirées mystérieuses*.

His duty, as he saw it, was "to arrest public attention; to startle, to make people talk and wonder; in short to let the world know that I had a Museum." So he situated his museum on Manhattan's Broadway, adorned it with fireworks and international flags, and targeted pedestrians from all walks of life, from the downtown working class to the uptown elite. He cashed in on the Jackson-era will to participate—to have Gypsy girls tell their fortunes, to have their heads read by phrenologists, to be taken in by elaborate jokes—but in the end every citizen was one more customer.

Barnum treated these customers with dignity. In his early years he courted the people's doubt, knowing their skepticism increased their investment and, in the end, sold more tickets. In 1842, for instance, when public was slow to challenge his "Feegee Mermaid" (a monkey head sewn to the tail of a fish), he published an anonymous notice in the papers that put the skeptics onto his scent: "Mr. Griffin, the proprietor of this curious animal, informs us that some persons have the impression that he is getting editors to call it a 'humbug,' for the purpose of drawing public attention to it, but he assures us positively that this is not the fact, no such clap-trap being necessary." This artfully lobbed missile of meta-promotion was aimed at only the sharpest readers, those who saw that the notice itself was the same "clap-trap" it was scoffing at.

Humbug, the way young Barnum presented it, relied for its effect on the public's curiosity. Whether gazing in wonder or laughing in ridicule (at Barnum, at the dupes, at their gullible selves), the crowd was engaged in a lively sort of fun that triggered their agency as free-thinking citizens. Indeed, as James W. Cook demonstrates, Barnum's hoaxes and museum pieces were among the many overt deceptions that appealed to the emerging middle class; magicians, trompe l'oeil artists, and other popular tricksters contributed to a culture of wonder and debate that energized the public during this period and engendered "a new way of thinking about popular culture—one in which deception (artful or otherwise) came to be understood as an intrinsic component of the commercial entertainment industry." For a time Barnum courted the people's imagination by daring them to find him out, but eventually, in the Gilded Age, as Americans became enamored of so-called realism, even he learned it made more horse sense to hide his trickery behind a gauze of convincing illusion.

But his hoaxes, humbugs, and American Museum wouldn't be Barnum's greatest legacy. In the decades after the Civil War, his international celebrity as Tom Thumb's promoter and ringmaster of "The Greatest Show on Earth" shot him to the forefront of American power. He headed up a campaign for mass spectatorship that ran roughshod over public debate. When postbellum intellectuals, as Bluford Adams has shown, decried the "Barnumization" of culture, they weren't referring to his humbug days, but to his legacy of tasteless commercialism. Even Mark Twain, a sometime friend, avoided all public associations, except when burlesquing the showman in print.

But Barnum knew there was no bad press. In his 1865 *Humbugs of the World,* he identified "business" as a breeding ground for "humbug." "All and every one protest their innocence," he wrote of his fellow businessmen, "and warn you against the rest. My inexperienced friend, take it for granted that they tell the truth—about each other!" Which of course is exactly what Barnum was doing. James W. Cook calls this statement his "greatest trick of all: to convince many of his new middle-class peers that humbug in the exhibition room was merely market capitalism by another name." Cook is right. Barnum was downplaying his infamous humbugs by putting them on a footing with commerce. But as with all of Barnum's best pranks, this one had at least one more twist. While amusing his readers with a straight-talk apology, he was distracting them from his open admission that his entire enterprise—all of show business, all of *business*—hinged on fraud.

He explains such fraud in *The Art of Money-Getting* (1880), though he may not have meant to. He warms us up with some Horatio Alger boilerplate (thrift, perseverance, diligence), then moves on to a bit of Gilded Age wisdom ("be systematic"). The prince of humbugs first tips his hand when he hits on the subject of advertisement, which is most effective when it tricks trusting consumers with reverse psychology, by placing plants in the audience, and other such assaults on the masses' gullibility. (After all, it's the "art" of money getting—as in "artifice," "artfulness.") But the kicker comes when Uncle Barnum is seeming most sincere, offering his cheerfully Christian advice that "politeness and civility are the best capital ever invested in business . . . the more kind and liberal a man is, the more generous will be the patronage bestowed upon him. 'Like begets like.'" Is he advising rough, raw, radical civility? Politeness born of "amicable collisions"? Certainly not. He is advising the softest, most lubricating kind. Barnum had mastered the show of civility, the air of fairness, the abuse of good manners to give the cozy impression that moguls like him had a chummy rapport with their millions of hood-winked customers, and his good example helped to radically reorient the American public sphere. Under Barnum's influence, "civility" became advertising, "politeness" became marketing, and rapacious corporations looked down from billboards with open arms and avuncular smiles. In the civil society Barnum inspired, citizens are greeted by upbeat clerks, appeased with impeccable "customer service," and flattered with the illusion that they are always right. If the customer is "happy," commerce clips along—and commerce is this civil society's purpose. But where is the fun, without that time-tested American friction? In the Gilded Age, promoters Barnumized fun's rough edges.

Such deception would work miracles for bigger and bigger business. One day it would make behemoths like McDonald's and Disney our household names and trusted friends.


THE POPULAR STORY GOES something like this: Thomas Dartmouth (T. D.) Rice, a journeyman actor from New York City, was making a show stop in the Ohio River valley (Louisville, Cincinnati, maybe Pitts-burgh), when he stumbled upon a nugget of comic gold. A disabled old black man (or was it a young boy?), with a hitched-up right shoulder and atrophied left leg, was out behind a barn throwing his body and soul into a folk song about "Jim Crow": "Weel about and turn about and do jis so," he sang, as if giving himself instructions. "Eb'ry time I weel about and jump Jim Crow." This was the late 1820s, and the enterprising Rice, knowing the vogue for strange new dances, stylized the unfortunate stranger's gyrations, crafted the lyrics to fit an Irish folk tune, and bor-rowed a black man's worn-out suit of clothes. Blackening his face with a chunk of burnt cork, he fashioned what he saw into a monstrous act that transformed mid-nineteenth-century American theater.

Rice wasn't the first. Blackface, a long-standing English tradition, had cropped up long before in American frontier towns where blacks and whites were forced to mingle and thus developed a begrudging sociability. Like the Patriots who dressed as war-whooping Indians, or the members of northeastern Tammany societies who performed elaborate Indian-inspired rituals as rallying points for an emerging middle class, young men who asserted their dominance through blackface both exaggerated racial differences to their own advantage and indulged in lewdness, by way of comedy, that was otherwise scorned or forbidden. Many of the early minstrels were outsiders and bohemians who enjoyed the carnival freedom of blackface, what Eric Lott calls "that fascinating imaginary space of fun and license outside (structured by) Victorian bourgeois norms."

America's growing white population was intensely curious about black culture, which could be seen in all of its public defiance from King Charles's Pinkster Days to Sundays on Congo Square. "Blackness," on the one hand, marked a moral danger zone where men were feared as sexual predators and women were identified, in the spirit of Sara Baartman—the wildly sensationalized "Hottentot Venus" who toured European stages until 1815—as essentially voluptuous, desiring animals. Blackness also stood for a culture of "fun" whose diction, humor, music, and dance loosely informed blackface minstrelsy's repertoire. Ironically, it marked a social freedom that was increasingly forbidden among middle-class whites. Blackface enthusiasts tried importing such "genuine negro fun" to the stage, a space of relative liberation, though all they offered was a cheap replica.

Edwin Forrest, perhaps the nation's first bona fide celebrity, wore blackface onstage in the 1820s, but it was Rice, with his limping "rockin' de heel" dance, who invented the overblown physical grotesquery that turned it into a national sensation. Whereas actual African-American dancing of the period was, as Hans Nathan notes, "improvised" and naturally "ecstatic," the theatrical heel-dancing inspired by Rice "demanded planned variety and . . . encouraged showmanship." Not spontaneous fun but deliberate comedy, minstrel dancing "stress[ed] jolliness and clownishness for their own sake." Rice's equally important innovation was his comic character, the bootblack "Jim Crow," whom he featured in dozens of songs, poems, monologues, and plays. This warm-blooded, hotheaded, fork-tongued fugitive dusts up trouble all over town—and throughout the society he's supposed to serve—whether he's charmingly pursuing "de holy state of hemlock" or insouciantly telling an uppity white mistress, who smirks at his interest in Shakespearean tragedy, that "he should like to play Otello—and smoder de white gal." In the 1830s, when T. D. Rice was indistinguishable from Jim Crow, he dominated theaters from New York to London with his popularization of the African-American trickster figure.

It's easy to be revolted by Rice's Jim Crow—a white man making fun of blacks for the amusement of other whites. He lampooned African-American skin color, facial features, and dialect. He exaggerated genitals, breasts, and curves that played on stereotypes of hypersexuality. But as W. T. Lhamon Jr. convincingly argues, Rice's Jim Crow, unlike the blatantly stupid clowns that Lhamon calls "Sambos," should be read for the deeply mixed messages that it sent to his "overlapping publics"— working class, middle class, bohemian, even black. Jim Crow was a "quick-quipping runaway who mocked slavery" and at the same time "pestered those who would enter into middle class aspirations or grasp at dandiacal pretensions." In the twentieth century he became associated with a truckling Uncle Tom figure, but in the antebellum period he was the original rebel who necessitated "Jim Crow" laws. Both the product of American racism and a critic of it, Jim Crow was pitched to heterogeneous audiences who laughed at different sides of his jokes: his burlesque of undereducated blacks, his attack on imperious and overeducated whites. Blackface may have "inspired the laughter of cruelty as well as the laughter of affirmation," as Gary D. Engle puts it, but the overwhelming evidence points to its cruelty.

For most minstrels weren't sending such a sophisticated message— most were showmen riding a wave of popularity. They played taverns and street corners. They jumped up during the intermissions of theatrical productions. P. T. Barnum, in his early circus days, always kept a blackface minstrel or two on hand. In the 1830s he blacked up himself when he couldn't secure good talent: once, behind the tent, he defended an employee against a local white man, who then turned his violent force on Barnum, thinking he was being disrespected by a black. On another occasion, having lost his star minstrel, John Diamond, to a competitor, Barnum allegedly scoured the Five Points dives until he landed a superior breakdown dancer. The best one, predictably, was a "genuine negro" who would have outraged respectable white audiences. This didn't stop the prince of humbugs. He blacked his dancer's face with cork and transformed William Henry Lane into the world-renowned "Juba," whose "regular break-down" in a New York bar would later command Charles Dickens's full attention:

> Single shuffle, double shuffle, cut and cross-cut; snapping his fingers, rolling his eyes, turning in his knees, presenting the backs of his legs in front, spinning about on his toes and heels like nothing but the man's fingers on the tambourine; dancing with two left legs, two right legs, two wooden legs, two wire legs, two spring legs—all sorts of legs and no legs—what is this to him?

Dickens doesn't name "this lively young negro, who is the wit of the assembly," but he declares him "the greatest dancer known," which in 1840s America was explicit enough. Lane is believed to have been the only professional black minstrel until small troupes began appearing in the late 1850s. Notable among "Master Juba"'s feats was to challenge his fellow Barnum alumnus "Master Diamond"—the other (and white) greatest dancer known—to at least three highly publicized dance-offs and ultimately to earn the latter's public respect. Of course Lane didn't perform *real* "juba," the patting kind. He had learned to dance the Irish jig and reel from a renowned black dancer, Uncle Jim Lowe, and thereby also elevated Catharine Market's challenge dances to the middlebrow stage at Vauxhall Gardens. At the same time he took potshots at T. D. Rice's grotesque tradition. In a cheeky announcement for an 1845 show, he promised "to give correct Imitation Dances of all the principal Ethiopian Dancers in the United States. After which he will give an imitation of himself—and then you will see the vast difference between those that have heretofore attempted dancing and this WONDERFUL YOUNG MAN."

Minstrelsy became an industry in the 1840s when Dan Emmett's sensational Virginia Minstrels inspired musicians across the country to form their own blackface ensembles—or "Ethiopian entertainments," as they were sometimes known. Emmett's stage-shaking variety show was built around the basic Jim Crow grotesquerie: five musicians in blackface arrayed themselves in a line, constantly bantering and strutting their antics, spontaneously breaking into theatrics and dance, and working it all up in outlandish dialect. Their first newspaper review called them "rare boys—'full of fun.'" When the English actor H. P. Grattan saw Emmett's chief competitors, the Christy Minstrels, perform in Buffalo in 1843, he was so astonished by "the fun of these three nigger minstrels" that he wanted to see it all over again. "The staple of [their] entertainment was fun—mind, genuine negro fun . . . the counterfeit presentation of southern darkies [whom] they personally wished to illustrate, and whose dance and songs, as such darkies, they endeavored to reproduce." This frantic endeavor to "reproduce" fun—"genuine negro fun"—dominated popular culture in the 1840s, seizing even the most respectable audiences. The Ethiopian Serenaders played the White House in 1844, starting a trend that in decades to come would amuse presidents Tyler, Polk, Fillmore, and Pierce. Like all popular culture, minstrelsy also headed west with the forty-niners, and by 1855 there were five professional blackface groups vying for San Francisco's gold.

Stephen Foster, composing hits in the 1840s and '50s, rebuffed "trashy and really offensive" lyrics by the likes of Rice and Emmett (Rice had rejected some of Foster's early numbers) and instead sold sanitized, sentimental songs to Christy's (increasingly mainstream) Minstrels. With upbeat tunes like "Oh! Susanna," "Beautiful Dreamer," and "Camptown Races," the so-called father of American music favored nostalgia for an "Old Kentucky Home" over a voyeuristic peep into the slave quarter's taboo frolics. The bet paid off, and the craze for his sheet music Fostered do-it-yourself minstrelsy in decent households across the land.

When Emmett formed Bryant's Minstrels in 1857, he introduced an unbeatable theatrical innovation. Dancing was of course a minstrel-show staple—Christy's employed both a "somersault jig dancer" and a (cross-dressed) "negro wench dancer"—and much of it, by the fifties, was tightly choreographed, often involving a call-and-response routine between the star performer and the ridiculous "end-men." But Emmett mined gold from an unrulier dance tradition that sprang the whole troupe to their feet. Clearly inspired by the ring shout and dances "for the eel" that were vanishing from urban public spaces, Bryant's Minstrels culminated their widely varied new sets—at Mechanic's Hall on Broadway, the main stage for American minstrelsy—with prancing, jigging, hand-waggling "walk-arounds" in which all of the blackface musicians and their large supporting cast climaxed in a jerky plantation-style hoedown. They clapped and shouted and mugged into the footlights. Children and dwarves provided Barnum-like diversity, and performers rotated in a counterclockwise motion that tried to replicate this African-American rite.

Tearing a page from Stephen Foster's songbook, Emmett published a volume of his popular "Walk 'Rounds" for folks who wanted to try it at home. In his introduction he vouched for his own authenticity: "I have always strictly confined myself to the habits and crude ideas of the slaves of the South."

But naturally there was nothing "genuine" about any of this "negro fun." The fundamental safety of blackface minstrelsy depended upon its *in*authenticity: that the participants *weren't* black; that the pleasure derived from their lewd gyrations was sequestered onstage, and done in jest; and that the threat of such unbridled pleasure—loud, brash, energetic, profane—was contained and controlled within a cartoon. Following the Civil War, when the rage for realism in popular culture combined with a loosening of race restrictions, more African-American minstrels took to the boards, and like their pioneer, William Henry Lane, they raised the bar for showmanship. For decades, however, they remained the victims of P. T. Barnum's original humbug, performing only as blacks in blackface.


THE PERIOD FROM the 1830s to the 1860s was one of widespread civic turmoil. Slave uprisings threatened Southern comfort; urban riots (over race, class, religion, elections, patriotism, banks, you name it) rankled tenuous northeastern civility; and Andrew Jackson's Indian Removal Act stirred up western race wars that would rage throughout the century. Though it didn't always erupt in violence, ideological turmoil was also rampant: from America's tiny towns to its overgrown cities, folks bumped chests over sundry issues that often erupted in bloody conflict—

Protestants fought Catholics, drys fought drinkers, abolitionists fought slave owners; an efflorescence of political parties and native-born religions created divisions within the growing ranks of aspiring middle-class conservatives and progressives; and a bold, ethnically diverse working class stormed the streets for their claims to popular sovereignty. The most colorful exponents of this latter demographic were the boisterous young denizens of lower Manhattan (as well as Philadelphia and Boston)—the Bowery "b'hoys" and "g'hals." Their nicknames approximated an Irish-American dialect, though this rowdy white subculture was multiethnic and many of them hailed from south of the Bowery—in the infamously seedy Five Points neighborhood. They were born to the fray—among pimps, prostitutes, thieves, and murderers, and in overcrowded tenements—and it was in their character never to back down. But they were also the era's most glorious dupes, for politicians and promoters alike.

With their flashy styles and political fury, b'hoys resembled eighteenth-century Jack Tars—right down to their rakishly knotted cravats. They split the difference between roughs and dandies: they wore short black jackets, double-breasted red flannels, flared black trousers, clunky work boots, and neatly brushed black top hats. They wore their pistols holstered and their bangs exaggerated, slicked with soap in a way that anticipated 1950s greasers. They chomped blunt cigars and strolled with a "swing, which nobody but a Bowery Boy [could] imitate." G'hals, for their part, were even more extraordinary, by dint of being streetwise working women in an age of compulsory domesticity. They worked long hours and partied at night. They trafficked in the latest gossip and slang and strutted in cheap, bright, extravagant versions of antebellum haute couture. They were recognizable from blocks away by bonnets that sprang out in all directions, "with a perfect exuberance of flowers and feathers, and gigantic bows and long streamers of tri-colored ribbons."

B'hoys worked as butchers, printers, shipbuilders, factory hands, and carpenters, but it was their universal identification as volunteer firemen that lent them their signature sartorial panache and their ferocious company loyalty. G'hals worked as bookbinders, milliners, and housekeepers, and often took sides with the combative b'hoys. B'hoys were early

America's most flamboyant gangsters. They pledged their allegiance to the violent street gangs that carved up turf from the Bowery to Five Points. The Dead Rabbits, Plug Uglies, Black Roach Guards, Bowery Boys, and other such clubs battled for turf, politics, and fun. As one former Bowery Boy recalled, "The gang had no regular organization, but were a crowd of young men of different nationalities, mostly American born, who were always ready for excitement, generally of an innocent nature." Veterans of the ongoing "recreational" riots that had broken out for years between fire brigades, b'hoys' greatest thrill, and highest prestige, came from fighting downtown fires and fighting other gangs and firefighters.

For all of their bare-knuckle differences, however, these mostly native-born children of Irish and other working-class immigrants rallied around their disgust for America's "aristocratic"—British, Whiggish—wealth. They took American democracy at its word, but they also believed it belonged exclusively to whites, as their bloody 1834 race riots, and widespread resistance to abolition, made clear. In the tradition of Jack Tars in the Sons of Liberty's taverns, they studied the incendiary editorials of proletarian activists like William Leggett. And as the Jackson Age wore on, and the Democratic Party became a factional circus under the big top of New York's Tammany Hall, they split up among the ranks of sexy new demagogues who prized them for their heedless streetfighting tactics. Levi Slamm's little militia of Locofocos (known in the press as "Slamm Bang & Co.") set out to "democratize" capitalism, but Thomas Skidmore's band of Workies pushed a communist agenda. In the 1840s, George Henry Evans's "Young America" movement had scores of b'hoys imploring busy New Yorkers to fulfill the nation's destiny in the West. "Thorough-going sporting-man" Isaiah Rynders led a thousand of his "Empire Club" b'hoys to rally for James K. Polk and bully Whigs away from the polls. And the pugnacious "underground" journalist Mike Walsh, a rabble-rousing Irish-born b'hoy himself, built an army of b'hoys he called the Spartans to bring about his "shirtless democracy." It suited the b'hoys' unresolved loyalties—cosmopolitan, racist, democratic, patriotic—that Walsh himself harangued for such inconsistent beliefs as Fourierist socialism, increased immigration, and the expansion of slavery into Texas. But it was his hobnailed tactics that pleased them most. Under his influence, they took politics to the streets—even road-tripping to Rhode Island in 1842 in a failed attempt to topple a state government that still restricted voting rights to landowners, the Dorr Rebellion.

B'hoys and g'hals were America's first fans. They frequented Barnum's humbugs and museums. They devoured dime novels and the sauciest penny papers. They were also incurable theater junkies who bullied their way en masse into shows and lectures. Voracious audience members whose eclectic tastes conformed to the era's new variety shows, they rallied for Shakespeare with the same avidity that they did melodramas and blackface minstrelsy. B'hoys and g'hals were pop-culture consumers, but they also spun their own turbines of fun—spoke out, wisecracked, and pulled practical jokes. They gambled, drank, and fought in the streets. And as cultural descendants of Irish immigrants who danced against blacks for eels and cakes, they frequented Five Points's rowdiest dance halls and put their own energetic spins on breakdowns, hornpipes, tap dance, and waltz. Up for adventure whenever, wherever, b'hoys were also—as Tyler Anbinder notes—"the first New Yorkers to leave for California when the gold rush began."

To be sure, in this primitive age of the theater—when crowd members drank, spat, yelled, tussled, and kept up an ongoing contest with the stage (and when balconies served as ad hoc brothels)—the b'hoys and g'hals, the most spirited patrons, saw celebrity fandom as an excellent reason to rumble. They took proud ownership of actors and plays and staged their own dramas in the peanut gallery. So it seems almost inevitable, in this age of humbug, that b'hoys and g'hals should soon become the *subjects* of popular culture. They were just too colorful, excitable, *ripe*. Just as stylish black "dandies and dandizettes" entered the national consciousness through 1830s and '40s minstrelsy (most notably under the guise of Zip Coon), b'hoys and g'hals made their stage debut in *Beulah Spa; or Two of the B'hoys* (1834). But they wouldn't become larger-than-life poster-board caricatures until the late 1840s, when Frank Chanfrau, a b'hoy turned melodramatic actor, fashioned a character, "Mose," from Moses Humphrey, an actual tough he had known as a fireman for the

Peterson Engine Company no. 15. Before long he had worked him into Benjamin A. Baker's play *A Glance at New York in 1848*. Chanfrau's more immediate inspiration, however, for this streetfighting butcher and red-shirted fireman were the kids who filled the pit in Mitchell's Olympic Theatre, where the play made its debut. So faithfully did he mimic their dress, gestures, and talk that the play's producer, William Mitchell, mistaking Chanfrau for a gallery rogue who had managed to sneak back-stage, tried to eject him on opening night.

*A Glance at New York* was a simplistic comedy—the travails of a country "greenhorn" taken in by a series of con men. Over the course of the play, Mose and his canny friends adopt the bumpkin, George, and defend him against grifters, sharpers, and thieves. But the story's real arc is the b'hoys' search for "fun"—the "capital fun" of cross-dressing in the g'hals' "uniform" and infiltrating their bowling alley; the "capital fun" of the bowling itself; their easygoing spree in the bohemian "Loafers' Paradise"; and, always, avidly, the pugilistic "fun" (the all-engrossing "muss") for which the tobacco-spewing and slang-slinging Mose itches, aches, parades, and spoils. His g'hal, Lize (Eliza Stebbins), is pegged with urban amusements of her own; she appears reading *Matilda, the Disconsolate* and urges Mose, in her Bowery dialect, to go to "Waxhall," "Wawdeville," and a "first-rate shindig." Mose and Lize strutted with a modern insouciance that tickled pit denizens right where they lived: they affirmed the audience in their own love of fun. "As may be supposed," one reviewer wrote, "it is received with shouts of delight by the thousand originals of the pit."

The play was such a runaway success—the biggest hit yet for the city's biggest-drawing theater—that it spawned a flash-in-the-pan "Mose" and "Lize" franchise, always starring Chanfrau as the beloved Mose. It packed the Olympic for seventy-four nights before Chanfrau moved the venture to his own theater, the Chatham, and began reaping the profits for himself. Chanfrau knew his rowdy clientele. But despite the fact that he was expanding the pit to accommodate nearly three-quarters of the hall, the unscrupulous *New York Herald* threw some humbug his way, calling his new theater "a pleasant place for family resort." The play had a surefire business model, and its crowd had a bottomless appetite for more, but the script left nothing to chance. Before the curtain falls, as Mose exits the stage to help his pal Sykesy "in a muss," he calls out to the pit: "Don't be down on me 'cause I'm goin' to leave you . . . if you don't say no, why, I'll scare up this crowd again to-morrow night, and then you can take another."

The trick worked. The play's immediate sequel, *New York As It Is,* sold a total of forty thousand tickets in forty-seven straight performances. It reheated the basic plot of *A Glance* and kept its promise of urban realism—in a soup kitchen and tenement fire—but also, for fun, a steamboat race and "dancing for eels" in Catharine Market. The next play, *Mose in California* (1849), jettisoned realism for topical hyperbole: the b'hoys take a ship called the *Humbug* through the Isthmus and get an exaggerated California education—grappling bears, defeating Indians, and landing an impossibly large chunk of gold. In subsequent plays the franchise flew off the rails, finally losing its wheels with *Mose in China* (1850), which closed in a month. As Chanfrau upped the ante to hold the Bowery b'hoys' attention, Mose transformed into an inner-city giant to steal even Davy Crockett's thunder. As David S. Reynolds and others have shown, "Onstage, the b'hoy gained superhuman powers. The gargantuan Mose used lampposts as clubs, swam across the Hudson with two strokes, and leaped easily from Manhattan to Brooklyn." To be sure, if Yankee peddlers and Kentucky woodsmen were comic icons of an earlier American character, b'hoys and g'hals (as well as some of their minstrel counterparts) stood for a roughneck cosmopolitanism that was spreading outward from the inner cities.

But b'hoys and g'hals have the dubious distinction of being America's first folk heroes to stand in line and buy tickets to see their own spectral images. The steps Chanfrau took to amuse these youths heralded a new age in American fun. His heroes were designed to flatter a demographic, and his theater catered directly to their class. The fact that his shows were loud and louche, maximizing audience participation, only showed how well this "Mose" understood his clientele's taste. Surely they thought they had invented this fun, and to a certain degree they had. But Chanfrau apparently had the last laugh, and it isn't clear whether the real b'hoys (who mortally hated fat cats like the one he was becoming) were warm to his elaborate gag. Quite possibly, like country greenhorns, they'd been had.

It wouldn't have been the first time. Politicians had been gaslighting them for decades. But in the year when Chanfrau baited his pit, the b'hoys' short tempers, high-value brawn, and mobbish fandom for true-blue American actors created a delicious new opportunity. For years they had championed the American tragedian Edwin "Neddy" Forrest against his archrival, William Charles Macready, England's greatest tragedian. On May 10, 1849, at the peak of the *Mose* craze, while Forrest played *Macbeth* to a capacity crowd at the downtown Broadway Theatre, a few blocks away, at the posh new Astor Place Theatre, with its high ticket prices and white-glove dress code, Macready also played *Macbeth*—but not to his typically tony audience. In the previous weeks, a loose consortium of troublemakers and Tammany Hall politicians—among them Mike Walsh, Isaiah Rynders, and the rapscallion journalist Ned Buntline, whose first dime novels would lionize the b'hoys—had

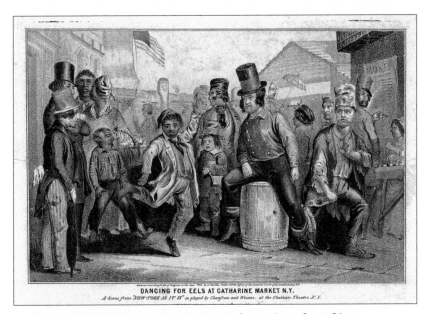

**DANCING FOR EELS AT CATHARINE MARKET N.Y.**
*A Scene from "NEW-YORK AS IT IS" as played by Chanfrau and Winans, at the Chatham Theatre N.Y.*

Mose in his full B'hoy regalia admires the finer points of an African-American jig—danced for eels at New York's Catharine Market.
("Dancing for Eels," F. S. Chanfrau & J. Winans in *New York As It Is*.
Courtesy of the Harry Ransom Humanities Center, University of Texas at Austin.)

distributed blocks of free tickets to the show. So while Forrest played his part with anti-British fervor, driving thousands of cheering minions to their feet, Macready, simply doing his job, incited a rain of witty abuse, rotten food, urban detritus, and theater seats. Afterwards leagues of b'hoys marched the streets, chanting in the voice of Shakespeare's weird sisters:

> When shall we three meet again
> In thunder, lightning, or in rain?
> When the hurlyburly's done,
> When the battle's lost and won.

The next night, when Macready accepted a petition from forty-eight prominent New Yorkers (among them Washington Irving and Herman Melville), asking him to retake the stage, ten thousand nativists flooded into Astor Place, and the result was the nation's bloodiest riot to date. Twenty-two were killed, more than a hundred injured, with the casualties due mostly to police suppression.

So, yes, Mose had fun. Commercial fun, criminal fun, loads of mobocratic fun. At his worst he did his henchmen's bidding and severely disrupted civil society—destroyed property, pummeled innocents, even allegedly gang-raped prostitutes. Luc Sante offers a grimly accurate explanation for the b'hoys' seeming "carnival": "the collected miseries of the people were acted out with torches and clubs and rocks . . . unable to imagine social stability as anything but repression . . . the rioters sought a permanent state of riot." No Sons of Liberty or Pinkster revelers, who strove for a permanent state of *democracy,* b'hoys outright rejected civility. They had a big appetite for American thrills—rough, raw, dangerous, dirty—but they failed to strike the playful balance that makes a party fun, the balance between individual and communal pleasure. At their worst they played in a danger zone between radical activism and criminality; they explored American fun's dark side. More vicious than eighteenth-century Jack Tars, who made surgical strikes on offending property; less principled than their revolutionary forebears, b'hoys seemed to justify ruling-class fears (as one Dorr Rebellion opponent put it) of "an aristocracy of the dram shop, the brothel and the gutter; not in the ruffle-shirt gentry but in the gentry who have no shirts at all." Bullying, wild, hell-bent for destruction, the Bowery b'hoys were a proven menace. Their self-serving pursuit of absolute freedom played right into their enemies' hands, justifying reform. What's more, their collective rage, combined with their love of popular amusement, made these kids an easy touch—vulnerable to politicians and entertainers alike, who stood to profit from their fury.

And so it follows that, in the 1850s, promoters, reformers, and city officials had only to cite the Astor Place riots when justifying strict civic rules—in theaters, on sidewalks, in municipal parks. Taste and decency had to be enforced, law and order had to be maintained, lest Mose and Sykesy and their Five Points thugs spread their mayhem across the land. Maine went dry in 1850, the same year P. T. Barnum opened his own tidy theater and debuted *The Drunkard,* William H. Smith's blockbuster temperance play. It would outsell even *A Glance at New York* and have a field day with the Five Points subcultures. With that decade's commercial blitz of Stephen Foster's sentimental minstrelsy and tsk-tsking novels like T. S. Arthur's *Ten Nights in a Barroom* (1854), in which King Alcohol brings a town to its knees, popular culture was cleaning up its act and catering to a new middle class.

B'hoys and g'hals fell out of vogue, but they didn't just vanish. In 1856, a year after the Dead Rabbit/Bowery Boy riot devastated lower Manhattan, Horace Greeley's *New York Tribune* sent their man George A. Foster to report on "the nightly revels at Dickens's Place," aka Uncle Peet's, the Five Points dance hall still known for the English author's visit some fifteen years before. The place hadn't changed much, despite once having burned to the ground. It "reechoed its wonted sounds of festive jollification." And on a Saturday night, all of America's outcasts were there. Among its usual multiracial clientele of "thieves, loafers, prostitutes and rowdies" were the expected Jack Tars and b'hoys and g'hals. Early in the evening the bar was mobbed, while female dancers, mostly black and "tidy and presentable," were "all agog for the fun to commence." When the little orchestra had warmed up and the gallants had stowed their wet chaw in their pockets, the whooping couples assumed their positions on the crowded, creaky planks. As Foster describes it, they were baited and caught by "Cooney in the Holler": "contorting their bodies and accelerating their movements, accompanied with shouts of laughter and yells of encouragement and applause, until all observance of the figure is forgotten and every one leaps, stamps, screams and hurrahs on his or her own hook." Foster orients this harmless riot within the district's violent history: "the dancers, now wild with excitement, like Ned Buntline at Astor Place, leap frantically about like howling dervishes, clasp their partners in their arms, and at length conclude the dance in hot confusion and disorder." But the sheer exuberance of Uncle Peet's celebrants shines right through the sneering prose, just as William Henry Lane's lightning-heeled expertise shone through Dickens's Victorian smirk.

Foster then notices an adjoining apartment, an implicit brothel, that was meant to cater to higher-brow clients—presumably to the wealthy slumming parties who would be slinking in great numbers into places like Five Points in the stuffier decades to come. "Champagne made of very superior pink turnip-juice is kept ready for the upper crust whenever the fun grows fast and furious and those with money have reached the 'damn-the-expense stage of excitement.'" Uncle Peet's effort to attract the swells shows that he was a man of his times. The b'hoys were evolving into the flashier "sporting set." And the rubbed-up fun of mixed dance halls was fast becoming a thing of the past, if also of the distant future.

# Barnumizing America

Barnum's American Museum prospered throughout the
Civil War: the giants, the little people, even the automatons were
dressed in Yankee uniforms. Patriotic dramas played two times a day.
And Barnum made his most profitable discovery yet, William Henry
Johnson—the "What Is It?"—a microcephalic African-American dwarf
whom he pitched to the recently Darwin-crazed audiences as the "missing link" between man and monkey. But in March of 1868, when the
museum burned for a second time, a holocaust that killed hundreds of
animals in their cages, the showman declared he was closing up shop.
He retired to a new mansion ("Waldemere"), then took a long, all-
American vacation hunting wild buffalo on the Kansas plains. He had
hardly been in retirement for a year, however, when he was approached
by William Cameron Coup, a young circus manager whom he'd gotten
started years before, and was tempted with the thought of starting a road
show. What began as a revival of his museum on wheels—reassembling
his pet performers and curiosities—soon hit the rails as "The Greatest
Show on Earth."

Barnum defended its claim to "Greatness" with a $100,000 chal-
lenge across his billboards: "ten times larger than any other show ever

seen on Earth." Only a fool would have taken him up on it. Even with its dozens of dormitories and stables and its ten big tops housing all his specialties—the Museum and the Laboratory, the Fine Arts collection and Menagerie—"Barnum's Magic City" could materialize overnight and accommodate ten thousand patrons at a pop. His decades of experience in keeping crowds moving ensured that nobody stood still for long, but was propelled from one attraction to the next—past Siamese twins, bearded ladies, frog swallowers, and dwarves, shedding nickels and dimes along the way as they were herded toward the roaring, high-flying Hippodrome.

In its first year his circus struggled on the roads, getting mired in mud and flooding rivers, but starting in 1872 they chartered trains—often sixty-five overcharged cars in length—and thereafter they struck all the midwestern towns where Barnum's name had only been legend. Despite severe setbacks, principally another fire in 1872 that killed most of his animals in a New York warehouse, his show kept growing every season, eventually merging in 1880 with that of his only competitor, John A. Bailey, to form a worldwide entertainment juggernaut.

The entertainment industry slavishly followed Barnum's methodology—for promotion, production, and transportation; it also enforced the standards of Victorian decency that he had adhered to long before the war. When in the 1830s he upstaged preachers to defend the virtues of entertainment, Barnum broke ground for a towering monoculture that throve on exciting, inoffensive pleasures. These pleasures were often peppered with dashes of folk fun (slang, risk, seeming rebellion), although even these zingers were mostly nostalgic, as if mischief belonged to America's past, which in many ways it did. For, to be sure, with the growing force of "middling folk" up north—white-collar suburbanites who earned regular salaries—the entertainments devised by Barnum and his adherents feasted on a lucrative new market. "Family fun," as these amusements have come to be called, were ostensibly nutritious and virtuous pleasures: they reinforced the tastes and mores that had been popularized during the Second Great Awakening. Family fun broadened the entertainment market with its daintier appeals to women and children. Perhaps more insidiously, it took citizens in moments of deep distraction and slotted them into postbellum America's increasingly corporate social structure.

But of course the mischief wasn't really gone: In the West, there were still jumping boomtowns. In the cities, there were untamed Bowerys that wisely preyed on leering slummers' wallets. But in a more pervasive sense, during the Gilded Age, American mischief went big time and came to characterize the culture industry—in both its methods and its champions. As Karen Halttunen argues in her classic book on the rise of the middle class, after the Civil War, the confidence men and "painted ladies" that antebellum reformers warned their children about gave way to heroic tricksters like the hero of Horatio Alger's eponymous *Ragged Dick*. Confidence men became capitalist icons. In what Halttunen calls the nation's "new corporate context" of acquisition and aspiration, "personality skills, such as that subtle quality called charm, were more useful to the ambitious youth than the qualities of industry, sobriety, and frugality" that reformers touted before the war; "executive ability and management— the art of manipulating others to do what you want them to do—was far more valuable than the ascetic self-discipline of an earlier era."

This new education redefined the citizen, not as an entrepreneur, adventurer, or rebel but rather—in the spirit of Mark Twain's middle-class hero, Tom Sawyer—as a lubricant in the capitalist system. If the system itself was based on trickery, the con man was its model citizen. Barnum said it himself: the "humbug in the exhibition room [is] merely market capitalism by another name." But if the heroes were con men, then the larger citizenry were their dupes, and family fun—one of the era's biggest-ticket schemes—had all the marks of a blurry shell game. Its customers stood in lines for tickets. They assumed their quiet places in rank-and-file bleachers. They bought cheap imitations of participation and liberty that made them feel like soaring athletes, daring cowboys, noble explorers. Before the Civil War, as many historians have shown, P. T. Barnum welcomed crowds to call his humbugs humbug. Afterwards, in an age of popular realism, his Gilded Age progeny flattered and dazzled their crowds. They assured them they were praying to see the real deal. In the exhibition room of the Gilded Age, corporate con men aimed to convince.

The recreation, amusement, and entertainment industries made lighthearted pleasures widely available—both to the city dwellers who benefited from the construction boom in parks, gymnasiums, vaudeville theaters, and arenas and to rural citizens who traveled from counties away when the big-top shows came to town. This cheap, modern, standardized "fun" not only filled the perceived social need for earlier American fun (the daring, primitive rebellions detailed in earlier chapters) but also—after the logic of P. T. Barnum, blackface, and "Mose"—often sold it in *replica*. Thrills that had been born out of sometimes desperate need, as they had been in slave quarters and mining camps, were repackaged as diversions for a growing workforce. They became "leisure" activities for weekends and holidays, and in eras since, their success has only grown. They have become so diverse, widespread, and profitable that they have spawned their own academic discipline, "leisure studies," which is a subdiscipline of both sociology and business administration.

Regulated and commercial family fun is, in its own right, "American fun." It reflects powerful strains in the national consciousness—capitalism and corporate administration, in particular—and it remains more prevalent now than ever. But far from reflecting a national tendency toward risk, struggle, and self-identification, it reflects the opposite in a tendency toward leisure, toward disappearance into the passive crowd. To be sure, this kind of Gilded Age fun is often the pleasure of *repressing* struggle, also of *dissolving* it. In the terms of this book's larger argument, the entertainments and amusements engineered during this period mark the first of modern fun's three "tributaries," all of which keep flowing today, usually mixing and commingling their respective social waters. The remaining two tributaries, the wildly playful and the radically political, will join the mainstream in later eras.

IN THE REPUBLIC'S EARLY DECADES, when a mostly rural population was struggling for survival, athletics were largely primitive pastimes. In the Northeast, sports, though generally less regulated than they had been in colonial Puritan communities, were valued most when they had something to deliver. Children's games like marbles and hopscotch were often linked with moral lessons, and adult diversions, like hunting and fishing, had obvious practical benefits. In Quaker Pennsylvania and throughout the American South, attitudes toward skittles, bowling, billiards, and a few other traditional European sports were typically more lax. In general, however, early U.S. citizens, mostly males, played roughly the same games that their ancestors had played—stoolball, ninepins, and, among the elite, tennis. The rules of these games were basic, the matches ad hoc. The balls and bats were crafted at home according to tradition or, by the 1820s, instructions in magazines. A "fitness movement" sprang up in that decade; this tentacle of the larger reform movement brought private male gymnasiums to East Coast cities and inspired the odd college to start a physical education program. Over the next twenty years, however, vigorous activities like rowing and gymnastics belonged almost exclusively to the upper classes. By the 1850s, baseball was becoming nationally prominent, but nobody risked mass-producing its equipment until after the Civil War, when soldiers on both sides had discovered the sport and baseball became the dominant sector of a sudden and booming "sporting goods" industry.

In the 1860s and 1870s, manufacturers doubled down on the sporting crazes that many Americans, as Stephen Hardy has shown, still shunned as "exotic and frivolous indulgences": croquet, football, tennis, bicycling, as well as baseball itself. Against lingering middle-class disapproval, however, sports bred new commercial opportunities. Americans swarmed new public courts and playing fields, and entrepreneurs were there to greet them, inventing new equipment, packaging uniforms, branding semiprofessional clubs and leagues, and selling tickets to athletic spectacles that hitherto had been limited to the horse track. Organized sports and softening attitudes toward games and sports made enduring changes to the postbellum republic. They improved citizens' spirits and physical health while making them behave in predictable patterns. They also served as ideological bait. Writing in 1869, upon the opening of New York's elaborate new Young Men's Christian Association, fund-raiser William E. Dodge Jr. justified the games typically found in barrooms (including "chess, draughts, billiards, and bowling") by saying "the devil should not have all the amusements" and by citing the growing Christian opinion "that every legitimate attraction should be utilized to gain the end desired." The "end," in this case, was winning young men's souls.

Sports had the potential for raw, pure fun. Football, baseball, track and field, and all of the exhilarating new athletic games demanded full-body engagement; they thrilled participants with heated contest; they hurled them into risk-filled arenas where natural talents were tested and sharpened. But two sweeping trends in the industrialized North, administration and commercialism, intervened to regulate and exploit these pleasures in the service of order, discipline, and profit. In contrast to spontaneous antebellum sports—played in open fields and on street corners and sandlots—postbellum sports, slotted by officials into newly founded ziggurats of clubs and leagues and organizations, helped to control the intimidating sprawl of an increasingly diverse and urban citizenry. Sports staged rivalries between schools and cities, turned youthful aggression into sanctioned competition, and channeled the American love of risk into games with ever more intricate rules. Organized sports revved up the citizens' activity, but they also corralled their spontaneity and rebellion into highly regulated channels. And they reinforced popular taboos that separated Americans by race, class, and gender: blacks and other minorities were excluded outright; whites were separated by privilege and ability and divided, more specifically, into the increasingly fine categories of "amateurs" and "professionals." For some, this latter division signaled the death of fun—by turning sports into work and spectacle. In 1884, Dudley Sargent, who would become the director of Harvard's Hemenway Gymnasium, decried "the growth of the professional spirit in our college sports" as "a most serious evil": in making his case, he cited the loss of "courtesy and generous competition" to "exhibitions of brutal violence" and excoriated the "demoralizing work" of professional training that turned athletes into de facto racehorses. E. L. Godkin, writing for *The Nation* in 1893, declared "the thing which produces most of the evils of football and other games"—among which he included humiliation and physical injury—"is the effort to improve them as a spectacle for the multitude."

Spectacle, naturally, was the whirring propeller of typical Gilded Age fun. And unlike rowdy Jackson-era audiences, whose obstreperous behavior was finally clamped down following the Astor Place riot, post-bellum crowds had to behave themselves. Indeed, the white-glove Astor Place Theatre itself—against which the b'hoys had violently rebelled—set the new high standard. In 1858, when Frederick Law Olmsted helped to design New York's Central Park, he wanted it "to embody his conception of democratic recreation," in John F. Kasson's terms, which meant he wanted it to be a scenic strolling ground for quality folk and "made little provision for the desire of working-class males to have 'manly and blood-tingling recreations,' 'boisterous fun and rough sports.'" From the 1870s to the 1890s, museums, opera houses, theaters, concert halls, even public parks, laid down the social law, enforcing dress codes, lowering noise levels, and imposing stringent rules of conduct. As Lawrence W. Levine and other historians have shown, well-heeled citizens "transform[ed] public spaces by rules, systems of taste, and canons of behavior of their own choosing" in an effort "to convert the strangers [read 'immigrants'] so that their modes of behavior and cultural predilections emulated those of the elite." But it was generally enough just to *emulate* the elite, for the audience promoters hoped to reach was the vast and aspiring middle class. The spectator's fun could be lively and flashy, but it took pains not to shock or offend, as it had to appeal to the nicer sensibilities of a widely imitated leisure class. If Barnum could meet such standards with the circus, which hitherto had suffered the lowest reputation, any entertainment was up to the challenge.

In 1885, when Benjamin Franklin Keith opened Boston's Bijou Theatre, he stepped into a well-worn variety-show tradition. He populated his stage with the same minstrels, jugglers, scientists, actors, gymnasts, preachers, and oddities he had been hawking for years as a barker for Barnum. What made him the founder of the new American vaudeville was an innovation he called "continuous performance"—the rotation of crowds through a twelve-hour cycle of repeating, "respectable" stage shows. He described the setup as a kind of banal paradise where "the show is [always] in full swing, everything is bright, cheerful and inviting."

The "fixed policy" for his "new scheme" was that "cleanliness and order should be continued" and that "the stage show must be free from vulgarisms and coarseness of any kind." He intended the theater to be "as 'homelike' an amusement resort as it was possible to make it," and in doing so he bundled low culture with high and stripped vulgar fun and the fine arts alike of their respective difficulties. By the turn of the century, the more homogenized his "homelike" industry grew, the more he came to value, in his own words, "light, frothy acts, with no particular plot, but abounding in songs, dances, bright dialogue and clean repartee." Such melodramatic pap, he discovered, was "the sort of entertainment which seems to please most."

Not everyone was pleased, of course. "The most dangerous acts of the trapeze have been withdrawn," William Dean Howells, nineteenth-century America's great tastemaker, moaned in 1903, citing the loss of high-risk spectacle as a harbinger that "vaudeville is dying." But in fact it kept growing into the early 1920s, around the time of Hollywood's rise, when the "Keith Circuit" commanded an annual audience of four million customers. And in the 1920s and 1940s, with the advents of radio and television, respectively, Keith's continuous performance was perfected. If Hollywood retrofitted vaudeville theaters for a new generation of movie palaces, these household devices, transmitting endless sanitary entertainment, perfected Keith's mission: "home" entertainment. Television's direct access to vaudeville-trained celebrities came to define the middle-class household.

THE GILDED AGE POPULATION was slow to get educated—from 1870 to 1890, the national percentage of high school graduates hardly budged from 2 to 3.5 percent—but its interest in newspapers, dime novels, and other print media fairly exploded. Indeed, during this same twenty-year period, daily news circulation increased by 222 percent, a growth that was boosted by new printing and transportation technologies, funded by flourishing advertisement opportunities, goaded by big-city newspaper wars, and—perhaps most forcefully—disseminated by the ingenuity of cooperative publishers like A. N. Kellogg and A. J. Aikens. These two Chicago moguls retrenched their businesses after the Great Fire of 1871 and syndicated hundreds of the nation's "country" newspapers. Otherwise unscrupulous about their papers' content, Kellogg and Aikens only required that the stories be tasteful, which mostly meant that crimes and scandals could not be reported in detail, but only summarized.

Mainstream journalism became less sentimental—and less blatantly sensationalized—than it had been at the birth of the penny papers. In this proud new era of straight-shooting realism, respectable papers didn't resort to antebellum-era hoaxes or to rollicking Wild West facetiousness. In the spirit of *postbellum* Barnumism, rather, the dramatic "facts" of modern life became popular entertainment. *Frank Leslie's Illustrated Newspaper* offered "pictorial reporting" of Ku Klux Klan killings, rough prison life, and the mob violence of the "Great Uprising" of railroad workers in the early 1880s. Also, the style of their lavish images, as the historian Joshua Brown has shown, became decreasingly stereotyped and more observant to meet public demands for authenticity. The news was also tempered with local-color sketches and comical human-interest pieces by the popular new regionalist writers—from northeasterners like Sarah Orne Jewett and Mary Wilkins Freeman to "southwesterners" like Mark Twain and southerners like Charles W. Chesnutt and George Washington Cable. Among this latter set, cutting his teeth as a self-proclaimed "cornfield journalist" for the *Atlanta Constitution,* was the amateur folklorist Joel Chandler Harris, a beat reporter whose renditions of African-American dialects and folk tales became widely touted for their apparent realism. In 1884, *The Nation* praised him for getting "very close to the untutored spirit of humanity." What sold newspapers, however—what helped the *Constitution* rebound from the financial panic of 1873—was his stories' delicious fun.

In the words of his daughter-in-law Julia, Harris was himself, as a boy, "like Brer Rabbit," the African-American trickster figure he would single-handedly transform into a mainstream national hero. Young Harris was small, quick-witted, and mean. Indeed, many of his biographers note how this poor, illegitimate, and physically slight child pulled vicious pranks on his peers and bullies—how he coaxed one into hogslop that was infested with fleas; how he shoved another into an active wasps' nest, causing him to be seriously stung; how he burned yet another about the neck with a spatula, much to his indulgent mother's delight. As a boy he aspired to be a professional clown, acting for a spell in a local troupe that called itself the Gully Minstrels, but later in life he would dismiss black-face as "represent[ing] nothing on earth, except the abnormal development of the most extraordinary burlesque."

It wasn't until 1862, however, when he was sixteen and working as a printer's devil on the Turnwold plantation in central Georgia, that Harris befriended Harbert and "Uncle" George Terrell, two older black slaves who would help to define his illustrious career. During this period he immersed himself in the slaves' daily lives, hunting rabbits with them, recording their language in dialect poetry, and slipping off at night with the master's children to visit the interiors of their cabins. His daughter-in-law steeps the tale in plantation nostalgia: "From a nook in their chimney corners he listened to the legends handed down from the African ancestors,—the lore of animals and birds so dear to every plantation negro. . . . The boy unconsciously absorbed their fables and their ballads, and the soft elisions of their dialect and the picturesque images of their speech left an indelible imprint upon the plastic tablets of his memory." Yet there is poignant realism in the shadows of this cabin. As a white boy who had grown up at the bottom of Southern society, Harris may have been, as Wayne Mixon suggests, more nostalgic "for a black world than a white one"—and more for a black *paternalism* than a white one.

For the Terrells were Harris's first father figures, and their nightly lessons in wily animals who capsized upright Southern mores shaped the way Harris would think. Brother Rabbit must have been a revelation for the boy, a sympathetic hero and a sort of family secret. He took the rabbit's lessons to heart. In the 1870s and 1880s, as he was tracking its stories, Harris employed his own trickster techniques to collect these tales from the source. When he was in the presence of blacks, and only blacks, as he once was in a rail yard waiting for a train, he would set out to gain "their confidence and esteem" by "listening and laughing awhile." Then he would tell a tale or two of his own. In the rail yard it was the "Tar Baby" story that threw the gathering crowd into "unrestrained laughter." Then it was "Brother Rabbit and the Mosquito" that "had the effect of convulsing them."

> The result was that, for almost two hours, a crowd of thirty or more negroes vied with each other to see which could tell the most and best

stories. Some told them poorly, giving only meagre outlines, while others told them passing well; but one or two, if their language and their gestures could have been taken down, would have put Uncle Remus to shame.

Harris feared these sources were fading fast. As he explained in 1881, most contemporary blacks were "unfamiliar with the great body of their own folk-lore," and even older ones who were "as fond of the legends as ever" lacked "the occasion, or the excuse, for telling them." So he caught them and stuck them like butterflies on poster board. When he began publishing in the *Constitution* in the mid-1870s, he put his hard-won tales in the mouth of Uncle Remus, the jolly but devilish former slave who animates "Brer Rabbit" (as Harris called him) for the ears of a white Southern boy, identified simply as "the little boy." Uncle Remus was, for Harris, the natural voice to tell these tales. "Only in this shape," he wrote, "and with all the local allusions, would it be possible to adequately represent the shrewd observations, the curious retorts, the homely thrusts, the quaint comments, and the humorous philosophy of the race of which Uncle Remus is the type." Only in this "shape," through this "type," could Harris convey his own experience, that of a dazzled and honored white boy glorying in stories of outrageous rebellion.

*Uncle Remus: His Songs and His Sayings* (1880) became one of the century's best-selling books. In the book's opening tale, "Uncle Remus Initiates the Little Boy," the latter's mother, Miss Sally, finds him leaning his head against Remus's arms, gazing into his kindly "weather-beaten face," and hearing about the time Brer Rabbit robbed her own garden to throw a dinner for Brer Fox—who in turn tries to make a dinner of Rabbit. But the lesson is that Rabbit always slips away. Rabbit always outwits Fox in the end, "en Brer Fox ain't never cotch 'im yit, en w'at's mo', honey, he ain't gwine' ter." The story never reveals Miss Sally's reaction to the glorification of her garden thief, but this bold "initiation," taking place right under her nose, tells young readers that these cautionary tales aren't intended for their mothers.

Of all the diluted "family fun" of the Gilded Age, Harris's Brer Rabbit tales may have been the most socially subversive. His tricksters didn't teach you how to climb the corporate ladder. Writing under the cover of a fawning old "darky" (Harris's word)—blacking up with the masquerade of hokey false innocence that middle-class audiences had applauded for decades—Harris celebrated the pranks, rebellion, flirtations, risks, jokes, fiddling, dancing, mockery, and indefatigable hedonism of "de funniest creetur er de whole gang." While overtly racialized through Uncle Remus's black culture and often impenetrable dialect, these naughty beast epics had a broad appeal for all of the nation's Victorian children: even in a world of starchy manners, where the rich and powerful call all the shots, they said the smallest and smartest creatures in the forest can, at their own risk, sport the highest prestige.

Children also liked it that Uncle Remus was black. Samuel Clemens was there in the spring of 1882, at the house of George Washington Cable, when a group of them came to hear Uncle Remus. They looked with "outraged eyes" upon the "undersized, red-haired and somewhat freckled" Harris, who was too shy to open his mouth in public. (Harris also had a stutter.) "Why, he's white," they complained. Clemens said he understood their outrage. As a fellow admirer of Uncle Remus, Clemens, like thousands of other readers, had come to believe they were "personal friends," and here was this stammering white journalist. This trickster's humbug was shocking even to the pupils of Brother Rabbit.

"Well, I tell you dis," Remus cautions in *Nights with Uncle Remus* (1883), "ef dese yer tales wuz des fun, fun, fun en giggle, giggle, giggle, I let you know I'd a-done drapt um long ago." There were serious lessons to be learned from Brother Rabbit, lessons never intended for little white boys. But even—especially—Brother Rabbit's *fun*, the same fun that electrified antebellum slave quarters, sent readers a penetrating message. The pursuit of pleasure on one's own terms—not P. T. Barnum's terms, nor B. F. Keith's—sometimes comes at a personal cost: embarrassment, hurt feelings, broken bones. But the benefits include a personal freedom that can't be bought at any price. Brother Rabbit was no "respectable" white trickster like Tom Sawyer, but once he had gotten into the American mainstream, he kept popping back up again—perhaps most tenaciously as Bugs Bunny.

..................

BOLDER THAN THE CIRCUS, rawer than vaudeville, more "genuine" than Uncle Remus, was Buffalo Bill's Wild West show. The show opened in Omaha in 1883 with a flagrant insult to Barnum's gimcrackery: "No Tinsel, No Gilding, No Humbug! No Side Shows or Freaks!" Here was *genuine American fun*—thrills, spills, and spectacular clashes between rowdy cowboys and noble savages. The Omaha headlines responded in kind: "Eight Thousand Attend the Initial Performances, and Go Wild With Enthusiasm—the Races, Fights and Feats of the Big Amusement Hit."

Colonel William Cody was no P. T. Barnum, no B. F. Keith. This ringmaster was himself the real, rawhide deal, at least according to his big-talking *Autobiography*, which appeared in 1873 as a realist foil to the various popular novels featuring the thirty-three-year-old legend. The story it told (and sold at the show) tintyped the West in grand escapades that appealed to middle-class American dreamers, and many of them appear to be true. When Cody was seven, in 1853, his father built a log cabin in the Kansas Territory, and the boy took an easy shine to frontier life. He aspired to the westerner's long-haired, buckskin-clad elegance, to "the belt full of murderous bowies and long pistols," a look he would eventually make iconic. His daily exposure to "the rare and skillful feats of horsemanship," he wrote, "bred in me a desire to excel the most expert," which eventually he did. He kept constant acquaintance with Indian boys who schooled him in archery and a bit of Kickapoo, and allowed him to "[take] part in all their sports." He told of a childhood fraught with violence, as between the "mobs of murder-loving men" who wanted Kansas open for slavery and opponents like his father, who was stabbed on a platform for making an anti-slavery speech. (This one was true.)

Then, of course, there was violence with Native Americans, but is it possible that Cody, fatherless and eleven, was overtaken by "red devils" and had occasion to kill his "first Indian"? Biographers dispute this story. Fewer, however, have challenged his claim to have ridden, at thirteen, for the Pony Express. This too-delicious-to-be-false episode, which stars young Cody making the Express's longest ride ever and working under Twain's favorite desperado, Slade, came to signify the Express itself—its youth, its danger, its daredevil audacity. Its reenactment was the signature event of his show; histories of the Express cited it as fact; and as late as 2000 a respected biographer honored it with a fastidious chapter, only to have it debunked in 2005, when Louis S. Warren showed with disappointing certainty that during those years Cody "was in school."

But even as he exaggerated his later-life exploits—tacking zeroes onto Indians' headcounts, decorating his gruesome buffalo slaughters with impossibly acrobatic flourishes—there was no disputing the frontier butchery that paid for his reputation. Strapping and handsome with his long flowing locks, sporting decadent weapons and fringe, Cody stood for western extravagance. He strutted the frontiersman's dangerous fun. He didn't swear, but he drank and fought, and he loved to stage a practical joke. In September 1871, on a buffalo hunt with General Philip Sheridan, Cody pulled an elaborate prank reminiscent of Dan De Quille's at Carson River. Having riled up "Mr. McCarthy," a New Yorker in their party, with rumors of violent Indians in the region, Cody arranged for twenty-some Pawnees, who were in league with a captain he knew, to "throw blankets around them, and come crashing down upon us, firing and whooping in true Indian style." The joke got out of hand, and "two companies of cavalry" were sent in pursuit, but Cody, as he told it, headed off disaster.

It was Cody's flair for such bullish theatricality that had him less than one year later exploiting the new road-show industry and staking his claim in the emerging star system. Thanks to Ned Buntline's dime novels—yes, Ned Buntline of the Astor Place riots—"Buffalo Bill" was now a household name, and easterners clamored to see the legend in the flesh. Accompanied by fellow scout Texas Jack Omohundro, Cody played out scenes from his personal adventures in *Scouts of the Prairie,* a play Buntline himself threw together in an afternoon. They fist-fought, wrestled, fired live rounds, and hurled hackneyed obscenities like "Death to the Indians!" But for all of the stage show's mawkish melodrama— which early reviewers mercilessly detailed—realism was Cody's ace in the hole. He would step out of character and mug for the audience. Between seasons, he would be back on the trail, hunting, scouting, and working up material that blended seamlessly into his dramas. Most notably, in the summer of 1876, he wrapped his season early to join the western wars that brought Custer's defeat at the Little Big Horn: adorned in his flashy stage clothes, he was out scouting Cheyenne warriors when he was stood down by the young Indian chief Yellow Hair (Cody called him "Yellow Hand"), who recognized his face and wanted to fight. Cody shot the man at twenty paces, and "jerking his war-bonnet off . . . scientifically scalped him in about five seconds." He branded this achievement "The First Scalp for Custer" and worked it into the next season's performance—"a noisy, rattling, gunpowder entertainment," he called it, "all of which seemed to give general satisfaction." In the years to come he expanded his cast to include fellow gunslinger Wild Bill Hickok and hand-picked Lakota actors from the Indian Territory.

By 1882 he had outgrown the stage. A national population, riven by the Civil War and waves of immigration, still struggling to recover from the Panic of '73, took comfort in this dashing frontier hero who bragged of America's manly triumphs. There was money to be made from his heroism. All he needed was an open arena and a good supply of cowboys and Indians. In recent years he had become partner in a ranch on Nebraska's Dismal River. Cody himself was a reckless horseman who groused about the "hard work" of ranching ("I could not possibly find out where the fun came in"), but he was fascinated by the cowboys' antics in their downtime: "broncho riding, roping, racing, riding wild steers, swimming contests." This was the genuine cowboy fun he imported for his show, along with "a bunch of outlaw cow horses." His hired Indian actors followed a similar pattern. Having learned on the boards that Native Americans could be sold as symbols of vanishing nobility (as well as of ruthless savagery), Cody joined the Barnums and other showmen who had been sensationalizing this culture for decades. His respectful treatment of the many Indians he hired for the Wild West show—to parade in full dress, to engage in staged battles, to compete in fair-and-square foot and horse races—earned him lifelong appreciation among various western tribes. With hard-won permission from the federal government, even the outlawed Sitting Bull joined his show for one year in 1885.

During its infamous first season, Buffalo Bill's Wild West caused a

national thrill, though it failed to lasso the respectable audiences that
Cody knew it would need to survive. As a large-scale road show it out-
shone Barnum. Cody borrowed some of Barnum's best tricks, such as
his techniques for moving animals in boxcars, but he traded the big-
top for the wide-open sky and told a manly, white-supremacist story
that, as Warren argues, soothed the anxieties of an urban middle class.
Against popular fears that boys and men were becoming "neurasthenic"
milksops, Buffalo Bill and his handsome "centaurs" celebrated the viril-
ity of the American male. Against the dread of runaway immigration,
his noble white cowboys staged glorious triumphs over the threat of
racialized others—over the Native Americans and Mexican "vaqueros"
who played his road agents and cattle rustlers. In truth, Cody's cast of
western toughs couldn't live up to this white-hat myth. They drank like
real cowboys all throughout the season, legendarily devoting one box-
car to liquor. They let their violence leak into the arena, publicly abusing their animals and their assistants. And the program itself showed
little restraint, promising spectacles of killing and "torture." Newspaper
reporters noticed less-than-savory crowds swarming Cody's bloodsport
spectacle, just the thing to keep nice families away.

But Samuel Clemens, America's first source for Wild West high
jinks, attended the show two days in a row and wrote Cody a fan letter
in 1884 that served as publicity for both mythmakers. "It brought vividly
back the breezy wild life of the Great Plains and the Rocky Mountains,"
he wrote, "and stirred me like a war-song." "The show is genuine," he
testified, "wholly free of sham and insincerity." Most stirring for Clemens, as he reported it, were the curiosities his book *Roughing It* had made
iconic, the "pony expressmen" he had glorified with shameless hyperbole
and the "bucking horses," which he claimed, in an allusion to his own
famous "Mexican Plug," were "painfully real to me, as I rode one of
those outrages once for nearly a quarter of a minute." Most potent for
Clemens was the show's nationalist splendor, its "purely and distinctively
American" entertainment. He signed the letter with his brand ("Yours
Truly, Mark Twain"), thus giving Cody tacit license to use it as a blurb.

Cody took note. He inflated the show's patriotic image and made it
worthy of this celebrity endorsement. He also enlisted showman Nate

Salsbury, who had gotten his start as a minstrel performer, to clean up the show's act for Victorian consumption. Salsbury forbade the cast to drink. He retained many of the show's original thrills—Bill's Express ride, his Buffalo Hunt, and the breathtaking Deadwood stagecoach attack that gave select audience members the rides of their lives—but he set it to the music of a cowboy orchestra, adding a dainty Virginia reel on horseback and for a "grand finale" having Cody and his cowboys save a white frontier family from Indians. Salsbury killed much of the show's genuine danger, and also its indulgence in reckless fun, but its new patriotic tribute to pure domestic values would have won even B. F. Keith's approval.

The show could now be sold as "America's National Entertainment" and boast its educational value for children. It also attracted a prized demographic that hitherto had eluded Cody: women. It wasn't until 1885, however, when he discovered the small, young, pretty, frugal, sprightly, demure, but sharpshooting Annie Oakley, that Cody was ultimately able, in Warren's terms, to "domesticate" the Western image. In Oakley's clever hands—the same hands that embroidered her stage costumes and served tea to reporters in her humble trailer—even the deadly, phallic rifle took its place as a household appliance. With the help of Oakley, the ruder Calamity Jane, and a supporting cast of female performers, Buffalo Bill's Wild West show cracked the mainstream code. No longer a celebration of the masculine abandon that galloped from one firefight to the next, it repackaged the frontier as a rousing triumph of the orderly American home.

While under Salsbury's influence, the Wild West show revived a lawless frontier that had only recently been declared "closed." In the popular imagination this extravagant lawlessness *belonged* to Americans. It bucked with the broncos, fought with the cowboys, and war-whooped with Cody's bona fide Indians. It roused the crowd's most savage wishes without ever making them enter the arena. The show no more threatened its audience's safety than did contemporary tableaux vivants (live still lifes of classical set pieces that flattered the upper classes with Old World culture), but its *sensations* were shocking, and it made the crowd feel radically American.

....................

THE MASS-PRODUCED AMUSEMENTS of the postbellum period justified the smirking sense of frivolity that is commonly associated with
"fun." These pleasures were fleeting and superficial—*by design*. Nothing was at stake, except the ticket price. As enjoyable as it was to laugh
at vaudeville or to gasp at the triple-somersaulting aerials of Barnum's
magnificent Matthews family, these were things you did "for fun"—
which is to say, for nothing at all. You took no risks, and took no part.
Even Cody's spectators who were pulled from the crowd to ride in the
Deadwood stage attack didn't experience deadly frontier action; it only
looked and felt as if they did.

Such fun was vicarious, as were its risks: spectators identified with
dexterous athletes, death-defying acrobats, and rough-riding (retired)
cowboys. Such fun was also voyeuristic, whether folks ogled the ribald antics of minstrels or the splendor of Native American powwows. It
required no talent, no personal investment. Such no-stakes fun (call it
entertainment) was readily transferable from the circus to vaudeville to
nickelodeon and carnival, where automated games of skill and chance
offered a limited sense of participation—shooting (corn kernels) like
Annie Oakley, galloping (on a carousel) like Buffalo Bill. This closed
commercial circuit made for a self-sustaining market. Its consumers were
unspecialized, indiscriminate, omnivorous, expecting little more than
varieties of distraction from one inexpensive venue to the next. The print
media benefited on all levels—selling advertisements, publishing pro-
motions, tracking and contriving celebrity gossip.

This system reinforced a severe double standard for what it meant
to "have fun": either, like Buffalo Bill, you achieve the impossible as
the star onstage or you achieve the bare minimum in the anonymous
crowd. Both were (and are) kinds of American "fun," and both tried to
approximate the participatory excitement that liberated early American
crowds—at Merry Mount or on Congo Square, or in the unadulterated cussedness of Virginia City. Day and night, in "continuous performance," performers replicated the merriment and daring of a bold young
nation inventing itself. Season upon season, in row after row, American

spectators took in the show, while the wide-open spaces for loose public pleasure quietly vanished like the western frontier.

Ironically, in the age of aggressive realism, the age of pragmatism and science, when the people had outgrown the midcentury gaslights of mystery, hoaxes, magic, and romance, the humbug of commercialism reached its adulthood. Fraud wasn't a laughing matter anymore. It also wasn't open to debate. Mark Twain verified Buffalo Bill's story, and the product these pseudonymous moguls sold was so much more flavorful than the real, dusty thing—funner than an actual "Mexican Plug," funner than a saddle-busting Dismal River roundup—so much funner that it handily passed the public taste test. Buffalo Bill's great sleight of hand, what had him out-Barnuming P. T. Barnum, was to engineer a pleasure so irresistible that nobody *cared* how real it was.

America hasn't been the same ever since.

THIS U.S. MARKET OF SEEING (and believing) achieved critical mass in 1893, at Chicago's World's Columbian Exposition. National religious leaders had convened months earlier, debating the exposition's general morality and lobbying to have it closed on Sundays, but in the end they conceded it was an excellent way to showcase their various orthodoxies. So the exposition surged seven days a week, and everybody was satisfied. Between May and October of that year, 21.5 million customers paid fifty cents apiece to gape in wonder at the plaster-of-Paris White City and to gawk along the fair's mile-long Midway Plaisance. The former was a temporary faux-classical metropolis devoted to the heights of civilization—plastic arts, music, technology, government. Charles Dudley Warner, Twain's co-author of *The Gilded Age,* lectured there and described a viral disease he called "Barnumism"—a "lack of moderation" and a "striving to be sensational" that was warping literature, sermons, and the press. Of course Barnumism defined the entire exposition, all of which was drawn to immoderate scale—outsize buildings, miniaturized nations—but the designers pretended it was kept to the Midway (at the farthest possible remove from the fair's art museum) where millions thronged along a Barnumesque esplanade of international "villages" and other gaudy attractions. The Midway offered a low-cultural universe in dozens of crass curios like Buffalo Bill's Wild West and the bluntly Orientalist Streets of Cairo, where the belly dancer Little Egypt became a household name and spawned lurid copycats across the country. But whereas the Columbian Exposition was mostly about looking (at a Hawaiian volcano, a squat Eiffel Tower) and also about listening (to lectures and sermons and world music, from Poland's Paderewski to African drummers), among its greatest hits were the oddball exhibits that invited full-body participation, especially the "captive balloon" rides soaring 1,500 feet above the city and George Ferris's wildly popular Big Wheel. This 264-foot-wide stroke of genius is said to have saved the exposition from failure. It was also the future of commercialized fun.

One of the exposition's millions of customers—a thirty-one-year-old honeymooner from Coney Island, New York—returned home determined to build a Big Wheel of his own. If any one American of his era *valued* the fun of participation, it was George C. Tilyou.

Coney Island had been Tilyou's grammar school and college. Raised in his father's resort, the Surf House, George was underfoot in the 1860s and 1870s when tourists arrived from the city dancing on pleasure boats and enjoyed what one guidebook called the "great democratic resort—the ocean bathtub of the great unwashed." As a youth, that is, he saw the real deal: the fun of New York's earliest "mixt Multitudes," dating from Easter Mondays in the early eighteenth century to any given summer day at nineteenth-century Coney Island. The West Brighton beaches were famously diverse (men and women; rich and poor; whites, blacks, Hispanics, and Jews) and overwhelmingly crowded with easygoing folks who mingled, frolicked, danced, sang, lounged, and dallied in the waves. According to a reporter for the *Brooklyn Standard Union,* they seemed to "abandon all the restraint imposed by the rules of decency and morality." Another reporter, from the *New York Sun,* wrote, "The opposite gender rush together at Coney Island and how they stay together and romp and tousle one another, and wrestle and frolic and maul each other, gray heads and youths alike, precisely as if the thing to do in the water was to behave exactly contrary to the manner of behaving anywhere else." By all reports Tilyou was a pious young man, but these radically playful surroundings may well have loosened his spirit, for he grew to be an expert on "fun"—at least from an entrepreneurial angle.

In his youth, when the iconic Old Iron Pier split the sweeping beach between the tony east, with its white and sprawling Manhattan Hotel, and the demotic west, where the Tilyous lived, a notorious sub-industry preyed on the crowds—swindling them with cons and three-card monte, picking their pockets while they ogled "panel girls." The Tilyous ran a respectable business, catering to well-connected families who took in the sea baths, clambakes, and beer gardens. George's later life as a titanic showman, however, suggests he took cues from both of these worlds, from the sharpers on the beach and his good, godly family.

As a boy he was as enterprising as young P. T. Barnum. He started small, at fourteen, selling vials of saltwater and cigar boxes of sand for midwesterners to keep as souvenirs. The next year he got serious and bought a pair of horses, built a rickety driftwood coach, and spent the summer hauling tourists back and forth between the boat landing and the center of Coney Island's amusements; his endeavor was so successful that he was quickly muscled out by the town's political heavy, John Y. McKane. In the early 1880s, when Coney Island hosted Buffalo Bill's first season and basked in the fame of its first roller coaster, George and his father opened a popular vaudeville theater and assembled a small real-estate empire. McKane, who by then was the corrupt police chief and notorious "King of Coney Island," had become the family's bête noire. His loose stance on prostitution and gambling, and his promotion of prizefighting and drinking on the Sabbath, helped West Brighton to become "Sodom by the Sea," a fact that the God-fearing Tilyous loathed. It was bad for the soul and bad for business. They were the only local businessmen to speak out against him, arguing in 1887 for middle-class reforms to make West Brighton a respectable resort. This stunt cost the elder Tilyou his lease, which officially belonged to the police department.

But George kept socking away his profits, and in 1893, full of big ideas from his Chicago honeymoon, on which he had failed to buy the Ferris wheel (it was relocating to the St. Louis fair), he took out a loan, ordered a smaller one built to scale, and posted some humbug along

Surf Avenue: "On This Site Will Be Erected the World's Largest Ferris Wheel." When it arrived, Tilyou's wheel wasn't half the size of the original, but it was higher and brighter than anything around. Soon there were knockoffs of the Midway Plaisance and Streets of Cairo, complete with camel rides and a fake Little Egypt. Following McKane's conviction in 1894 for rigging Benjamin Harrison's election, Tilyou's vision for Coney Island blossomed. His sights were set on "clean fun." More exhilarating than the roller coasters and the toboggan slides that had cropped up over the previous decade were his high-wire Aerial Slide and his Aqua Aerial Shuttle. The latter carried passengers on an 825-foot loop over the ocean's crashing waves. And more spectacular even than Paul Boyton's Sea Lion Park—which opened in 1895, featuring his world-famous Shoot the Chutes—was Tilyou's response to it two years later, the twenty-two-acre Steeplechase Park, a midway boasting fifty mechanical amusements and encircled by a gravity-powered wooden racetrack: "A ride on the horses," Tilyou's promo claimed, "is a healthful stimulant that stirs the heart and clears the brain. It straightens out wrinkles and irons out puckers. . . . The old folks like it because it makes them young again. Everybody likes it because it's cheap fun, real fun, lively fun."

As a Coney Island native, Tilyou knew that Americans liked to participate, even to put themselves at risk—bodily risk, social risk. Americans were drawn to anything daring, whatever raised eyebrows or got a laugh. "We Americans want either to be thrilled or amused," he said, "and we are ready to pay for either sensation." (This last bit, *payment*, was key.) So to jangle their nerves and make them look silly—to give them their nickel's worth—he sent them walking on the Earthquake Floor, zapped them in the Electric Seat, knocked them around on the Human Pool Table, splashed them through the Electric Fountain, rolled them around in the Barrel of Love, and sent them down the Funny Stairway, which, he attested, "caused laughter enough to cure all the dyspepsia in the world." Tilyou knew from a life on the beach that people loved to get lost in the crowd, so he threw in New York's largest ballroom and kept four bands in constant rotation. Perhaps his more genuinely *fun-making* machine—for riders and amused observers alike—was a contraption called the Human Roulette, or the Human Whirlpool, a ride later depicted in an esteemed Reginald Marsh painting and featured in Clara Bow's blockbuster *It,* where it was rechristened again as the Social Mixer. The ride was simply a wide spinning cone, surrounded by a dish. Its riders gamely clung to the center until—when the thing really got going—its centrifugal force scattered them around the margins in a tangled, woozy, democratized mass of heads, legs, arms, and torsos.

By the turn of the century Tilyou had Steeplechase Parks in Atlantic City, St. Louis, and San Francisco. One was even featured in the 1900 Paris Exposition.

Eventually he housed all of his head-spinning rides in the five-acre so-called Pavilion of Fun, a family-oriented steel-and-glass enclosure where drinking, swearing, even slang were forbidden. (B. F. Keith's standards for "polite vaudeville" were judiciously enforced.) Just as Cody sold his show as education, Tilyou promoted his rides' health benefits and bally-hooed their high moral standards. Bucking the island's lingering reputation as a "Sodom by the Sea," he enlisted local churches as evangelizing "sales people" and offered special deals to Catholics and Lutherans and

Patrons of George C. Tilyou's famous Human Whirlpool enjoy the gut-wrenching fun of centrifugal force. (Courtesy of the Brooklyn Public Library—Brooklyn Collection.)

eventually to troops of Boy Scouts and Girl Scouts. Apparently even his Blowhole Theater—which blew fast air up women's skirts and shocked men's privates for the hilarity of the audience—was winkingly excused under Tilyou's good name. As the historian Kathy Peiss explains it, by risking a bit of "flirtation, permissiveness, and sexual humor," while never slipping into outright obscenity, Tilyou discovered a winning "formula" and exercised a "sexual ideology that would become increasingly accepted by the middle class."

Tilyou knew fun's power to fling people together, and like an electrician he harnessed that power. Turning people loose on his maniacal machines, he zapped their restless American spirits in harmless, painless, ninety-watt jolts. And he probably provided some of the vigor he advertised: he pumped his patrons with perpetual shots of adrenaline, endorphins, and dopamine. By many accounts, Tilyou was a man who wanted to do some social good. He stood down scoundrels like John Y. McKane. He believed in his inventions and the virtue of commerce. He wanted to bring joy to modern society. At the same time, he followed all the Gilded Age guidelines: Barnum's self-promotion and "politeness," B. F. Keith's "continuous performance," the jostle and pitch of Cody's stagecoach, and the celestial scale of the Ferris wheel. And he upheld his era's standards of decency. He believed in his outfit, and it made him a mint. "Laughter," he said, "made me a million dollars."

But P. T. Barnum would have caught the humbug. Tilyou was such a subtle trickster that apparently he had tricked himself. The "fun" he hawked in his Pavilion of Fun wasn't the real American deal—hardly the antics, pranks, and parties he witnessed as a boy growing up on the beach. Maybe he didn't want it to be. Tilyou was selling a modern experience: cleaner, easier, with a quicker payoff. But unlike the old-style pranks and parties, this new stuff lacked fun's social function—or, worse, it *warped* it. Tilyou may not have seen it that way. He saw his park as unadulterated fun. So would his son Edward, who would call it a "gigantic laboratory of human nature" that allowed customers to "cut loose from repressions and restrictions, and act pretty much as they feel like acting—since everyone else is doing the same." A *feeling* of liberty may have prevailed at Coney Island, but the fun in this laboratory was a whole new species. Unlike the free-lance human pyramids that feature in countless Coney Island photographs, in which men and women in striped bathing costumes laugh and struggle to keep their balance, Tilyou's machines got in between the people and forced them to take passive, defensive roles: trapped them in the Soup Bowl, whisked them along cables and groaning tracks, rolled them up high on the Ferris wheel.

With fewer chances in the vertical city for wild, expansive, liberating fun, crowds flocked to the beach to frolic in the waves, as they had done in decades past. But now they were halted several meters short by Tilyou's acres of indoor distractions. (He was still selling sand by the seashore.) Tilyou's machines looked friendly and familiar—they were cousins to appliances, elevators, and subways. But their threat was insidious. They hit the citizens at the level of their pleasures and created new tastes, desires, *needs*. It was that old West Brighton trick of picking men's pockets while they gaped at "panel girls."

FUN WAS INSTRUMENTAL in forming the best of the early American character. Playful risk and playful rebellion helped to loosen Puritanical authority. They motivated peaceful crowd action in the revolutionary era. They liberated African Americans in the face of tyranny. They helped to civilize the violent frontier. Fun, in these cases, lubricated the conflicts natural to a budding democracy. It rewarded citizens for acting boldly, for breaking barriers and speaking out. It brought them into amicable collisions with people they may have considered enemies.

But the "fun" engineered during the Gilded Age rewarded distinctly different behavior. It rewarded waiting, watching, and buying. Early photographs of the Pavilion of Fun show neck-craning crowds standing placidly by while the daring few are jerked in circles. Tilyou's pleasures demanded submission, a submission even more extreme than at Barnum's circuses or in Keith's muffled theaters. His patrons were fixed, immobilized, trapped. But the mass of Americans were used to submission: no longer rebels, they were the stage rebel's cheerleaders; they weren't the cowboy, but his screaming fans; they weren't the prankster, but the prankster's dupes. As Americans became customers, consumers, and fans, the citizenry became ever more susceptible to the ingenious humbugs of bigger and bigger business. Not that many cared, however, not while they were having such fun.

Visiting Europeans sensed something was amiss. Maxim Gorky, having seen Coney Island in 1906, allegedly exclaimed, "What a sad people you must be!" Freud went there in 1909, the same year he concluded that America was "a gigantic mistake."

Whether mechanical amusements were healthy, as Tilyou contended, or insidiously damaging, their legacy was mighty in the century to come. Progressives pushed back in the name of hands-on playtime: starting in 1906, the newly founded National Recreation Association oversaw the widespread construction of free urban playgrounds—promoting kid-powered fun on swings, seesaws, and merry-go-rounds and, by their mission, "encourag[ing] positive citizenship through supervised playground and leisure time activities."

But the mechanical amusement industry, now a multibillion-dollar international juggernaut of interactive museums and theme parks, was only in its infancy, and already it was a formidable opponent.

There was more to turn-of-the-century fun, however, than what was found on Coney Island, and the best of it *wasn't* supervised. During these same decades, in Missouri and Louisiana, a volcanic new variety of fun was erupting. Pulling "walk-arounds" down from the minstrel stage, freeing tricksters from the storybooks, early jazz was black folk fun destined to shatter America's barriers—and to set people twirling all on their own.

# 7

# Merry Mount Goes Mainstream

A CCORDING TO LEGEND, jazz was born in the brothels of Storyville. There's some truth to this. The early practitioners of rhythmic, brass-based, syncopated music tended to frequent the twenty-five
barbershops—and countless bars, dance halls, and parks—in and
around the twenty-block New Orleans neighborhood winkingly named
after Sidney Story, the alderman who made prostitution legal there in
1897. And jazz has traditionally been connected with sex—and vice,
disruption, dissolution, and crime. The word "jazz," which gained cur-
rency during World War I, may possibly derive from the cant word
"jasm"—a mid-nineteenth-century version of "jism," which meant "pep"
and "vigor" in addition to semen. So Storyville's brothels make for an
attractive birthplace. But few musicians ever played the red-light district proper, where live music was shunned as a costly distraction from
the brothels' more lucrative services. They were just as likely to play in
churches.

The music is actually of uncertain parentage. Most likely, in the
words of James Weldon Johnson, jazz—"like Topsy," the ragamuffin
slave girl from *Uncle Tom's Cabin*—"jes' grew": just grew from early
black spirituals, field hollers, work songs; grew from the bamboulas on

Congo Square; grew (ironically) from blackface minstrelsy; grew from the herky-jerky ragtime piano playing that had traveled from the gut-bucket bars of Missouri to the World's Columbian Exposition of 1893; grew from the street-corner spasm bands that bashed out songs on wash-tubs, lead pipes, cigar boxes, and hair combs; grew from the bighearted call-and-responses in black Baptist churches throughout the South; and grew, most directly, from hip-swaying marching bands that drove miles-long parades throughout the Crescent City—wedding parades, holiday parades, funeral parades to raise the dead.

It also grew from turn-of-the-century black theater. Black-owned, -directed, and -performed minstrelsy had risen to prominence in the 1880s and 1890s, and even when it upheld the blackface cartoon of heedless African-American life, it slipped in innovative new dances and humor and served as a training ground for serious black performers. While some African-American productions of the 1890s shed the min-strel tradition altogether (1898's *A Trip to Coontown* and *Clorindy—the Origin of the Cake-Walk,* for example), others, like the comedy act of Williams and Walker, turned it inside out.

Looking back on this duo in 1925, the author Jessie Fauset contrasted Bert Williams's "kindly, rather simple, hard-luck personage" with George Walker's "dishonest, overbearing, flashily dressed character" and con-cluded: "The interest of the piece hinged on the juxtaposition of these two men." They hammed up this juxtaposition in a dance. In 1896, dur-ing their record-breaking forty-week run at Koster and Bial's Hall in New York, Williams and Walker ignited the cakewalk into the first inter-national dance craze. The dance was a play on the Virginia Minstrels' walk-around, which was a play on the *slaves'* play on Southern white marches—as well as eel dances at New York's Catharine Slip. The way Williams and Walker did it, the dance split ragtime music down the mid-dle: flashy Walker pranced out its marchlike rhythm, and shy Williams improvised the syncopated accompaniment. Something about the way they rounded the stage, leading their lively female partners; something about the mix of Walker's tidy strut (a variation on the stately, original cakewalk) with Williams's slinky, sliding "smooch" (a less polite move, with ring shout origins) made audiences scramble to try it themselves.

Suddenly walk-arounds stepped off the stage and reclaimed their place down in the crowd. That year the nation was overtaken by cakewalk sheet music, cakewalk piano rolls, cakewalk contests. Williams and Walker appeared in cigarette ads, and when they learned that their chief competitor, the performer Tom Fletcher, was giving dance lessons to the Vanderbilts, they delivered a challenge to the Fifth Avenue mansion: $50 would "decide which of us all shall deserve the title of champion cake-walker of the world." (The Vanderbilts never responded.) In 1899, the *Musical Courier* scorned this unruly "sex dance" as "a milder edition

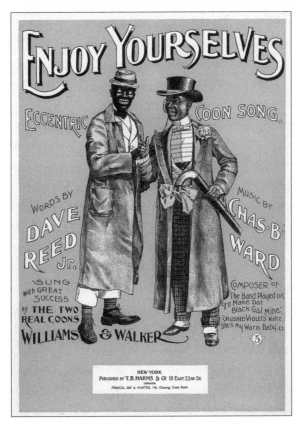

Minstrelsy and the Jazz Age overlap. On this 1896 sheet-music cover, Bert Williams and George W. Walker, originators of the global cakewalk craze, are racially exoticized for their "eccentric" fun. (Courtesy of African American Sheet Music, 1850–1920, Sheet Music Collection, John Hay Library, Brown University.)

of African orgies," but the people were having too much fun to care. In 1900, when John Philip Sousa brought the cakewalk to the Paris Exposition, the song "Bunch o' Blackberries" was, according to the *San Francisco Call*, "hummed, whistled, and played in almost every nook and corner of the French capital," and the dance itself—the "peregrination for the pastry"—was widely celebrated as "gay," "boisterous," and *"la plus illustre des fanfares américaines,"* even more illustrious, presumably, than George C. Tilyou's mechanical amusements.

Jazz was reaching its preadolescence when it sprang from the cornet of Buddy Bolden, the light-skinned, muscular, five-foot-eleven sport who is usually credited with being its first "king."

Born Charles Joseph Bolden in 1877, Buddy was raised in a mixed New Orleans neighborhood where working-class blacks, Irish, and Germans mostly got along. These groups divided along religious lines, but they mobbed the same street corners, and in the city's ongoing culture of celebration nearly everybody came together for barbecues, parades, and plein-air parties. Marches and dance music were the main attractions, and they provided Buddy's elementary training. Little is known about his early years. He may have attended Fisk School for Boys, with its vibrant choral and band programs, but most of his training would have happened by osmosis—from the ever-present fiddle bands, brass bands, and orchestras that were known to share a single stage in a night. Not long after he turned seventeen and had learned the cornet (from a kindly cook in the French Quarter), Bolden was incorporating all of these musical styles into his magpie horn-playing technique, a musical ventriloquism that incorporated anything from the junk collectors' calls to the fruit peddlers' chants.

By age twenty-two he was already known as the dance-band leader with the loudest horn in town. His horn invited wild hyperbole—people said it could be heard blocks away, even twenty miles away, and his folk-hero status increased in proportion. The only record Bolden ever made has been lost, but testimonies to his uncanny musical voice, and his idiosyncratic hooks and quirks, fill the pages of early jazz history. More generally, they survive in the work of his descendants: King Oliver, Sidney Bechet, Bix Beiderbecke, Louis Armstrong. What mattered most to this genial young fellow, who chatted in barbershops and caroused in bars and maintained an extramarital "harem" of prostitutes and brawling lovers, was the life of his music down among the dancers. Crushing opponents in nightly cutting contests; conning their hits overnight and blasting them back better; hearing and repeating the sounds of the people and tailoring syncopation to the dancers' needs, Bolden rose to fame—albeit local fame—right alongside the cakewalk craze. But Bolden had more of the Williams in him than the Walker. Absorbing the dance floor (not the parade), he improvised a brass-based ragtime that sparked "keen rivalry" among its dance members, taunted and tickled its demanding audience, and maximized the dancers' fun.

Bolden had some Barnum in him, too. He rolled his bandwagon around the neighborhoods, spreading his trademark with his loud, crackling horn—but the real local Barnum was named Buddy Bottley. Bottley was an enterprising balloon-ride operator who helped to manage Lincoln Park (the turn-of-the-century Congo Square where Bolden's band often performed) and staged competitions among Bolden's audience members. His carny ride fell out of favor when the crowd's "best dancer," "a cute little girl named Annie Jones," went up in his balloon and didn't return for a week, having been found in a swamp thirty miles away by "some Cajun trappers." Bottley and Bolden were "bosom buddies," two conspiring "lady killers" who dressed "like wealthy Southern gentlemen," yet Bolden was more in the line of Zab Hayward (kicking up Thayer's tavern floor) and Alfred Doten (touring the California gold fields with his banjo, fiddle, and obstreperous spirits). Steeped in folk culture, in love with the crowd, King Bolden was the avatar of old King Charles—because he was also a rebel. Jazz was disreputable, low-down, and dirty, and its practitioners wore their notoriety with pride. His honky-tonk music was *so* low down that it barely reached the bass clef of New Orleans's social scale. It was the scourge of the good Creole society that disowned Ferdinand LaMothe—the great ragtime pianist known as Jelly Roll Morton—for descending into Bolden's demimonde.

Upon the request of Lincoln Park's proprietor, Buddy's band could "keep it clean" for the "real high class, respectable, influential, colored people who would be having an affair in the main dance hall." But Bolden's fan base, whom he called his "Chillun"—"a bunch of youngsters . . . great dancers . . . fanatics," as Bottley's brother recalled—preferred it low and dirty. Case in point was his signature number, "Funky Butt." This ribald little tune, and the dance it inspired, was a dynamite cap of American fun: loud, rude, angular, *sensual.* The song was born one hot, sticky night when the band was playing Odd Fellows Hall. Willie Cornish, the trombonist, heard Bolden crack an impolite joke about the foul, *nasty* air. He spun the joke into a song that thrilled his sporting set:

> I thought I heard Buddy Bolden say
> Funky butt, funky butt
> Take it away.

Bolden's jazz headquarters, the Union Sons Hall on Perdido Street, soon became known as Funky Butt Hall, and the song itself became a mixing bowl for the people's defiant wit and slang. Bolden legendarily would change its lyrics "on the spot," improvising as always to suit the crowd's needs. The versions ranged from the political to the profane. Jelly Roll Morton's famous version softened the refrain—"You're nasty, you're dirty, take it away"—but it also took a swipe at the local judge who had convicted Bolden's various band members for the occasional misdemeanor. The Funky Butt's bard was the banjo player, Lorenzo Staulz, a wit, rhymester, and dirty-dozens maestro who "had the reputation of being the nastiest talking man in the history of New Orleans." Trombonist Frankie "Dusen and Bolden used to get a great big happy feeling when Lorenzo sang. He could sing 'Funky Butt' for an hour . . . because he would sing about all the notoriety whores, pimps, madams and even about the [white] policemen at the door." Duke Bottley recalled one especially hazardous verse:

> I thought I heer'd Abe Lincoln shout,
> Rebels close down them plantations and let all them niggers out.
> I'm positively sure I heer'd Mr. Lincoln shout.

Sidney Bechet, who started out in Bolden's original Eagle Band, recalled: "The police put you in jail if they heard you singing that song."

"Funky Butt" was the young black rebels' anthem, and the dance it inspired—exaggerating the city's earliest hip-grinding techniques—waved its unapologetic essence in the face of high New Orleans society. The funky butt *flouted* couth. Not at all orderly like the quadrilles and schottisches that sometimes shared the same dance floor; not proud and prancing like its fraternal cakewalk, the funky butt was purely a product of the folk—their street sounds (and smells), their vulgar jokes, and their ancestors' unassailable music. It enjoyed an easy place among other pelvis-driven dances that were fashioned by African Americans; as the blues musician Coot Grant recalled, these included "the Fanny Bump, Buzzard Lope, Fish Tail, Eagle Rock, Itch, Shimmy, Squat, Grind, Mooche . . . and a million others." But when Grant was asked to put the funky butt into words, she "hesitated and then explained: 'Well, you know the women sometimes pulled up their dresses to show their petticoats—fine linen with crocheted edges—and that's what happened with the Funky Butt.'" She went on to describe the dancing of "a tall, powerful woman" named Sue "who worked in the mills pulling coke from a furnace—a man's job," saying: "As soon as she got high and happy, that's what she'd do, pulling up her skirts and grinding her rear like an alligator crawling up a bank."

Bolden's fame crumbled in 1906, when he began to show symptoms of "dementia praecox, paranoid type"; he would spend the next quarter century in a mental hospital. While his musical contributions to early jazz are faint (he played mostly in B flat, and his riffs were just hints at the sophistication to come), his groundbreaking, ground-*shaking* take on ragtime, tailored to the whims of unbridled dancers, whipped up a genuinely *popular* culture that would define America's funnest era.

IN THE FINAL WEEKS of 1924, writer and *New York Times* editor Robert L. Duffus welcomed America's "Age of Play." Writing for *The Independent,* he attributed Roaring Twenties joie de vivre to factors long since held commonplace: shorter workdays, longer vacations, the boredom of factory work, and the chance to make more money while exerting less energy. Duffus, who in college had been the houseboy for Thorstein Veblen, eminent theorist of the "leisure class" and "conspicuous consumption," ran through a list of largely commercial diversions that pleased the primed and ready nation: contact sports, "recreation centers," playgrounds, movies, phonographs, "cheap automobiles," summer camps, et cetera. Praising Americans for altering their "ancient attitude," he argued, with a nod to current race theories, that their seeming shift from the "unceasing industry" of the "temperate zones" to the noncompetitive ease of "tropical and subtropical areas" was liberating them from the chains of conservatism and letting them get "nearer a frank and full enjoyment of life than any people that ever lived." At the heart of his argument, he pleaded with his readers to preserve what was "sacred" in all of this pleasure:

> I do not maintain that all [American] amusements are wholesome, nor that the excessive standardization and mechanization of work and play alike is without its dangers. . . . These evils are not to be cured by curbing the spirit of play. Reformers and educators must accept this spirit as more sacred than anything they have to give; they can help by guiding, not by restraining.

Duffus's appeal for a constructive response to the nation's sudden rush for enjoyment ("by guiding, not by restraining") placed him in a demilitarized zone of the Jazz Age culture wars, a tiny zone indeed. His vague reference to play's "evils" and "[un]wholesome" pleasures didn't exactly put him in William Bradford's old camp, the army of preachers and vice-squad bullies whose mission in the 1920s was to bomb America back to Plymouth Plantation. Nor, however, did his clarion call to America's "right to play" show him swinging drunk around the Maypole with the flappers, sharpers, and Lindy Hoppers who reveled in their own exciting permission. He wasn't overjoyed to live in what has been called "the Golden Age of the roller coasters"; to him, George C. Tilyou's chutes and wheels looked like the flip side of factory work. Nevertheless, in his socially reforming way, Duffus admired fun—not so much P. T. Barnum's fun, but the stuff the people came up with on their own. In it—"the spirit of play"—he saw the perfection of liberty. "The right to play," he wrote, "is the final clause in the charter of democracy. The people are king—*et le roi s'amuse.*"

Duffus made a charming case, but in retrospect his thoughts on play and democracy may have been too timid. In the 1920s, the struggle against cops, parents, censors, and even well-meaning reformers like himself was built right into the people's fun—certainly their most dangerous and democratizing fun. Essentially edgy, 1920s fun was had *in reaction* to cops, vice squads, racists—and especially to that popular villain, the "Puritan," who was widely viewed, in Frederick J. Hoffman's terms, as the embodiment of Freudian "repression," "a man ignorant and rudely affirmative, who forced his religion and its strait-laced moral code upon a growing country." But this villain also reflected a national reality, the long legacy of social, political, and legal institutions that anxiously defended what Stanley Coben calls the "Victorian character" in 1920s America: feminine domesticity, patriarchal manliness, Protestant faith, and white supremacy. If Prohibition was the tallest monument to this "character," then members of the Ku Klux Klan, which was gaining political dominance in Indiana and elsewhere, were its most vicious "guardians."

Caricature or not, this would-be "Puritan" became the fall guy for intellectuals, bohemians, flappers, minorities, homosexuals, and other outsiders who aimed to liberate their nation and—as is the subject of the following three chapters—its libido through unapologetically liberal pleasure. Even when their fun was outrageously silly—flagpole sitting, goldfish swallowing, utterly fluffy and superfluous slang—Americans flicked a tooth at the modern severity of pragmatism and professionalism. And rolled their eyes at squares like Duffus. The "guiding" he proposed—who needed it? The people were happy guiding themselves.

But for this reason the Jazz Age *did* advance democracy—widen it, energize it, *modernize* it. If Gilded Age entertainments, as we have seen, were designed to separate and segregate the people, then many of the risky new Jazz Age amusements, with which the culture industry struggled to keep up, did just the opposite. In the tradition of Buddy Bolden's Funky Butt Hall, and in their illegal and unregulated hideouts from Prohibition, the people engineered new pleasures of their own that not only fostered class and race mixing (in an otherwise politically volatile age), but also, most radically, gave new social power to many race and gender minorities who managed to have more fun than the majority.

The people's fun, in the 1920s, may indeed have been "the final clause in the charter of democracy." In the spirit of Merry Mount and the Pinkster Days, though now on a national scale, Jazz Age fun allowed average Americans to revel in their two basic freedoms at once—their individuality *and* their community membership.

Duffus was one of countless contemporaries to debate the worth of fun. This discourse itself was quite new, *modern*. In earlier eras, "fun" was treated as the ineffectual aside to pressing political and social issues. Jack Tar's pranks were instruments of revolution; African-American festivals and balls were quaint displays of primitivism; public drunkenness was the bugbear of reformers. In the 1920s, however, fun qua fun advanced to the forefront as either proof positive of the great American spirit or a warning of civilization's decline. Its presence was too great to be dismissed. It was also just too interesting. The voices in this debate were varied and forceful, and they addressed the subject in every medium. Duffus, Walter Lippmann, Constance Rourke, Max Eastman, and countless other intellectuals parsed, debated, and defended the value of fun. Preachers and lawmakers argued for and against it. Newspapers and magazines bulged with the subject and reveled in its culture wars. H. L. Mencken, the decade's most jaundiced culture critic, assessed his home state of Maryland's rage for fun as a dismal reaction against both a "stiffening, almost a deadening in" moral and political "manners." In such an overregulated society, he argued, "To be happy takes on the character of the illicit: it is jazz, spooning on the back seat, the Follies, dancing without corsets, wood alcohol." He blamed his contemporaries' "almost complete incapacity for innocent joy" on antics that to twenty-first-century Americans look exceedingly joyful and innocent, if also quaintly roaring.

Those who got closest and most embroiled in fun's details were the composers, musicians, novelists, poets, playwrights, comedians, filmmakers, actors, and painters who animated popular, pleasurable rebellion and tried to understand its social power. Down among the funmakers themselves—the dancers, drinkers, pranksters, and jokers who animated the "age of play"—were cultural leaders and innovators, especially young ones, who recognized fun as the great American difference and worked to elevate its dignity. Harlem's most brilliant "New Negroes" saw fun as a mark of racial pride. America's most daring "New Women" saw fun as a mode of liberation. Stars of both groups wrote poems, plays, stories, and songs that explored the risky pleasures of American rebellion. Jazz Age fun wasn't as simple as it looked, and as these rebels' works revealed (by slowing their era down to a vivid freeze-frame), the personal costs of having fun reflect the dangers of democracy itself.

Fun—once the province of discrete American groups—was touted in the 1920s as the great social mixer. In earlier eras it had strengthened social bonds to the exclusion of meddling outsiders: it had fortified Patriots against Royalists; it had fortified black communities against racist whites; it had fortified frontiersmen's homosocial bonds against the interference of feminine domesticity. In the 1920s, it still served such identity formation—as in helping young women break Victorian chains or galvanizing a growing black urban population. But in the social upheaval following World War I—America's sudden economic prosperity, African Americans' Great Migration, women's suffrage and growing economic freedom—new and more sophisticated kinds of earlier fun became instrumental in breaking boundaries down. Playful behavior and acts of rebellion carved inroads among long-divided races, classes, and genders who recognized at least one common opponent: Bradford's legacy, the American killjoy.

GILDED AGE–STYLE "family fun" flourished during the prosperous 1920s. Thanks to sophisticated new communications technology, it had grown sleeker and stronger since Barnum's newspapers announced the circus was coming to town. Silver screens dominated moviegoers' senses. Radio signals entered consumers' homes. But the pleasure being sold was basically the same: the passive reception of a performer's talent. The popularity of amusement parks dropped off during this decade, beginning "a steady decline" as early as 1921, but Americans tripled their consumption of entertainment in general, largely in the form of sports and movie tickets—but also of records, books, sheet music, and sporting goods, products that required some level of consumer engagement. The

U.S. population grew by 16 percent, from 105 million to 122 million, but annual spending on spectator sports more than doubled from $30 million to $65 million and on cinema from $301 million to $732 million.

Sports stars became the new folk heroes. Among those who dominated the public imagination—boxer Jack Dempsey; tennis star Big Bill Tilden; running back Red Grange, the Galloping Ghost—none of them matched the bleachers-packing celebrity of the Sultan of Swat, Babe Ruth, the rags-to-riches slugger whose fame was gaudily constructed by the press agent Christy Walsh. Adored for his athletic prowess as much as for his gustatory and erotic appetites, the barrel-bellied Babe—far more than his surly rival Ty Cobb—was the cheerful and beer-swilling epitome of fun, and his fans (who wasn't one?) loaded themselves down with his trademarked merchandise and spin-off items, the cars, dress shoes, fishing poles, and other products (most with no connection to baseball) buoyed up by his famous name. Baby Ruth candy bars appeared in 1921 and cashed in on the Bambino's fame for free—by claiming to have been named after Grover Cleveland's daughter.

"Each week about 100 million Americans went to the movies," writes 1920s historian Geoffrey Perrett, "a number equal to nearly the entire population. . . . By 1926 there were more than 20,000 dream palaces offering celluloid refuge." It would be difficult to overstate the impact Hollywood had on America's national consciousness—and self-consciousness— during the 1920s. The movies' "celluloid refuge" was even darker and more impersonal than B. F. Keith's vaudeville theaters, but thanks to their absolute passivity and total immersion the reclining spectators were consumed by pleasure. No longer victims of the worn-out material and lackluster performances of circulating road-show talent, Americans paid a quarter to be plunged into fantasy—titillated by Cecil B. DeMille's racy comedies, surrounded by D. W. Griffith's (racist) and Erich von Stroheim's sprawling histories, and—most important—indulged by the graceful, witty, glamorous, gorgeous, carefree, death-defying, and scandalous ectoplasms of Mary Pickford, Douglas Fairbanks, Theda Bara, Gloria Swanson, Rudolph Valentino, Charlie Chaplin, and all the royalty whose faces and antics towered thirty feet above the raked seating. Anyone with the price of a ticket claimed an evening's rights to the purity and danger of the world's biggest stars. The movies' dazzling fun blended in just fine with what Duffus called the "age of play." Nevertheless, for all of their vicarious excitement, they were also the era's most efficient means of keeping citizens stock-still in their seats, "gaping stupidly at idiotic pictures in monochrome," Mencken objected. "No light, no color, no sound!"

The new "Puritans" thought movies posed a moral threat. Movies set bad examples, gave bad ideas, and gloried in Jazz Age libertinism. In 1922, when critics raised a stink about his flapper fantasy *Foolish Wives,* von Stroheim felt they were infantilizing society: "My ears have run with their united cry: 'It is not fit for children!' Children! Children! God, I did not make that picture for children." But the conservative majority was an indomitable force, and that same year, as Hollywood sank into a scandalous mire—Mary Pickford's divorce; Fatty Arbuckle's (supposed) rape and murder of a young party guest; actor-director William Desmond Taylor's unsolved homicide—studio executives, in an act of contrition, founded the Motion Picture Producers and Distributors of America (MPPDA), their own homespun censorship and moral-conduct squad. With this very public and showy gesture, the largely Jewish film establishment tried to appeal to America's stern Christian establishment, in particular to the powerful Federal Council of Churches, overseers of upright civic organizations like the YMCA and the Daughters of the American Revolution (DAR) and the Boy Scouts of America. Lest the churches doubt Hollywood's sincerity in making peace with Main Street, the MPPDA appointed as its "czar" the sober and evangelical Will Hays, a former postmaster general who was winkingly known as the "Billy Sunday of the Republican Party."

Hays, their small-town-Indiana shill, enjoyed his warm California welcome. The Hollywood streets were "decorated with bunting and flags" and "big signs reading WELCOME WILL HAYS" (one of which, FBI sources reported, ended up hung over the door to Charlie Chaplin's bathroom). But his appointment and purpose, bunting and all, were flagrant acts of Barnumism. By assigning Hays as liaison to the churches, and by allowing him to loosely enforce his touted moral "Formula," the studios could forestall the conservative lobbies from ramming a censorship bill through Congress. Throughout the 1920s, even as Hays occasionally ceded ground by failing to grease the right clerical palms, the humbug worked. Movies remained classified, begrudgingly, as speech, and Hollywood was trusted to regulate itself. Hays's "Formula" was updated in 1927 to become the "Eleven Don'ts and Twenty-Six Be Carefuls," whose most egregious "Don'ts" would have been Middle American box-office poison anyway: anti-Christian profanity, "sexual perversion," "nudity," "miscegenation," "ridicule of the clergy," and, tellingly, "*white* slavery." *The Jazz Singer,* Al Jolson's blockbuster talkie that same year, much of which was played in blackface, seems to transgress the radically democratic "Don't" against "willful offense to any nation, race or creed," but as with all of the Hays guidelines, the "race" this one protected (and flattered) was white.

Hollywood's showy pact with the churches, like Barnum's own pact some ninety years before, was strategically commercial. The industry required such mainstream access as only the clergy's blessing could ensure; studios vied for block distribution, carte blanche contracts with the nation's theaters to screen their movies, good, bad, or ugly. At the same time, the movies had to please cosmopolitan ticket buyers: they had to be modern, daring, *fun.* With feckless Hays they had found the perfect Formula. With the fox guarding the henhouse, the fun went on: *Flaming Youth, Free to Love, Smouldering Fires, Flesh and the Devil.* Industry heavies like von Stroheim and DeMille trod on the Don'ts and ignored the Be Carefuls, and their blockbusting profits gave them moral high ground. They were just giving the people what they wanted. What is more, while DeMille's biblical pictures (*The Ten Commandments* [1923] and *The King of Kings* [1927]) may have been his raciest of all, in the end they were forgiven even for using illicit sex (Mary Magdalene's burlesque dance for a stony-faced Christ was trimmed and tamed but ultimately ran) because they sparked interest in religious film. F. Scott Fitzgerald, unimpressed by tame cinematic sex, refused to see any threat in it at all. "Contrary to popular opinion," he opined, "the movies of the Jazz Age had no effect upon its morals."

Unlike the rebels in Buddy Bolden's line who dove into the fray of 1920s fun, simple moviegoers were a sleepy majority. Their role was vicarious, identificatory at best; their pleasure was scopophilic, voyeuristic.

To this extent, they were less adventuresome than Buffalo Bill's cheering crowds. As consumers of the tabloid boom and of salacious and canned new fan magazines, they were silent investors in the dazzling star system that empowered Hollywood with a global reach. And yet by buying tickets, moviegoers (who were often also churchgoers) gave assent to changing national attitudes toward fun. Thanks to the humbug surrounding Hays's new Formula, even middling Babbitts were given mind-blowing lessons in risk, transgression, rebellion, and silliness, as well as in the defiant populism of the era's infectious tramps and flappers.

The deadpan slapstick of Charlie Chaplin and Buster Keaton remain our crispest images of 1920s fun. In *The Gold Rush* (1925), a masterpiece of the silent era, Chaplin's Tramp treks into the snowbound Klondike in search of turn-of-the-century riches but instead, like Mark Twain's self-satirizing argonaut, encounters adversaries societal and natural. In the end he gets both the girl and the gold, but not until he has known humiliation and near death by exposure, starvation, mauling, murder, and cannibalism at the hands of a fellow prospector who hallucinates that he is a chicken. Chaplin gleaned this latter setup, and another in which the Tramp eats his boot, from an account of the Donner party. "Tragedy," he later wrote of these scenes' dark comedy, "stimulates the spirit of ridicule, because ridicule, I suppose, is an attitude of defiance: we must laugh in the face of our helplessness against the forces of nature—or go insane." This statement may have been a coded reference to his personal misery that year. Having impregnated the film's original dance-hall heroine—a sixteen-year-old named Lillita MacMurray—he embarked on a two-year shotgun marriage that dragged his peccadilloes through the courts and tabloids, resulting in his nervous breakdown and the public's disgust and a divorce settlement that cost him more than a million dollars. Even H. L. Mencken, not much of a Chaplin fan, redirected blame (via Puritan metaphor) at the fickle Babbittry: "The very morons who worshipped Charlie Chaplin six weeks ago now prepare to dance around the stake while he is burned." True to form, Chaplin took refuge in "an attitude of defiance": throughout this crisis, his Tramp clowned around making his 1928 name-saving feature, *The Circus*.

For all of their seeming weakness, Chaplin's and Keaton's shambling protagonists were monsters of such defiance—Keaton's, in particular. Hapless, fumbling, ingenuous, and daring, Buster Keaton's assortment of long-faced straight men turn the roughest scenes into jungle gyms—from grapples with Virginia bootleggers in his 1918 short, *Moonshine,* to his astonishing array of silent features: the luckless Friendless roping (and befriending) cattle in *Go West* (1925); the weakling Alfred pretending to be a prizefighter in *Battling Butler* (1926); the dandy turned soldier wrestling a locomotive in *The General* (1926); the egghead turned acrobatic jock in *College* (1927); and, in *Steamboat Bill, Jr.* (1928), the delicate flower forced to hold his own against a roughneck riverboat crew and—in the finale, one of the most impressive sequences in all of cinema—a town-flattening tornado. Chaplin's and Keaton's sight gags in the face of misery encapsulate the Jazz Age spirit: humor, agility, audacity, and style were the best defenses against nature's foes, and on these strange terms such underdog clowns became the modern American heroes. Heightening their fun, their risky pleasure, was the fact that their lethal stunts were real—as were Harold Lloyd's and many of Douglas Fairbanks's. (Gary Cooper also got his start in stunts.) They tripped along cliffs, slid from great heights, jumped from trains, fell from buildings, forever holding their gullible mugs intact. But Keaton's antics set the standard. Trained as an acrobat in vaudeville, limberly drunk much of his time on set, he put his body in constant peril (discovering only decades later that he had once broken his neck) and trained newcomers to do the same. "I developed more stunt men than any studio in Los Angeles," he said. "I've taken the goddamnedest people and made stunt men out of them." But Hollywood's stuntmen, the stars and stand-ins, were only glamorous examples of a greater thrill-seeking culture that took the goddamnedest people (on airplanes, skyscrapers, flagpoles, dance floors) and made daredevils out of them. Stuntmen only made this fad more visible.

Hollywood's "It girls," for their part, took sassier, sexier, *steelier* risks. They dangled from the cliff of a steadfast social code that expected them to be either virgins or whores. Clara Bow, the "Brooklyn Bonfire," made it look like child's play. Born into abject poverty in a Sands Street tenement—some of the most violent and tubercular living conditions in turn-of-the-century America—as a girl she suffered constant hunger and frequent beatings by her severely epileptic mother and her vicious alcoholic father, a career busboy who dreamed of being a singing waiter. Shunned by other girls for being ugly and dirty, she excelled as a tomboy in her local street gang: "I could lick any boy my size," she boasted. "My right was famous." She and the boys got into "all sorts of crazy stunts. . . . Once," she recalled, "I hopped a ride on behind a big fire engine. I got a lot of credit from the gang for that." At the age of nine, she rescued her best friend from an apartment fire by rolling him in carpet, only to have him die in her arms. She quit seventh grade to cut hot-dog buns at Nathan's on Coney Island, then briefly answered phones for a Manhattan abortionist. In her teens she defied her mother and escaped her constant loneliness as most Americans did: she lived at the movies and devoured fan magazines, dreaming of one day becoming a star; she vanished into the movies' "distant lands, serene, lovely homes, romance, nobility, glamour," as she put it—into "everything that magic silversheet could represent to a lonely, starved, unhappy child." Then at age sixteen, in 1921, she got her one-in-a-million break. Armed with two "terrible" boardwalk portraits, dressed in her goofy tam and single shabby outfit, she beat out streams of other hopefuls to win Brewster Publications' Fame and Fortune Contest—for which distinction (in addition to winning a minor movie role) her mother tried to kill her with a butcher knife, *twice*. But her publicity shot was a revelation: auburn-haired, moony-eyed Clara was gorgeous.

More to the point, as was clear from her first screen tests, this lonely teenager was wild good fun. Despite her uncanny talent for crying on cue ("All I hadda do was think of home"), this strange new girl galloped like a mustang: "She is plastic, quick, alert, young, and lovely," wrote the contest judges. Throughout her intensely prolific career (fifty-four feature films by 1933), cameramen struggled to keep her in the frame as she romped and cavorted about the set—often making editors fill in with close-ups when they lost her altogether. Her unbound, vivacious, improvisational style reflected her genuine effervescence: playing the flapper daughter Kittens in *Dancing Mothers* (1925), she overrode the script's Hays-placating disapproval and "played her," in Bow's words, "as a girl out for havin' fun"—out, that is, for writhing on furniture, relishing liquor, gulping cigarettes, and flirting with men young and old at a pirate-themed speakeasy. In this otherwise dour cautionary tale about the modern family's disintegration, she's a spark plug, a sparkler, exquisitely out of place. But she also frolicked out of Chaplinesque "defiance," as she did during the filming of *Enemies of Women* (1923), when her mother was on her deathbed in an asylum: "In the picture I danced on a table. All the time I had to be laughing, romping wildly, displaying nothing for the camera but pleasure and the joy of life. . . . I'd cry my eyes out when I left my mama in the morning—and then go dance on a table." By all appearances, however, she did it wholeheartedly, and the critics adored her in the worst of movies.

She was right at home in tomboy roles—as a roustabout stowaway in *Down to the Sea in Ships* (1922), as frontier girls and gutter urchins, and like the male comic stars she did her own stunts. But her stock-in-trade was to play the "jazz baby"—the neighbor girl, newlywed, or college coed whose lip-biting desire and smoldering appeal threaten to torch the whole neighborhood. She perfected this role in Victor Fleming's 1926 funny adaptation of Sinclair Lewis's *Mantrap;* her lead character, Alverna, the Emma Bovaryescent wife of a clueless country bumpkin, cracks the ice under their cold Canadian town when she is tempted by a New York divorce lawyer. A serious social novel played for laughs (the joke is on frigidity), *Mantrap* showcased Bow's ultramodern talent for making sex fun: frolicsome, not fearsome; liberating, not damnable. "Alverna channels all her vitality in flirtation," Michael Sragow observes. "She stands for life amid a mob of pious zombies." For Bow eroticism wasn't an act; it was her most authentic mode. It gave her power and put her at ease. Fleming was ensnared by it on the set of *Mantrap,* at the same time Gary Cooper was, and the Hollywood gossip mill went berserk—because, true to character, she refused to be discreet. She liked them both. Where was the shame? In Hollywood, as she put it, she was "running wild"—"in the sense of trying to have a good time"—and moviegoers were the beneficiaries: "I suppose a lot of that excitement, that joy of life, got onto the screen, and was the sort of flame of youth that made people enjoy seeing me." All her bad name lacked was a brand.

So in 1927 her relentless producer, B. P. Schulberg, the same spin doctor who had trademarked Mary Pickford as "America's Sweetheart," enlisted the aging Elinor Glyn, a British romance writer who had become the decade's authority (after Freud) on sexual prowess, to ordain Clara Bow as America's "It girl"—*It* being the title of Glyn's recent novel. "It"— a winking play on id—referred to a sort of erotic chutzpah. Did Clara Bow have it? For a $50,000 promotional fee, Glyn allowed she did and fawned over the object of her endorsement. The honeymoon ended when Glyn's (unsolicited) etiquette lessons prompted Bow to call her "that shithead."

*It* (1927) is the film for which Clara Bow is legend and one of the decade's biggest box-office hits. In it, she plays downtown Betty Lou who works the fabric counter of a midtown department store. By dint of her pluck and flirty wit, she catches the eye of the dashing store president (Antonio Moreno), who eagerly tries to win her for himself. His uptown idea of having fun is to treat her to a night at the Ritz (where Glyn makes

Clara Bow: The Brooklyn Bonfire. (Courtesy of the Library of Congress.)

a stiff and stagy cameo)—though, predictably, their evening falls flat. She agrees to give him a second chance. Her idea of a "real good time" is to take him out to Coney Island. Among the rubbed-up Steeplechase throngs, he takes some encouraging but gradually loosens up. At a climactic moment in a romantic sequence that entails the usual carnival fun, she drags him into the Fun House, where they mount George C. Tilyou's Human Roulette. In *It* it's called the Social Mixer, and risk and democracy are part of its structure. The ride, as we have seen, is a broad, gently sloping cone, surrounded by a wide and generous dish. Patrons pile up onto the cone, and as it spins they cling tightly to each other, lest they be thrown off in all directions and ultimately be "mixed up" in the dish. In the film, the It girl and the president are the last two revelers left clinging to the center, gleefully resisting centrifugal force. She flies off first into the writhing rabble. Though he holds on with all his might, he accepts natural law that the center cannot hold and is flung into the spinning crowd (and our heroine's arms). But the whirling motor under the movie's hood isn't Tilyou's outmoded toy, it's Clara Bow's up-to-the-minute *id*.

And like her libido, her folksiness was real. She was more at home with working-class film crews than with her fellow superstars—who widely shunned her for her bad table manners, her coarse Brooklyn accent, and her refusal to put on the high-class airs that Hollywood's lowborn society affected. At the height of her fame and fortune, instead of buying the expected sprawling mansion, she moved with her infamously drunken father into a modest bungalow, best known for its lurid Orientalist boudoir, and she roller-skated up and down the driveway. When the rest of the "colony" wouldn't keep her company, she cold-called the Sigma Chi house of Morley Drury, the captain of the University of Southern California's famous "Thundering Herd," and spent the late fall of 1927 entertaining the entire football team (including the undergraduate who would become John Wayne)—whether in loud dance parties at her bungalow or in the Garden of Allah's jazz club and swimming pool. When she managed to break the thumb of an All-American tackle in a late-night game of touch football, the Herd's coach publicly rounded them up. The bad-news It girl was officially off-limits. But the twentieth-century g'hal from Brooklyn's mean streets kept thriving in her milieu of fun. "I like young people and gaiety," she said in 1928, "and have a lot of both around me whenever I have time."

Bow and her generation of so-called flappers—brash "New Women" like Bessie Smith, Louise Brooks, Zelda Fitzgerald, and Dorothy Parker—headed up a fun-loving jazz revolution that electrified the middling masses. For the real social mixer, of course, was sex, and the capacity to admit it if you *liked* it. But it was still risky business: the Victorian Age wasn't that long ago. All it took was the scorching Mae West, another frank rebel from Brooklyn's mean streets, to blow the lid off Will Hays's cooked Formula.

THE JAZZ AGE CAUSE CÉLÈBRE was booze. After the Volstead Act of 1920, the opposing sides of Main Street became radicalized into the temperate "drys" and the wild-living "wets." The drys, as ever, had the moral high ground, and now the law was on their side. The historian Paul A. Carter makes a reasonable case for Prohibition's "democratic faith," explaining how the Eighteenth Amendment "met all the tests of proper democratic action: the test of time, the test of full discussion, the test of decisive majority expression (forty-six of the forty-eight states had, after all, ratified the constitutional change)." When the law passed in 1919, the winning majority was mostly rural Protestants fulfilling the wishes of their temperance forebears, but they were met with such resistance from the growing minorities—most notably from blacks and Catholic and Jewish immigrants—that the law also signaled the decline, as Carter argues, of Protestant ideological power.

In the Jeffersonian spirit of hedonism and rebellion, the wets (or "Wild Wets," as they were punningly known) felt no obligation to honor a law that denied their self-defined right to pursue happiness. A rebel front comprising all ages, classes, races, and gender identifications attacked the new law from every angle and rallied around their fight for freedom. The playwright Dwight Taylor remembered this revolutionary sentiment being especially fervent in the literary world: "Our national heritage of freedom seemed in jeopardy, drinking became a patriotic duty, and the average American writer's reaction to the passing of the Eighteenth Amendment was to embark on a prolonged Boston Tea Party, in which he very often found himself acting like an Indian. Some of the outstanding editors and publishers of the period were enthusiastic leaders in the revolt." Even the socially conservative William Randolph Hearst, who once campaigned in San Francisco for "wholesome and decent fun," touted the values of old-school rebellion, saying of Prohibition: "If the American people had had respect for all laws, good or bad, there would have been no Boston Tea Party." Like the original Sons of Liberty, the wets used action, publication, and antics to demonstrate their right to play.

Bootlegging became a common hobby. Accessory stores opened nationwide, offering the necessary equipment and ingredients to fire up a bathtub distillery. All generations got in on the act. Often when their parents were sent up the river, children kept the home fires burning. Doctors padded their incomes writing prescriptions for alcohol. Even the American Medical Association, which in 1917 had declared prescriptions for alcohol had "no scientific value," changed their minds in 1922 and named twenty-seven medical uses for it. (In New York, counterfeit prescriptions sold for twenty-five to thirty dollars.) One of the law's biggest loopholes was sacramental wine. Protestants (who had voted in the act to begin with) usually used grape juice in their services; rabbis and Catholic priests could make a solid case—for purchasing a case. Few actual rabbis are believed to have abused the law, but its ambiguous wording allowed the non-rabbinical to don hats and beards and procure enough wine to supply fictitious congregations. With millions in agreement that the law was absurd, transgression itself became a stylish sort of fun and encouraged an epidemic of nervy pranks. An ambitious little still, with a running capacity of 130 gallons, was found bubbling away "on the farm of Senator Morris Sheppard, the author of the Eighteenth Amendment."

Some drys, for their part, got in on the fun. Harry S. Warner inverted popular wet rhetoric, calling Prohibition "the liberation of the individual from the illusion of freedom that is conveyed by alcohol." Izzy Einstein, a trickster detective of the Prohibition Commission, allegedly disguised himself as a rabbi and a jazz musician to nab bootleggers and crash speakeasies. But even without the formidable opponents of Al Capone, Lucky Luciano, and the rest of the syndicate, the drys were playing a losing game. "Stills were everywhere," wrote the ever-colorful Herbert Asbury, "in the mountains, on the farms, in small towns and villages, and in the cities. In New York, Chicago, Detroit, Pittsburgh, and other cities with large foreign populations the pungent odor of fermenting mash and alcoholic distillate hung over whole sections twenty-four hours a day."

Speakeasies were the staging area for the revolt. From exclusive nightclubs like New York's '21' to the nation's dives and roving gin parties, houses and their patrons shared the risks and taboos of resisting Prohibition. Whereas more "respectable" houses just violated the act, while enforcing erstwhile drinking ages, the majority welcomed anyone (except the cops) and offered the full menu of illegal vices—gambling, drugs, prostitution, cockfights. In the moral murk of the underground, it was hard to draw the line between fun and crime—a confusion that was often blamed on the liberal mixing of race, class, and gender. But mix people did. "Homosexuality, transvestitism, and interracial relationships," the historian Michael A. Lerner writes of New York's speakeasy culture, were no longer "discreetly hidden and visible only to those who actively sought them out" but rather "part of the amusement for every thrillseeker who ventured into the city's nightlife." A government survey of 373 New York speakeasies declared that 52 of them were "respectable" while the remaining 321 were veritable brothels where "hostesses" and other women employees were "connected with the business of commercialized prostitution." George E. Worthington, in a 1929 article for the *Survey,* distinguishes between the "disreputable night club" of his contemporaries "and its forerunners in the long history of *maisons de tolérance,*" San Francisco's traditional upper-crust bordellos: "To it come all classes and conditions of people." Another report suggested that most of Detroit's "vices" emanated from its socially open speakeasies: "Narcotics are said to be distributed among them, crime plots are hatched there, and there among the criminals mingle the members of respected families. I doubt," observes the author, Ernest W. Mandeville, "if the influence of one class on another, in this case, is an uplifting one."

This rollicking new underground wasn't limited by region; its subway tracks ran nationwide and picked up whoever wanted a ride. Transgression alone was the ticket price. The writer Carl Van Vechten, Jazz Age impresario, wrote regarding "the matter of cocktail parties" that "since the laws were passed prohibiting the sale of liquor, it could be said that more were held in one day in Manhattan than in a month elsewhere." Maybe so. But his cultural elite, centered on Greenwich Village, didn't have a monopoly on pleasure. Though many of their number had fled the Midwest (Van Vechten hailed from Cedar Rapids, Iowa), and though small-town contributions to Jazz Age fun were snobbishly dismissed as escapist and hypocritical by the ascendant bohemians of the Jazz Age, America's underground party life—with its cocktail-induced lurid behavior—reached even the remotest American communities, where popular support for Prohibition held strong. "Of the 113 establishments licensed to sell soft drinks in Sheboygan, Wisconsin," Daniel Okrent writes, "the two that actually confined themselves to nonalcoholic beverages went out of business."

So, sure, Americans everywhere broke the law to drink, and for many transgression became a virtue. It was fetishized, as it had been in the 1820s, as a noble sort of liquid democracy that enabled community and set people free. It was a lawless tongue waggled in the faces of the Dry Crusaders' electoral victory. Much as their forebears getting drunk and waltzing in the diggings may look frivolous in contrast to the European revolutions of 1849, the Wild Wets' drinking moonshine and dancing the Charleston look silly in contrast to the temperance activists' century-long effort to bring about the Volstead Act. But as the historian David J. Goldberg rightly claims, America was falling on apathetic times, and "in a decade that saw a declining interest in politics, Prohibition was one of the few issues that aroused strong emotions." It reheated the cooling public sphere. Drys argued America was safer and even more prosperous for being dry—as they had been predicting for decades. Wets argued that their "personal liberties" had been violated. Neither side backed down, and the press fairly crackled with joy.

But even among the most apathetic wets a revolution was afoot, whether most of them knew it or cared. While petty crime, prostitution, and murder were among the waste products of this hard-drinking

national demimonde, and while bohemians gloated over their own caricatures of bloodless, dullard Puritans, everyday folk in every region were
learning to have some antiquarian fun—the fun of being assertive, of
taking big risks, of rubbing themselves up against other mischievous citizens. Was this politics? Whatever else it was, it was—in flapper-speak—
the cat's particulars.

TWO ENTRENCHED VALUES of early American democracy—
individualism and communitarianism—were loosened up and mingled
in the 1920s public sphere. The cult of celebrity, of soaring individuals,
which arguably originates in the 1820s with the rising frenzy over Edwin
Forrest, had seized upon the national imagination. Movie stars, musicians, and athletes reigned supreme, and tabloids and fan magazines gave
fans a sense of participation in, ownership over their lives' minutiae—
the Fitzgeralds' escapades, Charlie Chaplin's every quirky move—and
they inspired adoring mimicry. These stars' public sightings caused mob
sensations that today are common only among pubescent girls. In 1927,
when a soft-spoken midwesterner named Charles Lindbergh had flown
in obscurity from America to France, which was experiencing *Les Années
Folles* of its own, the American poet Harry Crosby was there at Le Bour-
get airport to witness five hundred thousand fans mob his plane: "C'est
lui Lindberg, LINDBERG! [*sic*] and there is pandemonium . . . thousands of hands weaving like maggots over the silver wings of the Spirit
of Saint-Louis and it seems as if all the hands in the world are touch-
ing or trying to touch the new Christ and that the new Cross is the
Plane." Flight and celebrity—the twin peaks of 1920s individualism—
apotheosized Lindbergh, and all of the world's crowd wanted a relic.

Pranks, antics, and breathtaking stunts decorated 1920s newspapers;
rash individualism was on full display, as was a full-scale assault on traditional ideas of taste and safety. As if emboldened by the racy new improvisational techniques with which King Oliver (Bolden's successor) had
transformed early jazz—rhythms, scales, and novelty sounds that were
ugly and aggressive by *any* musical conventions—citizens everywhere
were going solo, "playing hot." The most daring Americans jitterbugged

on the edges of skyscrapers, tightrope-walked over city canyons, and performed a quirky sample of death-defying capers (fox-trotting, human-pyramid building, even tennis playing) high above the world on the wings of biplanes. Indeed, if the term "Roaring Twenties" derived from the new abundance of loud, fast, and relatively cheap cars—impressive sources of power and liberty for recently horse-saddled Americans—then the fact of *flight* soared in the popular imagination as the acme of fun and freedom. Europeans, Ann Douglas notes, still suffered from the shock of aviation warfare, but in far-off America airplanes glowed with heroism and adventure. "Only in America could you get mass-produced piggy banks, purses, fans, clocks, lamps, and (a rarer item) coffins shaped like airplanes."

As the twenties roared on, aerobats aped the hazards of war, making mortal danger look like child's play: aileron rolls, the simplest trick of all, involve a manually guided flipping of the plane. Flick, snap, and barrel rolls, however, call for all-out leaps of faith, requiring the pilot to gain enough forward velocity to throw the plane into autorotation, a state wherein the plane spins freely on its own. But hammerheads, or stall turns, are probably the most breathtaking of all: for this stunt, the pilot cuts the gas at the top of the climb, lets the plane flip back over, and shoots it toward the earth like a diving missile.

It must have been the hammerhead that Harry Crosby had in mind when he dreamed of diving his plane into Manhattan. But in his fantasy he doesn't pull back from the spiral. The Boston Brahmin poet wrote to his parents in 1929 that he "like[d] looping the loop and other aerial acrobatics" and that "there might come a crash but there is no crime in an explosion whereas there is I think a crime in ending life the way so many do with a whimper." He had survived a shelling at Verdun in which, according to Geoffrey Wolff, "his ambulance was vaporized," leaving behind "a young man's untouched body and gravely injured imagination." As Malcolm Cowley writes of Crosby, "Bodily he survived, and with a keener appetite for pleasure." Crosby and his wife, Caresse, the more esteemed writer of the two (and the inventor at nineteen of one of the first modern bras), were low-level aristocracy on the American expatriate literary scene and best known for running the Black

Sun Press. His appetite for sex, drugs, and luxury were extraordinary for any man, but exemplary of American trends at the time. Harry Crosby was nobody's democrat. An avowed "aristocrat" and "anarchist," and the spoiled nephew of steel magnate J. P. Morgan, Crosby was the portrait of 1920s hedonism, of the moguls and celebrities who sailed above the crowd and became symbols of dissolution and excess. While he never lived his dream of crashing into Manhattan, he satisfied another long-held violent fantasy when, in the final months of 1929, amid a spree of drinking, drugs, gambling, adultery, shooting, and aerobatics, he killed himself and his mistress in a room at the Ritz.

In vivid contrast to Crosby's murderous egotism was the crowd-pleasing showmanship of Hubert Fauntleroy Julian, the first African American to receive a pilot's license. Ann Douglas describes this avatar of Buddy Bottley as "a glamorous and charismatic man, a sheik-type, black America's more sophisticated version of Rudolph Valentino." A lover of jazz who neither drank nor smoked, this anti-fascist, pan-Africanist flier was called the "Lindbergh of his Race." Though he encountered rivalry, even sabotage, among a few of his Harlem neighbors, this Garveyite claimed racial identity as the primary motive behind his flamboyant stunts. He cut a swell image, swooping Harlem rooftops and parachuting into the city (once dressed like the devil and playing the saxophone), but because of his persistent difficulty getting financial backing he always flew a rickety craft. Julian was the exception that proved the rule: flight, while the gold standard of American fun, was a pleasure set apart for the elite.

For all the raging cult of personality, however, communitarianism, in a range of crowd pleasures, was just as characteristic of the era: it took the far-flung form of national trends (mah-jongg, crossword puzzles, bridge) and the more intimate forms of marathons and dance parties, which, unlike the mass spectacles and spectator sports also on the rise during this period, demanded lively participation from their multitude. A transcontinental footrace, commandeered by the stunt promoter C. C. Pyle, made its way eastward from California. A multiplex marathon in Madison Square Garden featured everything from twenty-four-hour talkers to round-the-clock rocking-chair rockers. Most notable, of course, were the dance marathons across the country that could drag on for weeks. But if marathons gave pleasure in diminishing returns, ultimately pleasing only victors like Vera Sheppard (whose story begins this book), the new dances themselves—the black bottom, tango, Charleston, *jitterbug*—never failed to satisfy. Jazz dance in particular was the chuffing locomotive pulling the boxcars of 1920s fun.

Kathy J. Ogren's excellent *Jazz Revolution* traces the broiling "controversy" between jazz's prudish 1920s opponents and the broad cross-section of easier-going Americans who were galvanized by this intensely sociable music. In attempting to explain the latter, she details the "participatory" qualities of jazz and their well-known roots in the earliest black folk culture—the "call and response" relations between the musicians, the "cutting contests" between soloists, the "bucking contests" between jazz bands, and the ongoing dialogue between crowd and bandstand. She argues that this black-identified form of music eventually grew so general that it "helped white Americans with diverse social backgrounds"—those who were bold enough to enjoy it—"explain their world." What she calls "Jazz emotions" were radical attitudes that helped people to break through "physical—and social—barriers" and opened new channels for community.

The musician and musicologist Roger Pryor Dodge, regretting the 1940s jazz trends toward purely improvisational bebop, praised early jazz as "dance-based music" that "completely drains the human system." One of the music's "strong supports," he argued, was "the pulse of a mob moving in time." To be sure, the most prominent jazz musicians had built upon Buddy Bolden's dance-driven example. They migrated in the teens from New Orleans to Chicago and ultimately in the twenties to New York City, never forgetting that dancers were their raison d'être. The two cultures riffed off one another and shared a spirit of competition. Dicky Wells recounts the "Trombone" and "Saxophone Supper[s]" that would take place at the informal Hoofer's Club below Big John's bar in New York: "All musicians would be sitting around the walls, all around the dance floor, maybe there would be forty guys sitting around there. The floor was for dancers only, and they would be cutting each other, too, while we were cutting each other on the instruments."

Vocalists had always ruled the musical stage, but by the mid-1920s, instrumentalists—especially Louis Armstrong with his Hot Fives and Sevens—were achieving unprecedented star status. Building on Bolden's showmanship and Jelly Roll Morton's virtuosity, Armstrong turned improvisation into a world-class art form. He soared to levels of creative prowess that teased and mocked his earthbound rhythm section. He injected individualist braggadocio—egomaniacal ecstasy—into what was at base a communitarian music. He shared the studio with vocalists, including Bessie Smith, whose "Reckless Blues," as Gary Giddens and Scott DeVeaux demonstrate, kept her "in control" and made Armstrong "alert to every gesture." He also squared off against his *own* astonishing voice. But at his best it was his horn playing that stole the show. It swooped aerobatically in and out of the clouds, "compet[ing]," as the composer Gunther Schuller puts it, "with the highest order of previously known musical expression."

But then the *dancers* refused to be grounded. It was during the mid-twenties that they too went solo, "played hot." Much as early jazz songs required constant negotiation between the soloist and the rhythm section, so did new dances inspire both soaring personal freedom and deeply erotic social interaction, the extremes of individualism and collectivism.

EARLY JAZZ DANCE HAD always left room for grace notes and novelties: hand flicks, eye rolls, kicks, and shimmies were all part of its essential pleasure. Rare couples dances like the breakaway and the Charleston already let partners split apart for a few bars and indulge in some lunatic expression, usually some kind of modified two-step, but they always returned to their basic steps, which, like the accompaniment itself, could be as strict and uniform as the waltz. Perry Bradford's 1919 "Original Black Bottom," however, which had flopped years before as the "Jacksonville Rounders' Dance" ("rounders" were pimps), was a single-dancer "challenge dance"—again, in the tradition of dancing for eels—that anticipated much zanier things to come. Sharing its rhythm with the original Charleston—which wouldn't gain wide acceptance until 1923, when it was featured in the all-black musical *Runnin' Wild*—the black bottom adorned a simple box step with early, slinky African-American moves—mooches, slides, hobbles, and twists that drove average Americans wild.

The 1924 instructional film *Let's Do the Black Bottom* provides a spurious history lesson that tries to be both flattering and comical to whites, who it also suggests invented the dance: "—funny how they got the Black Bottom idea—someone strayed from the Great White Way to the great open spaces and saw—" two black boys struggling in the mud, mimicking a cow doing the same. The film features a white girl in a modest white dress giving a plodding demonstration of stamps, double-stamps, and a stiff-legged strut. Strangely, it suggests she started the craze. "They heard her music," a panel reads, and the film insinuatingly cuts to two gleefully dancing black girls, to a dancing traffic cop, and to some startling footage of construction workers kicking and swaying on a skyscraper's beam. "All the world will soon be imitating that cow stuck in the mud." This latest effort in the long white campaign to appropriate African-American culture paled, however, in face of fact: all the world *was* learning the dance, and America's soaring new pleasure was black.

In the summer of 1928, twenty-some days into one of New York City's first non-segregated dance marathons, when the crowd on the enormous Manhattan Casino dance floor had dwindled down to four punchy couples, young gossip columnists Walter Winchell and Ed Sullivan zeroed in on dancer number 7, George "Shorty" Snowden. Their publicity drew fresh crowds of spectators who sponsored challenges between the couples. It was during one of these challenges that Shorty pulled a breakaway and electrified even the weary dance band. Onlookers may have assumed he was just going "squirrelly," a common term for marathoners losing their wits. But when Fox Movietone News got Snowden on film, magnifying his blurring feet, they knew they were seeing something new. An interviewer asked him what he was doing. He called it "the Lindy" and kept on dancing, but as he explained decades later, he was just doing what his friends always did up in Harlem, only possibly faster. "It was new to them, and I was sure having a ball, doing whatever came into my head." In other words, he was improvising.

When it caught on, the dance was often called the jitterbug, but

Snowden's invented-on-the-spot "Lindy" was uniquely inspired. It captured the dance's sheer modernity. He named it, of course, for Charles Lindbergh, who had been apotheosized since his transatlantic flight. The Lindy animated reckless grace, and for this it owed more in its style and spirit to Buster Keaton and Charlie Chaplin. It answered the jazz solo's fearless exploration and celebrated the thrill-seeking individual. In the months and years and decades to follow, when the *Spirit of St. Louis* possessed the dance floor and inspired Lindy Hoppers to leave the ground—with flips, rolls, throws, and swings—it reveled in the majesty of flight.

Back on Snowden's Harlem turf, the Savoy Ballroom, its owner, Charles Buchanan, who had previously prohibited dancers from doing even the Charleston (thereby spurring them on to invent the steps that became the Lindy Hop), quickly cashed in on Snowden's celebrity. He awarded Snowden a lifetime pass and rechristened the ballroom "The Home of Happy Feet." In no time the Savoy's 12,500-square-foot dance floor boasted, as Jean and Michael Stearns put it, the "'hippest' dance audience in the world" and was "the acid test of a true dance band."

All facets of Jazz Age Harlem glittered at the Savoy, where a cut-glass chandelier adorned the marble lobby and all of New York braved its dance floor. Soon the Savoy, an acre-wide rent party, was open to just about anything, including spectacular drag balls and dance marathons. (Its Chicago iteration, in 1926, was home to Abe Saperstein's "Savoy Big Five," the choreographed basketballers who would soon become the Harlem Globetrotters.) To accommodate the full range of its clientele, Harlem's Savoy held special nights—Mondays were "Ladies Night," Tuesdays featured the club's best dancers, Thursdays were "Kitchen Mechanics Night," Saturdays packed in so many dancers that it was difficult to move, and Sunday was "when celebrities and movie stars arrived." In an interview, Pearl and Ivy Fisher distinguished between the "segregated" Cotton Club and the "open" Savoy, where "everybody went—whites and blacks." Lucky Millinder's song commemorates the Savoy as a "joint" where people could "grab a cook or mechanic" and "let [their] feet go frantic," the great American dance floor where race and class tensions were sublimated into the having of fun.

From the beginning the Savoy sponsored bucking contests between its two opposing bandstands. Legendary black artists like Louis Armstrong, Chick Webb, and Fletcher Henderson went into hot but good-natured battle against white upstarts like Bix Beiderbecke and Benny Goodman. The jitterbugging thousands were the beneficiaries. With the advent of the Lindy, the bands' competitive spirit spread to the dance floor, where neither the richest nor the most famous but only the most talented could cut it up in "Cat's Corner," an area Snowden cordoned off in 1927 for only the hottest Lindy Hoppers.

# 8

# "Joyous Revolt"

*The "New Negro" and the "New Woman"*

J. A. ROGERS'S PROMINENT 1925 ESSAY "Jazz at Home" reads like a sporting response to Duffus's "Age of Play." Both writers argue for pleasure's social power, but while Duffus's "play" involves movies and board games, the raw pleasures Rogers attributes to jazz—"the nobody's child of the levee and the city slum"—pulse with rebellious electricity. "The true spirit of jazz is a joyous revolt from convention, custom, authority, boredom, even sorrow—from everything that would confine the soul of man and hinder its riding free on the air." Rogers admitted that jazz, like Duffus's less offensive "play," had begun to spread throughout American society, but that wasn't his point. It mattered more that jazz "spontaneity" and "the perfect jazz abandon" came most easily to "the average Negro, particularly of the lower classes," who "puts rhythm into whatever he does."

Black writers of the 1920s often expressed this opinion—for better or for worse. Race leader W. E. B. DuBois often regretted lower-class blacks' open displays of "jazz abandon." His friend and peer James Weldon Johnson, however, seemed delighted that "an average group of

Negroes can in dancing to a good jazz band achieve a delightful state of intoxication that for others would require nothing short of a certain per capita imbibation of synthetic gin." Rogers, rather resembling Duffus, takes a middle road. A social conservative among young black urbanites, he warned that jazz was a "poison for the weak"—especially for the poor black whose "amusement life is more open to the forces of social vice"— but allows that it also gives "recreation for the industrious" and "tonic for the strong." And for this reason, in spite of "its morally anarchic spirit, jazz has a popular mission to perform." Echoing his era's progressive arguments for physical recreation, he sees in jazz a civic virtue that transcends race, class, and gender because it is rooted in a most basic instrument—the human body.

Rogers sees this joy as a poison and a tonic, but unlike Duffus he doesn't want to interfere. Recklessly, democratically—at least in this essay—Rogers puts his trust in the people: "This new spirit of joy and spontaneity may itself play the role of reformer." His seemingly utopian vision, in which music and dance cause social reform, was at no time more plausible than in the 1920s, when the rhythms that freed slaves on Congo Square were helping to warm Americans' chilly attitudes— toward their own bodies and each other's humanity.

The stakes were much higher for Rogers than for Duffus, nothing lower than political equality for blacks. He hoped that jazz might do the work peaceably. For of course blacks felt more than "joy and spontaneity." For instance, in 1925, many felt deep reserves of rage. To be sure, the year before, W. E. B. DuBois, while acknowledging African Americans' "spirit of gayety," reminded readers that "the first influence of the Negro on American democracy was naturally to oppose by force—revolt, murder, assassination coupled with running away. It was the primitive, ancient effort to avenge blood with blood, to bring good out of evil by opposing evil with evil." Revolutionary figures like Marcus Garvey kept this violent history in the public eye, lecturing and parading in military dress. But during this highly racist period in American history, when eugenics was a popular academic position and the KKK, in 1925, had five million members nationwide, even the joyous revolt of jazz was an opposition by force: its practitioners stood down their frigid opponents with blatant sexuality and loud racial pride. Under such conditions "democracy" had to be bullish—especially if it was going to be fun.

But jazz wasn't destructive, jazz was creative. Published in a year when the pages of *Crisis* were filled with lynchings, evictions, and other evidence of prejudice, Alain Locke's landmark *New Negro* anthology, in which Rogers's essay appears, never ignored such vicious stakes but charted a more constructive heritage of African-American revolt—from spirituals, folk dances, and Brother Rabbit tales to their cultural grandchildren in the Harlem Renaissance. One contributor, the novelist and *Crisis* editor Jessie Fauset, traces the African-American "gift of laughter" as it comes down from slave culture, through the "jesters" and "clowns" of minstrelsy, to the twentieth-century all-black musicals, where it "radiates good feeling and happiness." When African-American comedians evolved from playing the "funny man" to what she calls "the state of being purely subjective," they could enmesh the audience in a common pleasure that acted a lot like a jazz performance—or like antebellum storytelling circles. When black performers can be comical on *their* terms, she argues, the audience "is infected" by the performer's "high spirits" and "excessive good will." "A stream of well-being is projected across the footlights into the consciousness of the beholder." Here, it seems, was the acme of Harlem Renaissance fun. At its finest moments, a culture born from struggle and trauma shot beyond resistance and mere rebellion. It struck syncopated harmonies of cross-racial experience—laughter, dancing, competition, and the impudent revolt of wild partying.

THE "NEW NEGRO" or "Harlem" Renaissance was a surge in African-American cultural production that culminated in the 1920s. Among its likely causes—black resistance to lynchings and segregation, a rising black middle class with greater access to education, the mainstream popularity of jazz—the widest dispersal was the "Great Migration" of southern blacks to northern cities, some 555,000 in the 1910s alone. The sudden removal of so many rural families brought mixed fortunes—increased economic opportunity in the wartime economy, increased economic privation due to overcrowding, as well as new waves of racial resentment. At its worst, during what James Weldon Johnson famously called the "Red Summer" of 1919—a year of severe labor shortages due in large part to veterans returning home en masse—twenty-five or more major race riots, most of them instigated by whites, erupted from coast to coast and resulted in dozens of lynchings, hundreds of other deaths, thousands of injuries, and an American society in disarray.

But even in the most cramped and impoverished neighborhoods of Washington, Philadelphia, and Chicago, a new African-American cosmopolitanism was taking shape. And if New York City set the era's highest standards for rebellious, socially integrated fun, Harlem was its Main Street. This predominantly black uptown neighborhood—whose population by 1925 was denser by a third than anywhere else in all of Manhattan—teemed with conflict. It was nobody's utopia. "Long before the stock market crash," writes the historian Jonathan Gill, "black Harlem had become a community in crisis, leading the nation in poverty, crime, overcrowding, unemployment, juvenile delinquency, malnutrition, and infant and maternal mortality." East Harlem, with its largely Latino population, didn't fare much better. But the runaway popularity of jazz—as well as Caribbean dance music—brought sudden revenue into the district, and while much of it stayed in the hands of white owners (such as the Mafia ownership of racially exclusive venues like Connie's and the Cotton Club), a lot trickled down to locally operated bars and dance halls. The influx of wealthy and middle-class whites was only New York's latest wave of slummers. Their presence was naturally galling to many Harlemites, who, while sometimes befriending them, also mocked, exploited, or ignored them.

Ed Small's Paradise, with its dancing waiters on roller skates, was nearly as posh and expensive as Connie's, but it was black-owned, color-blind, and popular for late-night Chinese food. As David Levering Lewis points out, Small's, like the Clam House and other clubs along the Mob-dominated 133rd Street "Jungle," sought "white clients enthusiastically, sometimes even fawningly," in hopes of getting a piece of the market. Farther uptown, at the more populist Panama, a large club with pianos and dancing girls, the clientele was deliberately split between "the more of a quiet reserved type of entertainment" downstairs and the "rougher"

type upstairs. The enormous Lincoln Gardens, however, traded ceremony for pleasure: one thousand patrons jammed the smoky floor and
balcony, drank $2 pints of "licorice-tasting gin," and were drawn like
moths to Louis Armstrong and King Oliver's Creole Jazz Band. "The
whole joint was rocking," recalled Eddie Condon. "Tables, chairs, walls,
people, moved with rhythm. . . . People in the balcony leaned over and
their drinks spilled on the customers below." Lincoln Gardens better
resembled jazz's natural habitat—the surging throngs in New Orleans's
steamy public halls. The most risqué (and fun) nightclubs such as the
"transvestite floor shows, sex circuses, and marijuana parlors along 140th
Street" were also least amenable to whites. More notorious white hedonists like Phil Harris, Mae West, and Carl Van Vechten managed to
"obtain entry" through "persistence, contacts, and money," but generally
these venues didn't welcome gawkers. The most famous sex circus on
140th Street was either Hazel Valentine's The Daisy Chain or 101 Ranch.
A jewel in the crown of Harlem's thriving gay and lesbian scene, celebrated in songs by Fats Waller and Count Basie, Valentine's show was
centered on sex celebrities like Sewing Machine Bertha and the transvestite "Clarenz" who performed acrobatics that "catered to all varieties
of sexual tastes."

Private "rent parties"—"Social Whists"—were the beating heart of
1920s Harlem fun. Neighborhood kids, Harlem celebrities, downtown
slummers, and working-class blacks could pay a small fee (ten cents most
nights) to stomp and dance to stride-piano maestros like Willie "the
Lion" Smith, James P. Johnson, Luckey Roberts, and Fats Waller. More
notorious "buffet flats" also marketed red-light favors, but rent parties
were most often just overcrowded blowouts. They were announced with
witty flyers, sold soul food and corn liquor, and helped overburdened
tenants raise some rent money by packing in just about anybody with a
thirst: "ladies' maids and truck drivers," recalled Langston Hughes, who
hit the rent parties nearly every Saturday night, "laundry workers and
shoe shine boys, seamstresses and porters. I can still hear their laughter
in my ears, hear the soft slow music, and feel the floor shaking as the
dancers danced."

Among America's brightest stars of the 1920s were three African-

American women—Ma Rainey, Bessie Smith, and Ethel Waters—who joyfully slaughtered any and all sacred cows: of lyricism, of beauty, of public decency. Bessie Smith, in particular, who trained under Rainey and then paved the way for Waters, earned her title as "Empress of the Blues" through exquisite musicality and thunderous personality. Born poor in Chattanooga in 1894, she was singing for coins by the time she was nine and performing for Rainey at age eighteen, when her voice already was clear enough, strong enough, to captivate audiences without amplification. Deep, rich, conversational, "creamy," Smith's voice brought listeners in close and animated her blunt confessions of poverty, promiscuity, and violence, often with a slashing sense of humor. And Smith lived hard. She fired gunshots at her abusive (but beloved) husband, Jack Gee, identified by the biographer Chris Albertson as a "semi-illiterate night watchman." She was stabbed by a man she'd knocked on his back. She constantly drank, kept a string of female lovers, and enjoyed a buffet flat in Detroit where Coke bottles and "lighted cigarettes" were sex-show props. She strutted out her antics in her hard-stomping blues, as in "Gimme a Pigfoot," in which she growls in pure exuberance over an illegal Harlem rent party. Wanting "to clown," wanting to send the piano player a drink because he's "bringin' [her] down," she calls for "a pigfoot and a bottle of beer," warning other revelers to "check [their] razors and [their] guns" because there's "gonna be rasslin' when the wagon comes." As hearty as any celebrity of her hard-living era, Smith freely mingled her dangers and pleasures. Accordingly, as the song roars to its infamous climax, she keeps on raising the stakes:

> We're gonna shim-sham-shimmy till the risin' sun
> Gimme a reefer and a gang of gin
> Slay me 'cause I'm in my sin.

In Harlem, more intimately even than in Hollywood, celebrities like Rainey, Smith, and Waters walked and partied among the people—as the finest examples *of* the people. Corroborating *Negro Digest*'s claim that it was "fun to be a Negro" during the 1920s and 1930s, David Levering Lewis describes the common "pleasure" of "seeing celebrities" such as

James Weldon Johnson, Fats Waller, Fletcher Henderson, Florence Mills, and countless other Harlem dwellers strolling through the "Campus," the name given to the intersection of 135th Street and Seventh Avenue. Celebrities heightened the frisson of the crowd, and in doing so with fellow feeling, as is evident in their populist songs and stories, they struck a syncopated jazz dynamic—a race, a dance, a competition—between soaring heights of individual freedom and the thumping rhythms of communal belonging. Bessie Smith and Louis Armstrong, for instance, were stars *because* they honored their racial community. They infused their every note with its heritage and invited the world to come along.

Among Harlem's celebrities who cherished their community while embracing their hard-won individual freedom was a rising generation of writers and artists. Musicians worked out their differences onstage in lively, showy cutting contests. These young intellectuals duked it out in print. Their poetry, novels, essays, and drama took bold new stances on African-American life. What resulted, among many other innovations, was American literature's most thorough debate over the harms and health of what this book calls fun—or what J. A. Rogers calls "joyous revolt." Following a century of blackface minstrelsy and primitivist fantasy, Harlem's young talents gave their own impressions and at last brought clarity and dignity to a subject—fun, raw fun, African-American fun—that historically had been dismissed as ridiculous.

IN THE MID-1920S, ranks started to form between the older generation of Harlem's elite—a black professional class whom DuBois identified as African America's "Talented Tenth"—and the younger generation of writers, artists, actors, and musicians who preferred to look beyond class differences. Much as it had been in revolutionary Boston, when John and Samuel Adams were divided over how the new rising citizens should behave, in Harlem the people's fun became a bone of contention. DuBois wanted to showcase the highest black achievements. With the influx of slummers and the nightlife boom, blacks were too easily fetishized as primitives—a loathsome stereotype that hung like sandbags on the project of racial uplift. The younger crowd resented this stereotype as well, but they were much more likely, in spite of such popular misperceptions, to look for redemption in the "joyous revolt" of "average" blacks. In it they often saw the vitality of the race.

Complicating matters was Carl Van Vechten. This white, gangly, forty-something Iowan threw some of the era's wildest parties and floated among the intercontinental elite—literary, artistic, theatrical, musical, cinematic. He and his wife, Fania Marinoff (whom Bessie Smith once decked for kissing her goodnight), were close friends with Gertrude Stein and Mabel Dodge. Their celebrity acquaintances included Clara Bow, Rudolph Valentino, and William Randolph Hearst. And at some point in 1922, Van Vechten became, in his own words, "violently interested in Negroes," an "addiction" that would lead him to spend the rest of the decade promoting black writers, musicians, and artists and giving distinguished white visitors "tours" of "authentic" Harlem.

It was right in Van Vechten's line to exploit Harlem's pleasures, as he did most infamously in his novel *Nigger Heaven* (1926), whose crude title and sensationalistic, salacious content caused an uptown uproar and made this onetime Harlem celebrity persona non grata. Despite its showy arguments against racism, the novel's fascination with Harlem's "Coney Island" thrills and its fantasy of gaily primitive Africans only gave readers more complex caricatures than had appeared in recent white American literature—than "the fat black bucks in a wine-barrel room" of Vachel Lindsay's poem "The Congo" (1915), than the "glistening African god of pleasure" who plays ragtime piano in Willa Cather's *My Ántonia* (1918). Despite its attempts at psychological accuracy, many of *Nigger Heaven*'s characters, especially the lascivious Scarlet Creeper and the sex-starved Lasca Sartoris, are astonishing cartoons of black hedonism.

W. E. B. DuBois called the novel "a blow in the face" and "an affront to the hospitality of black folk and to the intelligence of white." He took special umbrage at the novel's "caricature" of Harlem life, "the wildly, barbaric drunken orgy in whose details Van Vechten revels." But he, too, played an avuncular role to younger artists and was careful not to dismiss Harlem fun outright. He admitted "there is laughter, color, and spontaneity at Harlem's core" but wished that someone of Van Vechten's credibility would celebrate "the average colored man"—who attended

church and was "as conservative and as conventional as ordinary working folk everywhere."

The younger generation voiced their own ideas of "the average colored
man"—and they were neither Van Vechten's nor DuBois's. Two months
prior to *Nigger Heaven*'s publication, the twenty-four-year-old poet Langston Hughes, a Columbia University dropout, tossed a firebomb in support of black-cultural art. He called in *The Nation* for revolt against the
"race toward whiteness"—against petit-bourgeois black artists and their
"desire to pour racial individuality into the mold of American standard-
ization." Taking implicit aim at their darling Countee Cullen, a gay poet
who would marry DuBois's daughter in the most elite black social event
of the 1920s, Hughes (probably also gay) rejected the "smug, contented,
respectable folk" (like Cullen's parents) who scold their children not to
"be like niggers." Mocking the black middle class for their "Nordic manners, Nordic faces, Nordic hair, Nordic art (if any), and . . . Episcopal
Heaven," he urged young black writers to celebrate the "low-down folks"
who are in the "majority—may the Lord be praised!" The black urban
poor—who were not at all "conservative," by Hughes's description—
enjoyed "their nip of gin on Saturday nights" and lived by their sometimes
dangerous whims. "Their joy runs, bang! into ecstasy. . . . Play awhile.
Sing awhile. Oh, let's dance!" Even "their religion soars to a shout," since
"these common folk are not afraid of spirituals, as for a long time their
more intellectual brethren were, and jazz is their child."

Hughes had a personal investment in the subject. The people he
praised resembled his easygoing mother and stepfather, who made their
"money to *spend*" and "for fun"—as opposed to his racist and stingy
father who scoffed at "Fun!" and "was interested in making money to
keep." Hughes believed the people's fun told a truth all its own. Despite
its risks and indiscretions, the fun of profligate, low-down folk revealed
a vitality in black—and larger American—culture, if only the upper
classes would listen: "Let the blare of Negro jazz bands and the bel-
lowing voice of Bessie Smith singing Blues penetrate the closed ears of
the colored near-intellectuals until they listen and perhaps understand."
Many of Hughes's peers heeded the call, and their writings of the 1920s
and 1930s have deepened our knowledge of American fun.

The A-list of these peers—Arna Bontemps, Richard Bruce, Countee Cullen, Aaron Douglas, Zora Neale Hurston, Helene Johnson, and others—appeared that year in the sole issue of *Fire!!*, a journal "Devoted to Younger Negro Artists" that challenged Harlem's literary establishment—namely, Charles Johnson's *Opportunity* and W. E. B. DuBois's *Crisis*. Its only editorial was a review of *Nigger Heaven*, in which Wallace Thurman, the journal's notoriously hard-living editor, took pains to protect Van Vechten, a friend whose patronage is acknowledged on the journal's masthead. Thurman predicted that "Harlem Negroes, once their aversion to the 'nigger' in the title was forgotten, would erect a statue on the corner of 135th Street and Seventh Avenue, and dedicate it to this ultra-sophisticated Iowa New Yorker." (Van Vechten had recently been lynched there in effigy.) At the same time, asserting the magazine's autonomy, Thurman slams the novel's "effusions about Harlem" for being "pseudo-sophisticated, semi-serious," and "semi-ludicrous." He also scoffs at "ignoramuses" who put any stock in the veracity of *Nigger Heaven*. Against both prudery and sensationalism, *Fire!!* defended verisimilitude—the artist's duty to "delve into deep pots of raw life." The magazine's office was engulfed in flames, ironically incinerating most of *Fire!!*'s only issue and plunging Thurman deep in debt, but its brief flame illuminated a fearless new aesthetic with which W. E. B. DuBois parted company, and whose scene he called the "debauched tenth."

THE FREEWHEELING SPIRIT of jazz kept Langston Hughes moving in the twenties and thirties. He had an irrepressible sense of fun. Mae Sullivan recalls Hughes being "adorable" and "always a little boy." He was born in Missouri and often relocated with his mother and step-father—to Lawrence, Kansas; Lincoln, Illinois; Cleveland, Ohio. He spent two high school summers with his father in Mexico City, where he lowered a loaded gun he aimed at his own head because didn't want to "miss something"—such as the "top of a volcano" or local bullfights, which he later discovered "must be smelt" for their "dust and tobacco and animals and leather." Hughes survived to miss very little: he smelled, tasted, drank, and devoured the 1920s scene.

When he first arrived in Harlem, he wanted "to shake hands" with the "hundreds of colored people," but Columbia University, where he was racially shunned by his fellow students, was definitely "not fun." Having enrolled to please his father, he dropped out after a year. Working as a mess boy on a boat off Staten Island, he rebuffed an invitation from the famous Alain Locke, who had read his poems and wanted to meet him; Hughes preferred the company of his fellow Jack Tars. At twenty-one, pulling out on a boat bound for Africa, he cut himself loose from academia and his father by dumping all his books in the sea. In the years to come, his life was his own. Whether admiring his fellow crew-members' "gaily mutinous state," enduring hunger and racism in Paris, scorning the segregation within Washington's black community, or losing the patronage of Charlotte Osgood Mason for declaring he was not a "primitive," Hughes stayed cheerful in the face of adversity and took inspiration from a defiant working class.

During his year bussing tables in Washington, D.C., Hughes met Van Vechten and Vachel Lindsay, both of whom supported his writing and facilitated his celebrated return to New York. Downtown, he frequented parties of influential whites: Florine Stettheimer, Alfred A. Knopf, and Jack Baker (one of whose parties never took off because the black crowd was "hunched over" his vast erotic library, "trying to find out what white folks say about love when they really come to the point"). He was right at home chez Joel and Amy Spingarn and, naturally, chez Carl Van Vechten, who, Hughes wrote, never spoke "grandiloquently about democracy or Americanism" and never made "a fetish of those qualities" but rather "live[d] them with sincerity—and humor." Uptown, Hughes attended anything and everything: the spectacular (but doomed) Cullen-DuBois wedding, the magnificent jazz funeral of A'Lelia Walker ("very much like a party"), the sober and sophisticated parties at Jessie Fauset's, and all the "good-time gatherings" that he preferred—gumbo suppers at James Weldon Johnson's, bohemian gatherings at Wallace Thurman's. He excoriated the Cotton Club and its "Jim Crow policy in the very heart of [Harlem's] dark community"; like the majority of Harlemites, he hated the "vogue" of being black among the "influx of whites" who were "given the best ringside tables to sit and stare at the Negro customers—like amusing animals in the zoo." But he loved the "ball" to be had at Small's Paradise and the "gaudy" drag balls at the Hamilton and the Savoy. Above all, he loved rent parties, where the hosts were usually anonymous and which were "more amusing than any night club."

Many of his poems, moreover, like Bessie Smith's songs, were inspired by rent parties and cabarets, especially those published in his acclaimed first volume, *The Weary Blues* (1925), and in his generally despised (and unfortunately titled) second one, *Fine Clothes to the Jew* (1927). His earliest influences were Sandburg and Whitman, whose raw enthusiasm and populist voices suited his desire to reach a large public; also influential were the rhythms and phrasings of jazz and the blues, which helped him to express, as he put it, "the tom-tom of revolt against weariness in a white world, a world of subway trains and work, work, work; the tom-tom of joy and laughter, and pain swallowed in a smile." The first volume aestheticized "the Negro soul," depicting even "low-down folk" with an elegance and purity that was well received by the African-American press; the second volume looked unblinkingly at their pain, pleasures, violence, and vitality. In both books the commoner's daily abjection is soothed by rhythm and peaks of joy, but in the second, his rancor—and his candor—were called shameful, amoral, and disrespectful to the race. Time has told a different story. *Fine Clothes to the Jew,* writes the biographer Arnold Rampersad, "marked the height of his creative originality as a poet" and "remains one of the most significant single bodies of poetry ever published in the United States."

In the humblest and roughest ghetto scenes that make up *Fine Clothes to the Jew,* Hughes looked so intimately into average black people's private lives (as he felt he understood them), and into their psychology and sexuality, that the critics spat back, J. A. Rogers (the advocate of jazz's "joyous revolt") calling the book "piffling trash"—"unsanitary, insipid, and repulsive"; others calling Hughes a "SEWER DWELLER" and the "poet 'low-rate' of Harlem," and excoriating the "literary gutter-rat" Van Vechten, to whom the collection is dedicated, for being just the kind of reader to "revel in the lecherous, lust-seeking characters that Hughes finds time to poeticize about." (Notably, however, amid this firestorm, DuBois's *Crisis* published an appreciative review.) The book's proximity to the *Nigger Heaven* scandal, and its association with *Fire!!,* where two of its poems had been previously published, drew close attention to its depiction of fun and its intimate look at poor urban blacks, although neither can be reduced to sensationalism.

In contrast to all of the volume's portraits of abjection—of the "Bad Man" who says "I beats ma wife" and "beats ma side gal too" or of "Gin Mary," who regrets her prison sentence because she'll miss her gin—is the hot-handed banter of poems like "Crap Game":

> Lemme roll 'em, boy.
> I got ma tail curled!
> If a seven don't come
> 'Leven ain't far away.
> An' if I craps,
> Dark baby,
> Trouble
> Don't last all de time.
> Hit em', bones!

Here Hughes plays "hot" like a jazz soloist, ripping off riffs of casual street talk, capturing the sexy fun of the game while keeping the "Trouble" of its context. But when the poem pans back and takes in the crowd, more constructive pleasures emerge—Rogers's "recreation for the industrious" and "tonic for the strong": people are drawn into random contact by humor, music, and robust sexuality, revealing a Savoy Ballroom–style democracy that originates for Hughes in ghetto culture. This volume's "Laughers," a seeming nod to Walt Whitman's "The Sleepers," catalogues and rejoices in the poet's "people"—a catalogue that ranges from "Dish-washers" and "Crap-shooters" to "Nursers of babies"—for their hilarity "in the hands of Fate."

> Dancers—
> God! What dancers!
> Singers—
> God! What singers!
> Singers and dancers
> Dancers and laughers.

> Laughers?
> Yes, laughers . . . laughers . . . laughers—
> Loud-mouthed laughers in the hands
> Of Fate.

"Laughers" praises the people's audacity, and "Jazz Band in a Parisian Cabaret"—urging the band to "Play that thing!"—praises jazz for spreading that audacity into all corners of humanity: "Play it," says the poem,

> for the lords and ladies,
> For the dukes and counts,
> For the whores and gigolos,
> For the American millionaires,
> And the school teachers
> Out for a spree.

Hughes recognized a deep grammar in jazz. He saw the force in its folksy brilliance, in its polyglottal pleasures. It could lift a crowd above its differences to a common level of erotic pleasure:

> May I?
> Mais oui.
> Mein Gott!
> Parece una rhumba.
> Play it, jazz band!
> You've got seven languages to speak in
> And then some,
> Even if you do come from Georgia.
> Can I go home wid yuh, sweetie?
> Sure.

The "joyous revolt" that Hughes and his peers observed in twenties America—the "joy" that ran "bang! into ecstasy"—sprang from a range of sources. For the "Loud-mouthed laughers in the hands / Of Fate" who migrated by the thousands from the violent Jim Crow South to the overcrowded and rioting northern cities, jazz and jazz dance and folk humor and partying were mutual forms of racial affirmation—forms of what Chaplin called the "defiance" of "ridicule." For more affluent African Americans, especially those who were torn between racial identification and European-American class distinction, nightclubs and rent parties were weekend havens where Protestant rules were eased or suspended. For white slummers touring inner-city neighborhoods in hopes of experiencing "genuine" black fun, teeming dance floors were as close as most could get to losing themselves in the melting pot. And for the regular working-class denizens (whom J. A. Rogers called the "average Negro"), the years when "Harlem was in vogue" brought exposure, often *over*exposure, to pleasures their communities had known for centuries. These various groups were at odds. The dancers on these dance floors had cause for fearing, even hating, one another. And yet writers like Hughes and many of his peers, bearing witness to these parties, saw an eros that actually gained momentum from such cross-societal purposes. Its friction was exciting, part of the fun. In a decade when America's public sphere was threatened by political and racial conflict, the jazz band emerged like old King Charles as a radically civil rabble-rouser. It urged wallflowers to jump to their feet and stomp and swing in amicable collision. The fun it demanded wasn't for the timid, but those who acquired a taste for the fray were converts for the public good.

THOUGH SHE WAS BORN in 1900 to Alabama bluebloods, Zelda Sayre wasn't your average southern belle. Mouthy, vandalous, flirty, wild, wearing rouge and lipstick at age fifteen, she was only interested in swimming and boys. "Zelda just wasn't afraid of anything," said a male companion from those years, "of boys, of being talked about; she was absolutely fearless. . . . But she did have a bad reputation." In high school she dated soldiers from Camp Sheridan and Camp Taylor, and she cajoled her entire senior class into skipping school on April Fool's Day, a prank that got all of them briefly expelled. Two months after graduating, voted "the Prettiest" in her class, she met a handsome first lieutenant from St. Paul, Minnesota, whose affections she would toy with for the next two years.

Zelda resembled the fiery heroines in Scott Fitzgerald's undergraduate fiction; Scott better resembled his hesitant heroes, or the eponymous *Romantic Egotist* of his first unpublished novel. He traveled regularly by bus to see her in Montgomery, and she didn't hide the fact that he had stiff competition. Her letters described escapades with up to "ten boys," and when he tried to gall her with stories of pretty girls, she gave him maddening permission to pursue them. Everyone warned him against marrying a "girl who," as he wrote, "gets stewed in public, who frankly enjoys and tells shocking stories, who smokes constantly and makes the remark that she has 'kissed thousands of men and intends to kiss thousands more.'" But the event happened anyway, on April 3, 1920. *This Side of Paradise* had been published a week before, and straightaway the newlywed Fitzgeralds kicked off the spree of high jinks, scandals, and nonstop parties with which their generation would identify. That month they chaperoned a party for Princeton undergrads that ended in drunken brawls. (Zelda held court from her bathtub.) Tracked by gossip columnists and autograph hounds, they were evicted from their honeymoon suite at the Biltmore and evicted from the Commodore for more parties and pranks; eventually they escaped to the Connecticut countryside.

Carl Van Vechten, who was twice their age, befriended the couple during these years and sometimes brought them to Harlem speakeasies, an unlikely destination for the white-supremacist Scott. Carlos, as Zelda liked to call him, seemed unimpressed by Scott, a lightweight drinker who "was nasty" when "drunk." But Zelda, he declared, "was an original. Scott was not a wisecracker like Zelda. Why, she tore up the pavements with sly remarks. . . . She didn't actually write them down, Scott did, but she said them." Scott also mined her diaries for material, quoting them verbatim in his first three books. And while Scott himself was certainly an "original"—the iconic American writer of the 1920s—his own sense of fun wasn't all that new. American males had been skylarking for centuries. But Zelda's was revolutionary. When he published *Flappers and Philosophers* in August 1920, winning sympathy for a girl who bobs her hair, it was Zelda's philosophy that stole the show.

"Flapper" was a British term from the 1910s, but its twenties iteration was all-American, and Zelda Sayre Fitzgerald was flapper royalty. She called the first flappers "young anti-puritans" who religiously followed "the flapper creed—to give and get amusement." She touted the flapper's defiant performance: "the art of being—being young, being lovely, being an object." And this reluctant belle from Montgomery, raised in the heart of KKK country, paraded the flapper's cross-racial curiosity: "The flapper springs full-grown, like Minerva, from the head of her once-déclassé father, Jazz, upon whom she lavishes affection and reverence, and deepest filial regard." For the flapper, in all her essential whiteness, signaled young women's freedom from—and theatrical rebellion against—all of the white patriarchal institutions that stood between females and their fun. Buddy Bolden's racial and sexual language let the flapper speak pleasure to power—if not miscegenistically (though flappers did that too), then culturally and symbolically.

In 1922—the same year *Life* featured a full-color "Flapper" as a butterfly in a see-through dress; the year *Flapper* magazine ("Not for Old Fogies") declared "Flapper Styles Will Prevail!"—Zelda published her "Eulogy on the Flapper." It was a pat flapper move: morbidly ironic, reported as if from beyond the grave. Writing for *Metropolitan,* the same magazine that had just serialized *The Beautiful and Damned* and elected the Fitzgeralds the first couple of fun, she honored the "deceased" flapper as a young woman of singular integrity. She praised her for keeping "mostly masculine friends," for wearing "a great deal of audacity and rouge . . . into the battle," for flirting "because it was fun to flirt," and for sporting "a one-piece bathing suit because she had a good figure." In short, she described the dangerous young woman who had seduced F. Scott Fitzgerald.

The flapper, poor thing, had died of popularity. This icon of female urbanity, Zelda mourned, was being imitated by "several million small-town belles." Flapping had been democratized, and the girl in the crowd didn't understand its original "philosophy." Which was? "The desire for unadulterated gaiety."

But by all remaining evidence, by 1922, the average flapper's "gaiety" was still "unadulterated"—she smoked, swore, danced, drank, strutted her flesh, and petted heavily. She wrung all the fun from her supersaturated moment and generally kept "Old Fogies" on guard, just as Zelda Sayre used to do. Only now the party was out of control. Even rural girls were acting cosmopolitan. Women everywhere were "absolutely fearless." And in 1927, the year of the It girl, F. Scott knew the flapper wasn't dead. He updated the term with Clara Bow, calling her "the quintessence of what the term 'flapper' signifies . . . pretty, impudent, superbly assured, as worldly-wise, briefly-clad and 'bard-berled' as possible. There were hundreds of them, her prototypes. Now, completing the circle, there are thousands more, patterning themselves after her."

THE "NEW WOMAN" MOVEMENT, like the "New Negro" Renaissance, gave a variety of new perspectives on the 1920s wild party. Its scofflaw fun, more often than not, was edifying and liberating—and for that reason thrilling, joyful, and scary. Contributing new tactics to their larger constituency of "Wild Wets," who reignited Merry Mount's old battle with Plymouth, women reimagined American rebellion according to their out-group identity. Joining forces among themselves, "New Women" took strength from leanings and attributes that had always been dismissed as weaknesses. Much as African-American comedy, music, and sexuality were embraced by younger black artists as sources of distinction, so too did women's bravado and eroticism, which had been scorned or exploited throughout American history, suddenly become ammunition—and the height of fashion.

Whether they were sensuous bohemians, emasculating flappers, lightning-tongued hedonists, or the singularly incendiary Mae West, the leonine New Women of the 1920s put the dusty old guard on notice: pleasure was a source of dangerous power, and having fun defined the citizen in ways not unlike the right to vote—it connected the individual to community, it gave groups of citizens bold expression, and it came with weighty responsibility.

THE POET EDNA ST. VINCENT MILLAY was the original flapper of 1920s letters. Raised poor in turn-of-the-century rural Maine, she was taught to be bold by a liberated mother who evicted Edna's no-account father. In 1912, at the age of twenty, she sent a palpitating lyric to a national contest that led to a scholarship at Vassar. Upon graduating, emboldened by her successful first book, *Renascence and Other Poems,* she moved into a garret in Greenwich Village where they called this classical beauty "Vincent" and made her the toast of thriving bohemia. The avant-garde sniffed at her traditional verse forms—which looked dowdy next to mavericks like Stevens, Eliot, Pound, Stein—but her second collection, *A Few Figs from Thistles,* earned her acclaim as "the unrivaled embodiment of sex appeal, the It-girl of the hour, the Miss America of 1920." And her third collection won the 1923 Pulitzer Prize, the first one ever given to a woman, after which her international renown was secure: she was adored by fashion magazines, mobbed at train stations. Now, for anyone who didn't already know, Millay was the voice and mind of the New Woman—not only boasting the flapper's "unadulterated gaiety" but vividly disclosing her insatiable desires.

In his 1923 *Love in Greenwich Village,* which recounts young New York's rampant sexual mores, Floyd Dell, whose marriage proposal Millay rejected, recalled her "liv[ing] in that gay poverty which is traditional of the village" and which afforded her and all her fellow bohemians "the joys of comradeship and play and mere childlike fun." The erotic content of her early lyrics typified her sybaritic times—as did her smoldering imagery of cigarettes, "jazzing music," and her iconic candle:

> My candle burns at both ends;
> It will not last the night;
> But ah, my foes, and oh, my friends—
> It gives a lovely light!

The flapper conjured up in her poems could be fickle ("And if I loved you Wednesday . . . I do not love you Thursday"), unrepentant ("'I've been a wicked girl . . . I might as well be glad!'"), or casually brutal ("I see with single eye . . . Your ugliness. . . . I know the imperfection of your face").

Emasculating wit such as Millay's was one of the flapper's most fearsome trademarks. As the *New York Times* warned in 1922, the flapper "will never make you a hatband or knit you a necktie, but she'll drive you from the station hot Summer nights in her own little sports car. She'll don knickers and go skiing with you . . . ; she'll dive as well as you, perhaps better." The flapper was as known for her sexual exploits as for turning the whole thing into a joke. ("The tittle-tattle of ingénues' luncheons," complains Dr. Osterhaus in Warner Fabian's *Flaming Youth*, "would enlighten Rabelais and shock Pepys! And the current jokes between girls and their boy associates of college age are chiefly innuendo and *double entente* [*sic*] based on sex.") And the public knew the truth behind Millay's lines. She moved freely among romantic encounters and refused to choose between women and men. Her poems traded, with similar caprice, between biting irony and love-struck agony. If her persona looks vulnerable in her most devastated love sonnets, it is because she yields to a sexual pleasure that racks her wanton frame.

Proof positive that she had fun with this dangerous image are the articles she published in *Vanity Fair,* under the pseudonym Nancy Boyd (read "nancy boy")—a trickster figure who, in the spirit of Mark Twain's Virginia City persona, made a prank of her celebrated identity. She especially enjoyed her perceived femininity. In one such piece, she masquerades as "An American Art Student in Paris" and is shocked to see "Edna St. Vincent Millay" sitting next to her at a café "eating an enormous plate of sauerkraut and sausages"—when she had "always imagined her so ethereal."

Firebrands like Zelda and "Vincent"—and Hollywood "It girls" like Colleen Moore, Louise Brooks, and Clara Bow—gave middle-class women exciting new permission to wear their sexuality how they saw fit; to act as bold as, if not bolder than, men; to *drink* as much as, if not more than, men; to indulge in masquerade—and call it masquerade; and to speak with a frank and silly new language that was neither ladylike nor manly, nor sensible.

Following their examples, of course, was risky. Paula Fass's landmark study of 1920s white youth culture suggests the flappers' most daring ambitions, especially those regarding sexual behavior, were regularly tempered within college peer groups, which tended to enforce their own limits on sex. But peer groups were far more permissive than parents. While most youth still scorned premarital intercourse, "petting parties," a mild prelude to the group sex of later decades, legitimized kissing, necking, and fondling. Women who took the flappers' lead faced serious consequences from college administrators. In 1925, after Bryn Mawr's president designated smoking areas for women, many more college administrators redoubled their prohibitions. Northwestern's dean of women gave no quarter: "Any girl I catch smoking anywhere and at any time will not be permitted to remain in college." Women's natural resistance to such stifling laws was backed by two ameliorating forces: the press and the markets. Student newspapers mocked their administrators' folly, noting women had already made smoking an "art" and supported women's rights "to indulge her tastes just as men had always done." One by one, over the course of a decade, women's "indulgences" cleared traditional hurdles: makeup, hemlines, dancing, kissing. Smoking was one of the last in line, since drinking was forbidden to everybody. And as with many of the New Woman's rebel props—haircuts, short skirts, dance steps, makeup—this taboo, too, was soon to be monetized. In 1929, the magisterial spin doctor Edward Bernays spun this fun new vogue (at the behest of tobacco companies) into a national symbol of liberation: he staged an Easter parade in New York City where women were photographed openly smoking their "torches of freedom."

The flapper, for whom fun was a cause in itself, deserves much credit for the New Woman revolution. The flapper knew women weren't supposed to have fun, and she joined the long American campaign of turning prohibitions into playthings. Not only did she claim this right, she perfected it, and her often arcane talk was as modern as the barrel roll. It boasted the highest critical standards for gaiety, liberty, class, and style. "A Flapper's Dictionary," printed in the July 1922 *Flapper,* listed 163 need-to-know terms for the girl "with a jitney body" who also had "a limousine mind." It distinguished the "Brooksy" ("Classy dresser") from the "Brush Ape" ("a country Jake") and the "Fire Bell" ("Married woman") from the "Fire Alarm" ("Divorced"). While it called the flapper's father a "Dapper" (he was the one who furnished the "Hush Money"), it was otherwise vicious to the older generation—to "Father Time" ("Any man over 30"), the "Face Stretcher" ("Old maid who tries to look younger"), and all the "Alarm Clocks," "Fire Extinguishers," and other chaperones.

The glossary gives a peek into the flapper's high standards. She liked "Smoke Eaters" (girl smokers) and "Floorflushers" ("dance hounds"), and most certainly "Weeds" ("Flappers who take risks"). These are all "Ducky," the "Cat's Particulars." But she snubbed "Bush Hounds" ("Rustics and others outside the Flapper pale"), warned against kill-joys ("Wurps," "Cancelled Stamps," "Crepe Hangers," "Lens Louises"), and called out the worst kinds of men by name: "Gimlets," "Weasels," "Oilcans," "Slimps," "Monologists," "Finale Hoppers," "Airedales," "Pillow Cases," "Mustard Plasters," "Dewdroppers," "Walk Ins," "Corn Shredders," "Rug Hoppers," "Bell Polishers," and those "Cellar Smellers" with noses for the cheapest booze. "Whangdoodle" was her racy name for jazz, and her lexicon was warm on all sorts of "Barneymugging" (sex)—whether it happened in a "Petting Pantry" (movie theater), somebody's "gas wagon," or any big "Blow" ("Wild Party") where the "Biscuit" ("pettable flapper") chose to "Mug" with her "Goof" or "Highjohn." She was chilly toward that old "Eye Opener," marriage. She called her fiancé a "Police Dog" and her engagement ring a "Handcuff"—it might as well as have been a "Nut Cracker" ("Policeman's nightstick"). Her wit in general ran deep: "Dogs" were feet and "Dog Kennels" shoes. "Meringue" was her idea of "personality." But beneath all the smoke and meringue and makeup was a steely eye for realism. Male gold diggers were "Forty Niners," bootleggers were "Embalmers," and undertakers were "Sod Busters." "Munitions" were the flapper's "Face powder and rouge."

Dorothy Parker, the era's most legendary wit, held the fast-talking flapper in high esteem. She admired her unassuming danger:

> Her girlish ways may make a stir,
> Her manners cause a scene,
> But there is no more harm in her
> Than in a submarine.

The *Times* called Parker's poetry "flapper verse" for being "wholesome, engaging, uncorseted and not devoid of grace." To this extent Parker resembled Millay, whom she worshipped and to whose finer poetry she aspired. But nobody accused her of being "ethereal." While Millay played the victim of her own gluttonous heart, Parker, who was as notoriously promiscuous, flaunted her genuine morbidity, making several attempts on her life and ultimately medicating herself to death with "small sips" of Johnnie Walker neat.

When a bartender once asked her what she was having, she replied, "Not much fun." The sundry works of Dorothy Parker—ranging from plays, essays, reviews, and doggerel verse to some of America's most poignant fiction—were an ongoing meditation on fun, and on its miserable casualties. Throughout the twenties she was the life of the party, covering the scene from New York's Algonquin to Paris's Les Deux Magots, with frequent stops in the Hamptons at the Swopes estate, the rumored template for the Gatsby mansion. But for all of her promiscuity and celebrated drinking, Parker's most reliable fun seems to have come from *jeux de mots*. When asked to use "horticulture" in a sentence, Parker quipped, "You can lead a horticulture but you can't make her think." A lingerie caption she proposed to *Vogue* read: "There was a little girl who had a

Risk-loving flappers dance the Charleston—in high heels—on the ledge of Chicago's Sherman Hotel, December 11, 1926. (Courtesy of Underwood & Underwood, CORBIS images.)

little curl, right in the middle of her forehead. When she was good she was very, very good, and when she was bad she wore this divine nightdress of rose-colored mousseline de soie, trimmed with frothy Valenciennes lace." (It was rejected at the last minute.) Her poetry ripples with such irreverent merriment, often erring on the side of the singsong but always with vitriol marring its surface. Her finest work ventures outside the submarine and lingers, dangerously, in the chambers of the sea. W. Somerset Maugham said her novella "Big Blonde"—which reads like Parker's own "Eulogy on the Flapper"—had "all the earmarks of masterpiece." It's about an over-the-hill flapper named Hazel Morse. In it, Parker's mermaid wakes up human and, like Eliot's Prufrock, drowns.

As so many twenties writers would have it, under all the booze, whangdoodle, and fun was a sneaking insecurity that belied both the sheik's and the flapper's confidence: fun was a cover-up that made matters worse. The deep distractions of the 1920s seemed to lead death-driven wild partiers, like Parker and Harry Crosby, ever farther from, not "nearer to," the "frank and full enjoyment of life" identified by Robert L. Duffus. Most likely, it was the Parkers and Crosbys whom reformers like Duffus had hoped to "guide." The wild-spinning fun, like Tilyou's Human Roulette, tossed weakly clutching citizens into the ditch. Throughout the story "Big Blonde," for instance, people clamber together in pursuit of reckless fun; in the end, the damaged ones—like Hazel, the eponymous Big Blonde herself—seek "drowsy cheer" in the sweet and absolute slackening of death.

The way Parker represents it, indeed the way she seems to have lived it, these two communities—the partygoers and the suicides—were on a continuum of risky pleasure that characterized Jazz Age extremity. At the era's illegal and extralegal wild parties, where only cops and parents weren't welcome, citizens were not only exposed to risk; they welcomed it, pursued it, demanded it. They laughed at tedious common sense. They flouted laws, civil and social, and tested the limits of decency and safety. It took resilience under such conditions for the average citizen to keep it together—to keep from succumbing to addiction and violence; to keep from knuckling under to tyrants.

The streetwise flapper put a premium on resilience. She tested her mettle in this risky age, and she expected other women to do the same. But as Parker demonstrates in "Big Blonde" and elsewhere, fun for fun's sake had special dangers for women, who lacked advantage in the world of men. Whether she was valued for her sex, her wits, or her fun, the woman's role at the party was often to entertain, even when what she wanted was only to amuse herself.

Dorothy Parker would die of a heart attack, but until then she was chronically suicidal. Like her Big Blonde, Hazel Morse, she once took an overdose of the sedative Veronal. Another time she consumed a bottle of shoe polish. It was in her character to turn even her suicide attempts into stunts and practical jokes. Having slashed herself with her husband's razor, she greeted bedside visitors with blue ribbons tied to her bandaged wrists. After an overdose of sleeping powders, she sent a telegram from the country estate where she was recovering: "SEND ME A SAW INSIDE A LOAF OF BREAD."

Gallows humor sets the tone for the Big Blonde's failed suicide. Approaching her beloved vials of Veronal, Hazel feels "the quick excitement of one who is about to receive an anticipated gift." Drinking down the pills she intones once more, "Here's mud in your eye."

But of course she doesn't die. That would have been a happy ending. "You couldn't kill her with an ax," is her doctor's diagnosis. Like Parker's, Hazel's fate is to keep on drinking.


MAE WEST, for her part, had nerves of steel. She stuck up for society's most despised citizens (prostitutes, gays, cross-dressers) and always managed to come out on top. Born in 1893, raised poor and tough in Bushwick, Brooklyn, she learned from her mother, a corset model, to market her sex appeal for a self-respecting profit. She learned from her father—a livery stableman who may have been a two-bit boxer—how to pump iron and judge a good prizefight. She hit the boards at six, and "by the time she was a teenager," Lillian Schlissel writes, "she was all strut and swagger, moving around the stage like a bantam-weight fighter"—a strut she would fashion into the pugilistic saunter that shook the 1930s silver screen. It was in her teens, in Coney Island's saloons and theaters, that she earned an Ivy League acting education. Having dumped her first husband at age nineteen, she acted with Jimmy Durante on the boardwalk, took comic cues from Bert Williams (the slinky half of Williams and Walker), conned songs from JoJo the Dog-Faced Boy, modeled her style on the "wildly uninhibited antics" of Eva Tanguay, and studied the rapid-fire comic banter of Jay Brennan and of the unapologetically gay Bert Savoy, who impressed her with his repertoire of heroines (in drag) and his dangerously irreverent zingers. This coterie of mismatched male, female, and female-impersonating influences—a boxer, a cakewalker, a circus oddity; comedians both gay and straight—inspired a fearless new fun in her stagecraft that could make even the flapper blush. And West's love of sex wasn't an act—she claimed to have had it nearly every day of her life.

She cast herself as a "jazz baby" in her first play, *The Ruby Ring* (1921), and in the title role of her co-written second, *The Hussy* (1922), but by the mid-1920s, when she had entered her thirties, she dropped the flapper dress for a whore's lingerie. Piqued by young Clara Bow's *The Fleet's In*, she adapted a low sex comedy called *Following the Fleet* (in which Montreal prostitutes do just that) into a morally shocking play called *Sex* (1926). *Sex* featured West as her heroine, Margy, a slang-slinging prostitute who proves, in the end, to be more upstanding than Clara, a Connecticut socialite who slums at Margy's brothel. What made *Sex* unforgivable was that, of all the sex comedies playing off-Broadway, this one gave moral high ground to the whore, even stating Margy would "make a better wife and mother than" Clara. The production featured sailors dancing an all-male jig. West herself did a "shimmy shawabble" that she claimed to have learned on Chicago's South Side. The critics, siding with high society, greeted *Sex* with a collective Bronx cheer: "vulgar," "nasty," "infantile," and "as bad a play as these inquiring eyes have gazed upon in three seasons." But the theatergoing public held a different opinion, making it off-Broadway's most successful play of the season.

Her next year's production joined the recent gay-comedy vogue and cashed in on a new, leering interest in drag balls. The play, *The Drag* (1927), drew in part upon West's circle of gay men and went beyond its potentially salacious subject matter to give a sympathetic and jubilant look at gay culture. Her great risk, once again, lay in her sympathy, this time with a sexual orientation that, as her play acknowledges, was scorned as "degenerate" and "criminal." Much as *Sex* ennobles prostitutes by society's highest standards, *The Drag* describes a gay couple as being "happier" than any "normally married couple." The story hinges on two contentious old friends, a doctor who speaks generously of the "born homosexual" and a judge who believes "people like that should be herded together on some desert island." The doctor's daughter is unhappily married to the judge's elusive son, Rolly, who, predictably, is secretly gay. Mae West's own melodramatic typecasting suggests that, against the play's defense of homosexuals, Rolly and other gays have questionable morals (he freely deceives his wife, he is killed by his rejected ex-lover), but *The Drag*'s dominant picture presents the gay community as close-knit, witty, and defiantly fun. A drag queen, Duchess, defending herself for powdering up in front of the cops, says that "they like me," and then with innuendo: "They all know me from Central Park."

West's cops are stand-ins for the 1920s vice squads that came down hard on sexual deviance and put special heat on West herself. In *The Drag* they're also the peak of excitement. In the culminating drag party—the dance spectacle that made the play's money—cross-dressers boast about previous jail time and burst into excitement when the joint is raided: "It must be the wagon, let me in first!" "I had to stand the last time!" "I don't care, I had a gay time!" "I had a grand time!" "I had a gorgeous time!"

On February 9, 1927, trying to forestall *The Drag* from ever opening in New York City, the Society for the Prevention of Vice raided *Sex* and two other racy plays. (The lenient "jazz mayor," Jimmy Walker, was on vacation.) West and her cast were hauled away in a van and released on $14,000 bail. She and her two producers, refusing a plea bargain, reopened the show with "a restraining order against police interference" and enjoyed several months of lavish profits while awaiting their obscenity trial. Each of the three was found guilty, fined $1,500, and sentenced to ten days behind bars—a high-profile incarceration with which Mae West, like P. T. Barnum some seventy years earlier, had a lot of fun. She reported in a limo, dined with the warden, and bragged of having done her time in a silk negligee.

She rewrote *The Drag* as *The Pleasure Man,* making changes to evade the censors but keeping its big draw, the drag ball, intact. *The Pleasure Man* was raided right away, and West and her producers were forced to bail out a cast of fifty-nine. The obscenity trial lasted fourteen days, but after the media had had their fill, the case was thrown out. In the end the trial was just another wild party. Having scored this major free-speech victory, though to the tune of $60,000, West summed it up: "Let's see some other son of a bitch do that."

Mae West came from tough American stock. She didn't shrink from the fight—she courted it. In the heat of battle—onstage, in court—West was at the top of her game, dropping her foes with delicious rejoinders, losing herself in a shimmy shawabble. Not just a writer, actor, or producer, West was an impresaria, a *force*. And she wasn't just in it for herself. Unlike Zelda, she was no elitist. Like Bessie Smith and Clara Bow, she was loyal to her people and eager to spread their fun around. She harnessed the power of despised Americans and made it desirable even to the middle class. Critics scoffed and censors pounced, but the people kept coming back for more. For her fun wasn't meant to please the elite. Her fun was at home down among the crowd. It was the fun of outcasts, rebels, and commoners, and it was open country for any citizen who was unafraid, unashamed, unflappable.

# 9

# Zoot Suit Riots

F. SCOTT FITZGERALD'S STUNNING ESSAY "Echoes of the Jazz Age" (1931) looks back on the early 1920s as years when "a whole race"—first the young, then everyone else—fell under the erotic spell of jazz and went "hedonistic, deciding on pleasure." Soon "people all the way up to fifty, had joined the dance." Eventually, and Fitzgerald implies *inevitably,* fun lovers started vanishing "into the dark maw of violence"—insanity, murder, suicide. Fitzgerald's perspective is typical of his elite white peers, who often presented fun as a prelude to catastrophe. It also makes for a tidy, boom-and-bust story. If the twenties were (in his words) "the most expensive orgy in history," a party fueled "by great filling stations full of money" that roamed from Palm Beach to the French Riviera, then it follows from this ruling-class reasoning that the end was near when the rich turned neurotic (somewhere around 1927); nearer still when they had to travel with "citizens" who had the "human value of Pekinese, bivalves, cretins, goats" (around 1928); and that the whole kaleidoscopic soap bubble had to pop with the great crash of 1929. Jazz may have turned the ignition, but money, by this argument, filled the tank.

And there's truth to it. America's excesses during the "age of play" fattened the movie, music, games, sports, tobacco, and travel industries. Bootlegging gave the crime syndicate unprecedented new power. Already-rich rentiers like Harry Crosby reached scary heights of extravagance and danger. And during its meteoric rise in 1929, the stock market itself became a source of excitement that attracted many first-time lower-to-middle-class gamblers. Hence, in the story of 1920s prosperity, the great crash was a cultural climax—what Crosby recorded in his diary as "exciting story millions lost in an hour suicides disorder panic." The big losers were bankers and celebrities, and as usual their failures filled the tabloids. But as John Kenneth Galbraith cautioned, "only one and a half million people, out of a population of approximately 120 million and of between 29 and 30 million families, had an active association of any sort with the stock market. And not all of these were speculators." At least in the short term, John Q. Public was largely untouched.

By the same token, then, the mass of Americans who embraced the twenties' vogue for witty, acrobatic, joyous revolt didn't need buckets of cash to do so. They didn't require biplanes and Stutz Bearcats. Like Pinkster revelers and argonauts before them, they fashioned their fun from what they had at hand—they bobbed their own hair, staged their own stunts, bubbled their own bathtub gin. It was the fun of improvised participation, and superstar tramps like Charlie Chaplin and Clara Bow inspired even the lowliest of citizens to join in. This latest iteration of American fun wasn't born of Gilded Age luxury. It was born of Buddy Bolden's reckless innovations, it was an all-hands showdown with Plymouth Plantation, and it emboldened crowds for any eventuality. This will to party was the twenties' cultural legacy, the playful one, that handily survived the crash of '29. Speculators jumped hand in hand from skyscrapers, and broken-down celebrities slipped away into asylums (Chaplin and Bow included), but once it had been released onto an eager mainstream, the risky, rebellious fun of the people stumbled its way through the economy's rubble. When speculators went bust, big-time bootleggers, whose business kept bubbling, snatched up their half-million-dollar yachts for a song (for as little as $5,000 apiece) and "decorated them with pretty girls in bathing suits." Prohibition was repealed in 1933, but the struggle for a pious America raged on. Dance marathons—which had only grown longer, wilder, and more dangerous since their inception in the early twenties—were widely banned in 1934. And that year the Hays Office finally got serious.

IN THE EARLY 1930S, with the advent of sound, movies were more salaciously fun than ever, assisted in large part by a *pair* of Brooklyn bonfires—Clara Bow (returning from her breakdown as a hot-tempered, whip-cracking, half–Native American gambling addict in the border-crossing talkie *Call Her Savage*), and the censors' bête noire herself, Mae West, whose 1933 film debut, *She Done Him Wrong,* based on her Gay Nineties comedy *Diamond Lil,* did to Hollywood what she had done to Broadway: dragged it through the seamy underworld, once again bedeviling viewers with a gleefully unrepentant Bowery madame, this time Lady Lou. Kindled by West's sulfurous legal history, bellowed by gusts of rave reviews, and promoted with an actual stunt still shot in which the famed evangelist Billy Sunday gamely threatens her with a barroom chair, *She Done Him Wrong*'s brushfire swept the nation, engulfing even southern and remote midwestern markets. It was also nominated for a Best Picture Oscar.

*Variety* called West "as hot an issue as Hitler." For now she had a formidable opponent. There was a new pastor in the parish, Catholics, who had stopped playing along with the studios' ruse. Following the Catholic Church's uproar against MGM's 1927 picture *The Callahans and the Murphys,* which comprised a shameless stream of Irish-American slurs, Hays had deputized U.S. Catholics to form the Legion of Decency, tasking them with writing the 1930 Production Code. Later known as the Hays Code, these new rules held films to high moral standards: criminals had to be detestable, crimes had to be punished, and only intimations of *marital* sex were permitted, and never between members of different races or (it didn't even need to be stated) same-sex partners. Until 1933 and Mae West's unprecedented onscreen eroticism, the Code—like the 1920s Formula—was distorted and ignored by its enforcers. But as Marybeth Hamilton puts it, despite the Hays Office's attempts to make Lady Lou into a contemptible cartoon, "West's acting style had subverted all [their] efforts to veil Lou and her surroundings in comedy." Her character was real, born of the streets, and her effect was terrifically seductive—especially to young women, which of course was the Legion's greatest fear.

That same year, Henry James Forman's hand-wringing book, *Our Movie-Made Children,* tried to arm priests, parents, and reformers with evidence that impressionable girls—especially reform-school girls— had been aroused and damaged by Hollywood eros. Forman opens fire on the youth who provide him testimonials. He smirks at the "young Negro high-school girl" for wanting to "possess" Clara Bow's "It." He makes examples of "tots" who identified with "robbers" over "coppers" and eventually went on to join "the racket." American kids were blazing out, having fun, and Forman blamed Hollywood: "When a girl tells of learning to handle a cigarette like Nazimova, to smile like Norma Shearer, to use her eyes like Joan Crawford, she is not necessarily an immigrant's daughter. She is merely a daughter of Eve." But the apparent foreigners and de facto whores were, to judge from these testimonials, mostly self-confident adolescents who, like Clara Bow herself, were finding their comfortable place in the crowd: " 'I have learned from the movies,' a high school girl boldly announces, 'how to be a flirt, and I found out at parties and elsewhere the coquette is the one who enjoys herself the most.' " They have learned from motion pictures how to banter, talk back, and "hug," and as one boy reports, "how to kiss a girl on her ears, neck and cheeks, as well as on her mouth." Kids were getting a sexual education and, yes, they were *using* it—as were at least 33 percent of the five hundred students who took Forman's survey. (He suspected the actual percentage was higher.) He scorns the "sixteen-year-old girl" who "so pertinently, so pathetically" calls such acquisitions "talents," but fairly clearly she is no Mae West. She is just reporting what her peer group values. Unlike Bowery b'hoys who did their demagogues' bidding, many of Forman's "movie-made children" come across as lively, thoughtful citizens: some speak critically of the movies' strong influence, others see movies as helpful primers for fine-tuning what they would probably do anyway—which is to say, have the kinds of taboo fun that had been defining American youth for over a decade. Forman sniffed that some parents even "may desire this species of schooling for their daughters." But parents who took Forman's anxious position went on the rampage.

Responding to public outcry, fearing reprisals, but still determined to cash in on West, Paramount severely vetted Mae West's sexuality— making her next heroine, in *I'm No Angel* (1933), a gold digger instead of a nymphomaniac. The Hays officials were delighted by the results, and fan magazines joined the general humbug, touting West herself as a humble church lady, but her mounting success was her greatest threat—to men in particular, as Hamilton argues. It was her brazen attitude, not her canned characters, that was causing all the damage. Girls filled the theaters at women-only viewings and took to imitating her walk and talk. A new generation of self-sufficient flappers, less dependent than ever on (often financially strapped) men, took notice that pleasure, pluck, and slang could be slung and shot like John Wayne's pistols. This threat wasn't lost on the Hays Office, who well knew their public's double standard: "The very man who will guffaw at Mae West's performance as a reminder of the ribald days of his past will resent her effect upon the young, when his daughter imitates the Mae West wiggle before her boyfriends and mouths 'Come up and see me sometime.'" Hence, though she stayed onscreen throughout the decade, West became the Hays Office's pet project. When they responded to Catholic pressure in 1934 and began to apply the Code in earnest, her trademark ruffian was reformed as the heroine of schlock morality tales.

The Great Depression shared a calendar with the golden age of Hollywood, an era of glitzily luxuriant escapism when Fred Astaire glided with Ginger Rogers, the Three Stooges and Marx Brothers redefined silly, and Busby Berkeley mastered the mass human ornament. This decade of the Dust Bowl, soup lines, and Hoovervilles deserved to be soothed by such crowd-pleasing frivolity. Yet its best filmic statement on Jazz Age fun looked economic misery full in the face. *Modern Times,* Chaplin's 1936 masterpiece, and his extravagant farewell to the silent era, butts the same Tramp who braved the Yukon up against the worst the thirties could dish out: factory drudgery, workers' revolt, unemployment, abject poverty. First called *Commonwealth,* then *The Masses,* it reflected the auteur's growing anti-capitalist stance. Defiant as ever—in a movie whose tagline is "humanity crusading in the pursuit of happiness"—his Tramp takes refuge in ridiculous play and lives on the constant lam from the cops. A portrait of Marx's original reified laborer, the Tramp develops a manic repetitive-stress injury from tightening bolts on Electro Steel Corp.'s assembly line. After bodily rotating through the machinery's cogs, he emerges a pranking and sex-crazed imp who cranks random levers until the turbines blow and squirts oil from a can into the factory president's face.

In and out of asylums and jail, in and out of work, he falls in love with a fellow rebel, "a gamin child of the waterfront" played by the flashing-eyed Paulette Goddard. They escape together from a police wagon, knocking a cop unconscious along the way. A Bonnie and Clyde of puckish fun, the Tramp and the Gamin pursue their happiness on the fringes of law and civil society. Exploiting his temporary job as a department store night watchman, they freeload at the lunch counter and cut loose in the fourth-floor toy department, where, blindfolded and roller-skating backward, the Tramp cuts breathtaking capers along an unguarded ledge. Compromising their dream of a middle-class home, they call her shanty along the docks "paradise" despite its tin-can tableware and collapsing walls, floors, and furniture. When at last they get their break as performers in a dinner theater—the Gamin as a dancer, the Tramp as an outlandish singing waiter (Chaplin's mockery of his first speaking role)—cops apprehend the Gamin for vagrancy and send them packing once again. In earlier versions, to placate the Hays Office, Chaplin sent his Gamin to the convent. In the final version, they march off into the sunset—poor and pursued but defiantly smiling.

ONE LEADING LIGHT of the Harlem Renaissance wouldn't publish her first book until long after Harlem had fallen out of vogue. Zora Neale Hurston, by many accounts, lived in constant pursuit of "fun"—or what she herself called "the terrific kick that comes from taking a chance." This self-proclaimed "Queen of the Niggerati" contributed to *The New Negro* and was a founder of *Fire!!*. She cut a spirited image on the 1920s scene—whether crashing swanky hotels dressed as an "Asian Princess" or speaking out against Marcus Garvey's anti-Americanism. But she didn't make her name as a folklorist and novelist until deep into the Great Depression. What she uncovered then was a cultural revelation. In contrast to Dorothea Lange's dismal photographs and Steinbeck's down-trodden Joad family, Hurston's treasure trove of jokes, tales, songs, and novels showcased, among many other features, the fun of rural southern blacks—a population too low on the national class ladder to have been helped by the boom or even hurt by the crash.

Though Hurston frequently lied about the year of her birth (some-where between 1891 and 1903), it is known that she grew up in all-black Eatonville, Florida, "a city," as she characterized it, "of five lakes, three croquet courts, three hundred brown skins, three hundred good swim-mers, plenty guavas, two schools, and no jail house." Her father was the town's sometime mayor who thought blacks shouldn't have "too much spirit," but her mother told her to "jump at de sun," advice driven home by the many dancers, drinkers, fighters, partiers, and athletes she so admired around town. Among this fun-loving population, she held the cutthroat storytellers on Joe Clark's porch in highest regard. Only the threat of a hickory switch could get her to leave before a story's cli-max. For young Hurston their stories shone like fact. In addition to the rattlesnakes, gators, and bears that added thrills to Eatonville's daily life, "God, Devil, Brer Rabbit, Brer Fox, Sis Cat, Brer Bear, Lion, Buzzard, and all the wood folk walked and talked like natural men." Even decades later, when she studied at Barnard under the famed anthropologist Franz Boas, her childhood enthrallment with jokes and folktales shaped the way she thought, worked, and played. Langston Hughes himself (swal-lowing his lingering bitterness over a plagiarism dispute) remembered her as the "most amusing" of the "niggerati" and cited her "side-splitting anecdotes, humorous tales, and tragicomic stories" as proof. In her pur-suit of such folklore in the 1930s, she got down to the root-ball of Jazz Age fun.

It was while working for Boas—and later for the Guggenheims, the Works Progress Administration (WPA), and her rich white "godmother," Charlotte Osgood Mason (whose primitivist demands didn't irk her as much as they did Hughes)—that Hurston kept returning to the Deep South, and later the Caribbean, and sharpening her techniques for collecting materials. After her initial failure in 1927, when Boas scolded her for gathering old news, she learned to exploit her southern charm and, most important, her secret weapon: being black, she could penetrate the "feather-bed of resistance" that kept out white colleagues like Boas and John Lomax.

Learning to suppress her "carefully accented Barnardese," Hurston went native in Polk County, Florida. She packed a revolver, frequented job sites and jook joints, nearly got herself killed by a bluesman's ex-lover, and spent years getting acquainted with the humor and hoodoo that inform her (uneven) first novel *Jonah's Gourd Vine* (1934), her folklore collection *Mules and Men* (1935), and most of her writing to follow. The fun she saw there eased even the hardest of lives. Lumberjacks were "poets of the swinging blade" and phosphate miners "Black men laughing and singing." Railroad workers, swinging hammers, sang a steady chant:

> Oh, let's shake it! Hank!
> Oh, let's break it! Hank!
> Oh, let's shake it, Hank!
> Oh, just a hair! Hank!

Orange pickers manned their ladders, "singing, laughing, cursing, boasting of last night's love" and didn't "say embrace when they [meant] they slept with a woman." And at night in the "jooks" the rhythm kept rolling and the people kept "balling," the sexually inflected black slang term that Hurston translated as "having fun": "Dancing the square dance. Dancing the scrunch. Dancing the belly-rub. Knocking the right hat off the wrong head, and backing it up with a switch-blade." The dancing and joking, often tinged with violence, sometimes erupted into the dozens—that "risky pleasure," Hurston calls it, of trading verbal blows about an enemy's family members until the weakest and least witty eventually lose their cool. Clarence Major calls the dozens a "test" of "emotional strength." Dozens were likewise the forte of Lorenzo Staulz,

Buddy Bolden's profane vocalist who could challenge his whole audience to verbal jousts. This cousin to cutting contests, this ancestor to rap music's chest-bumping rivalry, becomes in Hurston's writing the razor's edge of fun. Its graceful slices, dodges, and parries sharpen the wits, strengthen the self, and delight any onlookers—right up to the brink of violent collapse. "If you have no faith in your personal courage and confidence in your arsenal, don't try it."

In *Their Eyes Were Watching God* (1937), widely regarded as one of the most important twentieth-century American novels, it's the dozens that sets Janie, the protagonist, free. Confined in her marriage to Joe Starks, Eatonville's big-talking mayor (a combination of Hurston's father and what she called "Negrotarian" race leaders like DuBois), Janie is "classed-off" from all of Eatonville's fun—its storytelling sessions, its "contest[s] in hyperbole," its hilarious funeral for Matt Bonner's mule. Only when she hears Joe mocking her aging body does she sling the razor tongue of a Ma Rainey or Bessie Smith. Verbally, she does "the thing that Saul's daughter had done to David." She castrates him in front of the other men:

> "Talkin' 'bout *me* lookin' old! When you pull down yo' britches, you look lak de change uh life."
>
> "Great God from Zion!" Sam Watson gasped. "Y'll really playin' de dozens tuhnight."
>
> "Wha—whut's dat you said?" Joe challenged, hoping his ears had fooled him.
>
> "You heard her, you ain't blind," Walter taunted.
>
> "Ah ruther be shot with tacks than tuh hear dat 'bout mahself," Lige Moss commiserated.

Joe Starks, never recovering his pride, ultimately withers and dies. After a brief mourning period, Janie lets down her hair and meets a fun young drifter who goes by Tea Cake—based on a twenty-three-year-old undergraduate with whom Hurston had an affair. Eatonville scorns him for being beneath Janie's station, but she loves him for asking her to play checkers—or go fishing, attend barbecues, or just fool around. Uninterested in Janie's class or money, he takes her into his world of migrant workers in the Everglades, or what they call "the Muck." Down off her pedestal and among the vibrant crowd—America's *least-valued* crowd of "permanent transients with no attachments"—Janie discovers an unlikely paradise of "pianos living three lifetimes in one" and "Blues made and used right on the spot." Free to be herself within this civil society of "dancing, fighting, singing, crying, laughing, winning, and losing," she finally gets to join the fun.

IN MODERNIZING FOLK CULTURE, Buddy Bolden & Company had gotten it ready for war. They had weaponized it. For the "age of play" wasn't an easygoing time. It staged some of America's great social struggles—between drinkers and drys, blacks and whites, women and men—and often these struggles came to blows. But even in this age of outsize personalities who spoke their minds and strutted their stuff, the technologies of fun, born of slave society, taught everyday Americans to spin their conflicts into pleasurable collisions. The stock market crashed, and the flood of rich slummers soon dried up in Harlem, but jazz, and its joyous revolt, just kept growing.

Throughout the 1930s, swing dancers goaded jazz bands to grow bigger, blow louder, and new copycat Savoys sparked urban dance scenes all across the country. But Cat's Corner, in Harlem, was still the engine room. In the late 1930s it was ruled by King Leon James, a tall, lanky member of the Jolly Fellows street gang and winner of the Harvest Moon jitterbug contest. Even on the jumpingest Saturday nights, the corner stayed empty until the King strolled in with his chain-swinging, coin-flipping entourage. The scuffle started at the base of the pecking order (the "scrubs") and always ended with the King himself, after which followed a respectful intermission.

One night, when the King had finished his set, a seventeen-year-old scrub named Albert Minns swept his partner into Cat's Corner. He imitated the King's new moves like a pro (plagiarism that was punishable by broken bones), but then he added trickier moves of his own, flying acrobatics like the "back flip," "over the head," and "snatch"—moves that eventually got "the Lindy off the ground" and anticipated the marvels of 1980s break dancing. The stunt was certain to earn a drubbing by the other Jolly Fellows—had the King not been so duly impressed. The prank's success, if nothing else, showed the power of audacity within the Savoy hierarchy. It helped, of course, that Minns could dance. The two were combining efforts within a year, and Al Minns himself went on to rule Cat's Corner. The fame Shorty Snowden originally brought to the Savoy had hardened into landmark, legend, so much so that a mock-up of the ballroom was erected at the 1939 New York World's Fair, where the Lindy Hop was canonized.

The Lindy or the "jitterbug" wouldn't take hold until 1936, the year it was associated with the white clarinetist and bandleader Benny Goodman—the year, that is, that jazz became "swing." The word spread fast: suddenly the jitterbug whipped and flipped on screens, stages, and dance floors nationwide. Around this same time, the flamboyant street culture that had gotten its start at Harlem's Savoy was changing the dancing and dressing styles of America's inner-city youth—in particular, young African-American "hepcats" and Latin American pachucos and pachucas. Loyal to their idol Cab Calloway, the men in these subcultures wore sleek, wide fedoras and flashy two-tone round-toe shoes. The men crafted loose and flowing suits, the women long skirts and flapping cardigans, all of which dramatized the Lindy's power and grace. The dance and its styles were a proud performance—of strength, invention, high spirits, *talent*—and it coursed from the Savoy and L.A.'s Diana Ballroom to the high streets and sidewalks of America's cities. Possibly as a nod to Cab Calloway's scat singing, they self-identified as "zoot suiters." But they were no stooges, no Bowery b'hoys—though black ones "conked" their long hair with slickening products in a style reminiscent of the old soap locks. Perfecting Buddy Bolden's dance-music tradition, they gave to jazz as much as they took: moves, style, attitude, *jive*. No "movie-made children," these kids were the *authors* of popular culture.

In an age when Hollywood was marshalling its forces to wipe "miscegenation" off the silver screen, swing dance was proving more effective than ever at bringing races and ethnicities together—close together. Malcolm X, who had been a zoot suiter at the Savoy in the early 1940s, looked back on its electric, multiracial fun: "I just about went wild! Hamp's band wailing, I was whirling girls so fast their skirts were snapping. Black girls, brownskins, high yellows, even a couple of the white girls there. Boosting them over my hips, my shoulders, into the air. . . . Circling, tap-dancing, I was underneath them when they landed—doing the 'flapping eagle,' 'the kangaroo,' and the 'split.'" The historian Luis Alvarez explores the pleasure and tension generated by swing dancers' racial mixing. In Los Angeles, major dance halls represented a full sample of the region's complex demographics: blacks, whites, Mexicans, Filipinos, Chinese, and Japanese. "Many zoot suiters," he writes, "broke public taboos against integration and racial mixing by socializing together and participating in [overtly diverse] public events"; the results themselves were often mixed—dancing, competing, sometimes

Sandra Gibson throws the legendary Al Minns in the Savoy Ballroom's Cat's Corner, 1939. (Courtesy of Cornell Capa, Magnum Images.)

rumbling—but the building up and breaking of tension was engineered into this subculture's fun, its "sheer enjoyment," eros dancing and tangling with thanatos.

Throughout New York City, not just in Harlem, swing bands drew radically diverse crowds: "every couple, almost," Dizzy Gillespie (who zooted, too) said, "was a mixed couple one way or the other. That was the age of unity." Swing was especially popular, he observed, among black and white Communist Party members. But larger society didn't share that love. In the early 1940s, when their subculture gained force and their styles and attitudes became more visible, zoot suiters and pachuco/as took it from all sides. Zoot suits themselves, constructed of ample fabric, were declared illegal in 1942—for hoarding textiles during wartime. Disliked by whites, disowned by adults who hated their flash, zoot suiters inhabited, as Shane White and Graham White have shown, the abject new category of "juvenile delinquency." Even J. A. Rogers, the journalist who touted jazz's "joyous revolt" in Alain Locke's *New Negro* anthology, decried zoot suiters in 1943 as the "revolt of callow youth against convention and authority." Zoot suiters strutted the worst of jazz's "morally anarchic spirit."

Their racial mixing was also seen as a threat, as unpatriotic, disgusting, enraging, especially by white U.S. soldiers and sailors, who were often forbidden to attend jazz clubs. Indeed, in May 1943, when city health authorities ordered the Savoy shut down, claiming its "role in facilitating the spread of venereal disease among servicemen," investigative reporting by the local black press unearthed a different motive: "Mixed Dancing Closed Savoy Ballroom." Their case was sound. In comparison with the downtown sex clubs and brothels that somehow eluded the authorities' notice, the Savoy, as they put it, looked like a "Christian youth center."

Later that same month, a long-running tension between zoot suiters and service members (often with the assistance of cops) erupted into the so-called Zoot Suit Riots—just the latest wave of race riots to spread throughout Los Angeles County. Having long been ridiculed by soldiers and sailors as femmes, cowards, and national enemies, a group of Mexican-American zoot suiters clashed with eleven service members in L.A.'s Alpine neighborhood, breaking the jaw of one of the sailors. On June 4, following a few similar clashes, two hundred or more sailors entered East L.A. in a fleet of taxicabs, armed with bludgeons and patrolling for zoot suits. They attacked the first boy they saw and unleashed four days of unchecked violence against randomly identified Mexican Americans and blacks, many of whom were beaten and stripped naked—whether they wore zoot suits or not.

THIS EXUBERANT ERA WAS grimly bookended between the Red Summer of 1919 and the Zoot Suit Riots of 1943 (or possibly the 1958 closing of Harlem's Savoy Ballroom)—but certainly *not* the crash of 1929. When it is reviewed not for its evidence of economic prosperity but for, as Fitzgerald's catchphrase implies, its aerobatics of playful rebellion, the Jazz Age gets its due as a coming-out party for the fiercest exponents of American fun. Morals were loosened, wits sharpened, boundaries busted, the citizenry *widened.* The voices of long-muffled women and minorities rang out louder and more joyfully than anyone's. Bodies that had been suffocated for decades by Victorian ruffles, bustles, and "character" were suddenly half naked, inebriated, and jitterbugging in public.

If F. Scott Fitzgerald was determined to read fun as a prelude to disaster, as a chancre in the rose of civilization, then the Zoot Suit Riots may fit his vision: their victims were bold young men and women who pushed too hard against American standards at an intensely conservative and patriotic time. In their opponents' view, they *courted* disaster. Their clothes were outrageous, their colors too loud. Their walk was too cocky, their talk too ethnic, and their gymnastic dancing *just asking for it.* Strutting their pleasure and cultural difference, they drew civic fire in a time of war, when the dominant culture enforced a campaign against racial enemies in the Pacific and ideological ones in Europe. The zoot suiters' fun was a threat, an affront, to the steamrolling myth of white American sameness that was rising to prominence at that time. To this extent, their risky fun was the perfection of 1920s popular culture. Theirs was the playful resistance of outsiders who claimed and flaunted their brilliant contributions—of Buddy Boldens and Louis Armstrongs, of Clara Bows and Mae Wests, of Shorty Snowdens and Bessie Smiths. It was the ludic defiance of Chaplin's Tramp in the face of destruction natural and social. To the same extent, from the streets to the dance floors, their fun was the perfection of radical 1920s social mixing, of Thomas Morton's original vision for Merry Mount that began to take shape by the grace of jazz. Zoot suit culture, with all its contests and conflicts, boasted a civility that the Bowery b'hoys lacked. It sported a style that touted the individual and highlighted racial discrepancy—but it welcomed everyone into the fight. The America it boasted was defined by struggle. The fun it promoted was passed around among agile individuals and swinging throngs. And the danger it presaged was the boys from Plymouth coming to chop that Maypole down.

So they did, but it wasn't disastrous.

For joyous revolt had carved a riverbed that is deeper and wider now than ever.

# A California Education, Redux

I N  A  G R A I N Y  C O L O R  M O V I E  from 1964, the novelist Ken Kesey spray-paints a campaign slogan across the top of his psychedelic school bus: "A Vote for Barry Is a Vote for Fun." The Merry Pranksters, as his band of funmakers called themselves, drive backward through the center of Phoenix, wearing red-white-and-blue sport shirts and frantically waving American flags from the roof. This lavish send-up of Barry Goldwater (that year's archconservative presidential candidate) happened early in the LSD-lidded Pranksters' serpentine cross-country bus trip—a joy ride that delivered the new Wild West lunacy to the boring, buttoned-down East Coast "establishment." The Merry Pranksters' "Vote for Fun" (similar in its irony to Paul Krassner's star-spangled 1963 "FUCK COM-MUNISM" poster) inaugurated a raffish participatory politics that all but obliterated the voting booth: it was a politics of sex and drugs and pranks, rooted in a cheeky sense of humor. As playfully rebellious as Merry Mount; as heedless of its consequences as Twain's and Barnum's hoaxes; far wilder and more irreverent than Timothy Leary's later *The Politics of Ecstasy* (1968), the Pranksters' "Vote for Fun" campaign (as it might as well be called) gave rise to an excitable generation that aimed to change the course of world power, and to have an insanely good time doing it.

By 1965, thousands were already on the bus, already in the "pud-ding," throwing in their lots with a noisy youth culture whose soul was somewhere between the Rolling Stones and radical New Left political activists. By 1966, *hundreds* of thousands had achieved at least a good contact buzz. And by the summer of 1967, all hell was breaking loose. Love (as they called it) was in the air, kind of, sure, although so were smoke, anger, drugs, satire, and dangerous levels of factionalism. But if this mostly young, white, middle-class movement had a fuzzy politi-cal agenda, their common target, *cops*—the apparent tip of the estab-lishment's spear—was in clear focus. Police were uniformed, impassive, and armed. Police curtailed the search for absolute freedom in practi-cally every form: free voices that joined in mass protest; free minds that explored psychedelic limits; free bodies that fell out of line and loitered, went vagrant, got naked, had sex in public, and refused to be conscripted into military service. As such, police contested this new youth culture's boundaries, just as the British had those of the Sons of Liberty, and the skirmishes along that disputed border were playful, coaxing, witty, and violent, much as they had been in the 1760s. Increasingly, the skirmish was a good in itself. On the one hand it was proof that the youth were serious and the cops were as tyrannical as they suspected. On the other hand, by 1968, the skirmish in all its forms—protest, satire, pranks, disobedience, as well as hand-to-hand combat—became the practice of liberty. The fight for rights was exhilarating fun. It was the thrill of democracy in action.

When one reads memoirs, journalism, literature, comedy, pam-phlets, history, and court cases from the 1960s, when one watches the movies and listens to the songs of one of the nation's most culturally rich eras, the popular story comes into focus, as does its place in the his-tory of fun. Yes, America's largest, most prosperous generation to date resisted and often rejected their parents, the "Greatest Generation" that had fought in World War II and revived U.S. patriotism. Many ran away from home, dropped out of school, got high, got lost, and followed the cues of demagogues and charismatic radicals into what came to be called the "counterculture"—radicals like, for one, Ken Kesey. En masse, but in different and colorfully imaginative ways, they raised arms against the "establishment" that their parents' generation seemed to embrace: the seemingly hydra-headed power structure that encompassed everything from banks and corporations to the U.S. military, organized religion, big media, university administrations, all forms of government, and even, as the decade got wilder, radical political organizations. This David-and-Goliath struggle, to the extent that it was one, became the latest reprise of Merry Mount's rivalry with the militant stodginess of Plymouth Plantation. In it, fun was more than a liberating practice or a widespread communal value—though of course it was both of those things too. More than ever, more pointedly than even during the Jazz Age, fun was conceived as both a civic practice and a sort of paramilitary tactic. And more than any time since the American Revolution, fun—*raw* fun, risky and rebellious—was overtly linked to patriotism.

But patriotism itself had to be recovered. In love with a different "nation" than their parents had been, Thomas Morton's latest descendants weren't loyal to institutions that had to be defended by military force. They weren't true to government or business. These latest patriots, often with naïve and reckless exuberance, rose up in support of the Declaration of Independence's wild ideals—a pursuit of happiness and national felicity for the individual and collective alike. From Ken Kesey's "Vote for Fun" to Jimi Hendrix's deconstruction of the "Star Spangled Banner" at Woodstock (1969), these flag-waving, flag-wearing, flag-burning citizens voiced their loyalty to an unsung America of rebels, merrymakers, outlaws, and freaks.


THE MERRY PRANKSTERS' new American rebellion didn't appear ex nihilo: the ice had already been cracking for some time.

Twenty years earlier, during World War II, a culturally conservative freeze had set in. The Zoot Suit Riots were just a warning shot: that same month, June 1943, California governor Earl Warren ordered 110,000 Japanese evicted from their homes and relocated into internment camps, arguing, "We don't propose to have the Japs back in California during this war if there is any lawful means of preventing it." He urged other governors to follow his lead. By contrast, the early forties had been a watershed era for the rights of women, whose decades of social and political progress had worked in concert with national need; all at once they were regarded as essential wartime personnel—especially in the distinctly unladylike field of heavy manufacturing. The free-spirited flapper had paved the way for her muscle-bound daughter, Rosie the Riveter, the socialist-realist icon for a multiracial workforce of tough and capable independent women. But shortly after the United States ended the war—by expediently vaporizing two Japanese cities—the nation's love affair with women's labor ended.

Over the next two years, the early baby boom years, two million women were summarily fired. Over the next five years, not coincidentally, the number of new houses built annually increased more than twelvefold, from 114,000 in 1944 to 1.7 million in 1950; this progress was accelerated by the likes of Bill Levitt, a Long Island subdivision entrepreneur whose elimination of skilled labor in favor of non-union workers and whose elimination of complicated basements in favor of mass-produced concrete slabs helped to generate "Levittowns," suburban human parking lots with minimal public space ("one swimming pool was built for every thousand houses") that could accommodate 80,000 inhabitants at a pop. The result, in general, was a cookie-cutter culture wired for prosperity and gender division. The middle class had come into its own, with all the exigencies of suburban mediocrity. Men in suits, enjoying the machine-made "freedom" of Herbert Marcuse's uncritically minded "one-dimensional" society, rode shiny new escalators through middle management's middle floors while women, now housebound, took conservative advice from recently empowered guides like *McCall's, Good Housekeeping,* and *Ladies' Home Journal:* they wore feminized styles, devoted themselves to high-output child rearing, and gratefully endorsed new labor-saving devices like clothes dryers, garbage disposals, dishwashers, vacuum cleaners, trash compactors. No longer socially acceptable wage earners, women became the vanguards of a new consumerism. The Airstream contours of a capitalist republic called for team-spirited conventionalism: millions of homes had tiny-screen televisions playing vaudeville's latest incarnation, and garages and carports housed late-model automobiles.

A paranoid new patriotic trend—which had been codified as early as 1939, when an archconservative representative from Texas created the Special Committee on Un-American Activities (soon to become the notorious HUAC)—made "American" (read "capitalist") an ideological imperative. After World War II, assisted by the virulently anti-communist Truman Doctrine (that required government on all levels to create loyalty review boards), by a crushing 1946 Republican victory in both houses of Congress, and by widespread wiretapping under FBI director J. Edgar Hoover, the national consciousness was seized by fear of freedom haters both foreign and domestic—a fear that touched every level of government and society and that those who witnessed it frequently described, in the words of the Red-scare historian Ellen Schrecker, as "paranoia, delirium, frenzy, hysteria."

In 1947, the languishing HUAC was energized by an incoming class of young Republicans, chief among them Richard M. Nixon, who staged an investigation of the culture industry. Naturally Hollywood was their highest-value target. The movie moguls, who had grown increasingly unnerved by their industry's worker guilds, played right into their hands. Better than anyone, they knew the public imagination: much as they had co-opted the "decency" wars over the previous two decades (disingenuously censoring their own palpitating flappers for threatening America's delicate morality), so too did they betray their own writers and actors—Communist, former Communist, or just suspicious—for smuggling left-wing and Soviet-sympathizing propaganda into the nation's innocent playtime. True to form, they sold them out in a spectacular way. The red-baiting Motion Picture Alliance for the Preservation of American Ideals (MPAPAI) served a list of suspected Communist sympathizers to the HUAC, which that September subpoenaed forty-three witnesses for a media-blitzed hearing in Washington, D.C. Hollywood was represented by high-profile "friendlies" (conservatives like Ronald Reagan, Jack Warner, and Walt Disney, who testified against his own subversive cartoonists for trying to paint even Mickey Mouse red) and a defiant band of nineteen "unfriendlies," ten of whom—the infamous "Hollywood Ten"—refused to take the Fifth Amendment, believing they were protected by their right to free speech. They ended up serving time in prison, to the destruction of their careers and the general suppression of

American filmmakers' creativity. In November of that year, Hollywood's executives and their New York financiers met at the Waldorf Astoria Hotel, where they devised the "blacklist" that would govern moviemaking for more than a decade and usher in the vicious age of Senator Joe McCarthy's witch hunts.

While the economy boomed, thanks in large part to America's first big ideological war in the Pacific, a small group of queers, bisexuals, college dropouts, carpetbagging Buddhists, and autodidactic intellectuals crisscrossed the continent in search of real fun. They came to be known as the Beat Generation, though they were little more than a roving clique. Energized by the sheer spontaneity of bebop; exhilarated by Benzedrine, marijuana, and booze; outraged by their government's Cold War xenophobia; and enthralled by their libertine friend Neal Cassady, who had slept with many of the beats and their wives, these renegades chased restless, kinetic new joys and stamped them in the titles of their trademark books: *Go, Howl, On the Road.* For Jack Kerouac, in his disgust with U.S. law and order, Mexico City was the Xanadu of fun: "This was the great and final wild uninhibited Fellahin-childlike city that we knew we would find at the end of the road." Such fun was a vanishing point for the beats, and it would kill more than one of those who tried to reach it, but even their car crashes, overdoses, and deadly enthusiasm are quaint, exuberant, even innocent—in contrast to the 1960s counterculture they came to inspire. Fittingly, Neal Cassady himself drove the Pranksters' bus.

The Merry Pranksters also grew from rock 'n' roll—the latest iteration of African-American dance music whose rhythm and message sprang from the hips. In 1950s America, safe and sound in air-conditioned suburbia, congregating at amusement parks and drive-ins, middle-class teens guzzled American prosperity and strutted their youth in a runway show of styles, slang, and backbeat music. Their parents tried to contain the fallout radiating from Elvis Presley's hips—chaperoning sock hops and hosting basement dance parties, packaging it through Dick Clark's weirdly stiff *American Bandstand*—but the randy energy of rock 'n' roll had poisoned the country like Bikini Atoll. *Rebel Without a Cause* (1955) created Elvis, who had memorized every line of James Dean's dialogue and studiously mimicked his clothes and walk. (To cultivate his rebellious neo-soap-locks look, Elvis also mimicked "cross-country truckers," whom he called "wild-looking guys," moved his body like black bluesmen, and bought flashy clothes from a black store on Beale Street.) But the movie gave Americans in general, not only enterprising young Elvis, a glossary for reading this troubling new fun. (Even Jack Kerouac was called a "literary James Dean" in *Time*'s 1957 review of *On the Road*.) On the one hand, by glamorizing greaser culture, *Rebel* branded switchblade duels and "chickie runs" (a deadly combination of drag racing and chicken that the movie served to popularize) as "kicks" that could turn young Natalie Wood into a fountain of surging hormones. On the other hand, however—by James Dean's angsty/playful example—it popularized a silly, carefree honesty that Sal Mineo's character, Plato, calls "fun." This latter fun, had by our three heroes in an abandoned mansion—on the run from their parents, the hoodlums, and the law—momentarily frees these bewildered kids from the fakey manners of the Eisenhower era. With its bright-eyed innocence, this lighthearted fun seems centuries away from the pants-down decadence of the late 1960s, but it was in fact in the whirl of such James Dean carnival, at Gregg's Drive-In in Springfield, Oregon, that young Ken Kesey's legendary pranksterism first appeared. Prosecuted for sticking a potato into some killjoy's exhaust pipe, he explained himself in court with a spirited defense of the exhilarating American Saturday night.

Ken Kesey wasn't your average political activist. Like Thomas Morton holing up thirty miles north of Plymouth Plantation's solemn religious experiment, Kesey ran a South Bay den of iniquity while the students at Berkeley were getting serious—in particular, in 1964, taking on the University of California Regents and forming the powerful Free Speech Movement (FSM). Kesey had a different take on his revolutionary times. The Students for a Democratic Society (SDS), founded in 1960 at the University of Michigan, branched out among the nation's campuses to promote what its influential "Port Huron Statement" (1962) called "participatory democracy" and the people's "unfulfilled capacities for reason, freedom, and love." They devised and debated new, revolutionary, political theories, and they valued the university's capacity for conflict, saying that students and faculty "must make debate and controversy, not dull pedantic cant, the common style for educational life." Their leaders were good students in suits and ties who wanted to work within the system. (Their more popular archenemies were the Young Americans for Freedom [YAF], founded by young conservative William F. Buckley.) And most important, the civil rights movement, which had exploded in 1955 following Emmett Till's grisly murder, overcame setbacks, hatred, and violence through extraordinary self-control. Its member organizations maintained a steady regime of protests, marches, and voter registration campaigns—not stopping when they had achieved the Civil Rights Act of 1964, which legislated equal rights for women and blacks. These movements were principled and serious. Martin Luther King, a sober and religious race leader in the line of Frederick Douglass and W. E. B. DuBois, believed civic and legislative rights were greater and more enduring than personal freedoms. He demanded strict moral discipline from the movement, and he got it—as would Malcolm X, whose 1965 *Autobiography* was the story of a zoot suiter's reform.

Kesey? Not so much. He was all *about* personal freedom. Like many of the young white men who would form the sixties counterculture, his basic political rights were secure. In the spirit of the rebel *without* a cause, Kesey took pleasure in rebellion proper—against bugbears of authoritarianism and narrow-mindedness—and flew off in search of *absolute* American liberty: sex, drugs, rock 'n' roll, bullhorns.

A talented young actor and wrestler, Ken Kesey came to Stanford University's Writing Seminars in 1958 and moved with his wife, Faye, a fellow working-class Oregonian, into the woodsy enclave of Perry Lane, the same bastion of bohemian exclusivity where Thorstein Veblen had lived at the turn of the century. Kesey, with his junky dooryard and bad table manners, finally alienated the colony's tweedy elite when, in the fall of 1959, he participated in CIA-funded laboratory experiments with LSD, a drug unheard-of by the rest of world, then passed it around among his neighbors. The history of American fun often entails forbidden booze. At Merry Mount, on the wharf, in the Wild West, in speakeasies during Prohibition, alcohol is the illicit social liberator that puts people in the mood for dancing and pranks. Cocaine had amped up the hip jazz crowd; marijuana was popular among mid-twentieth-century Mexican Americans and beats. But the designer drug Kesey brought home to Perry Lane, and which attracted curious hipsters from all around Northern California (Allen Ginsberg, Neal Cassady, Robert Stone, Larry McMurtry, and Jerry Garcia were among the now-familiar names), was proof that rebellious American pleasure had entered the nuclear age. To the acid taker, its benefits seemed limitless. As a passport to lunacy and cosmic amusement, it left alcohol to a quainter time. Kesey was eager to get its message into the world. He served it to guests in his venison chili.

With the proceeds from his first novel, *One Flew over the Cuckoo's Nest*, the weirder passages of which he wrote on LSD, Kesey established his own psychedelic Merry Mount, in a redwood forest outside the "Wilde West" town of La Honda. He equipped his log-cabin lodge for wild parties and guided head trips into the woods, where loudspeakers, light shows, and avant-garde "Funk Art"—like the copulating male and female sculptures that orgasmed with garden hoses—anticipated the 360-degree "happenings" that would typify the coming era. Among the dropouts, drifters, writers, and heads who answered Kesey's open invitation, Kenneth Babbs—an honors English major and an NCAA basketball star who most recently had flown choppers for the Marines in Vietnam—"introduced the idea of *pranks*," writes Tom Wolfe, "great public put-ons they could perform." The American institution of pranks, which dated back to the scroll of lascivious verse that Morton tacked up for Plymouth's delectation, was just the trick for rousing a nation lulled to stupor by professionalism and obedience. But it was one thing to keep shocking the rustic folks of La Honda, another altogether to take their show on the road and electrify the keyed-up U.S. citizenry. With the introduction of a 1939 school bus, every inch of it painted with Day-Glo mischief, wired inside and out with microphones and loudspeakers for an ongoing dialogue with clueless America, what began as a road trip to New York City, where Kesey's second novel was being released, was transformed into a "superprank."

They startled pedestrians and gas station attendants with flamboyant costumes and bemusing nicknames—Hassler, Dis-Mount, Lord

Byron Styrofoam. Kesey wore a pink miniskirt, pink socks, and pink shades and wrapped his head in Old Glory to become "Captain Flag"; he demanded salutes along the Jersey Turnpike. Cassady, the lead-foot chauffeur, was "Sir Speed Limit." They staged impromptu games with red rubber balls and "tootled" passersby with flutes from the roof of their bus, interpreting their expressions with merry riffs. Inside the bus, among the Pranksters themselves, their only edict was to *"go with the flow"* and let each have his or her own trip—even if that meant going clinically insane, as happened to a couple of them. Most of them, however, just rode the white water. On Lake Pontchartrain, New Orleans, they haplessly stopped at a segregated black beach, where the Prankster named Zonker was nearly trounced for being white (his wide, tripping grin saved his hide) and where a crowd of blacks surrounded the bus for an impromptu party, "doing rock dances and the dirty boogie" to a blaring Jimmy Smith record—until the cops shoved the bus along. And in Millbrook, New York, paying a highly anticipated visit to Timothy Leary's League for Spiritual Discovery, they encountered a surprising culture clash. Expecting a summit of the nation's (microscopic) psychedelic community, they arrived at the peaceful upstate retreat in a torrent of American flags and loud rock. But they could have been crashing Plymouth Plantation for all the warmth in the LSD's welcome. Leary, who had been kicked off Harvard's faculty for turning students on to acid, was taking a contemplative three-day trip and would meet only with the celebrated Cassady. His followers regarded them with beatific dismay. Ignoring the chilly reception, Babbs elbowed in and led everyone on "the first annual tour of the Prankster's Ancestral Mansion." West Coast fun was coming home to roost. Or as Leary's colleague Richard Alpert (aka Baba Ram Dass) expressed it at the time: "I feel like we're a pastoral Indian village invaded by a whooping cowboy band of Wild West saloon carousers."

As far as the Pranksters were concerned, Leary and his followers were establishment types just playing another social "game." The Pranksters wanted to change the game—as quickly and as often as they pleased. All that mattered was that they stayed "out-front." So long as they were as frank and freaky as their most natural selves, they permitted themselves—and each other—to be as rude as they pleased, fostering a roughneck sense of civility that was as old as the California hills. This rollicking attitude liberated these youths as much as their drugs did.

In the culturally uptight year of 1964, the Pranksters' mere existence was a prank. The powder in their rifles, of course, was LSD, gunpowder which they wanted to give to the natives. And even though their drug hadn't yet been made illegal, they enjoyed a de facto outlaw status. Not long after the Pranksters returned to La Honda, cops and Feds staked out their compound, providing a new source of childish amusement. A sign on the lodge called the chief narc by name: "We're Clean, Willie!" Communiqués were sent over loudspeakers in the woods. "It was fun," Wolfe writes, "the cop game." Even the raid, when it happened, was "high farce, an *opéra bouffe*," full of great setups for comebacks and wisecracks. Kesey may or may not have been caught flushing some marijuana, but fourteen of them were arrested all the same, mostly for satirically resisting arrest. The upshot was a wave of sympathetic publicity among San Francisco's embryonic counterculture—for whom Kesey became a "hipster Christ" and "modern mystic." In the tense months to come, awaiting his trial, unwilling to lie low, he posted a red-white-and-blue banner across the entrance to his property, stating, "THE MERRY PRANKSTERS WELCOME THE HELL'S ANGELS." It hailed what would become a three-day blowout.

On August 7, 1965, the infamously violent and racist biker gang, some of whom Kesey had met through Hunter S. Thompson, came rumbling into La Honda past ten flashing squad cars and were greeted by a crowd of Perry Lane regulars, along with curious Bay Area intellectuals like Alpert and Allen Ginsberg. But the meeting wasn't frosty like the Ancestral Mansion tour. When the beer got flowing—and then the LSD, which the Angels were encountering for the first time—it better resembled the miners' ball that J. D. Borthwick observed at Angels Camp. Sidestepping all their cultural, ethnic, and ethical conflicts, the bands of outlaws locked (figurative) elbows and had a rowdy California frolic. The Pranksters even joshed the Angels, who found it refreshing. Lord Byron Styrofoam ad-libbed a fifty-stanza blues, and eventually everyone was joining in the chorus:

Oh, but it's great to be an Angel,
And be dirty all the time!

And what fun it was to be an outlaw, with cops and Feds surrounding your premises and thousands more Americans starting to get the joke.


THE MERRY PRANKSTERS WEREN'T the era's *premier* pranksters— that distinction goes to the San Francisco Mime Troupe. This so-called street theater company, started in 1959 by R. G. Davis, was a funmakers' training camp for the as-yet unchristened Haight-Ashbury district. Put off by commercial theater and what he called "the inordinate boredom of middle-class life," Ron Davis, a political activist from Ohio University, combined his leftist beliefs, his stateside training in modern dance, and his French training in traditional mime to found an improvisational and radically participatory new American drama. In the spring of 1960, he quit as assistant director of San Francisco's groundbreaking Actor's Workshop (convinced that they had sold out by accepting a Ford grant) and revived the Renaissance form of commedia dell'arte, originally a "working-class" drama that, as he described it, "pleased its audience by farting and belching at the stuffier stuffed classes." Appropriately, commedia, with its grotesque masks and satire, had also taught Thomas Morton his best tricks.

If Morton tailored the commedia to suit his New World conditions, the Mime Troupe repurposed its sixteenth-century scripts to surprise even post-beat San Franciscans—turning, for instance, bubbly medieval rounds into Mexican political songs. Many of their techniques were fashioned from early jazz. Like Buddy Bolden's dance-based music, they kept an ongoing dialogue with the audience, which Davis called their "guinea pig." And they played the commedia's characteristic *"lazzi"* (stock comic routines) like "riff[s] of jazz from show to show," reinventing them each time with new stunts and pratfalls. Improvisation and what Davis called "participatory fun" were essential to both street theater and jazz. In both art forms, "riffs or bits and gags are played out" according to "intuition and feel," and the crowd's reactions drive the performance. The Mime

Troupe began their show as they assembled their wooden stage; they also included the audience in their warm-up exercises, blurring, then erasing, the line of spectatorship. To clinch the deal, their performances were free, a feature that guaranteed a big bohemian following.

Their first outdoor performances were held in Golden Gate Park, at the mercy of the Park Commission, whose censorship they routinely ignored. By the summer of 1965, however, when their reputation for causing trouble rose with the tide of political unrest, the commission was paying much closer attention and closed Giordano Bruno's *Il Candelaio* (1582) after three performances, calling it "indecent, obscene, and offensive." Not entirely persuaded, the troupe widely advertised a fourth performance that drew a crowd of more than a thousand. Strangely, they hadn't erected a stage. Davis, dressed in character as Brighella, announced that the permit had been revoked, engaged the crowd in a lively debate, and started the show as such: "Ladieeeees and Gentlemen, Il Troupo di Mimo di San Francisco, presents for your enjoyment this afternoon . . . AN ARREST!" He leapt with a flourish, was arrested as promised, and " 'guerrilla theatre' was born."

The Mime Troupe's theatrical acts of rebellion were right in step with the season. Adding teeth (and a grin) to the radical politics of Berkeley's FSM and the straitlaced SDS (with whom the troupe shared a Howard Street loft); marrying Lenny Bruce ribaldry with the fun-loving audacity of the long-haired, costumed, and free-living "hippies" (who had only recently discovered the Haight-Ashbury's surplus of cheap, colorful Victorian mansions), these populist entertainers turned willing outlaws would soon become the leaders and gadflies and conscience of a roiling Bay Area counterculture. But they lay low for most of '64 and '65, writing scripts and leisurely rehearsing plays while the rest of the world seemed to catch fire. While: race riots sparked off in Rochester, Philadelphia, Cleveland, Los Angeles, and elsewhere. While: U.S. troops dropped bombs on Vietnam. While: Bob Dylan went electric, the Beatles discovered sitars, and an amateur chemist named Augustus "Owsley" Stanley III, living in Berkeley, allegedly cooked up enough LSD to turn on San Francisco's every man, woman, and child—twice.

Pine Street, where the Haight-Ashbury community began, was home to freaks in nineteenth-century dress. They reactivated their mansions' gaslights. They smoked (and dealt) marijuana. But that was about it. In early 1965, nightlife was scarce; Tracy's Donuts was where you went for food. So it almost makes sense that a contingent of young anachronists, following an art band called the Charlatans, pioneers of psychedelic music and style, should have decamped to Virginia City, Nevada—Mark Twain and Dan De Quille's old Comstock Lode haunts—where a Berkeley beat named Chan Laughlin had opened the red-velvet Red Dog Saloon, devoted to campy Wild West fun. "This is an Old Western town," Laughlin told his crowd, "and we're more Old Western than anybody else. Remember when your feet hit the floor in the morning, you're in a Grade B movie."

Freaks flocked in from states away. Milan Melvin remembered it as "an outlaw enclave" for an "eclectic mixture" of the new western riffraff: "revolutionaries, outlaws, hustlers and hookers and go-go dancers and anarchists and beatniks and musicians and Indians. You know, quality people. People you could trust." The Red Dog scenesters got deep into their roles—they shot jiggers of bourbon and stray jackass rabbits; the men wore chaps, the women wore garters, and the vivacious chanteuse Lynn Hughes served as the saloon's official "Miss Kitty." The Charlatans, whose acid rock blended early blues with Appalachian old-time folk, may have been the most deliberate of them all. With their cowboy garb and rough demeanor, they openly defied the British Invasion vogue being slavishly followed by their contemporaries: "We knew we were American, so we decided to be . . . American."

The Red Dog's adherents were the avant-garde of 1965: they were high at all times and held legendary Monday-night LSD parties that attracted bands from up and down the coast. They advertised with drippy art nouveau posters and inaugurated Bill Ham's sound-sensitive "lightbox," a contraption that used colored lights and a chicken rotisserie to splash trippy prismatic designs on the walls. And yet to maintain that *1860s* Washoe thrill, they also went around lethally armed, from the pistol-packing bartenders to the rifle-toting Charlatans; for a couple of weeks that summer, Mark Unobsky, the saloon's proprietor, paid everyone's wages in firearms. Their arsenal notwithstanding, however, the Red

Dog's band of longhair outlaws was genial, jovial, and self-regulating. "The bottom line," Laughlin recalled, "is that almost nobody started any trouble, and very, very few persisted after Washoe Mike [Jones]"—the massive but gentle Native American bouncer, dressed in a purple velvet sash and black top hat—"pointed out to them the benefits of being peaceful."

Like the Pranksters and the Mime Troupe and the countless new communes springing up all across America, the Red Dog crowd was one more "tribe" that banded together in the name of freedom. Doyle Nance, a resident carpenter, said the participants came "from all phases of life" and made the place itself "a fireball. . . . You come inside the Red Dog Saloon and you just *knew* you'd entered someplace that was completely different." But Virginia City was still the Old West, so when some Nevada teens were caught with marijuana, the California interlopers fell out of favor. And when one of their number was seen in the street portaging an armload of guns, V.C. sent its calling card: a tombstone decorated with the managers' names. Late that savage summer, after a visit from the Merry Pranksters, who brought along one of their own trademark happenings (what they were now calling "acid tests"), the Red Dogs followed in Mark Twain's footsteps: skulking off in fear to San Francisco.

Back on Pine Street, four Red Dog alumni, living in what they called the "Dog House," kept the Virginia City scene humming by hosting weekly "Tribute" dances at Longshoreman's Hall near Fisherman's Wharf. Their parents provided the seed money; they called themselves "the Family Dog." For the inaugural dance—a tribute to Marvel Comics hero Dr. Strange—they booked the Charlatans (who performed in dusty Comstock style), two new mod bands called the Great Society and Jefferson Airplane, and a satirical DJ called "the Moose" to serve as the evening's MC. It was a rock show that starred its theatrical audience: costumed kids mingling with Hell's Angels and Allen Ginsberg and inventing snaky, trippy new dances. The second dance party, "A Tribute to Sparkle Plenty," was just as fun and peaceable and weird; the Airplane didn't perform, but they showed up on acid, as did Jerry Garcia's band, the Warlocks, angling to get booked for future events. The third dance,

"A Tribute to Ming the Merciless," resulted in broken windows and teen-age fisticuffs while Frank Zappa, leading his L.A. band, the Mothers of Invention, "improvised lyrics about the fights on the floor."

But that same night, November 6, 1965, a much more significant event went down in the Mime Troupe's scruffy practice loft. Five days earlier, Ron Davis had been found guilty for the truncated *Il Candelaio* performance, a conviction that added to their financial woes, so their business manager, a talented young businessman named Bill Graham, who had spent his childhood fleeing the Nazis, cruised the streets in a rented white Cadillac and pamphleted a festive "Appeal" for the troupe, a rock show starring the Airplane and the Fugs that was all the sexier for its anti-censorship cause. Outside the warehouse, hopefuls snaked around the block. At the door they were met by a sliding donation scale—from $48 (for the affluent) down to just anything (for the broke). Inside the loft, the walls were Day-Glo, donated fruit dangled from the ceiling, art films were "liquid" projected onto hanging bedsheets, and as the Haight-Ashbury historian Charles Perry puts it, hundreds of "people who'd never heard of the Family Dog dances or Kesey's acid parties came out and experienced the same wide-eyed, unforeseeable freedom to act as strange as they felt." The Appeal "represented," as Bill Graham remembered it, "the artistic community coming together"—the writ-ers, artists, actors, jazz and rock musicians, all of San Francisco's sun-dry scenes; at the time he had also exclaimed: "*This* is the business of the future!" Davis remembers Graham being "slightly hysterical about collecting this money." The cops tried to shut it down at twelve, but Graham, in all his cocksure diplomacy, fibbed that the crowd was still waiting for Rudy Vallee and Frank Sinatra; he then bartered with the crowd to give up their places to the hopefuls waiting outside. As such, he kept it jumping till dawn, when Allen Ginsberg led the cleanup crew in a few kitchen-yoga mantras.

The Appeal broadened the base of countercultural fun. SDS activists met folkies and hippies, and everybody felt the acid-test vibrations that would shake like earthquakes in the months and years to come. More profoundly, however, it marked Bill Graham's debut as the P. T. Barnum of psychedelia. The next month he held a much a bigger appeal—"for

Continued Freedom in the Arts"—at the capacious Fillmore music hall in the mostly African-American Fillmore district. And in January 1966, he promoted the Pranksters' gaudy "Trips Festival"—a two-night, three-ring acid test. The Trips Festival handbills read like Mime Troupe (even SDS) boilerplate, announcing "a more jubilant occasion where the audience PARTICIPATES because it's more fun to do so than not. . . . Audience dancing is an assumed part of all the shows, and the audience is invited to wear ECSTATIC DRESS and bring their own GADGETS." "Maybe," the handbill mused, "this is the ROCK REVOLUTION." It was likewise the culmination of the Pranksters' master plan (to freak out as many Americans as possible), but Graham wasn't looking for trouble. The festival was billed as a "non-drug recreation of a psychedelic experience." Still, it was a Prankster event. The light shows, op-art, Thunder Machines, acid rock, and six thousand open-minded participants rather begged for LSD—which California had outlawed months before. So if you wanted it, it was in the ice cream.

And the festival *did* offer participatory fun, just like the poster said. A mob the size of a midwestern town wore self-expressive costumes, danced improvised dances, dropped acid, spoke into randomly distributed microphones (when they weren't being hogged by Babbs and Cassady), and got a taste of the Prankster and Red Dog scenes. The message was that fun and expression are one, but in fact the array of weirdish attractions better resembled Barnum's traveling show, where paying customers gaped in awe at the wonders of the world—at bands, at spectacles, at Stewart Brand's multimedia piece *America Needs Indians,* the Native American awareness show that had become a staple of the acid tests. Much of the spontaneity and danger was canned; only the freaks were real. Jerry Garcia described it as "old home week" for "every beatnik, every hippie, every coffeehouse hangout person from all over the state," all of whom were "freshly psychedelicized," some of whom were "jumping off balconies into blankets and then bouncing up and down." Kesey, who had been convicted only days before for the La Honda bust, was forbidden by the judge (and by Graham) to attend. Naturally, he attended anyway, wearing "a gold lamé space suit with a helmet." A scene described by Charles Perry, Graham, and others suggests a changing of

The Trips Festival's psychedelic fun with toilet paper and drugs in San Francisco's Longshoreman's Hall, January 1966. (Courtesy of Gene Anthony, © Wolfgang's Vault.)

the counterculture's guard. When Graham caught Kesey at the back of the hall, giving free admission to some Hell's Angels cronies, he let him have it: " 'Goddamn son of a bitch, I'm busting my fucking balls out here to make a dime and you—' Kesey simply closed his bubble helmet." As Kesey recalled, "It was one of those balanced-up helmets. I just nodded and it went *plop*."

It was Kesey's last stand. He bolted to Mexico to beat his drug charge. But Graham, who had turned the biggest profit of his life, was only getting settled. Within a month he had held his last Mime Troupe benefit and was staging for-profit shows at the Fillmore, under the Barnumesque title "Bill Graham Presents." Following a marketing strategy that hadn't missed a step since the Gilded Age, Graham seized on the vogue for Day-Glo art nouveau posters and sound-and-light spectacles. It was Chanfrau's "Mose" franchise all over again: Graham repackaged the latest California fun in an on-the-spot Wild West show. The big magazines and television played right into his hands, inadvertently advertising the far-out hippie scene and making San Francisco, over the next three years, the preferred destination for America's restless youth. Along with the head shops and other Haight Street storefronts, the constant rock shows at the legendary Fillmore—and at Red Dog Chet Helms's Avalon Ballroom—turned the counterculture into big business. With similar alacrity, as they had with bootlegging during Prohibition, crime syndicates bullied into the hippies' pot market, and Owsley, who still owned the LSD game, was branching out to Los Angeles, New York, and elsewhere. Whatever the rebellious origins of these pleasures, they were quickly becoming mass entertainment.

IN THE SPRING of 1966, while new white argonauts poured into the Haight, the Mime Troupe rehearsed its most disruptive prank yet. They wanted a break from sixteenth-century Italy; they wanted to do an all-American show. They ran a stunningly tone-deaf attack on stereotypes called *A Minstrel Show: Civil Rights in a Cracker Barrel.* Ron Davis got the idea when he discovered "that minstrel shows were a part of our cultural heritage from 1830 to 1920 and, at its peak, there were three hundred floating companies, from town to city, amateur and professional." As usual, he *meant* to stun: "We were not for the suppression of differences," he explained. "Rather, by exaggerating the differences we punctured the cataracts of 'color blind' liberals, disrupted 'progressive' consciousness and made people think twice about eating watermelon." In other words, whereas early minstrels used black stereotypes for white entertainment, the Mime Troupe used them to poke fun at whites and what Davis called "tolerance." In both cases, of course, African Americans themselves were simply tools, cartoons—objects, not sources, of biting comedy.

*A Minstrel Show* generated little new material. Most of its jokes, songs, and walk-arounds were lifted wholesale from nineteenth-century playbooks. The show corked up both whites and blacks (there were always four of each on stage), a seeming innovation to "unnerve" the audience and "fuck up their prejudices"; but Barnum's sleight of hand had already been a staple of postbellum minstrelsy, when blackface was the closest black performers could get to legitimate theater, and in neither century did blacks in blackface go far, of course, in fucking up anyone's prejudices. On the contrary, blacks' identity disappeared into blackface: their actual presence was traded for a joke, and in both centuries for jokes that were written by whites. Perhaps more pernicious yet, then, were the Mime Troupe's *new* caricatures and stories, which seemed to update prejudice for the civil rights era. They added an aggressive Black Panther–like "Nigger" and the story of a verbally abusive black "Stud" who picks up a fawning, vulnerable white "Chick." They also resurrected "Uncle Tom," with full knowledge that this fictional figure had been "lambasted" by the civil rights movement; as if by turning him into T. D. Rice's Jim Crow, they made him a "wise conniver" and, in Davis's words, "learned to respect him." The show recounts a comic black history "lesson" that makes revered African Americans (from Crispus Attucks to George Washington Carver to Martin Luther King) the butts of crude and easy jokes. (The lessons behind such slurs and insults never come to light.) At center stage was the white MC, Robert Slattery, not in blackface. And though Davis called him the "thing to be attacked"—"white America in the middle of these screaming, ranting darkies"—he had a "great, mature, stone WASPish face like a fine Clark Kent" and he made "the perfect ringmaster." No ridiculous screaming and ranting for him. Dramatically, symbolically, he kept the old hierarchy firmly intact.

*A Minstrel Show* met with some trouble in its two years on the road. Only two black actors stayed on for the duration; others either failed to meet Davis's standards or were, he implied, just too sensitive. The show was frequently closed on college campuses as it made its first West Coast tour, but only for the script's graphic sexual content. Ironically, its controversy raised its prestige among the "color-blind" progressives it had meant to shock. The Student Nonviolent Coordinating Committee of California, for instance, called it "a courageous and creative act." The ACLU stepped in that September when three of its actors were arrested in Denver. And drama critics welcomed it with rave reviews—not only in the *New York Times* and *The New Yorker* but also in the left-wing *Nation* and *People's World*. White liberals, as it turned out, loved to be shocked, even at the cost of African-American dignity. What's more, it was hip to throw their support behind the vaunted S.F. Mime Troupe. The performance scholar Claudia Orenstein praises the play as offering "an empowering vision of black power . . . rather than merely a derogatory one." (On the contrary, the play embraces the derogatory.) She misses the mark by suggesting that the play "deconstruct[s] and subvert[s] black stereotypes" (it *reconstructs* them), but she also misses the troupe's dark purpose. "People thought we were on their side," Davis wrote in 1975. "People thought it was a civil rights integration show. Not so, we were cutting deeper into prejudices than integration allowed." They were *exacerbating* racial trouble. It was dirty work, but *A Minstrel Show* did it—all in a divisive sense of fun.

*A Minstrel Show* marked only the edge of a chasm between San Francisco's white hipsters and struggling blacks. Despite their attempts to understand each other, they were basically taking different trips. The largely black Fillmore neighborhood borders on the Haight, but the black and hippie communities had little to do with each other; in addition to historic race and class tensions, their needs and values were often opposed. Many blacks resented a young white movement that was bent on mocking, rejecting, and destroying all the middle-class privileges they had yet to achieve: suburban homes, political hegemony, and (perhaps most galling) good education. Hippies called blacks "spades," a hip and allegedly non-derogatory epithet—but an epithet all the same. It was hip for hippies to *appreciate* "spades," kind of like the Mime Troupe did. The journalist Nicholas von Hoffman wrote in 1968, "[T]he hippies use black people as whites always have in America, as the people who are truly affective, emotional, sensual, and uninhibited." For many white hippies, blacks were *real;* they were rebellious company to keep, in theory. But as von Hoffman observed, less than fifty blacks living in the Haight had "become a hippy." And as the sociologist Lewis Yablonsky witnessed at a Haight-Ashbury town hall meeting—where the citizens wore flamboyant costumes; where kids and dogs tussled in the marijuana smoke—*real* black fun could be a tough sell. A well-known black activist named Scooter, joined by a line of thirty black men, stood up to promote tickets for a community dance. He could hardly contain his hostility: "We don't want violence or trouble. But we could have it, baby.

*We want for our kids the things you people have put down. We want good food, jobs, houses, and cars. Dig?* . . . The honkies downtown, the Birchers and the bigots like they're all buying tickets. None of you hip people buy tickets. Don't you love us?" The room applauded, and a few bought tickets (for $1.50—a buck less than a typical Bill Graham ticket), but most people said they were hard up themselves.

On September 27, 1966, in the African-American neighborhood of Hunter's Point, cops chased Matthew Johnson, a black teenager suspected of stealing a car, trapped him against a chain-link fence, and shot him in the back. This murder—and its immediate dismissal by city government—touched off two days of riots and vandalism and a military-style retaliation from the National Guard, 1,200 of whom had been mustered in Candlestick Park. An unseasonable heat wave elevated tensions. The Guard marched and drove tanks down Third Street, soon shooting into buildings with automatic weapons and drawing gunfire, rocks, and bottles from the locals. In the end, 44 were injured, 146 arrested; $100,000 in damage was done, and a citywide curfew was enforced. Just as the hippie community was starting to thrive, the San Francisco black community—like so many others in late 1960s America—was plunged into devastation that would plague it for decades.

In the aftermath of the Hunter's Point riots, SDS and other activist groups staged protests outside the Mission Street Armory. They also marched their cause down Haight Street, waving signs reaching out to the "Psychedelic Community," some of whom heckled their own messages in return: "Go back to school where you belong!" Emmett Grogan, a twenty-two-year-old Duke University dropout from Brooklyn (a Mime Trouper who spuriously claimed the army had discharged him for clinical schizophrenia), was amused to see activists butting heads with Haight-Ashbury merchants over the correct response to the curfew. The activists wanted to make it a cause; the merchants wanted to keep the peace. Grogan, along with Mime Troupers Billy Landout and Peter Berg, preferred to stir up the conflict itself. Letting themselves into the SDS offices to liberate the mimeograph machine, they ran off a series of nose-thumbing screeds that have since been known as the Digger Papers. Maintaining their anonymity (like the Sons of Liberty); pulling pranks in the spirit of Holland's anarchistic Provos and Antonin Artaud's "theatre of cruelty"; naming themselves after seventeenth-century English rebels who "defied the landlords" and "defied the laws" (as the traditional song about them goes) and redistributed food among the poor, these new Diggers deplored private property and reveled in nonviolent disruption. The Digger Papers accosted the general public from telephone poles and storefronts; they called bullshit, usually with excellent humor, on everyone from the Learyites' *Oracle* to the Berkeley-based radical activists. The most commonly reproduced Digger Paper, called "Take a Cop to Dinner," burlesqued a campaign by Haight Street's commercial association (HIP) urging hippies to sit down and eat with the cops. It accused all of society—"Pimps," "Racketeers," drug dealers, the "Catholic Church," "Establishment newspapers," et cetera—of pandering to the police. Its joke was built on parallel structure:

> Places of entertainment take cops to dinner with free booze and admission to shows.
> Merchants take cops to dinner with discounts and gifts.
> Neighborhood Committees and Social Organizations take cops to dinner with free discussions offering discriminating insights into hipsterism, black militancy and the drug culture.
> Cops take cops to dinner by granting each other immunity to prosecution for misdemeanors and anything else they can get away with.
> Cops take themselves to dinner by inciting riots.

All of the Haight (especially the ridiculed merchants and leaders) wanted to know who the Diggers were, so the Diggers responded in their papers and by personal telegram: "Regarding inquiries concerned with the identity and whereabouts of the DIGGERS: We are happy to report that the DIGGERS are not that."

Within a week the Diggers were backing up their papers with bold community action. Most notably, they tapped San Francisco's food surplus (some stolen, some donated, some day-old leftovers) and prepared ten-gallon milk cans of hot stew and wooden crates of green salad to serve to the rising numbers of street people. It was called "Free Food Theatre," it was passed through a one-story-tall yellow "Frame of Reference," and it happened every day at 4 p.m. under a eucalyptus in the Panhandle. "It's free because it's yours!" pamphlets announced. A hundred or so customers appeared every day, recognizable by their bowls and spoons. Grogan and the others spent their days foraging, and a group of women (some of them Antioch College dropouts) ran the primitive kitchens, in keeping with hippies' typically retrograde gender roles. The *Berkeley Barb,* one of the Bay Area's new radical newspapers, followed the Diggers' operations closely and saw their high spirits and irreverence rub off on the patrons. When a reporter asked who the Diggers were, a girl smiled and responded: "Are you a digger?" Another kid shouted " 'FUCK THE DIGGERS!!!' . . . and everybody laughed and repeated it." They horsed around with apples and stew, shouting "Food as Medium!" But mostly the people got their fill, then passed around their cigarettes. Free food could be counted on every day at four, despite occasional meddling by cops and the Health Department (who were told it was just a "picnic"), but as the numbers of patrons doubled and quadrupled, the Diggers made the hungry work for it—making them chase down their famous gold bus (known around town as the Yellow Submarine) or pry their own dinner from the hot, hammered-shut milk cans. For at bottom these liberators were Mime Troupers, pranksters.

Throughout the fall of 1966, as capitalist horse sense took root in the Haight, the Diggers waged war on private property. Disgusted by condescending "charity," insisting they weren't "helping anybody" but only "doing [their] individual thing," they stepped up their free food efforts; they worked with the Human Switchboard to find free "crashpads" for the homeless, and they turned a six-car garage on Page Street into the first of their "free stores." Named for the empty picture frames left behind in the garage, which they painted and nailed into a puzzling mosaic, The Free Frame of Reference, as the first store was called, posted a surprising policy: Everything is free, and "you're in charge." Everything: kitchen supplies, furniture, knickknacks, books, a surplus of white oxfords that the Diggers tie-dyed, even a box of "free money" in place of a cash register. It was impossible to shoplift; those who tried were instructed to take more. Peter Coyote, who managed the Cole Street free store, called A Trip Without a Ticket, described the Diggers' stores and stunts as effects of their "life acting" philosophy. Their message was unequivocal activity: "The Diggers attracted actors (trained or not) who wanted to employ these skills in their everyday lives, constructing events outside the theater that were 'free,' financially and structurally, so that they might exist outside of conventional expectations and defenses." Any American had to be shocked by their willful anti-consumerism. But Roy Ballard, the twenty-seven-year-old civil rights activist who managed the Fillmore's Black Man's Free Store, took a more practical stance: explaining the hippies' fantastical ideas for restarting their parents' game from scratch, he said "the white kids are more advanced but also less realistic." Of all their theories, pranks, and pipe dreams, only free merchandise made sense to him.

The Free Frame of Reference was the operating base for the Diggers' wild ideas. That Halloween, they moved their yellow frame up the block and staged a show with two nine-foot-tall puppets by the sculptor La Mortadella. Five hundred spectators spilled out into traffic. When the cops failed to break up the crowd, they mirthlessly tried negotiating with the puppets and inadvertently "tickled the people silly." In the end the cops seized the Diggers (their first arrest) and couldn't quite get over the puppets—assuming that they were made to "hurt people." "Will you look at how fuckin' big they are!" Five performers were booked for "creating a public nuisance," but Grogan remembered it as a "fun bust." When the charges were dropped two days later, Grogan, Berg, La Mortadella, and the others were pictured pulling Marx Brothers antics (ass-kicks, obscene European hand gestures) above the fold in the *San Francisco Chronicle*.

On Thanksgiving the Diggers opened their garage doors for a public "Meatfest," and on December 16 they held their Death of Money Parade, a lugubriously fun, full-participation charade in which Mime Troupers (without R. G. Davis's blessing) dressed like reapers, dwarves, and lepers; in which girls in togas passed out pennywhistles and hand signs (reading "Now!") and pallbearers shouldered a black-draped coffin. The Hell's Angels—who had become Haight Street's sometime protectors since the Pranksters had turned them on to acid—provided a rumbling escort. Competing groups led the crowd in nonsense call-and-response: "Oooo!" and "Aaahhh!"; "Ssssh!" and "Be cool!" "A Munibus driver," Grogan remembered, "got out of his coach and danced in the street with a girl, and his passengers disembarked to mix in the fun." And despite the lack of a parade permit, the cops wisely honored the chants of four thousand insistent revelers: "The streets belong to the people! The streets belong to the people!" In the milling aftermath, however, when they busted Angels Hairy Henry and Chocolate George for ostensible parole violations, the crowd marched a noisy candlelight vigil in their favor ("We want Hairy Henry! We want Chocolate George!") and filled the Death of Money casket with bail. Two weeks later, Hell's Angels showed their appreciation by hosting a "New Year's Wail" in the Panhandle— free music, free beer, the first free party of 1967.

Most of the Diggers hailed from New York, but like the forty-niners they administered a California education. For all of their disruptions and childish absurdity, the Diggers were a force for civic good in a generally outlaw society—a subculture of runaways and distracted idealists who exposed themselves to rampant hepatitis, VD, meth addiction, poverty, drug wars, rape, and frequent abuse by pimps (who seized on "free love" teenyboppers), Hell's Angels (who treated weak hippies like servants), the Mafia (who bullied dealers into their drug trade), and, constantly, cops and Feds. Unlike the self-interested Merry Pranksters, the Diggers fought for community values in a rough and improvised society. They organized free food and shelter and arranged for free medical and legal services. "The Digger Papers" offered free ideas on starting everything from free banks and automotive garages to "Balls, Happenings, Theatre, Dance, and spontaneous experiments in joy."

This Haight-Ashbury ethos, this Port Huron–style democracy played out in real time with "spontaneous experiments in joy," metastasized throughout the country during the middle 1960s. More than popular music, itinerant teens, and alarmed reporting from the mainstream media, the "underground press" deserves recognition for disseminating the exciting news. The underground press gave unguarded voice to the ethics, pleasures, habits, styles, and generally leftist politics of the era's urban and

Haight District denizens help Diggers celebrate the "Death of Money,"
December 17, 1966. (Courtesy of Gene Anthony, © Wolfgang's Vault.)

college-town youth cultures. Sold by mail or in the nation's newsstands,
cafés, and head shops (which likewise boomed, not coincidentally, after
America bombed Vietnam), the undergrounds mixed radical politics
with the hip new formulas for public pleasure: folk, rock, free love, gathering, and all the modern ways to get high. Originating in L.A. and the
San Francisco Bay Area but soon spreading to most mid-sized American
towns, cheaply produced and distributed by amateurs—indeed, often
identifying their publications with revolutionary-era broadsheets—these
typically mimeographed "newssheets," as the historian John McMillian
has convincingly argued, espoused an SDS-influenced "participatory
democracy." Their tone, like that of the rude and bawdy "underground
comix" with which they shared a readership, was decidedly irreverent,
reflecting the youth culture from which they sprang. They mimicked
the scrappiness of *Mad Magazine,* one of the 1950s' few mainstream outlets for biting satire and cynicism, and of the lavishly offensive *Realist,* a
perfectly obscene New York magazine that gleefully skewered America's
sacred cows—and whose founder, Paul Krassner, "demand[ed] a blood
test" when accused of fathering the underground press. But even as they

took root in many regions and "scenes," Virginia City's *Territorial Enterprise* was the dominant code in their DNA.

For they made reporting an instrument of fun. More than just satirical opinion papers, they mixed the community-building populism of the 1830s "penny papers" with the out-group pride of the 1860s Washoe papers and supported local countercultural activity; they became what McMillian calls "community switchboards." They fostered the Diggers' lifestyle of "Free." They helped hard-up folks in their teens and twenties track down food, clothing, shelter, wheels, health care, and lawyers. They also provided an open forum for the pursuit of drugs, music, protest, street theater, and all the bare facts of a purely groovy life. The underground papers were crucial to off-the-grid living, and in the summer of 1966 they expanded their reach by forming an "anarchistic organization" called the Underground Press Syndicate, or UPS. This national organ for the "Fuck Censorship press" allowed the undergrounds to swap their materials, inspired twenty-five new newssheets in just half a year, and led to a total national circulation of 250,000 by the start of 1967. The undergrounds aligned themselves with the Sons of Liberty, and they proved to have a similar effect. They helped lefties, hippies, dropouts, and heads form thriving "scenes" across the country.

Fittingly, in the spirit of their nineteenth-century antecedents who refused to take fact-based journalism too seriously, it was one of the original and most influential undergrounds, the *Berkeley Barb,* that authored the 1960s' biggest hoax, the "Electrical Banana." In the *Barb*'s March 3, 1967, issue, Ed Denison, the music columnist, offered a tongue-in-cheek recipe for dried banana peels and suggested that smoking them had a cannabic effect. Denison, also the manager for Country Joe and the Fish, had smoked banana peels with the band a few months earlier; the only effects they had felt, as he well knew, came from the LSD they were taking. His article's recommendation for "50 mg. of acid swallowed" said as much. But the underground press seized on the story, and quickly *Time* and *Newsweek* joined in. Suddenly there was a run on bananas in supermarkets from Berkeley to Cambridge, Massachusetts. In the spring of '67's loamy cultural soil, the rumor sprang up like dandelions. Watering it was Donovan's song "Mellow Yellow," which had been throbbing on the airwaves since January. Its third verse made the cryptic prediction: "E-lec-trical Banana is gonna be a sudden craze, / E-lec-trical Banana is bound to be the very next phase." Even though Donovan would later specify that *his* banana was a yellow vibrator, his phrasing gave the rumor serious weight. And in May, the Velvet Underground's first album, signed *Andy Warhol*, boasted a peel-able banana sticker—though it had been produced too early to be related. Coincidence? Who cared? It all became part of the big banana craze. As with the great Moon Hoax of 1835, or with Dan De Quille's 1867 "The Traveling Stones of Pahrangat Valley" (which fooled geologists in far-off England), the people were too tickled to ask serious questions (banana smoking became a short-lived fad), and the scientists who tested it, like the U.S. Food and Drug Administration, proved themselves to be total squares. To those in the know, sometimes a banana wasn't just a banana. Thus did bananas become the people's icon in the early months of the Summer of Love. Bananas were represented by a half-crooked, half-obscene finger gesture. Bananas inspired a "banana pledge" at the Central Park Be-In. Bananas also provoked U.S. Representative Frank Thompson (D-N.J.) to join the fun and propose the Banana Labeling Act of 1967.

THE DIGGERS BELIEVED spontaneous fun was essential to a free citizenry. They goosed the public with pranks and jokes, and nearly every Sunday over the next couple of years—making good on their protests against Bill Graham and Chet Helms, whose concert halls they often picketed—they employed their skills at outdoor production and staged free concerts in Golden Gate Park, where they always served free food for the masses and featured bands that charged admission at the Fillmore. Reminiscent of the 1760s Stamp Act protests, where citizens of all classes swarmed into the streets to liberate themselves in masquerade, these Sunday gatherings attracted them all: "aborigines, Tonto, Inquisitor-General Torquemada, Shiva holy men, cowboy bikers, every shade of gender bender, flower children, urban junkies, stockbrokers with cautiously expressed face-paint, dentists on dope, real estate agents disguised as flower-children"—as Peter Coyote recalled. But these Sundays in the park didn't protest anything. They simply *were:* the liberated people in all their glory. The first such party, the famed Human Be-In on January 14, 1967, was fortified with five thousand free turkey sandwiches (turkeys courtesy of Owsley Stanley) and what seemed like the lowest-key American fun. A sea of humanity filled the Polo Field in Golden Gate Park for no other reason than just to hang out. Everybody did their own groovy thing—"took drugs, danced, painted their faces, dressed in outrageous costumes, crawled into the bushes and made love, fired up the barbecues, pitched tents, and sold wares—crystals, tie-dyes, hash pipes, earrings, hair ties, and political tracts. Fifty thousand people played flutes, guitars, tambourines, tablas, bongos, congas, sitars, and saxophones, and sang, harmonized, and reveled in their number and variety, aware that they were an emergent social force." Hell's Angels babysat missing children, and afterwards everybody picked up the litter.

Everyone liked the Be-In but the Diggers themselves. It was too white, too commercial (thanks to drug dealers and the Diggers' archenemies, the Haight Independent Proprietors [HIP]), and too stage-focused on celebrities like Timothy Leary, Richard Alpert, and a sensational new radical named Jerry Rubin. (Emmett Grogan called it "the love shuck.") So they planned a weekend-long happening of their own—"The Invisible Circus: The Right of Spring"—to educate the district about having fun. It was advertised by word of mouth and a limited number of psychedelic red pamphlets and slated to start on February 24 at Glide Memorial United Methodist Church on Ellis and Taylor, whose young black minister, Cecil Williams, had been widening his congregation in recent years to accommodate "San Francisco's diverse communities of hippies, addicts, gays, the poor, and the marginalized."

But even this ultra-hip church wasn't ready for what the Diggers and their co-conspirators, the Mime Troupe and the Artists Liberation Front, had in store. The chapel was split up into zones, each one vying to outdo the other in its "improbable and outrageous" activities. The basement hall was piled three feet high in shredded plastic and divided into a free-love recreation room and a cafeteria serving acid-spiked Tang. The church offices became dedicated "love-making salons"—tricked out with mattresses, "lubricants," and dead bolts. A rather stuffy lecture on pornography was interrupted, from behind, by a penis appearing through a glory hole and got much more interesting when a couple was carried in for a live sex demonstration. Naked belly dancers burst in through a paper wall, someone played Chopin's "Death March" on the organ, and revelers and reporters coursed in by the thousands. Congas, laughter, and microphoned voices echoed in the candlelit air; Hell's Angels copulated in the pews with a woman dressed like a nun; prostitutes brought their johns, transvestites coupled, and the writer Richard Brautigan wrote and published "Flash!" bulletins of everything he witnessed, with the help of his "John Dillinger Communication Company" toiling away in the basement. "Several couples," wrote Grogan, who was prone to embellishment, "were draped over the main altar, fucking, as a giant, naked weight lifter towered above them, standing on top of some sort of tabernacle in a beam of light, masturbating and panting himself into a trance."

Grogan praised the "surreal harmony" of this "incredible Fellini wet-dream": "everyone moving, watching, seeing it all, and no one afraid, but laughing joyfully, happy, and then a scream followed by a hushed silence with everything still for a moment until the person who screamed would laugh and give away the joke." Coyote, who was home sick for the Circus, reported from hearsay a similarly surreal sense of harmony: "Permission was the rule, and despite the chaos, the conflagration of taboos and bizarre behavior, no one was hurt, wounded, shunned, or scorned." No one, perhaps, but Glide's dismayed deacons, whose church had been thoroughly defiled and who had been misled as to the nature of the happening. With some help from the cops, Glide doused the party's flames before dawn, at which point the attendees moved their circus to the beach and watched the sunrise in the jittery manner, as one might assume, of the stragglers at the end of *La Dolce Vita*.

Wild fun was had at the Invisible Circus, Merry Mount's blasphemous mission accomplished, and in this extreme case of American fun, Coyote's "safety-valve" metaphor seems perfectly appropriate: "it was simply like letting steam out of a pressure cooker: once accomplished, it was not necessary to repeat."

Some Haight-Ashbury pressure may have broken, but the party was far from over. And from then on out, the Diggers' indefatigably antic spirit didn't always keep the peace, not even at the laid-back Sunday gatherings in the park. By the spring of that year, 1967, when banana peels were smoldering, when resistance to the draft was starting to catch fire, the crowds grew bigger and more intense. Peter Berg, known to fellow Diggers as "the Hun," had recently alerted media outlets that the nation's teens would converge on San Francisco; with this prank, he created what the historian Alice Echols calls the "disastrous Summer of Love"—when the Gray Line Bus Company ran a national "Hippie Hop Tour," when "seventy-five thousand kids spent their summer vacation in the Haight," and when commercialism, addiction, racial tension, and rape ran rampant among the disorganized masses. Some Mime Troupe members, under Berg's leadership, seized on the chance to stir things up. During one of the late-spring parties in the Panhandle, while Janis Joplin played and people got peacefully high on the lawn, the politically moderate young writer Joan Didion observed Peter Berg and others, all in blackface, working the crowd with plastic nightsticks. On their backs they sported antagonistic signs: "HOW MANY TIMES YOU BEEN RAPED, YOU LOVE FREAKS?" and "WHO STOLE CHUCK BERRY'S MUSIC?" They distributed flyers that warned "by august haight street will be a cemetery" because by "summer thousands of un-white un-suburban boppers are going to want to know why you've given up what they can't get." At one point they surrounded an African American, prodded him with nightsticks, and "bar[ed] their teeth." The hostility was lost on one cheery kid, who told Didion that it was a "really groovy" thing called "street theatre," but it wasn't lost on a small group of blacks. One of them said, "Nobody *stole* Chuck Berry's music, man . . . Chuck Berry's music belongs to *every*body." When a blackface girl badgered him about the meaning of "everybody," he responded, simply, "Everybody. In America." In one phrase he accounted for the spread of black fun from the earliest slave circles to events like this one.

But these minstrels weren't interested in *that* kind of fun. They wanted blacks to attack the hippies in the name of economic justice. The blackface girl shot back at the black man: "What'd *America* ever do for you? . . . White kids here, they can sit in the Park all summer long, listening to the music they stole, because their bigshot parents keep send-ing them money. Who ever sends you money?" The black man didn't take the bait; he simply told her such tactics weren't "right." Predict-ably, their prodding came to nothing. For much as *A Minstrel Show* had updated stereotypes for the civil rights era, so did Peter Berg's black-face agitation grossly oversimplify African-American rage. To be sure, it wasn't irritating street theater, it was Matthew Johnson's murder by a cop that had touched off the Hunter's Point riots.

# Revolution for the Hell of It

Tʜᴇ ʏɪᴘᴘɪᴇs, American fun's most notorious activists, found their
soul in underground journalism, in ornery rock 'n' roll, in Che
Guevara's street politics, in Herbert Marcuse's Freudian Marxism, in
Marshall McLuhan's media theory, and in the Mississippi "Freedom
Summer" of 1964. They were also inspired by the Diggers' troublemaking. Like the Artists Liberation Front (founded by Mime Troupe members among others), the Yippies wanted to marry radically democratic
politics with pranks, street theater, disruption, absurdity, and sophisticated media blitzkriegs. Their fun resounded on a global scale.

Kurt Vonnegut called Yippie leader Abbie Hoffman a "holy clown."
Dashing, wild-eyed, raven-haired Hoffman had been (like Kesey) a college wrestler, also a psychology T.A. at Berkeley, a deeply committed
activist in the civil rights movement, and was a divorced father of two
boys when, at age thirty-one, in 1967, he moved in with his new girl-
friend, Anita Kushner, on New York City's Lower East Side. Kushner,
then twenty-five, had also studied psychology, had also worked for the
Student Nonviolent Coordinating Committee (SNCC), and was, in
his words, "a born rascal." Their neighborhood was the center of East
Coast radicalism, and soon the couple became its radical royalty, open-

ing their doors to wayward youths and the likes of needle-popping Janis Joplin. Like the Haight-Ashbury, the Lower East Side drew what Hoffman called the latest "waves of immigrants" into its run-down tenement houses: "They came not by sea, but from within America," and they lived under the same septic conditions. Most of these "immigrants" were disaffected youths, prey to dealers and pimps. The older crowd of activists, like Hoffman and Kushner, mentored them and helped them to get organized. This older crowd also provided free professional services, in an effort to wriggle themselves out of what Hoffman called the "strait jackets" of their careers: "Actors created street theater groups. Lawyers volunteered time for serious busts. Medical students set up a free clinic." Leaders and organizers learned the ways of the street and in turn became "instigators" of hippie "style and values." East Village radicals like the clean-cut Hoffman grew their hair as a sign of resistance, and commitment. Not a costume they could wear on the weekends, bushy hair, as Hoffman saw it, welcomed the kind of abuse typically hurled at blacks and Puerto Ricans. During their early months together in New York, Hoffman, Kushner, and their friends ran a free store that was frequently raided by cops. In California Diggers fashion, they didn't advertise its address; they made interested patrons find it themselves.

In March 1967, they attended Central Park's Be-In, and Hoffman dressed as a gold-painted Easter Bunny. In April they formed a sixteen-member "Flower Brigade" and marched in a pro–Vietnam War parade; trailing a troop of Boy Scouts from Queens, identified only by flowers and flags, they were set upon by a "Flatbush Conservative Club contingent," who punched them, kicked them, spat, hurled beer cans, and—rather quaintly—tore up their flags. In May, they booked a tour of the New York Stock Exchange under the Digger code name George Metesky—New York City's "Mad Bomber" of the forties and fifties. They arrived in a group of eighteen pranksters and showered the trading floor with money that Hoffman had earned as an employee of the city's Youth Board program. His message was that he didn't do such work for the money and that, more important, "money should be abolished." As predicted, they caused a money-grubbing frenzy that briefly stopped the ticker tape. A tourist who had joined them in the prank "got the point":

"I'm from Missouri and I've been throwing away money in New York for five days now. This is sure a hell of lot quicker and more fun."

Hoffman and Kushner got married in Central Park, during New York's own Summer of Love, and were celebrated by three thousand invitees. And on October 21, during the biggest antiwar demonstration of the decade, they joined student leader Jerry Rubin in diverting some two hundred thousand peace activists from the Washington Mall, across the Potomac, and up to the Pentagon. They intended to "levitate" it and "exorcise" its evil spirits. Though this mystical activity had a solemn purpose—complete with witches and Allen Ginsberg's Tibetan bells—Hoffman and friends played up its antic side. Anita dressed as Sgt. Pepper, Abbie as a Native American Uncle Sam, and they distributed two truckloads of "water pistols, smoke bombs, Halloween masks, and noisemakers" among the protesters. The water pistols were loaded with disappearing purple ink, a mystery fluid that, in the months before, they had led the straight press to believe was an on-contact psychedelic aphrodisiac called "Lace"—slyly rhyming with the "Mace" that police had threatened to use on the crowd. America watched with rapt attention: Would they levitate the Pentagon? Would Lace cause the biggest orgy in history? All of their witchcraft and pranks and flowers, however, didn't soften the military's head-bashing response—an armed offensive on the peaceful crowd that they called "the Wedge."

The Yippies were born on New Year's Eve 1967, when Abbie, Anita, Jerry Rubin, Nancy Kurshan, and Paul Krassner—stand-up comic and the illegitimate father of America's underground press—were smoking some high-grade Colombian. Inspired by the Diggers' recent "Death of Hippie" parade, they sought a political identity—or, in Marshall McLuhan's terms, "a myth"—that would captivate the press by capturing their own purely antic spirit. "Yippie!" was a hurl of crazy joy that could be broken down into Y.I.P., or Youth International Party. "We would *be* a party," Krassner wrote, "and we would *have* a party"—"the kind of party you had fun at," Hoffman later told the court. "Yippies say if it's not fun," Rubin wrote, "don't do it." "What does Yippie! mean?" Hoffman asked in his incendiary book *Revolution for the Hell of It.* "Energy—excitement—fun—fierceness—exclamation point!" Years later, when he was on the lam from the Feds, his thoughts on the subject seemed to deepen: Yippies didn't seek the "eternal bliss" at the end of capitalism's rainbow. But nor could he support the utopian bliss he had once witnessed at Antioch College, where ROTC had been banned and students had free rein—communing with teachers, taking drugs, having open sex and "naked swim-ins in the gym pool." He couldn't see the fun in it. "Everything was so beautiful, I was completely bored after three hours. The school lacked the energy that comes from struggle." Yippies pursued the joy of the fray. "With Yippism," he wrote, "the distinction between work and play collapsed. It blended fun with struggle." Yippism courted the *old* American fun: revolutionary struggles, Pinkster Days struggles, argonaut struggles with a reformed middle class. Yippism courted fun *with stakes*.

By contrast, the Merry Pranksters' "Vote for Fun" was an idle threat. To the Yippies, some of whom had risked their lives to register voters in Mississippi, American elections meant serious business—just the kind of high-stakes fun they were looking for. So they set their sights on the 1968 Democratic Convention in Chicago. Ideally, they would finish off a moribund system, and the work would be outrageous fun.

The Yippie! revolution wasn't meant to be violent. Not demagogues like Mike Walsh and Company who sicced their b'hoys on decent society, the Yippies imagined a cavalier revolution by which citizens enjoyed themselves to the fullest and allowed all others to do the same. These anarcho-democratic officiants would have wed American individualism with free-loving communalism. Its love child, had it come out that way, would have been Rubin's "Festival of Life," a shindig that, as they described it to bemused Chicago Park District officials, would feature a free, cooperative gathering in Lincoln Park. Kids would sleep on the grass, enjoy a hundred rock bands and guerrilla performers, and share their food, bodies, ideas, wampum. The Yippies said they had no interest in marching on the convention; the festival's open lifestyle would send its own message. They signed the application, which requested portable kitchens and latrines, "For Fun and Freedom."

But they sent the American media a racier image. If the summer before they had directed traffic to their sexy Lace hoax by inviting reporters to a demonstration (actors squirted each other with Disappear-O and copulated on the spot), now, in anticipation of the convention, Krassner, who had achieved national fame by publishing scandalous JFK material, used a foolproof strategy as their media spokesman: "If you gave good quote, they would give you free publicity." His wisecracks and one-liners spread their message like pollen, sprouting Yippie chapters on the nation's campuses. As unscrupulous as he could be when provoking media, even Krassner opposed Abbie Hoffman's slogan, "Kill your parents!" But Jerry Rubin took it up anyway, and it put his face on the front of the *Enquirer:* "Yippie Leader Tells Children to Kill Their Parents!"

Jokes like this were no joke in the spring of '68, when violent youth revolutions shut down Paris and Prague and the assassination of Martin Luther King Jr., on April 4, caused the decade's most devastating wave of race riots, a major one occurring in Chicago itself. But the Yippies liked needling the public's paranoia. That same month, when asked by Mayor Daley's office why he wanted a street permit, Krassner invoked that season's hippie exploitation movie, *Wild in the Streets,* in which kids spike the water supply with acid and overthrow the government. (This didn't endear Yippies to the Park District.) And yet their political commitment was sincere—and not merely anarchistic. When LBJ dropped out of the presidential race due to unbeatable competition from Robert Kennedy, leaving the Democrats with an antiwar platform, they nearly called off their demonstration. As Abbie Hoffman put it, RFK was "a direct threat to our theater-in-the-streets, a challenge to the charisma of Yippie!" There were even rumors that he had "turned on." But then when he was assassinated in June, leaving the likely candidacy to LBJ's pro-war vice president, Hubert Humphrey (and not to Eugene McCarthy, for whom many left-wing hippies had shaved their beards and gone "Clean for Gene"), Yippie! was back in play. Then, when Humphrey trotted out his "Politics of Joy" slogan, it felt as if they were being scooped. Yippie! pulled out all the stops.

Their publicity tempted the nation's youth with "a huge rock-folk festival for free" that would restage the Pentagon experience in Chicago. As an answer to the Diggers' recent "Death of Hippie" parade, they rakishly promised the "Death of Yippie" ("a huge orgasm of destruction atop a giant media altar"), the birth of "Free America," and promised thirty-some performers and a gamut of constructive activities—"workshops" on drugs, draft resistance, commune building, guerrilla theater, and underground media. They demanded SDS-style participatory politics in theater-of-cruelty language: "It is time to become a life-actor. The days of the audience died with the old America. If you don't have a thing to do, stay home, you'll only get in the way." They admitted that they were still negotiating for a permit and acknowledged the risk of violence: "This is the United States, 1968, remember. If you are afraid of violence you shouldn't have crossed the border." But violence wasn't their bag. Unlike the typical sixties "be-ins," many of which they had organized themselves, the "Festival of Life" promoted active community in which everybody and nobody was a leader. The festival was also presented as a chance for radicals to bury the water pistol with hippies. Oh, and they nominated their own presidential candidate: Pigasus the Immortal, an actual pig purchased from an Illinois farm.

Things didn't go as beautifully as planned. The "Festival of Life" was a fine idea, but an urban war zone between roiling Chicago cops (not the nation's gentlest police force) and revved-up kids from all factions of the movement (Yippies, Black Panthers, SDS, and countless other groups) wasn't conducive to spontaneous peace and love, certainly not without a permit. Only three or four thousand participants showed up—possibly ten thousand at its culmination. The week leading up to the Yippies' abortive festival reads like *Fear and Loathing in Chicago*. The Yippie! "leadership," true to their message, spent the preliminary days "zonked out of their minds" on hash-oil cigarettes that they prepared for general distribution. They also distributed thousands of Yippie Leader buttons. Tailed the whole time in a "slow-motion car chase," they eventually asked their undercover shadows for a friendly restaurant recommendation. While demonstrators arrived from across the country in busloads, their lawyers were still haggling with the city for a permit and Yippies staged the first ad hoc march—delivering "peace offerings of apple pies" to the Lincoln Park precinct office. When the *Chicago Tribune* printed the headline "Secret Yippie Plans Revealed," Hoffman went them one better and mass-distributed leaked information about the delegates' accommodations; he labeled it "SECRET PLANS REVEALED" and whipped up a mild terrorism scare. Their candidate Pigasus was nominated with fanfare, and his "wife," a sow named Piggy Wiggy, was turned out in the park for "a merry, greasy romp" that ended when she was "apprehended by Chicago's Finest."

During the week of the convention, against the backdrop of massive demonstrations in Grant Park organized by David Dellinger and the National Mobilization to End the War in Vietnam ("the Mobe"), the Yippies held extraordinary power over the literal-minded authorities. Thousands of National Guard members, for instance, were tasked with defending the water reservoirs to ward off a (scientifically impossible) acid-trip outbreak. The entire police force was put on duty and taunted and baited by out-of-town kids. Hoffman put a Yippie! smiley face on it, summing up the week as a "Perfect Mess" in which "everyone gets what he wants" and "only the system suffers." In other words, Chicago wasn't equipped for a "Festival of Life," and the "system" perceived its anarchically tinged liberties as a clear and present danger. Whether the Yippies were demagogues or jokers, their antics were instrumental in creating this "Mess." Mounting tensions and pranks were fun, but they must have contributed to the violent outcome, much as they had at the Boston Massacre. At least that is what federal prosecutors would argue.

Said violent outcome erupted on August 25, a Sunday afternoon, when MC5, the proto-punk band from Detroit, had finished playing in Lincoln Park and a mock political rally for LBJ was under way. Hoffman was threatening to defy the city's orders and send in a truck to serve as a stage when a wedge formation of cops, impatient to enforce that night's 11 p.m. curfew, came bashing into the crowd with clubs and tear gas. Many crowd members were eager to fight back. Todd Gitlin, the Harvard-educated former SDS president, identified these aggressors as Bowery b'hoys of sorts—real revolutionary muscle:

> "greasers," motorcycle toughs, no-nonsense Chicago working-class teenagers, along with a handful of Chicago organizers simulating them. Even more than the runaway slave-surrogates of Abbie Hoffman's revolutionary dream, the greasers were as far as you could get from middle-class values and still be white . . . their presence was a sign to be taken that the white movement was getting serious.

What began as a turf war, in this case between the cops and these "Park People," would be broadcast for America over the next three days, when the fight culminated in and around Grant Park, as the great, gory show-down in the cops-and-dissenters game that had begun four years earlier in Mississippi and Berkeley. Gitlin also gives a colorful account of the cops, whose astonishing lack of scruples and restraint knocked the wind out of the nonviolent movement:

> They charged, clubbed, gassed, and mauled—demonstrators, bystand-ers, and reporters. They did it when there were minor violations of the law, like the curfew; they did it when there were symbolic provocations, like the lowering of an American flag; they did it when provoked (with taunts, with rocks, and, at times, they claimed, with bags of shit); in crucial instances, like the assault outside the Hilton Hotel Wednesday evening, they did it when unprovoked.

Amped up on adrenaline and lack of sleep, Hoffman kept heading back into battle. He had been clubbed and clobbered many times by police in his years as a political organizer, and he had always emerged on the side of rough civility, but the events in Chicago finally soured him. On the big day, Wednesday, the cops interrupted his breakfast with Anita and Paul Krassner; he had scrawled "FUCK" on his forehead with lipstick, to keep his pictures out of the papers. They seized him, hauled him "right across the table, through the bacon and eggs," and embarked on a thirteen-hour tour of the city's precincts and jail cells—"without food, phone calls, or lawyers," he remembered, "while cops beat the shit out of me." He "laughed hysterically through the beatings," being "so winged-out from not sleeping and all the tension." They succeeded, in the end, in hiding him from his lawyers and preventing him from joining the Michigan Avenue throng.

"I don't think I was much of a pacifist after Chicago," he wrote.


NEVER MIND *Hair,* the so-called Chicago Eight (then Seven) trial was the countercultural performance of the sixties. Guerrilla theater stared down courtroom farce to decide the civil dispute of the era: the Movement vs. the Establishment. The eight defendants seemed finically chosen to represent the world of dissent: SDS leaders Rennie Davis and Tom Hayden (who had authored the "Port Huron Statement"); graduate students Lee Weiner and John Froines; portly fifty-four-year-old Christian socialist David Dellinger; Yippies Rubin and Hoffman; and—briefly—Black Panther Bobby Seale. "Conspire, hell," Hoffman quipped. "We couldn't agree on lunch." The most colorful figure, however, was the judge. Seventy-four-year-old Justice Julius Hoffman, a trickster in his own right, whom Abbie called his "illegitimate father" and Rubin called "the country's top Yippie," was a blatant right-winger who mugged for the court and openly distorted judicial procedure—refusing to admit the defendants' "self-serving" evidence, showily favoring the prosecutors' motions, and overtly manipulating the jury's deliberations. But his behavior in this case was nothing new. As one Chicago lawyer noted, Julius Hoffman "regarded himself as the embodiment of everything federal" and routinely saw the "defense" as the "enemy."

The Eight were charged with crossing state lines with intent to incite a riot, a clause in the Civil Rights Act that had been proposed by a southern senator to prevent out-of-staters from organizing voters. The trial, set in Chicago's black-steel federal office towers designed by modernist Ludwig Mies van der Rohe, was one of the hottest tickets in America. Continual protests raged out front; people lined up for days to get in. The courtroom itself was theater in the round. The spectators were a vibrant and heckling crowd of canny reporters, ornery hippies, Black Panthers in uniform, out-of-town luminaries, and starstruck oglers, as well as the defendants' vocal associates and worried close relations. The marshals, whom the judge kept in constant play, manhandled spectators, defendants, and lawyers. The divided jury—all but one of them women—guardedly expressed their amusement and outrage. And the stars of the show, the colorful defense, maintained their slouchy, slovenly outpost alongside the prosecutors' businesslike table: they lounged in boots and leather jackets, headbands, armbands, and brightly colored clothes; their backpacks and belongings—food, wrappers, magazines, radical literature, and once a bag of pot "in a silent dare to the court"—covered their four pushed-together tables and spilled over onto the courtroom carpet. When they weren't heckling, stage-whispering, vamping, sleeping, or passing out jelly beans among the spectators, the Eight kept busy writing the speeches and correspondence with which they made their case to the public. Justice Hoffman, for his part, played the trickster with a range of voices and kept the room on edge for months.

One of the trial's observers, John Schultz, described it as a campaign to win "allegiances" through laughter. The Yippie! defendants used guerrilla theater to heighten the hilarity. Abbie Hoffman and a marshal played tug-of-war with a Viet Cong flag that had been hanging from the defendants' table. And on the day that Mayor Daley testified, Abbie Hoffman sauntered up to him, Wild West–style, and said, "Why don't we settle this right here and now—just you and me? The hell with all these lawyers." (Even the draconian mayor laughed at this one.) The most significant comedy, however, arose from the proceedings themselves. Reporters who had covered the riots were consistently amused by the prosecutors' egregious distortions. And anyone sympathizing with the defense enjoyed the government's and prosecutors' unfailing lack of humor. When an undercover cop denied that "Pigasus" was "satire," she set herself up for a round of jokes: "Did you support Pigasus?" ("No." Then: "Certainly not.") "Did you oppose him?" ("No.") "You were neutral, right?" ("Yes.") As Schultz describes it, this "completion of the game was so perfect that the laughter was wide and silent, a part of the game, never letting her know the import of what she had said."

This ongoing trial of the government's (minus Judge Hoffman's) lack of humor delivered a verdict on the riots themselves. The people—represented by the Yippies—were exercising their freedom to crack a few jokes, to pull a few pranks, as Americans had been doing for centuries. So long as they weren't hurting anyone, they were well within their rights. But the government's dullness in the face of humor—resorting to violence instead of to wit—showed what tyrants they had become. And it showed their failure at playing the dozens. David Stahl was the young deputy mayor who had "stalled" (Abbie Hoffman's pun) in awarding the permit, arguably creating the conditions for a riot. At issue in his testimony was whether he took "seriously Abbie and Jerry's statement about tearing down the city." When he said that he did, and Hoffman and Rubin "laughed quietly together" at the table, he seemed to come to his senses: Should he defend the government or his personal dignity? Should he take the fall like Attorney General Bunker in Carson City's great landslide case? When the questioning attorney gave him a second chance, asking, "Does Mr. Hoffman often speak in jest?" Stahl got it right: "I believe," he finally said with a smile, "that's a matter of broad public knowledge." This display of temporary sanity earned him laughs from "both sides."

Judge Hoffman, always the master jester, knew better than to step into the Yippies' trap. Too old and smart to play the straight man, instead he played "Mr. Magoo," as the defendants took to calling him. He willfully mangled their lawyers' names—especially that of Leonard Weinglass, whom he routinely called "Fineglass," "Weintraub," "Weinrus," and "Weinrub." And unlike the tetchy prosecutor Foran—who complained of the courtroom's annoying "mirth"—he mildly rebuked and smirked at the defendants while asking the recorder to note their high jinks. But he held back his whopping punch line for the end, when, while the jury was deliberating, he delivered an uncommonly brutal list of 175 counts of contempt, earning the ultimate seven defendants a combined sentence of fifteen years and five days behind bars. Judge Hoffman's most vicious prank, however, was reserved for the only black defendant, Bobby Seale—whose special elimination reduced the "Chicago Eight" by one.

Though Seale was a professional drummer and stand-up comic, he didn't condone the other defendants' horseplay. From the beginning he wanted to win through "revolutionary discipline." In October, when the court refused to wait for Seale's lawyer to recover from gallbladder surgery, Seale chose to defend himself and grew increasingly incensed with Judge Hoffman's prejudicial treatment, demanding "constitutional rights" and not "jive bargaining operations," a position the defense lawyers corroborated. Invoking a single case in which a defendant in a murder trial had been restrained after threatening the judge's life, the judge had Bobby Seale gagged and shackled to his chair. When he could still be heard demanding his rights through the gag, his mouth was sealed with adhesive tape. In a year when mainstream white America was widely alarmed by the furious Panthers, Hoffman's graphic binding of its founder like a slave was the trial's most resounding stunt.

Bobby Seale was then tried separately and sentenced to an unprecedented four years for contempt.

On December 29, 1969, in the final hours of the sixties, Abbie Hoffman testified for himself. In explaining how Yippie! came about—that it was meant to be "the kind of party you had fun at"—he made it clear that this was a solemn idea. Hoffman had told Rubin, he testified,

> that fun was very important. . . . It was a direct rebuttal of the ethics and morals that were part of the religion of the country; that the Protestant ethic was designed to keep people working in a rat race, that people couldn't get into heaven, they were told, unless they kept working, unless they tried to keep up with the Joneses—that work had lost its joy and that there was a whole system of values that told people to postpone their pleasure, to put all their money in the bank, to buy life insurance, a whole bunch of things that didn't make any sense to our generation at all and that fun actually was becoming quite subversive.

At the end of the trial, when five defendants were convicted of the major charges, Abbie Hoffman, one of the guilty parties, addressed his statement to the forefathers pictured above the bench. "I know those guys on the wall," he said. "They grew up twenty miles from my home in Massachusetts. I played with Sam Adams on the Concord Bridge. I was there when Paul Revere rode right up on his motorcycle and said, 'Pigs are coming.'"

As it had been for Paul Revere, on his motorcycle, American freedom is at its most exciting when it is being threatened—whether that perceived threat comes from the government or from the people: at that moment Old Glory cracks like a whip, to the right and to the left. Conservative Americans declared their patriotism to the nation's reigning authority—as did the two hundred or so "hard hats" who, in May 1970, achieved brief star status for bashing student protesters and raising the flag the kids had lowered for the Kent State massacre. But the trickster politicians of the 1960s—scofflaws like the Pranksters, Diggers, and Yippies—pledged their allegiance to unchecked freedom and waved American flags in support of "fun—fierceness—exclamation point!" In 1969, awaiting his conspiracy trial, Abbie Hoffman was the first American to be charged under a new law against desecrating the flag, for wearing the same stars-and-stripes shirt that he had been sporting for years. He told the appellate court that he had been off to testify to the House Un-American Activities Committee and had worn the shirt "to show that we were in the tradition of the founding fathers of this country, and that that committee wasn't."

As in all the battles for unofficial freedom examined in this book, the sixties fight over the meaning of America was exhilarating and brief, and it delivered many casualties. Some fell to drugs—like Neal Cassady, who overdosed walking Mexican train tracks, or Emmett Grogan, poignantly, who OD'd on the train to Coney Island. Some ran from the law, like Abbie Hoffman, who spent many years as a fugitive from the FBI, and some ran from themselves, like Jerry Rubin, the once self-proclaimed "P. T. Barnum of the Revolution" who later became, rather fittingly, a self-proclaimed Yuppie. Many were injured and killed in protests, but hundreds of thousands more were killed fighting the Red scare in Southeast Asia. These two conflicts—the civilian and the military—had at least this much in common: their results at the time looked disastrous, futile. And yet the Yippies' crowd actions in 1968, and their courtroom antics in 1969, for all their fun and ostensible frivolity, made America reconsider its commitment to freedom—to its limits, its dangers, its pleasures, its *struggle*—without asking its citizens to sacrifice their lives. While the U.S. government was defining democracy abroad with napalm drops and carpet bombing, the Yippies were defining it with fun at home. Equipped only with irony, satire, and farce, they stirred up fights that stress-tested the nation's most powerful institutions.

Like the commercial amusements of the Gilded Age and the "joyous revolts" of the Jazz Age, the fierce freedoms and antics of the 1960s counterculture carved a new flowing "tributary" into the mainstream of American fun. Nineteenth-century innovators like Barnum and Tilyou founded an entertainment empire that still dominates the American experience: Broadway, Hollywood, television, Vegas, Disneyland, spectator sports, video games, and so on. In their genius for promotion and mass production, they poured the cement for commercial ventures—nay, pleasures—that inform a major part of the American experience. Likewise, Jazz Age innovators like Buddy Bolden and Mae West modeled high-spirited popular rebellions that got average citizens out of their seats, dancing like fools and shooting their mouths off: their liberation of the unruly American self stimulated a resistive, mainstream youth culture that renews itself with every generation: with folk, with rock, with punk, with rap. And in the sixties playful innovators like the Merry Pranksters, Diggers, and Yippies blew the lid off American freedom. They initiated a radical new American politics that inspires even disempowered citizens to challenge the system, to rewrite the rules, and to enjoy the hell out of political participation. Their playful tone and love of irony has inspired dissenters ever since: nonviolence, they insisted, isn't enough; the people need to flaunt their freedom with jokes, pranks, costumes, music; as did the Sons of Liberty, they found their freedom was best expressed through fun.

Yippies stayed in the news during the early 1970s, most notably for throwing pies at bigwigs, but their grips on the media and the youth culture slackened. Before long they were just another sixties relic.

And yet their "revolution for the hell of it" transcended their historical moment. As connoisseurs of "struggle," "participation," and "fun," they understood the basic principles that got Paul Revere on his motorcycle. Even more than the Merry Pranksters and Diggers, they brought these principles to the nation's attention and made them relevant again. The historian Gerard J. DeGroot, echoing those who dismiss the Sons of Liberty's high jinks, sees only frivolity in the Yippie! program. "The recipe for revolution was effortless and simple: having fun, dressing up, and getting high would somehow create a better world." But there was nothing effortless about it, nothing simple. "Revolution for the hell of it" was truly infernal. It meant walking directly into the furnace of power—the New York Stock Exchange, the House Un-American Activities Committee, the Pentagon, the federal courtroom, the "wedge" of police—and throwing a kamikaze party. As Abbie Hoffman testified to Judge Hoffman, "fun actually was becoming quite subversive." The vision of such civil impudence—like dumping tea in Boston Harbor—is as inspiring now as ever. As Americans have shown from the nation's beginning, having fun in the house of power can indeed create a better world.

# 12

# Mustangers Have More Fun

B Y EARLY 1968, the three tributaries of American fun—the commercial, playful, and radically political—were mingling beyond
distinction in mainstream American popular culture. Case in point was
that spring's big-budget, major-release movie *Wild in the Streets,* whose
LSD-terrorism plot was invoked by the Yippies to needle Mayor Daley's
office. The movie's ingenious doomsday fantasy—lavishly edited with
split-screen technology and psychedelic stars-and-stripes effects—both
celebrates and satirizes the counterculture's efforts to politicize acid-rock
debauchery.

The actor Christopher Jones, a James Dean manqué who had played
Jesse James for two seasons on television, stars as the miscreant teen Max
Flatow—a bomb-building, acid-cooking rebel without a cause who lives
for sex, flirts with his mother (played by Shelley Winters), and Oedipally
dynamites his father's Chrysler before running away to rock-star freedom. At twenty-two, he has become multimillionaire Max Frost. He has
a sprawling mansion in Beverly Hills and ownership of "14 interlocking
companies." A dreamy and commanding Jim Morrison–ish heartthrob,
Max is "a leader of men and of little girls" whose multiracial rock band
and blissed-out entourage includes a fifteen-year-old Yale Law School

grad and his wisecracking drummer, "Stanley X," played by Richard Pryor. The movie's election-year satire kicks in when California's Democratic senatorial candidate, John Fergus (Hal Holbrook), a well-meaning and affable RFK stand-in, recruits Max to promote his cause célèbre of lowering the voting age to eighteen. Commandeering Fergus's stage, Max promotes his own idea that citizens twenty-five and younger are in the American majority ("We're 52% and we make big business big") and that the voting age should be lowered to *four*teen—an idea encapsulated in his catchy pop song "Fourteen or Fight." Max thus wheedles the candidate into a compromise ("Fifteen and Ready"), and so begins a rock 'n' roll government takeover, thanks to Max's fan base of teenage "troops."

The takeover itself is unstoppable fun. Hundreds of thousands mob the Sunset Strip (reminiscent of recent sit-ins that had defied the strip's curfews) and stage "the biggest block party in history"—to the shock of geriatrics watching on TV. A rock revolution sparks off in California, where, as a TV pundit opines, "the pursuit of happiness has long been replaced by a headier flight back into pubescence," but soon it has intimidated all of the nations' legislatures into lowering the voting age. Max quips that he has become "King," Stanley X retorts that he has "sold out," and their irony highlights the movie's constant references, now comical, now earnest, that link youth suffrage to civil rights and the Revolution: For, indeed, are these starry-eyed youth "citizens" supporting a democracy or a monarchy? Do they want to participate in the nation's governance or idolize a boyish rock star? The movie literalizes the Pranksters' "Vote for Fun" in a speech to Congress by Patriot-tricorne-lidded Sally Leroy. The child star turned acidhead/nudist, now the nation's youngest senator, druggedly beats her tambourine and plays to cheering kids in the gallery: "America's greatest contribution is to teach the world that getting old is such a drag. Youth is America's greatest secret weapon."

To unleash this weapon, she proposes the minimum age of fourteen for all public offices, including the presidency. ("Amend!" becomes young America's rallying cry.) To ensure that the grizzled senators give their support, Max and his entourage dump LSD in D.C.'s water supply and wheel them in one by one—bug-eyed, cackling, wildly tripping—for one wigged-out special session. Only Senator Fergus, who prefers being "good old patriotic drunk," is bummed out by the acid, dismayed to see democracy's institutional collapse. The rest of the disabled senators are on "a happy trip, a *voting* trip" that opens the gates for Max Frost's election—as the 1968 *Republican* candidate because, as his advisers argue, "They've been looking for a hero since they lost Eisenhower." Anyway, Reagan and Nixon would look "dumb" with long hair, and "nobody's going to take the country this year with short hair."

The joke here, initially, is that both parties are the same, and that rock stars are, in essence, the greatest demagogues. Both parties serve the ruling-class establishment, and Max only needs an expedient way in (he wins by the largest margin in history). But the joke suddenly darkens when Max, as president, out-tyrants even Nixon by becoming a militant fascist-for-fun. He makes thirty the mandatory retirement age and sends everyone over thirty-five to concentration-camp-style "retirement homes," where they wear blue robes with peace-sign patches and are forced to trip on acid every waking hour. His teenage goon squads notwithstanding, President Maximilian Frost, cruising the open country in his silver Rolls-Royce, enforces a Diggers-style democracy: he disbands the military, Secret Service, and FBI ("Protection—who needs it?"); he gives free food aid to Third World countries; and he uses the nation's "immense wealth . . . to create the most purely hedonistic society the world has ever known." But the results are unambiguously dystopian: Senator Fergus hangs himself from a tree, and his orphaned daughter (a premonition of the hippie-hating punk generation) scorns Max, now twenty-four, for being "old." This insult haunts him in the closing scenes, when he encounters a band of sneering minors who have taken his lesson to heart: "We're going to put everyone over ten out of business."

Historically, having fun had been an underdog position—it was the practice of Patriots, slaves, and forty-niners who enjoyed and empowered their out-group identities. Likewise, in the 1920s and the 1960s, whether flappers or hippies, Lindy Hoppers or heads, Americans who embraced rising cultures of fun positioned themselves against an established power structure that gave their pleasure an illegal edge. Historically, as this book has shown, that illegal edge defined American fun. It kept it nimble, resistive, reactive. It kept it witty, inventive, evolving. It kept it from devolving into flabby complacency. But *Wild in the Streets* warns what could happen if youthful fun were to gain both market share and electoral power, if rock revolution became *real* revolution and youth pursued psychedelic hedonism unchallenged: it wouldn't be much fun anymore. By this doomsday scenario, the combative attitude that characterizes fun (and deploys it against a closed-minded ideology) could slacken and lose its purpose; sex, drugs, and rock 'n' roll would no longer signal rebellion but simply empty mainstream entertainment, and the aggression that historically was channeled through hilarity into forms of civil disobedience could come to behave as dominance, even tyranny, if nothing were there to keep it in check. Whether or not this warning had merit, it spoke to popular worries in 1968: hippie fun had become big business. Once-outlawed breeds of pleasure and license were looking like the norm. The "counterculture," to this extent, was looking a lot like the "establishment." And the acid tests, protests, and witty street theater that were amusing sideshows of the mid-1960s were exploding that spring (or so it seemed to many) into full-scale riots. To consumers of *Life* and the evening news, the fact that fun had become political, as temperance had in the nineteenth century, suggested that one day it could be *enforced.*

*Wild in the Streets,* for a million-dollar send-up of populist fervor, delivers a pretty lucid verdict on the competing properties of late-sixties fun. On the one hand, the movie captures the counterculture's efforts to make having fun a matter of right. Having fun, as these rebels had learned from history, was the essence of American freedom, the essence of American youthfulness, the essence of a mixed and open society, and for these noble reasons it was the worthiest antidote to an aging, conservative, exclusive establishment that recruited young soldiers to defend an ideology. Having fun represented the best of democracy, the power of people to struggle together, as kids throughout history tended to know best. On the other hand, more cynically, the movie also captures fun's serious limits—limits the counterculture often blithely ignored. Hardly a substitute for good governance, hardly an ideology in itself, the right to have fun, especially as it was touted by the hippie generation, was also a highly volatile position that could easily give way to self-gratification, mob rule, or—for the stargazers of the "rock revolution"—mindless demagoguery. And even ostensibly political fun was vulnerable to commercial forces; to the Bill Grahams, drug dealers, and tour-bus companies that capitalized on the Summer of Love; to the fashion, publishing, and record industries that mass-produced hippie accoutrements; indeed, to American International Pictures, which cashed in big on the fun revolution with their part-flattering, part-satirical *Wild in the Streets:* "We're 52% and we make big business big."

Much as jazz and its Wild Wets acolytes drove 1920s popular culture, the counterculture's fashions and rock and politics drove the late 1960s vibe. It was a heady, contradictory, psychedelic moment in which the entertainment industry was alternately rejected (by Yippies and communally living hippies); aestheticized (by Robert Rauschenberg, Andy Warhol and his Factory); and freely and easily embraced by the mainstream for giving open access to their exciting times. With the Barnumesque alacrity of Bill Graham Presents, the late-1960s culture industry flipped the people's raw fun from the streets to the department-store shelves, often so fast it wasn't clear which had come first. To be certain, *Wild in the Streets* was just the best of the new movies exploiting the hippie aesthetic and message: *Hallucination Generation* (1966), *Riot on the Sunset Strip* (1967), *The Love-ins* (1967), *The Trip* (1967), and *Psyche-Out* (1968). The Monkees, 1966's made-for-television fake American Beatles, had become the real thing by 1967—and the entertainment industry's latest test-tube teens. Mose and Lize for the Acid Age.

*Laugh-In,* the comedy duo Dan Rowan and Dick Martin's TV show, took its name in 1967 from the protest movement's be-, sit-, love-, and teach-ins; it held prime-time airways for the next six years and emulated the scene with its weekly mod dance party (interlarded with hip-to-the-minute political jokes) and vaudeville-style sketches in a hippie vein. *Laugh-In* was the scrubbed-up, aging-teenybopper face of a late-sixties comedy renaissance, which had sprung from Mort Sahl's comic radicalism and Lenny Bruce's lacerating irreverence and had generated a star system of rebel stand-ups: Woody Allen, Mel Brooks, Joan Rivers, Bill Cosby, and the unflappable Dick Gregory, who would respond to hecklers who called him "nigger" by saying the management was contractually obligated to pay him $50 every time an audience member said the word: *"So will you all do me a favor and stand up and say it again in unison?"* In contrast to what was playing in the clubs—profanity, obscenity, anarchy, drugs—the comedy that made it onto *Laugh-In, The Smothers Brothers Comedy Hour,* or *The Steve Allen Hour,* for all of its certified drollery, and for all of its acid-rock optics, was as safe and clean (and hip) as B. F. Keith's continuous performance. Because it ran at the pleasure of its commercial sponsors.

Soon even the (ostensibly) radical press wanted its slice of American pie. San Francisco's *Rolling Stone,* an acid-culture magazine founded in 1967, aimed higher than the region's gutter-punk undergrounds by bringing the "things and attitudes that [rock] music embraces" to a broad national audience—initially about six thousand readers. And when Detroit's edgier *Creem* appeared in 1969, it was already mocking rock's "things and attitudes" with a hipper-than-hip *Mad Magazine* tone, but also for a national audience. It became hard to tell the underground press from the straight. *The Whole Earth Catalog,* 1968's most radical *New York Times* best seller, ironically eschewed commercialism altogether. This shabby-looking clearinghouse of hippie enterprises everywhere was fashioned by a Stanford biology graduate, Stewart Brand, after the recently issued L.L.Bean catalogue. It was tabloid-sized, like *Life* and *Rolling Stone,* but it had the mimeographed look of the underground press and was devoted to a Digger-like economy. It positioned itself against "government, big business, formal education, church" and advertised the books and "tools" of a handmade, hands-on, self-starting ethos: "personal power . . . power of the individual to conduct his own education, find his own inspiration, shape his own environment, and share his adventure with whoever is interested." Despite the *Catalog's* hackneyed plea for subscribers ("save 25% off the cover price," complete with blow-in cards) and its promotion of many mass-market books, its theme was low-impact, self-sufficient community: dome houses, tipis, kibbutzim, yoga, survivalism, recycling, camping, organic farming, solar energy, home auto repair, and home health care. It also featured the farther-out ideas of the era: ESP, cybernetics, self-hypnosis, dolphin psychology, student rebellion, space travel, even personal computing. Its advice was practical, and its tone ran the gamut from sanctimonious to satirical, but its emphasis on action and getting involved was decidedly fun. A poem in its pages by R. Buckminster Fuller says, "God is a verb, / the most active," and a poem lifted from the pages of the *Realist* suggests repurposing consumer society's "garbage" as an imaginative way to "act out our fantasies, use it for unimaginable gratifications." *The Whole Earth Catalog* delineated the perimeter of a garbage-producing culture, and many of its advertisers gave an exit strategy, but at bottom it was just another catalogue, and amusing reading. As if acknowledging that its readers were *by definition* consumers, its pages also recommended *Consumer Reports*.

The commercial embrace of '60s fun didn't stop at the entertainment industry. In 1963, the agency Batton, Barton, Durstine, and Osborn made advertising history by marketing an entire generation. They branded the baby boomers fun: "Come alive! You're the Pepsi generation! This is the liveliest, most energetic time ever . . . with the most active generation living it. You're part of it. Pepsi-Cola is part, too. . . . It's the official drink of everyone with a thirst for living!" By 1965, emboldened by the success of adman Bill Bernbach's creative innovations, marketers, advertisers, and manufacturers of all kinds suddenly saw the folly in scorning youth rebellion, as buttoned-down advertisers routinely had just a couple of years before. From the mid-sixties onward, at the same time the counterculture was finding its feet, Madison Avenue was reforming its strategies and changing its culture to appeal to youth. Ironies and humbug abounded. 7UP was the psychedelic "Un-Cola," and airlines and liquors sneered at conformity, but the auto industry took the cake. Dodge promoted the "Dodge Rebellion," Ford said "Mustangers have more fun," and Oldsmobile betrayed its own stodgy image: "Today, millions of *Life* readers are getting young ideas. The '68 'youngmobiles' from Oldsmobile are here." Kids were indeed "the 52%," a target market that had come of age—but they weren't necessarily playing along. For instance, in the March 4, 1966, *Time*, an issue that featured a teen dancing the Watusi to sell the idea that "Sugar swings," an article covering America's recent countercultural parties, "Happenings Are Happening," reported on the "spectators" who "joined" the Merry Pranksters' Trips Festival's "fun": one was dressed in "a toga made from an American flag," another wore a sign that read "You're in the Pepsi Generation, I'm a pimply freak."

By 1967, as Thomas Frank shows in *The Conquest of Cool,* the ad industry was reorganizing itself to maximize the popular new kinds of fun—by absorbing them into its corporate structure. The people's war on "organization" and its stuffy "technocracy" was infiltrating the biggest firms. The "establishment agencies," as they came to be known, scooped up talent from the upstart startups and nurtured what Frank calls "a stripped-down, flexible, 'democratic' arrangement" among its staff "that privileged creative nonconformists." What resulted was a culture of "rebellion" and "democracy" safely ensconced within *advertising,* an industry that half a decade earlier had been following the social protocols of insurance and banking. This move gave the industry a friendly new face that flattered (and exploited) the Pepsi Generation. It slaked their thirst for edgy fun.

This creative new wave in advertising—like the racy new big-distribution movies, the trippy new music dominating the airwaves, the op-art fashions filling department stores, and all the hippie-themed variety shows playing on prime-time television—did more than disguise the old-guard interests of its "establishment agencies." It was part of a speedy cultural revolution that was changing the agenda of the establishment proper, as *Wild in the Streets* had warned. The draft carried on, and the Nixon administration and many college administrations did little to endear themselves to America's youth: these enemies held a valuable, ugly status for a generation that identified with rebellion. But other powerful institutions, likewise Vietnam War profiteers, saw the gain in kids' rebellious pleasure. They built it into a monoculture that sold its thrilling rebel *feeling* (if not necessarily its *fact*) to the masses. In an era when government was the towering bugbear, big business stood to turn a profit off the youth rebellion against it. It was the Gilded Age all over again: risky fun made safe for unlimited consumption. And the institutional thresholds for what was safe—set by censors, marketers, producers, sponsors—had gotten so high by 1969 that it seemed as if the Merry Pranksters were finally driving the bus.

When in fact they were nowhere to be found.

...................

NINETEEN SIXTY-NINE WAS a dark year for fun. That year youth actions turned more subversive, also caustic, and Abbie Hoffman (who was turning to violent anarchism) would be arrested seven more times. That year the vogue for what Yippies called "monkey warfare"—water pistol antics and the like—had been replaced with something closer to the real thing by an SDS faction of highborn bomb throwers who called themselves the Weathermen. "These hip outlaws made revolution look like *fun*," Gitlin writes—criminal fun, to be sure. Weathermen enjoyed orgies and acid, like old-school hippies, but their heroes were that year's Hollywood gunslingers—Butch and Sundance, Bonnie and Clyde— and their objective wasn't to end the Vietnam War (that cheerful hippie dream had passed) but to move it onto American soil. In October of that year, they spearheaded the "Days of Rage"—three days of incendiary actions in Chicago that they hoped would rouse the black population, but the Panthers, who denounced them, didn't take the bait. A few days later thousands of supporters from a march on the Washington Monument rained projectiles on the Justice Department. The grand marshals of the parade, Abbie Hoffman and Jerry Rubin, had a special gripe with that particular department, by whom they were currently being tried for conspiracy.

In June 1969, in New York City, a routine police raid on a West Village gay bar—recalling the raid in Mae West's play *The Drag*—was met with unexpected resistance. Patrons of the Stonewall Inn, unwilling to skulk away in shame, vigilantly gathered along the street to watch for signs of police brutality. At first it may have seemed as if rebellious fun would prevail: As the crowd grew in number, their resistance turned vocal and theatrical. Evacuees performed for the cheering crowd, and drag queens, as they boarded the patrol wagon, directed quips and come-ons at the cops. And while at first only a few dared to shout for "gay power," a virtually unknown concept at the time, before long the crowd sang "We Shall Overcome" and, dissatisfied with the standard protest song, "began to camp on the solemn lyrics." Their antic satire in the face of oppression had a distinctly Sons of Liberty cast.

But it was the cops' rough struggle with a powerful lesbian that touched off the legendary Stonewall riots. They hit her with a billy club, she escaped their squad car twice, and the mostly male crowd erupted in violence, starting the riots that would rage for four days and end in bloody clashes with police. In the months to come a young movement would form, led by activist groups like the Pink Panthers and the Cockettes, a guerrilla street-theater troupe whom John Waters called "insane hippie drag queens on and off the stage." Like many of that year's rebel actions, however, Stonewall was an act of grim determination; there was nothing lighthearted about it.

THE THREE "TRIBUTARIES" of American fun, springing from three different eras, could be said to constitute three kinds of citizens: consumers, partiers, and activists, respectively. By the late 1960s, these three fun-loving citizenries showed significant overlap: advertisers trumpeted radical slogans, protesters chanted rock lyrics, and everybody knew it was cool to have fun. "Rock revolution" was a shibboleth of the era, and there was truth to it. Rock stars motivated the newly gathering people like prophets and presidents of earlier eras. The Beatles called for calm in "Revolution," but Berkeley demonstrators, not knowing the words to old left-wing solidarity songs, ignored the message. They sang and marched to "Yellow Submarine." The Rolling Stones' "Street-Fighting Man" became a rallying cry. It equated rock 'n' roll with violent resistance: "My name is called disturbance. I'll shout and scream, I'll kill the king, I'll rail at all his servants." John Sinclair—the manager of MC5, the headlining band at the "Festival of Life"—echoed a popular sentiment when he called "rock and roll music . . . one of the most vital revolutionary forces in the West—it blows people all the way back to their senses and makes them feel good, like they're alive again in the . . . monstrous funeral parlor of western civilization."

If the fictional President Maximilian Frost was the satirical composite of these "revolutionary forces," Woodstock was the reality. In August 1969, American fun's three rivers swirled together into a muddy whirlpool. Four hundred thousand rock fans piled onto a dairy farm in Bethel, New York, for what was billed as a three-day festival of "Peace & Music." In the weeks before the event, Abbie Hoffman and fourteen other Yippies staged a mock police raid on the commercial offices of Woodstock Ventures, the show's promoters. They urged them to make it a free political happening, something along the lines of their "Festival of Life." To no avail, of course. But neither would it succeed as a commercial enterprise: Woodstock Ventures didn't have the means to reap even half the intended ticket sales. On the days of the event, hippies, refusing to act like consumers, gushed by the thousands through holes in the fence. And yet, as a laid-back be-in of drug-culture youth, rolling in the mud and standing in line for the woefully insufficient latrines, it worked well enough, which, after the riots in Chicago the summer before, must have been a relief. At this mass experiment in spontaneous community, the carefree partiers carried the day. Folks stripped naked, took drugs, had sex, and a general feeling of camaraderie reigned. Nobody was killed, and a baby was born. And yet whether or not it turned a profit, Woodstock smacked of what Yippies called "the old America," a land of easy entertainment. Which is to say, it was a big rock concert.

As a political event, Woodstock was shallow: it lacked the purpose, organization, and will of the era's clearly focused demonstrations. "For the most part," as the rock critic Ellen Willis observed, Woodstock attendees "took for granted not only the discomforts but the tremendous efforts made by the state, the local communities, and unpaid volunteers to distribute cheap or free food and establish minimum standards of health and safety." A pacifist collective called the Hog Farm distributed free food and supplies. "Movement City" was Woodstock's camp for radical politics, but most attendees didn't take much interest. They were just there to have some fun. At one point during the show, while the Who performed, Abbie Hoffman, zonked on acid, jumped up on the stage, grabbed the mic, and said it was a "pile of shit" that everybody was lounging around while MC5 manager John Sinclair, that outspoken proponent of the rock revolution, languished in prison for marijuana possession. Irony carried the day: Pete Townshend, the king in his castle, knocked the court jester of radicalism over the head with his infamously dangerous guitar. The blow sent Hoffman "crumpl[ing]" to the stage, affirming his own claim that rock stars were the "real leaders" of the revolution.

But what sort of "revolution" were they leading? Proto-blogging the event in his book *Woodstock Nation,* which he rushed into print before the conspiracy trial began, Hoffman recorded his experiences down among the dirty, tripping crowd. He drew a sharp distinction between "the za-za world" of the "ROCK EMPIRE" and the millions of people who were moved by it, "Woodstock Nation" itself. "Clearly I love their music and sense in it the energy to liberate millions of minds. On the other hand, I feel compelled to challenge their role in the community, to try and crack their plastic dome." Outside this dome of wealth and celebrity, Hoffman saw Woodstock citizens like himself "running around setting up hospitals in the hills of the NATION and trying to wreck the government that claims it owns our land." He also saw a multitude of others, just having a good time in the rebellious pulse of the crowd, and he believed this collective pleasure in itself, the Artaudian "festival of the streets," was a positive source for change, the heart of what he called a "cultural"—as opposed to "political"—revolution. By his argument, whereas "politics breeds organizers," cultural revolution encourages "outlaws" to strike out on their own. In keeping with this outlaw mission, Woodstock Nation stood in opposition to what he called "PIG NATION." It stood for liberty, rebellion, and fun.

But the cultural revolution had already happened, sometime in the middle sixties, and Abbie Hoffman had been one of the players. Woodstock Nation was up and running, but it wasn't quite what he wanted it to be. Thanks to promoters, advertisers, movies, television, rock stars, and popular fashion, it rather resembled the frictionless freedom that had bored him at Antioch College: even the most radical fun had somehow become the status quo, and the mass of young white citizens felt entitled to it. It left some Americans wanting more—bomb-throwing Weathermen, acidheads turned heroin addicts, even the hardened Hoffman and Rubin—but what they wanted wasn't exactly fun.

THAT SAME MONTH, in California, the "rock revolution" lost what moral force it may once have had. On the eighth and ninth of August, in the canyons of Los Angeles, a cult called "the Family" that had made a religion out of the Beatles' *White Album* (1968) followed the orders of its leader, Charles Manson, and went on a gruesome killing spree—most notably stabbing to death the actress Sharon Tate, who was eight and a half months pregnant at the time. Among the messages they scrawled in their victims' blood were references to "pigs" and the song title "Helter Skelter." And in December of that year, at a free rock concert at San Francisco's Altamont Speedway, Mick Jagger looked on in apparent nausea while some Hell's Angels, who had been hired as security, stabbed a young black man to death by the stage.

The late-1960s rock revolution had dubious democratic potential. Not lively and kinetic like the "jazz revolution," where bands and dancers goaded each other to higher levels of personal achievement, the rock revolution was a spectator sport, demanding nothing but echoes and applause. Not risky and kinetic like the pranks of the era, it welcomed passive participation. Rock led its would-be revolutionaries out beyond the law, and often it just left them there.

But Woodstock featured at least one band of outlaws whose star-spangled spectacle and outright audacity flooded all three of American fun's rivers—the commercial, the wild-partying, *and* the political; a music whose excitement and fat, driving bass lines set a fast, funky pace for decades of American culture to come. The concertgoers had slogged in the mud for three days, sodden with hunger, overcrowding, and confusion, when, on Sunday night, in a plasmatic flash, the eye-poppingly dramatic Sly and the Family Stone, San Francisco's latest pop sensation, jolted them with, as Steve Lake described it, "Sly's ecstatic exuberance": "Half a million clenched fists and peace signs rising into the air in a massive human tidal wave of approval." Sly Stone's joyous revolt of self-affirmation met the people more than halfway, surrounding them with ripping horns, thrilling organs, wicked guitars, and a rhythm section that, like the drums on Congo Square, didn't follow but *led the way*. What could the people *do* but dance? The songs sang imperatives of acceptance and action. They used mockery and irony to put bigotry down. But their tone was so open and irresistible that their politics didn't divide. They just conquered.

Like most of the funk artists his music would inspire, Sylvester Stewart came of age fighting in civil rights conflicts. Born in 1943 and raised in racially mixed Vallejo, California, he divided his time between leading street gangs, participating in local race riots, and crafting a jumping pop-music style that yoked his talents on drums and guitar. His star rose fast. He was signed by Autumn Records in 1964, and while he popularized his eclectic tastes as a Bay Area disc jockey—mixing soul, folk, and the new psychedelia—he was forming a multiracial band that, as Greil Marcus describes it, vaulted right over the race and gender hypocrisy that plagued the Haight-Ashbury free-love experiment: "There were whites as well as blacks, women—who played real instruments—as well as men: 'The Family.'" While the Mime Troupe went rummaging in America's back closets for its ugliest instruments of racial division, Sly and the Family Stone—a "tribe" and a "family" in the hippies' best sense—unearthed the nation's cultural gold, the rhythm and blues and dance and humor that the minstrels could only envy and mimic. Sly refined these minerals using bebop complexity, made it sparkle with Sgt. Pepper–grade costumes, and tricked it out for his postmodern age. The Family Stone was ultrasophisticated fun, the newest groove, the latest craze, twinkling with the kinds of signifying tip-offs that educated Louis Armstrong's most attentive listeners. But it was also pungent with earthy rusticity, with sledgehammer clangs, gospel moans, trickster myths, and the honky-tonk revelry that Zora Neale Hurston found in Polk County, Florida. It was the newest of the new in an age oversaturated with creativity and novelty; "Sly Stone *owned* pop music," Rickey Vincent claims, "from 1968 to 1970"; the brash egalitarianism of infectious hits like "Everyday People," "Stand!" "Fun," "Life," and "Thank You (Falettinme Be Mice Elf Agin)" added a futuristic glimmer to the Panthers' "Black Power." In these songs, black solidarity and soul emerged as America's postnuclear worldwide weapon, the bomb that would bring us together. And yet for all these songs' aggressive novelty, the listener sensed how *old* they were: *centuries* old.

The Family Stone released three albums and several singles proclaiming the virtues of radically inclusive fun—the joys of self-pride and rolling crowd power. Their honey-toned anthem, "Hot Fun in the Summertime," briefly lifted '69 above its culturally disenchanted fug. By early

1970, however, the angst would reach even jubilant Sly Stone. Addicted to cocaine, prone to missing or canceling shows, he soon moved on from the people-moving music that had dominated the world's discotheques. His dark and moody album, *There's a Riot Going On,* has since been recognized as the spiritual soundtrack of the blaxploitation era, when sex and flash and criminality met with heady self-examination. But the high-spirited fun, it seemed, was past.

Or was it? Sly Stone's personal story turned somber, but his early music spawned a nationwide phenomenon of ecstatic, erotic, space-age dance music that answered to Buddy Bolden's call sign: funk. The matrix for disco, hip-hop, and techno, the new code for funk was written in 1970 by George Clinton and his Wizard of Oz–like theatrical offspring, Parliament and Funkadelic. Kicking off a decades-long Vote-for-Fun campaign, these P-Funk All Stars played for keeps.

To give one solid example, in "Chocolate City"—Parliament's 1975 vision of a black-occupied White House featuring Muhammad Ali, Aretha Franklin, Stevie Wonder, Richard Pryor, et al.—Clinton exhorted his fun-loving Americans with a prescient rhetorical question: "Who needs the bullet when you've got the ballot?"

# 13

# Doing It Yourself, Getting the Joke

THE SOUTH BRONX WAS a war zone in 1971. Three-quarters of all kids dropped out of high school, an estimated eleven thousand belonged to violent street gangs, and ongoing turf wars, drug wars, and race wars raged among the Puerto Rican majority and African-American minority. That December, Cornell Benjamin, a leader of the dominant gang, the Ghetto Brothers, was stomped to death for urging rival factions to bury their hatchets. Remarkably, instead of murdering the aggressors, the Ghetto Brothers only pummeled them, turned them loose, and called an historic summit at the Bronx Boys Club. Police snipers surrounded the block; TV crews filmed the scene inside, while members of the borough's major and minor gangs, many of whom had grown acquainted through lethal combat, filled the gymnasium in bristling détente. In Benjamin's honor, the Ghetto Brothers and other gang leaders broke the attendees into caucuses and discussed the tenets of a binding treaty. Afterwards they joined their hands as one group: "Peace!" they said, in resounding unison.

The peace treaty didn't fix the Bronx—the police redoubled their gang-fighting efforts; kids kept settling scores with blood—but in its aftermath the gangs started to disintegrate. Some fell to drug abuse or lost group cohesion. The Black Spades and the Ghetto Brothers, two of the biggest, reconstituted themselves for community action—registering voters, securing health services, and, most auspiciously, throwing block parties.

Clive Campbell, an eighteen-year-old Jamaican immigrant, caught this new wave of urban creativity and restarted American popular culture. Or should bragging rights go to his sister Cindy? In the summer of 1973, she needed money for the freshest back-to-school clothes, so, in the spirit of 1920s rent parties, she hired out their building's recreation room, bought cheap cases of Olde English 800, papered the neighborhood with James Brown–flavored flyers, and put her brother in charge of the music. Souping up their father's sound system with tricky wiring that made it the loudest thing these kids had ever heard, Clive—known as Hercules around school for his pumped-up body, and as "Kool Herc" in his graffiti tags—laid the foundation for a style of party making that would coronate *DJ Kool Herc* the king of the Bronx. That night, behind his decks, after activating the crowd with some funk and soul, he read their excitement like Buddy Bolden. He developed a technique right there on the spot to bring their dancing to a fever pitch. Listening for the licks, beats, and breaks that freaked dancers out the most, he repeated, layered, and *compounded* those breaks, hour after groovy hour, channeling the flashing electricity of gangland into the rhythmic frenzy of hip-hop.

"Forget melody, chorus, songs," he recalled. "It was all about the groove, building it, keeping it going." Kool Herc's spinning was masterful and coy—he took to soaking labels off records (an old Jamaican trick) to keep other DJs from copying his tracks. But it wasn't just his magic spin. On the mic, as MC, Herc flirted with the crowd—giving shout-outs, rapping rhymes, fashioning with his friends a singular slang as flashy and fresh as the kids' funky clothes, as their sparkly tags. Herc's name took flight. Cindy used her clout in student government to throw a party on a cruise boat, and by the next summer they had graduated from rec rooms to block parties. The police ignored large swaths of the Bronx, rendering street permits unnecessary, so Herc plugged his sound system into streetlamps. He took ownership of the streets, as he had learned to do with cans of spray paint. Soon the Campbells were hosting big throbbing parties like the ones they remembered back in Kingston. In the same open air where gangs used to rumble, Herc's booming voice gave permission and warning, promising to shut down at the first sign of trouble. Under these radically civil conditions, practicing Sons of Liberty restraint from violence, they could rage all night. Rolling from break to break to break, the indefatigable parties "broke daylight."

The violence wasn't gone. The violence was *evolving.* Inner-city dance in the early 1970s ignored the smooth trends in the discotheques. The hip kids adopted the lightning-flash footwork of the Black Power, "Say It Loud" godfather of soul. What James Brown did onstage started in his blurring, stamping feet then rocked and shimmied up his twisting frame. The full-body athleticism of B-boys and B-girls—break dancers or "breakers," the new Bronx wave—copied James Brown's fiery bodywork and merged it with the styles of their favorite combatants, most notably Bruce Lee and Muhammad Ali. The block-party scene of Herc and his rivals became the battleground for B-boys and B-girls. Their "crews," like gangs, competed for turf. But their combat also signified a repertoire of "comic moves," including, according to the music journalist Will Hermes, "*Monty-Python*-style funny walks, Charlie Chaplin penguin-stepping, and assorted pantomime riffs."

Afrika Bambaataa, the son of Jamaican immigrants, had been a leader of the Black Spades during the truce of '71. He knew the strategies of turf warfare. A charismatic community leader and popular DJ, he politicized Herc's endless groove; blending a black pride philosophy with the B-boys' and B-girls' nonviolent rivalry, he came to "preside," as the hip-hop historian Jeff Chang puts it, "over a ritual of motion and fun." Under Bambaataa's influence and discipline, hip-hop "organization" eclipsed old-school gang warfare. In 1975, when police killed his cousin Soulski, Bambaataa's constructive response was to turn gangland into "Zulu Nation"—a ferocious crew of rappers and breakers who spread their Zulu motto throughout the tristate area: "Peace, Love, Unity, and Having Fun."

Like the Lindy Hopping of King Leon's Jolly Fellows, who ruled Cat's Corner at the Savoy Ballroom, Zulu fun, despite its peaceful message, imported all of street fighting's danger, strength, endurance, wits, bravery, skill, and ruthless vengeance into the breaker's "cypher," a ring of support and feverous competition as old in its heritage as African storytelling. In the cypher, on the street, whether on scraps of linoleum or on bare concrete, B-boys and B-girls, in their best athletic dress, pushed the limits of flesh and gravity to spin, pop, twist, stop, glide, slide, float, and fly—better than their rivals and always on time. Cuts and abrasions were the battle trophies of this latest rebel fun. But: the smoother the surface the finer your style. And: "If you break on the cement," B-boy Tiny Love testified, "you're, like, a raw motherfucker." So, just as taggers tagged train cars and billboards as prominent tableaux for their illegal art, breakers employed the marble floors of lobbies for impromptu breaking sessions, until security shoved them along. B-boy Trac 2, looking back on that era, remarked "how innocent and pure" he and other preteens "were in that environment . . . with all those abandoned buildings." For at-risk kids, devalued by society, break dancing was "very empowering. It allowed us to be who we are and express it the way we wanted to express it." B-boys and B-girls of the mid-1970s, whether Zulus or otherwise, were the vanguard of a self-sufficient youth culture that didn't look to cops, teachers, social workers, or parents to show them how civil society works. Their "play" didn't ask for the "guidance" Duffus advised to an earlier generation. The America they had inherited needed major improvements. They set out to fix it as kids do best—by having fun.

Of course it was the old Gilded Age scam that pure fun can be simulated, packaged, and sold back to the people as mass amusement. DJs like Kool Herc, Afrika Bambaataa, and the newest innovator, Grandmaster Flash, had come to accept that their dance-party subculture could never get bigger than block parties and discos. It was a rolling, organic urban experience that required hip-hop's "four elements": DJing, MCing, breaking, and tagging. Like Zulu Nation, it was all about *unity*. Rapper Chuck D, who was a teenager at the time, remembers thinking hip-hop could never be recorded. "'Cause it was a whole gig, y'know? How you gon' put *three hours* on a record?" But then in December 1979, just as hip-hop was dying of old age in the Bronx, a studio found three unknown rappers, called them the Sugar Hill Gang, pressed a fifteen-minute track called "Rapper's Delight," and captivated the world with a bright and tinny echo of hip-hop's original street-level bomb.

IN THE 1970s and early 1980s, young Americans, in cliques and crews, fixed their own society by urging each other to scary new heights—of personal style, of cool expression, of musical power, of physical daring. Discontent with the rebellious styles in stores, kids aggressively reconstructed fashion with scissors, markers, paint, and rejects. Unwilling to trust TVs, magazines, and newspapers to report the news that really mattered, they commandeered photocopiers, Diggers-style, and connected their subcultures through posters and zines. Unamused by the machinery, toys, and playgrounds that were sold to them by the older generations, they went where they wanted and crafted new tools. And unsatisfied with the entertainment industry—with the overproduced hits of hard rock and disco, with the deeply entrenched trends in both movies and sports—they made their own music, invented their own dances, shot films in Super 8, and, inspired by their era's athletic mavericks, pushed sports into unimaginable new territory.

Doing it yourself (or DIY, as it came to be known) was nothing new for Americans. Plymouth and Merry Mount were DIY colonies, though with contrary ideas of what "it" was. The Sons of Liberty were DIY revolutionaries, determined to build government from the streets. Antebellum African Americans, deprived of society's most basic freedoms, designed and sustained DIY liberties as durable as the U.S. Constitution—which, for that matter, was another big DIY project. And the pioneers in covered wagons, the Mormons pulling handcarts, the forty-niners over land and sea, and the millions upon millions of intrepid immigrants were all of them DIY adventurers, leaving behind what was safe and familiar to break something new from the frightening unknown. Historically, DIY is the American way. But its new rising spirit among 1970s youth, who picked up when the sixties counterculture tuned out and made use of what was already at hand, grew in large part from American failure: the inner-city devastation of "urban renewal" projects, the energy crisis, soaring unemployment, runaway crime rates and drug addiction, the moral collapses of Vietnam and Watergate. Many kids whom the system neither helped nor gave hope to made their lives meaningful all on their own. They built their civil society from the urban rubble and, as kids do, made it wild fun.

In the early 1970s, while Clive and Cindy Campbell were jacking into streetlamps and hosting their game-changing block parties, teenagers were risking their lives for fun along the embattled Los Angeles shoreline, where crews and gangs carved up turf south of Wilshire Boulevard—from the mean streets to the breaking waves. At the turn of the century, the tobacco millionaire and real estate developer Abbot Kinney had turned the marshland south of Santa Monica into a Coney Island–style seaside resort. Coursing with Old World canals and gondolas, it earned its name, Venice of America. After 1967, when its last theme park shut down, the derelict pier and its surrounding streets gave way to typical early-seventies decay: gang wars, arson, drug dealing, vandalism. But churning in the center of its waterfront ruins was a *natural* source of thrilling amusement: the wildest break in Los Angeles, growling through the broken rib cage of the Pacific Ocean Park pier. Among the radical surfers who braved Hell's Angels and deadly chunks of urban detritus to surf underneath the P.O.P. was a band of fearless, long-haired teens sponsored by the Zephyr Surf Shop—the legendary Z-Boys. Home movies of the era show several kids at once fighting to own a curling wave, swerving and clashing between dock pilings and rebar and executing life-saving cutbacks. Locals chucked bottles and dropped concrete blocks onto outsiders who tried to crash their waves: "Death to Invaders" and "Invaders must die" read the in-dead-earnest spray-painted warnings. But the greatest hazards lurked underwater. "You could get impaled on a fallen roller coaster track or, like, a piling," Z-Boy Tony Alva recalled. Under the jagged P.O.P., these most radical Californians fairly butchered the Beach Boys' chipper "Fun, Fun, Fun." In the same breath they openly mocked the wreckage of George C. Tilyou's crumbling amusement-park legacy.

The Z-Boys were twelve Asian-American, white, and mixed-race youths, many of them "discarded kids" from low-income, single-parent households. One of their most talented members, Peggy Oki, was a girl. The Zephyr shop was their "clubhouse," and their den-mothers-of-iniquity were the owners, Skip Engblom, who organized their time and pushed them, in his words, to act like "pirates"; Jeff Ho, a professional surfer who shaped and painted surfboards to mimic graffiti and low-rider street styles; and Craig Stecyk, also a surfboard shaper, as well as a budding journalist and sports photographer whose articles in the mid-seventies for *Skateboarder* magazine made the Z-Boys national celebrities.

For the Z-Boys didn't earn their fame on the waves—they earned it on the pavement. In the afternoons, when the surf at P.O.P. was flat, they imported their hell-for-leather style to the wavy asphalt basins of local elementary schools. With the recent invention of polyurethane wheels, skateboarding, a trend that had vanished in the early sixties, was enjoying a rebirth with American kids. The Z-Boys took cues from Ho and Stecyk and crafted performance skateboards of their own from chunks of lumber and old furniture. Like B-boys and B-girls mimicking Bruce Lee, the Z-Boys aped their surfing idol, the shortboarder Larry Bertlemann. Riding low to the ground, fluid, and *fast;* dragging and planting their hands for leverage (like Bertlemann did on the waves), the Z-Boys reinvented skateboarding for extreme velocity, danger, and style.

The Z-Boys were children of a DIY culture; their mentors, and the rogue sport of surfing in general, demanded quick-thinking ingenuity. Their own guerrilla moment came in 1976, when California suffered from an historic drought and L.A.'s ubiquitous swimming pools were drained. The Z-Boys combed streets and surveyed canyons with binoculars, searching for empty pools to ride. When they found one, they would unload pool-draining equipment from their trunks and post high lookouts for cops—who often came and ran them out. "Part of the thrill was knowing the police could come at any time." The rest of the thrill, of course, was skating—carving high-speed, surflike turns in the cavernous deep ends of forbidden pools. Under these intense new conditions, each skater ground out an inimitable style (risk and style being the highest achievements), but the Z-Boys' searing competition, combined with their ganglike group cohesion, kept them raising their collective standards—for individual performance, for rebel pride. Their practice had the conviction of politics. "Skaters," Stecyk wrote that year, "are by their very nature urban guerrillas: they . . . employ the handiwork of the government/corporate structure in a thousand ways the original architects could never have dreamed of." The Z-Boys' example of the guerrilla skater enthralled the nation's kids, who followed their story, who imitated their Vans and skater hairstyles, and who scoped their hometowns for auspicious pavement. Skateboarding, like break dancing, inspired America's youth to flaunt their skills in full public view. It showed them reinhabiting the failing public sphere in creative, daring, and exciting style. "Skateboarding is not a crime" became a common tagline, a postmodern echo of the Declaration of Independence, which dared to declare a higher law. But in 1977, *Skateboarder* reported a weird new twist on the timeless feud between cops and punks: in response to a mouthy young skater's taunt ("Bet you can't ride it, pig!"), an L.A. cop shed his sidearm, took the punk's deck, borrowed Adidas from one of the "rowdies," and turned out some "highly technical freestyle routing," topping it off "with a stylish crossover dismount." He told the kid "to tighten his mounts as well as his act."

Some of the Z-Boys achieved international fame. Tony Alva bucked corporate sponsorship and, at age nineteen, started his own popular line of skateboards. Stacy Peralta used the proceeds from his co-owned skate-equipment company to found the Bones Brigade, a Zephyr-style team for the next generation of radical skaters. The Z-Boys' personal achievements aside, their greatest contributions were to the future of sports. In the fall of 1977, when Tony Alva shot up over the lip of a swimming pool and magically sculpted a turn in the air, he broke into an aerial frontier from which the sport has never returned. With the advent of makeshift half-pipes—and then with publicly sponsored skateparks—the guerrilla efforts of these L.A. daredevils blazed trails for an awe-inspiring realm of sports. From the Z-Boys' innovations came the aerial-based X Games in which skaters, snowboarders, BMXers, skysurfers, and others still push the limits of soaring midair.

Of course, with the professionalization of such sports, as was the common complaint in the 1880s, a good part of their original fun drops out. Like professional football, baseball, and basketball, the X Games

Z-Boy Shogo Kubo goes vertical in the Dogbowl, Santa Monica, 1977. (Photograph © Glen E. Friedman.)

are now big business, subject to the limits of corporate sponsorship and intense regulation. It is fitting, then, that Jay Adams, the wildest Z-Boy with the most original style, the group's surefire punk, should have lost interest when the others went pro—when, in his words, "guys didn't seem like they were having as much fun" and skating became "more of a job." At the same time, however, the urban-guerrilla side of skating—and of BMXing and break dancing and newer activities like European parkour (PK), which turns urban landscapes into aerobatic playgrounds—has inspired kids ever since with its fun of exploration and rebellion. For all the skate parks cropping up across America, the nation's parking ramps, sidewalks, and staircases still smack and growl under polyurethane wheels.

DIY WAS A PUNK TERM. DIY was a punk *ethic.* DIY was the punk rocker's exuberant raspberry at a corrupt, bankrupt, and fucked-up system—a wholesale rejection of the commercial dream. Punks, in the tradition of American pragmatism, shitcanned ideals; they scuffed the cleats of their steel-toed Doc Martens on hippie-dippie idealism. To punks, *real* punks, even the authorities (cops, presidents, whatever) weren't considered a worthwhile menace—they were just a lurid joke. And if you didn't get the joke, you weren't punk. You were just a poser, a weekend warrior in safety-pinned jeans. And the only thing worse than a poser (who was never punk to begin with) was the sell-out, the punk who *becomes* a joke.

In December 1970, writing for *Creem,* the rock critic Lester Bangs bemoaned the decadence of rock in his article "Of Pop and Pies and Fun." Designing "A Program for Mass Liberation," he scorned the new wave of self-important commercial rock in favor of the half-naked, howling Iggy Pop and his loud, simple, ridiculous, and generally offensive band, the Stooges. Bangs praises the Stooges for their "crazed quaking uncertainty" and "an errant foolishness that effectively mirrors the absurdity and desperation of the times." A grim message? Certainly. A warning? Not really. In 1970 Americans were tired of warnings. Instead, in the Stooges, America's third proto-punk band (alongside the Velvet Underground and MC5), Bangs also observed "a strong element of cure, a post-derangement sanity." Bangs's prospective "Program" involves audiences throwing pies "in the faces of performers who they thought were coming on with a load of bullshit." It also praises the Stooges for their self-mocking "courage" to admit to fans that their show was a "sham" and "the fact that you are out there and I am up here means not the slightest thing." Obliteration of the sacred stage had a long American history: in the Jackson Age, b'hoys and g'hals behaved as if they owned their celebrities; in Buddy Bolden's Jazz Age, musicians and dancers kept a hot rapport; and for a few minutes in the West, in the early sixties, the Mime Troupe and the Charlatans rose to meet their crowds in edgy showdowns of shared satire. The "rock revolution" reclaimed the stage, but Bangs wanted both sides to crush it, both the prankster crowd and the puckish rockers. All he requested was a shared sense of "fun"—the joy of smashing the Gilded Age myth of celebrity-centered enjoyment. His "Program," in a word, was punk.

In the early seventies, Andy Shernoff, a mouthy adolescent from Queens, started a disorderly fanzine, *Teenage Wasteland Gazette,* while studying music at SUNY New Paltz. Not given to the usual fanzine fawning, the *Gazette* took a cheeky *Mad Magazine* stand on the sex, drugs, and general damage of the rock 'n' roll lifestyle—which is to say, it reveled in it. It invented fake bands. It reviewed fake shows. So true was it to the dangerous fun of rock that it received the unprintable castoffs of major rock critics like, yes, Lester Bangs and the gleefully anarchistic Richard Meltzer, who reported in its pages on a blow-out party where furniture, records, and art were destroyed; where sex was had right out in the open; where Meltzer scrawled obscenities on the walls; and where the host, "Handsome Dick Manitoba" (this was his parents' house), met the cops at the door wearing "a jock strap with red lipstick swastikas drawn all over [his] body." Out of such orgies and the wasteland revelry of the *Gazette,* America's first bona fide punk band was born. Disgusted by the decadent softening of rock by noodlers like Emerson, Lake, and Palmer; tickled by the New York Dolls' rude camp theater; enthralled by the raw-boned, three-chord assaults of MC5 and the Stooges, as well as by the equipment-wrecking spectacles of the Who, Shernoff and Manitoba and some friends from Queens and the Bronx—the genuine teenage wasteland where hip-hop was born—formed the brash, hilarious, reckless, gross, and supremely adolescent Dictators. Asked how they settled on that name, Shernoff said it was the "funniest."

They had been practicing for half a year in a farmhouse in the Catskills when, thanks to Meltzer's connections, some producers from Epic Records took their DIY rock 'n' roll parody seriously. *The Dictators Go Girl Crazy!,* released in 1975, struck a sweet harmony between insult and irony. The album's signature track, "Master Race Rock," reads like Manitoba's lipstick swastikas—or Mel Brooks's "Springtime for Hitler": if you didn't catch the wisecrack from a song that precedes it ("We knocked 'em dead in Dallas / They didn't know we were Jews"), you might think they were Nazis, but that tension is the point, and the offense is the joke. Stepping on toes was the Dictators' stock-in-trade; they devoured sensitive types like White Castle cheeseburgers. "Hippies," after all, as this song opines, "are squares with long hair, they don't wear no underwear." The band's comedy roars in their mock-macho choruses, ripples in Ross Funicello's lead guitar, and rides on vocalist Shernoff's comic timing. Only a loser wouldn't get the joke. Still, not to be underdone by losers, they giddily, idiotically, spell it out: "We tell jokes to make you laugh, we play sports so we don't get fat."

The most auspiciously punk gesture on *The Dictators Go Girl Crazy!* may be its two cover tunes—blistering guitar tributes to Sonny and Cher's number-one 1965 hit, "I Got You Babe," and the Riviera's number-five 1964 hit, "California Sun." These covers poke fun at the seventies' *American Graffiti* nostalgia and refine rock 'n' roll's essential nonchalance. In the tradition of Thomas Morton's satires nailed to the Maypole, or of Alfred Doten's correspondence about Wild West bacchanalia in the pages of the *Plymouth Rock,* the Dictators' Benzedrine-pitched pop-rock tributes revel in their unwelcome intimacy with an audience that they have every intention of offending. Such rankling punk parodies send an all-American message: We're in this together, like it or not. All of us are tapping the same cultural keg, so we may as well enjoy our differences. The Dictators' most obvious musical inspiration was the bubblegum surf-pop of the early 1960s. Like the Z-Boys, however, they gleefully rubbed their feet on early surfing's beach-blanket innocence. The album's closing number, "(I Live for) Cars and Girls," rips off the Beach Boys' trademark "Ooooo-wheee-aaah-ooooo" and relocates the party to teenage wasteland. It opens, "I'm the type of guy / who likes to get high / on a Friday afternoon." The lifestyle this song equally razzes and celebrates entails pretty much the same reckless hedonism that nearly killed Jan Berry of Jan & Dean, but the Dictators mock and embrace its anarchy: "Cars-girls-surfing-beer / Nothing else matters here!" It's California fun by way of the outer boroughs, where kids were never promised anything, and its tongue-in-cheek patriotism looks ahead to the anti-neotraditionalism of Reagan-era hardcore: "It's the hippest scene, it's the American dream, and for that I'll always fight!"

Kids were slow to catch on. The Dictators went right over their heads. Critics dismissed them as novelty rock, which of course they were, but four guys from Forest Hills, who attended their shows and imitated their streetwise dress (leather jackets, T-shirts, jeans, and sneakers), understood their subversive force. Posing as a dysfunctional family called the Ramones, they turned surf-punk shtick into performance art, and by 1976 they were dominating the art-rock scene that had coalesced around a lower Manhattan bar called CBGB-OMFUG. The Ramones tempered their humor with gormless cool and punched it out in one- to three-minute anthems: "Blitzkrieg Bop" ("Master Race Rock" redux), "Beat on the Brat" (drubbing rich kids), "Let's Dance" (punk tribute), "Judy Is a Punk." If the Dictators gave the lie to their chuckleheaded rock with smarting swipes at the oil industry, the Ramones, despite the aggressive idiocy of songs like "Now I Wanna Sniff Some Glue," mocked their own political and historical educations with smartass polemics like "Havana Affair": "Now I'm a guide for the CIA / Hooray for the USA!"

Early New York punks—often suburban social dropouts who adapted the modern-primitive looks of their working-class (and largely unemployed) English brethren—embraced these bands' overeducated stupidity as the antidote to so much bullshit: hippie earnestness, disco excess, government corruption, bourgeois materialism. In the tradition of 1960s undergrounds and the *Teenage Wasteland Gazette,* with a contact buzz from the English *Sniffin' Glue,* they published and distributed handwritten fanzines that flouted all taste, decorum, and polish. Transatlantic/transcontinental zines like *New York Rocker, Maximum Rock 'n' Roll, Ripped and Torn,* and Legs McNeil's superlative *Punk* were aggressively childish and obscene publications. Interviewers insulted bands (and vice versa). Editors insulted readers. Badly written articles and badly drawn cartoons espoused nihilism, drinking, insolence, vandalism. But even as they promulgated the anarchic lifestyle that (ironically) brought punks closer together, zines also functioned like Sons of Liberty screeds in defining the punks' civil society. As the historian Tricia Henry has shown, zines intervened as a sort of conduct manual between unruly bands and their audiences, whose most creative response to angry acts like the Sex Pistols could be to spit or throw beer bottles. While the mainstream press liked to sensationalize punks' garish public fury, making them a caricature of society's decay, the zines, which knew better, showed readers "that there was a line between good-natured, high-spirited fun and senseless, destructive violence." The enemy wasn't the bands or other punks. The enemy was boredom. Even, *especially,* Johnny Rotten—the "I is anarchy" *porte parole* of violent 1970s punk—stressed the carefree pleasure of his profession: "Rock 'n' roll is supposed to be fun. You remember fun, don'tcha?"

And yet, in the late 1970s, while the Dictators and the Ramones were remembering fun and Sid Vicious, late of New York, broke any and all rules and laws, there remained a skittish disconnect between the surly, stylish fans and the bands and zines making all the noise. In England, it was popular for punks to "pogo," a thuggish, jostling, hopping dance that matched the music's 4/4 time. Stateside, however, at CBGB and elsewhere, arty crowds would stand by in toleration while a shrill, pounding, and screaming ensemble like Cleveland's excoriating Dead Boys—which Nicholas Rombes calls "one of the first punk bands to drive off the cliff"—showered them in abuse. Lester Bangs's "Program for Mass Liberation" had not yet come into its own.

But then sometime around 1980, rather appropriately in San Francisco and Los Angeles, American punks remembered their California education and the crowds themselves got in on the act. As a new breed of "hardcore" punk bands (the Dead Kennedys, Germs, Circle Jerks, Black Flag) hit the gas and sped the music up to 8/4, 8/8, and faster (and gnarlier), a furious synergy gushed up from the crowd and rose to meet the action onstage. With the birth of the mosh pit—that sloshing mass of unchecked youth that chewed like a blender in front of the band— punk became a full-contact sport. Suddenly punk was American fun. This rude and sweaty new California fun lacked the skill of the B-boys' cypher, lacked the soaring elegance of the Z-Boys' aerials, but what it shared with both of them—and with the 1850s miners' ball that J. D. Borthwick saw at Angels Camp—was a raw, reckless, rebellious pleasure that pulled the outcast crowd together. What all of these revelers shared, throughout history, was respect for radical civility: a rough balance of individual and communal pleasures. Mosh-pit fun pushed civility to its limits. Lifesaving rules were honored in the pit (they would pick you up if you fell to the ground), but mostly (and this was the point) all bets were off. If you joined the mosh pit, you were in it for pushing, thrashing, kicking, head-butting—whatever. Buddy Bolden invented early jazz by reading the crowd. Punk musicians dove right in—riding, surfing, often *fighting* the crowd.

Hardcore fulfilled the Dictators' promise of unsafe, unclean, politically tainted fun. From 1979 to 1982, hardcore metastasized throughout America's urban centers, growing its most pernicious cells up the East Coast's I-95 corridor—from the turf of D.C.'s Minor Threat and Bad Brains to Boston's Negative FX and Gang Green. Self-sufficient "scenes" cropped up around hardcore, much as they had around hippie "tribes." Connected by word of mouth, DIY publications, and late-night shows on college radio stations, the hardcore explosion enthralled American youth with its virulent amateurism. Hardcore dropped all pretense of art. Anyone, it seemed, could throw together a band, write some deliberately terrible songs, and successfully enrage a crowd.

Punks hated money with all the fervor of the Diggers and Yippies. Crafting a barter-and-forage economy, they parasitized the system they scorned and lived bare lives of urban primitivism. They gathered their food, clothing, and furniture from curbs, dumpsters, and alleyways. If hippies "dropped out" and inhabited crash pads, punks went them one further and "squatted"—overtaking abandoned buildings where

An early 1980s mosh pit at Merlyn's Club in Madison, Wisconsin. (Photograph © Hank Grebe.)

they "pirated" plumbing and electricity and burned indoor bonfires for heat. Often these "punk houses" assumed an identity—around a band, around a purifying belief system like veganism or "straight edge" (the refusal to drink or take drugs). Punk houses let the squatters form radically defined communities in the cracks of mainstream civil society. Punks were clannish like hippies had been, but their larger subculture wasn't defined by psychedelia and peace-and-love "being." Restless, irreverent, and violently pissed off by the stark incongruities of Reagan's America (union busting, runaway unemployment, material excess, "trickle-down" economics), punks, for all their competing identities, were defined by the rage and blistering ironies expressed in their anti-rock-star music. To listen to their scorching diatribes, it is clear that hardcore punks, like their predecessors the Dictators, held hippies and other rockers in contempt. But for this reason, they showed a sneaking kinship with the Merry Pranksters, Diggers, and Yippies. Jello Biafra, the Dead Kennedys' superlative frontman, recalls the band's only Bill Graham show, when they opened for the Cramps and the Clash. Graham was still playing the hand-wringing chaperone. Biafra: "I did my usual swan dive in a crowd of about 3000 jocks, and when I emerged, the only clothes left on my body were my belt, shoes, and socks. I did the rest of the show *nude* while Bill Graham smoldered by the edge of the stage."

By the sociologist Ryan Moore's interpretation, punk culture was an "exclamation point" on the sixties counterculture's "decline into impotence." Which is to say, the subcultures were syntactically linked—by rock, by rebellion, by DIY resistance. But like Z-Boys' surfing and skating in the debris of California's failed leisure class, hardcore punks gloried in the rot of the hippies' flower-waving optimism. They grinned bloody grins of pessimism.

A hardcore punk show was frightening to witness. To cops, to parents, to the uninitiated, the mutual destruction between the stage and the crowd signaled the failure of civilization. The punk show was a rehearsal of raw social violence that flaunted its bloodshed and broken bones. And as the historian Lauraine Leblanc shows, hardcore punk's mosh pit—Jello Biafra's "3000 jocks"—was intensely masculine. The gender-inclusive art-punk scene of the late 1970s had given way to a physically aggressive arena where women were assaulted as freely as men (to this extent, the violence was democratic) but also, often, groped—a fact, however, that didn't stop a rash of female hardcore bands from forming. The mosh pit wasn't pretty. It was a consensual bloodsport for self-selecting thrashers. And yet, for this reason, it was the practice of anarchy, whose danger was as attractive to the leftist and pacifist as it was to the most divisive, racist skinhead. In the mosh pit these strangers could thrash like bosom enemies in spite of their ideological differences. To the uninitiated, the mosh pit looked mirthless, *merciless,* the polar opposite of fun, but for the willing and exhilarated participants—who dove back in, night after night, with the stamina of ring dancers on Congo Square—thrashing was the sheerest, funnest expression of all the outrage that made punk punk. Thrashing was the hardest-core way to show that you got (and could take) the big cosmic joke.

ONE MORE STORY. (One more joke.) America's original punk allegory was published by Nathaniel Hawthorne in 1831, four years before his "May-Pole of Merry Mount." Now a staple in high school literature courses, "My Kinsman, Major Molineux" tells the revolutionary-era tale of Robin, a "shrewd youth," who comes to Boston from his home in the sticks expecting a break from his kinsman, the governor. As it turns out, Major Molineux is nowhere to be found. Robin starts asking around, and at first he is puzzled by the citizens' coarse reactions. Shouldn't his connections get him some respect? He is indignant toward the gentleman who offers to throw him in the stocks. Despite his Puritan upbringing, he feels warmth for the drinkers he finds conspiring in a tavern, and vows to join them when he has earned some money, but they turn hostile when he mentions his kinsman. Next, a pretty wench in a "scarlet petticoat" tries to drag him through her door, insisting his kinsman dwells within, but then a night watchman scorns their impropriety and prods Robin along, leaving him more frustrated than ever.

Long story short, he spends the night in the streets, bemoaning his outcast fate and listening to an approaching band of merrymakers. Talking with a stranger about this "multitude of rioters," he proposes that they, too, should take their "share of the fun." But when the musical procession rounds the corner, he is quickly intimidated by their savage democracy: some are "wild figures in the Indian dress," others "fantastic shapes without model," and all of them—both spectators and participants—raise "shrill voices of mirth or terror." More to the point, at the head of their procession, carted along like an obscene punch line, is Major Molineux himself, "in tar-and-feather dignity."

The crowd goes silent while Robin takes it in. The disgraced kinsman is pitiable, to say the least: "His whole frame was agitated by a quick, and continual tremor, which his pride strove to quell, even in those circumstances of overwhelming humiliation." But then as Robin locks eyes with his elder, "a bewildering excitement" fills his head, and as the members of the crowd start to chuckle, then to laugh, the "contagion" of hilarity soon envelops Robin:

> He sent forth a shout of laughter that echoed through the street; every man shook his sides, every man emptied his lungs, but Robin's shout was the loudest there. The cloud-spirits peeped from their silvery islands, as the congregated mirth went roaring up the sky! The Man in the Moon heard the far bellow; "Oho," quoth he, "the old Earth is frolicsome to-night!"

As in his tale of Merry Mount, Hawthorne seems ambivalent about all this fun. "On they went," he continues, "in counterfeited pomp, in senseless uproar, in frenzied merriment, trampling all on an old man's heart." And in the orgy's postcoital aftermath, Robin rather dejectedly wants to return home, but a crowd member urges him to stay on a few days, suggesting his participation in the "congregated mirth" may help him to "rise in the world, without the help of [his] kinsman, Major Molineux." Robin has contracted the wild power of the people. In getting the joke, Hawthorne seems to say, he is on his way to becoming a citizen—a DIY citizen, of course.

The story's "senseless uproar" and "frenzied merriment" pretty accurately depicts the seventeenth-century "rough music" with which colonists tarred and feathered outcasts. The fun was scary, one-sided, sadistic, and often it did the Puritan authority's bidding. Rough music was in most cases glorified bullying, and it seldom advanced democratic virtues—even when it was employed during the Revolution to overthrow Royalists. But the governor's humiliation is only part of the pleasure. Hawthorne tells us how to become an American citizen. You become a citizen by getting the people's joke. In Robin's case, the joke is complicated. He comes to town thinking he will cash in on the monarchy. But at the same time he develops a taste for the people's joys—their taverns, their brothels, their riotous fun. So when it turns out that authority has fallen, and that the joke is on him, he finds himself laughing louder than anyone because self-rule is what he wanted all along. The rioters crack the joke, but Robin takes it best because it means most to him.

And so it has gone throughout American history. The "Merry, Merry Boyes" got Thomas Morton's joke that Plymouth Plantation was a joyless prison—and that people were made for frolic and freedom. The American colonists got the Sons of Liberty's joke that England didn't have a clue—and that government should rise up from the streets. Antebellum blacks got Brother Rabbit's joke that the master was himself a trickster, if a duller one—and that the purest freedom was in having fun. And the forty-niners got each other's joke that the United States was turning stiff and stodgy—and that civility was only stifled by manners. All of these American citizenry-building jokes took aim at some humorless authority or other: if you laughed at the joke, you either got it or *took* it, or—as in Robin's case—both. More powerful and personal than even ideology, these American jokes created steely citizens out of their most chest-racking pleasures. They hard-wired an electric sense of humor into the national character.

Their twentieth-century beneficiaries got the big American joke: that fun—especially fun in the midst of struggle—is the personal and communal experience of freedom. All it requires is a cavalier attitude toward killjoys, tyrants, limits, and timidity. In these terms, the 1920s and the 1960s were arguably the nation's *funnest* decades. They were also decades of extreme upheaval. This is no coincidence. But while many Americans responded to upheaval (clashes in values, race-and-culture wars) with hardheaded resistance and bloody rioting, the ones who got the joke had the times of their lives. (It was like surfing in the rubble under the P.O.P. pier.) All the better if a square majority thought they could shut the rebels down—that was what made it a joke to begin with! That was what made it a laugh riot! Laughter, in these cases, is a powerful metaphor for how such citizens responded to struggle: with ebullience—dancing, capering, cracking jokes. Laughter, as such, is the perfection of citizenship. It is the joy of the one joining the joy of the many in a powerful wave of common purpose.

"Congregated mirth." "Joyous revolt." "Revolution for the hell of it." These are fundamentally American phrases. They capture citizens being born of laughter at moments of widespread social struggle: the Revolution, the Jazz Age, and the sixties, respectively. Such snapshots of citizens coming of age, and recognizing their exhilarating power, have inspired Americans during the barren periods, when democracy itself can look like a joke, but these images may be more than inspiring snapshots. They may be the nation's most enduring icons, alongside Old Glory and Lady Liberty. For as the post-colonial theorist Frantz Fanon brilliantly argued, a nation's "consciousness" and its most binding "culture" isn't created during the easy times, the peaceful times, when it can seem as if the arts and the public flourish. They are created during the periods of highest struggle, when the people's liberties are under attack and their identity is under reconstruction. So it is that Americans have embraced fun—*the playful practice of threatened liberties*—during the eras examined in this book. So it is, too, that the blackface minstrels and the Buffalo Bills who amused Americans during times of leisure simulated and packaged pure American fun. As these entertainers seemed to know, such wild acts of liberty and rebellion were among the nation's great treasures, and audiences loved to kick back and relive them.

But nostalgia isn't the same as fun. Nostalgia, a dreamy and passive pleasure, may even be the death of fun: it is the vicarious enjoyment of your *ancestors'* fun. The pioneering youth of the 1970s showed a healthy sense of the past: They dismantled it. They made it useful in the moment. Funk artists cracked gunpowder from black culture's firecrackers; they packed it into a big, fat space-age bomb. B-boys and B-girls used their parents' records to jimmy a head-spinning street-corner art form. Z-Boys stripped the hotdogging from sixties surf culture and retrofitted it for their urban reality. And punks, inspired by primitive rock 'n' roll, repurposed its native thrills and rebellion to suit their own fuck-you attitudes. Each of these classes of DIY pioneers spawned a billion-dollar industry that, left to its own devices, would have erased its humble origins. But the fun they invented was so pure, so raw, that it still hits the people where they live—not out of nostalgia, but in practice. The practices themselves have become global ambassadors for radical American fun. George Clinton's P-Funk All Stars are as mad as ever, and they still inspire insanely grooving crowds. Skateboarding and its many extreme-sport spin-offs still inspire thrashers young and old to shred, carve, rail-slide, and fly. The heritage of punk is visible everywhere—from the mainstreaming of piercings and tattoos to the guerrilla distribution of music. And breakdance crews, taggers, MCs, and DJs have become unshakable institutions among the world's youth; indeed, hip-hop (in its many cross-pollinating forms) has become the global instrument of celebration and protest. To be sure, hip-hop was the dominant cultural expression during the 2011 Arab Spring uprisings.

The legacy of these 1970s thrills raises an important question: Is it still fun if you're paying for it? Is it still fun if you buy a Burton skateboard and carve the half-pipe at your local skatepark? The answer, of course, is yes. It's a scream. Even wearing the regulation pads and a helmet, you can tear it up on your $200 deck, and you can hone your thrashing skills. But it isn't the fun of DIY invention, urban exploration, physical danger, and civil disorder that the Z-Boys enjoyed in 1976. It is fun within serious limits, and for all of its thrills it is (by contrast) scripted. And rather obedient. The fact that there are public skateparks and high-performance skateboards signals progress: America has embraced this sport, as it did bicycles in the nineteenth century. Towns want to make skating safe and acceptable. The economy has more opportunity to grow. America is better off for all of this. Yet such government and commercial intervention in a sport that was born of radical liberty means that the fun itself has changed; it has become mediated. For the skaters who take pride in their flashy store-bought equipment have already missed the Z-Boys' joke: Skating is a guerrilla activity. It's the fun of beating, not supporting, the system.

P. T. Barnum said it himself: all of business is humbug. How else could business turn a profit, if it didn't trick you with advertising? If it didn't hook you with its product? This particular brand of humbug was perfected in the late 1960s, when merchandise was developed and marketed and sold to make Americans feel like rebels. Now, as then, customers always pay for this privilege, and purveyors keep it safe (and generally clean) to curb their liability. They can't afford customers taking *real* risks. Plus it's bad for business to encourage *real* rebellion. And yet, marketers know Americans love fun—they have known this for centuries. And they know that Americans, especially kids, crave autonomy and participation, so they simulate the DIY experience at franchises like the Build-A-Bear "workshops," where kids construct teddy bears from limited options, or "DIY" restaurants, where customers pay to grill their own steaks, fry their own pancakes, make their own Bloody Marys. These pay-to-play stores and restaurants are, in a sense, more active, more "fun," than their traditional competition: that's their big selling point. But in both cases (as Barnum knew) the joke is still on you: the personalized bear is a standardized mishmash, the personalized food is often inedible. As Las Vegas knows, the house always wins.

In the history of radical American fun, pleasure comes from resistance, risk, and participation—the same virtues celebrated in the "Port Huron Statement" and the Digger Papers, in the flapper's slang and the *Pinkster Ode*. In the history of commercial amusement, most pleasures for sale are by necessity passive. They curtail creativity and they limit participation (as they do, say, in a laser-tag arena) to a narrow range of calculated surprises, often amplified by dazzling technology. To this extent, TV and computer screens, from the tiny to the colossal, have become the scourge of American fun. The ubiquity of TV screens in public spaces (even in taxicabs and elevators) shows that such viewing isn't amusement at all but rather an aggressive, ubiquitous distraction. Although a punky insurgency of heedless satire has stung the airwaves in recent decades—from equal-opportunity offenders like *The Simpsons* and *South Park* to Comedy Central's rabble-rousing pundits, Jon Stewart and Stephen Colbert—the prevailing "fun" of commercial amusement puts minimal demands on citizens, besides their time and money. TV's inherent ease seems to be its appeal, but it also sends a sobering, Jumbotron-sized message about the health of the public sphere.

Computer screens are more pernicious yet, since they seize on our native DIY desires. They offer narrow, *fascinating* involvement—in a safer, simpler, duller realm. In this age of iPhones, iPads, and so on, tiny screens shape our consciousness from early infancy—when babies have yet to find their footing in the risky, exciting world of things— and cleverly precede our 3-D reality with flashy, lifelike 2-D simulacra. Before we can draw or read or write, we swipe and tap and click like pros. After that, from early childhood to post-retirement, we learn to funnel our entire lived experience through chintzy hand-held pixillated screens—snapping photos, shooting videos, e-mailing, texting, tweet- ing, updating, mapping, Googling, Foursquaring, ad nauseam. Our free time (mealtime/playtime/facetime) is forever interrupted by "snack" entertainment: bite-size junk-food games and gifs and sugar-salty puffs of news. At night, our quiet and docile crowds resemble eerie blue can- dlelight vigils, but our downturned faces are staring at Facebook. And when Google has its way—coming soon!—all of us will see the world through the hyperreality of screen-colored glasses.

In the digital assault on American fun, video games pack the big- gest wallop. Video games, which can be the *products* of extraordinary creativity, replicate high levels of risk and participation (warfare, car crashes, zombie invasions) when in fact the players—like Build-A-Bear customers—fashion their avatars from the designers' choices and spend hours, years, within prescribed worlds that demand nothing obvious in the way of personal stakes. Most deceptive may be the so-called interac- tive games—Wii (with its no-impact, weightless, plastic pantomime of rackets, bats, clubs, and jump ropes); *Guitar Hero* and *Rock Band* (whose would-be rock stars spend hundreds of hours becoming "expert" at punching colored buttons in sequence); and the cynically named *Dance Dance Revolution* (whose would-be Vera Sheppards, Shorty Snowdens, and B-boys tap out buttons instead of executing gravity-defying moves). Are the thousands of hours Americans clock with their thumbs and fore- fingers . . . fun? Or does the fun soon corrode into compulsive behavior? An endless rat maze of binary decisions? The video-game proponent Jane McGonigal, one of *BusinessWeek*'s "ten innovators to watch," argues that video games are what she calls "hard fun," a term she coins from the phrase "hard work," because they create "positive stress" for the gamer and a sense of accomplishment. In particular, they generate an "emotional rush" of "pride," which game designers call by its Italian name, *fiero,* and which is "one of the most powerful neurochemical highs we can experience." This habit-forming rush of "hard fun," she argues, can motivate gamers to inhabit "alternate realities," to have "fun with strangers" under disguised identities, and ultimately, she believes, to reengage with fellow citizens in the real world. She even argues that video games will make us "dance more."

All while staring at a television screen. The student of American fun, *real* fun, has to ask "Why?" Why would a vigorous and youthful and (to consider the costs of such equipment) *prosperous* population sacrifice its enjoyment to the screen? To the habit-forming tricks of a game designer? Clearly, as with any kind of fun, the *pleasure* of gaming is a reason in itself, possibly the only reason. But what sort of nation does this amusement foster? What sort of "global happiness"? A twitchy one, to be certain, and sedentary. Even for all of the vaunted worldwide connectivity of multiplayer systems, for their celebrated "fun with strangers," gaming fosters physically isolated citizens, an atomized citizenry that finds it harder, not more inspiring, to break free from their screens and to engage face-to-face. To the student of American fun—of lively, risky, rebellious action that has set people free for four hundred years—it all just looks so *safe.*

When in fact it isn't. McGonigal, in describing the neurochemistry of *fiero* (the gamer's emotional benefit), locates the sensation in the "reward circuitry of the brain . . . which is most typically associated with reward and addiction." As McGonigal only passingly acknowledges, *fiero*'s relevance to addiction is real, and a serious problem among game-playing youth. Sure, *fiero,* as a neurochemical fact, is a thrill that arises from any accomplishment, from an ace serve in tennis to scientific triumphs (cut to NASA's astrophysicists wild-partying over a Mars landing, particle physicists popping champagne over the Higgs boson discovery), but the mind-blowing humbug of video games is to deliver higher and stronger *fiero* for lower levels of accomplishment, and to keep it coming in rapid doses. What is more, the effects that enhance this often violent experience make it larger, and larger than life. Games have amplified television's habit formation by making it minimally interactive and by overpowering the brain's reward center: after winning the World Cup, or World War II, or saving the world from aliens or zombies, gamers lose interest in real accomplishments. Or they become intimidated: after spending months in front of the television, perfecting your free throw becomes a distant achievement. Like the lethal "Entertainment" in David Foster Wallace's novel *Infinite Jest,* video games dead-end their players' willpower into a cul-de-sac of absolute withdrawal.

Tom Bissell tells a harrowing tale in his brilliant book *Extra Lives:* his video-game addiction led to a cocaine addiction that allowed him to play more video games. A recent Google search for "Video Game Addiction Treatment" yielded 207,000 hits and treatment centers around the world. The American Psychiatric Association has the condition slated for inclusion in its next edition of the *Diagnostic and Statistical Manual of Mental Disorders,* but the research is in its infancy. Video gamers feel the thrill of reward, but what "rewards" do they actually reap after hours, days, and years of "hard fun"? And what rewards does the nation reap? McGonigal acknowledges such hazards, and she also mentions an industry-specific anomie called "gamer regret," but in downplaying them she rather games the facts, hailing a new generation of games that "go beyond flow and *fiero*" and "provide a more lasting kind of emotional reward." This may be so, but such nutritious fare doesn't account for video games' runaway popularity; first-person-shooter junk food does. She also says that "very big games represent the future of collaboration," and she may be right. The student of fun thinks it's too soon to celebrate.

IN 2010, the Supreme Court's *Citizens United v. Federal Election Commission* ruling declared that corporations merit the free speech of any legal citizen and thus are allowed unlimited political broadcasts. That same year, the "American" corporation General Electric earned $14.2 billion worldwide, $5.1 billion of that in the United States, and paid $0.00 in U.S. taxes. GE even claimed a $3.2 billion tax benefit. When these figures hit the news, the public was outraged, but GE's spokesperson was unflappable: "We did not owe any," she said. According to the Supreme

Court decision, corporations deserve all the rights of citizens, including a bully pulpit for electing government leaders, but at the same time their immense collective power—especially when they assume "multinational" identity—lets them shirk the citizen's basic responsibilities. This fact spells despair for the nation's vitality—if its "vitality" (as the word denotes) rests with actual human beings. Hence, in March 2011, when GE recanted and announced that they were returning their $3.2 billion "refund," the Associated Press immediately published the story. What great news! GE revealed that it had the conscience of an everyday citizen! But the press release was a hoax, of course. It was the latest coup of the ingenious Yes Men, a pair of trickster citizens who have been calling out corporations since the 1990s. In this case, all the nation got back from GE's staggering profits was congregated—if bitter—mirth.

Our nation's vitality doesn't rest with corporations. It rests with people—not only as voters but as active citizens with the potential energy of "physical bodies," as Saul Alinsky, legendary activist extraordinaire, writes in his classic *Rules for Radicals*. Bodies are the agents of political action, especially among those whom he calls the "Have-Nots," those whose resources are "no money" and "lots of people." His advice for activating the citizens' bodies might as well be a recipe for American fun: "Use the power of law," he suggests, "by making the establishment obey its own rules. Go outside the experience of your enemy, stay inside the experience of your people"—or, in other words, if you're an American colonist in the 1760s, bewilder the British by parading your freedom and acting like Samuel Adams's "True Patriots." Alinsky goes on: "Emphasize tactics *that your people will enjoy*. The threat is usually more terrifying than the tactic itself"—emphasize tactics, that is to say, like the decades of fun on Pinkster Hill and, a century later, in the Savoy Ballroom, enjoyable tactics that may have threatened uptight contemporaries but ultimately harmed nobody. "Once all these rules and principles are festering in your imagination," he concludes, "they grow into a synthesis." And that synthesis—that prank, that party, that hoax, that joke—could plant the seeds of what the moral-sense philosopher Adam Ferguson called "national felicity," the rough, raw, and widespread fellow-feeling that can keep a nation feeling young and that can, in the best cases, unite its citizenry, from the least of the have-nots to the richest of the haves.

Our nation's vitality rests with people. It rests with prisoners and illegal immigrants; with the homeless, unemployed, and poor; and with the ever-dwindling middle class as well as with presidents and CEOs. Rereading history, where the people are heroes and creativity flourishes in times of greatest struggle, one sees the vitality of American democracy cropping up in some low-down places: trading posts, dockyards, mining camps, taverns. Most remarkably, America's most original culture, America's most *durable* culture—now an immeasurable international rhizome of hip-hop, techno, rock, dance, style, slang, humor, sports, whatnot—got its roaring start in the southern slave quarters, among Americans who valued possibly more than anyone the liberty and equality that they were denied. Among people who held tight to their forbidden African heritage while embracing their new American conditions. Among people who were witty enough to tell the joke, nimble enough to get the joke, and tough enough to take the joke.

Doing it yourself is individualist fun. Getting the joke is collectivist fun. Together they foster a strong, smart nation. American democracy hasn't been fortified by passive citizens, not by the obedient, gullible, or accepting, not by citizens who wait to be governed and not by thugs doing demagogues' bidding, but by active, resistive, DIY citizens who take pleasure in agency and group definition. It's a fundamentally American idea: citizens should be defined as much by their *fun* as by their work or service or duty. It's also a distinctly American phenomenon that these four principles (work, service, duty, and fun) can and should be one and the same—as they were for the "Mohawks" storming Griffin's Wharf, as they were for the Yippies showering the NYSE with cash, as they were for the Yes Men writing GE's press release. They may not have known it at the time, but when, in 1973, Cindy and Clive Campbell threw their back-to-school bash and urged the crowd to new levels of ecstasy, they were doing the work of exemplary citizens, honoring the past and providing for the future. For all they knew they were just having fun, but they did it with a shrewd and playful creativity that unleashed the people's constructive power.

Americans in recent decades—gender activists, in particular—have been deliberate in binding these four principles. In 1985, the Guerrilla Girls, a pseudonymous collective of female artists, took on the overwhelmingly male New York arts establishment with comic posters, a "penis count" at the Met, and other street actions—all executed in gorilla masks. (Their antic movement is still going strong.) Also in the 1980s, New York's drag balls, whose heritage stretches back to the Savoy Ballroom, gained new force and splendor and acceptance, thanks in part to Jenny Livingston's documentary, *Paris Is Burning* (1990), and to this day are a spinning disco-ball hub for the nation's transgender community.

In the early 1990s, B-girls and Riot Grrrls pushed back *hard* against male-chauvinist rap and punk. On Thursday nights in L.A.'s Leimert Park, for example, at the hip-hop institution called Project Blowed, female MCs like Venus, Tasha Kweli, and the legendary Medusa—considered "the queen and high priestess" of the L.A. underground—defeated men and women in fierce rap battles and on the floor in break-dance cyphers. Flashing her double-W hand sign and honoring the long heritage of African-American women, Medusa—like Bessie Smith, with whom a male competitor once respectfully compared her—also made daring claim to her sexuality, even in rap battles with tough male opponents quick to write her off as a "ho." But her deft lyricism and ferocious irony put the best of rappers on their back feet. As the hip-hop scholar Marcyliena Morgan demonstrates, Medusa's "crowd-pleasing anthem," "My Pussy Is a Gangsta," flips the street code and satirizes both men and women: men, by "us[ing] gangsta, a hiphop term associated with misogynistic, predatory, and sadistic men," to refer to "a woman's sexual and reproductive organ"; women, by calling out the ones who wield their "femininity," as Medusa puts it, "to their extreme advantage."

Also in the early 1990s, when macho hardcore had lost its momentum, giving way to less political (and more commercial) speed metal, the Riot Grrrl punk scene launched in Washington State and shot across the country. Technically and musically masterful Grrrl bands—spearheaded by the likes of Bikini Kill and Bratmobile—revitalized the punk ethos for a new generation of do-it-yourself, up-yours, uncompromising feminists. If NOW inspired the "second-wave" feminists in 1966, rejecting the counterculture's cavalier tone in favor of unambiguous anger, then Riot Grrrls energized the young "third wave" with all the irreverence, obscenity, and swagger of the hardcore punk movement. They resuscitated Lester Bangs's "Program for Mass Liberation," rejecting the music industry's love affair with grunge and running with small labels like Kill Rock Stars; mocking "beergutboyrock" and needling self-important male rockers who lacked what the band Sleater-Kinney called "rock 'n' roll fun." Riot Grrrls' new wave of fire-breathing zines (*Fuckapotamus, Something Smells, Puberty Strike, Teenage Gang Debs*) sported creativity, power, and comedy and declared independence from male-dominated rock. Riot Grrrl attitude made a comeback in 2011, when women staged "SlutWalks" in seventy-six cities around the world and reclaimed their miniskirts as symbols of power. "When was the last time feminism was this much fun?" *The Nation*'s Katha Pollitt asked. Riot Grrrl–inspired stunts made world news in 2012, when three members of Pussy Riot, Russia's multicolored-balaclava-sporting feminist punk collective, were sentenced to two years of penal-colony time for performing their anti-Putin, putatively blasphemous "Punk Prayer" in a Moscow cathedral. That same year, oversize-underpants-wearing female "Volunteers" staged disruptive pranks and playfully resistive feminist street theater throughout the People's Republic of China.

A look back over the past half century shows a groundswell of ethnic- and identity-based groups whose long-standing parties, conventions, and parades broke the levees in the eighties and nineties. For more than a century "Mardi Gras Indians"—New Orleans neighborhoods and gangs paying tribute to Native Americans who sheltered blacks during slavery—have staged once-violent, now intensely playful showdowns of masquerade and mimicry. For generations a New Year's Day Mummers' Parade has strutted and blared its outlandish mummery through the center of Philadelphia. Gay Pride parades, originating in the 1969 Stonewall riots, have grown the world over into weeklong hootenannies. Plus: Chicanos' Cinco de Mayo, black Texans' Juneteenth, Trekkie conventions, Civil War reenactments, underground-comics fairs, Coney Island's Mermaid Parade, San Francisco's Folsom Street leather fair, Deadhead tribes, sock-burning sailors, grrrl-powered roller derby leagues, and the riotous Sturgis Motorcycle Rally whose participant population every year since 2000 has eclipsed that of South Dakota, in whose Badlands the party goes down. While the nation's teenagers blow major bucks on the official holidays of Homecoming and Prom, they still fight for their rights to unchaperoned dances, heedless house parties, and, most fun of all (sorry, administrators), Senior Skip Day and Senior Prank.

And in the long tradition of revolutionary-era broadsides, Washoe newspapers, sixties undergrounds, and punk-rock zines, a DIY bonanza in fun information dominates the Internet. On blogs, YouTube, Facebook, Twitter, Urban Dictionary, people get the joke. These technologies and more—many of them "free," if not always in the Diggers' purest sense—have excellent potential for creative fun: they foster public debate and media parody; they get people producing their own films and music and forming networks without corporate sponsorship; they allow strangers to throw spontaneous parties on sidewalks and department-store floors—the site, indeed, of the first millennial flash mob, when some one hundred citizens answered the call to pile onto a rug at the flagship Macy's. Whether triggering nonpartisan pillow fights in Union Square, or politicized ones at the NYSE, the swarming trends in the millennium's first decade seemed to marry the nineteenth-century mass hoax with the twenty-first-century mass prank.

The American ringleader of this global circus, a not-for-profit P. T. Barnum of hands-on high jinks, is the neo–Merry Prankster Charlie Todd. Influenced by such twentieth-century troublemakers as situationist Guy Debord, comedian Andy Kaufman, his mentors in the Upright Citizens Brigade, and, naturally, Abbie Hoffman, Todd founded an organization called Improv Everywhere—a Web-based collective, based in New York City, devoted to "causing scenes"—or what they called "missions" performed by "agents." Starting small in 2001 with spoof celebrity sightings and bemusing performances in downtown Starbucks, they stepped up their game in 2006 by swarming a Best Buy with employee look-alikes. Their instructions, which forbade agents to bring cameras (and being spectators), made this caveat: "only show up if you are wearing the proper dress and are ready to participate and have fun." Eighty agents turned out in khakis and royal-blue polos; otherwise they made for a "really diverse group of agents," which as Todd recalls "added to the fun." Harmless chaos ensued. It tickled agents and customers and "lower-level employees" alike. But as Todd had discovered with other retail pranks, "the managers and security freak[ed] out." (The cops, when called, were superfluous: as usual, their prank was perfectly legal.) In 2007, in Grand Central Terminal, 207 agents froze in place for five minutes, and Improv Everywhere's name went viral: agents repeated the prank worldwide, morning talk shows wanted replays (Improv Everywhere pranked them for the favor), and commercial interests staged copycat ads—passing the joke on to unwitting consumers.

But Improv Everywhere—and its many affiliates in the Urban Prankster global network—keep switching the rules. Best known for its annual No Pants! Subway Ride, which boasted four thousand participants in 2012, and also for its free downloadable MP3 missions, which gather thousands of strangers in New York's parks for conga lines and squirt-gun fights, Improv Everywhere holds tight to its cheeky motto of "caus[ing] scenes of chaos and joy in public places." In the oldest American tradition, it exploits general gullibility and the desire to play along. Their book signing in Union Square by long-dead playwright Anton Chekhov played beautifully to all different members of the crowd: the "clueless" were amazed, the "misinformed" were baffled, and clued-in citizens got the full joke. No wonder Improv Everywhere's bumptious high jinks have been embraced by the "Fun Generation," as Anand Giridharadas pointedly calls them. Their way of "doing, doing, doing" is fiercely witty and radically inclusive. "The golden rule of pranks," for Charlie Todd, is that "any prank should be as much fun for the person getting pranked." Which is to say, with an excellent prank, all of society gets activated, and only the killjoys miss the joke.

Improv Everywhere is radically civil, not overtly political, and it acts on the distinctly millennial impulse to seize on any chance for fun. Indeed, even the terrorist attacks of 9/11 raised the stakes for collective fun, which historically has comforted Americans in crisis. *The Onion*, with its schticky midwestern irreverence, lived up to its slogan as "America's Finest News Source," when, having taken a respectful break during the week after the attacks, it rose above the sanctimony, jingoism, and fear-mongering that dominated the "serious" twenty-four-hour news cycle and galvanized, broadened, and soothed their readership with a flash of *real* patriotic fun. They put crosshairs on a map of the United States and gave it an all-American headline: "Holy Fucking Shit—Attack on America." Who, after all, didn't get *this* joke?

Post-9/11 fun also rose from the streets. Antiwar activists staged festive protests, while smaller tribes of merry pranksters—Green Dragons, Billionaires for Bush—gloried in the myopia, irony, and hypocrisy generated by Bush doctrine politics. Antic activism in the face of tragedy came, for many, to define this century's first decade. Down in New Orleans, five months after Hurricane Katrina, twenty-seven krewes honored Congo Square's spirit by holding defiant Mardi Gras parades, many of them mock-celebrating the sorest spots of the catastrophe—the flood damage, the looters, FEMA, the "Sewerdome," all of the natural and social disasters that tried to drag the city down. By making their agenda delightful and comic, or by following Saul Alinsky's "rules for radicals," these aggrieved citizens and political activists invited even their opponents to participate and laugh—if not necessarily to get the whole joke. And for several weeks in the winter of 2011, thousands of Americans seized the Wisconsin State Capitol—chanting and singing in exhilarating defiance of the governor's assault on state workers' unions. The Occupy movement, formed in the rubble of the worst financial crisis since the Great Depression, spread this fight-the-power fun all across the globe.

OVER THE COURSE of four centuries, as if in pursuit of Thomas Morton's wild dream, Americans have rigged up delightful new ways of busting down barriers that keep them apart, on sandlots and street corners, at parks and on beaches, forever diving back into the skirmish with other fun-loving, party-throwing, pranks-pulling, footballing, jitterbugging, motorcycling, double-dutching, masquerading, spray-painting, scav-hunting, zombie-parading, "yarn bombing," tough-mudding, melon-launching, banner-wielding, nation-building . . .

And over the course of four centuries, in the spirit of William Bradford, some of the nation's most authoritarian citizens have marveled at America's lust for freedom. Sometimes they have tried to get involved, like slave masters joining the dance with their slaves, and sometimes they have matched the rebels' wits, like Justice Julius Hoffman crossing swords with Abbie Hoffman during the Chicago conspiracy trials. But time and again, much to their dismay, authoritarians' efforts to quell American liberty have only inspired wilder and wittier outbursts.

FOR THE PAST THREE DECADES, out in Mark Twain's old Washoe Territory, in the week preceding Labor Day weekend, up to seventy thousand wild-minded citizens of the world have met in the Black Rock Desert, where they've built a flammable Wild West town devoted to the thrills of radical civility. In agreement that activity is the lifeblood of community, trusting in each other's basic decency, trusting in each other's appetites for pleasure while shedding any semblance of law, the risky citizens of Black Rock City found their town on maximum fun: artists build makeshift theme-park rides, acrobats and fire-breathers roam the desert floor, composers and musicians stage avant-garde concerts, massive dance parties rumble round the clock, bicycles circulate, "mutant" cars parade, costumes sparkle, nudity abounds—as do comedy, drugs, good manners—and the ever-present torches and camp- and bonfires grow in significance as the last night approaches, and the crowds crowd together, and the towering wooden man that has loomed all week like a hollow frame of law and order is torched at sunset with weapons-grade fireworks. This great conflagration inspires the citizens to join in the hollering fire-making frenzy and, like Bradford's "Maenads or mummers," to burn their own art and clothes and garbage into the echoey, smoky black sky.

What began in 1986, on San Francisco's Baker Beach, with twenty partiers burning an eight-foot-tall driftwood anthropomorph, has exploded into a multimillion-dollar incendiary city, typically pushing radically civil fun beyond all recognizable limits. It has become an international destination, a mass-media darling, an academic cottage industry. Who knows but that Burning Man—as unlikely as Hollywood or Washington, D.C.—may actually be here to stay? Who knows but that Americans may need it? Its critics are legion. Many call it silly, dangerous, perverse. Others call it self-parody, a commercial sellout, or say it has lost its authenticity. But the participants still dive in and have a ball. And every year there are more of them. In a related trend, this one truly commercial, the rave craze of the late 1980s and early 1990s, when guerrilla youth gathered in derelict urban spaces for Ecstasy-flavored all-night dance parties, has unearthed yet another entertainment gold mine: at events like the Electric Daisy Festival, where three hundred thousand ravers crowd the Las Vegas Speedway to dance to the latest celebrity DJs, the rage for electronic dance music (EDM) eclipses even Woodstock-inspired music festivals. It's all the latest in Barnumism, without a doubt. But is that all? Burning Man, EDM, and the viral pranks of the Cacophony Society and Improv Everywhere may signal another change in mainstream tastes. At a time when billions are staring at smartphones, glued to Facebook, shackled by ever more sophisticated shackles to their ever-larger television screens, people may be growing weary of being spectators. Maybe they're intrigued by the chaos of the crowd. Maybe they see possibility down there. Who could blame them? Who could blame them for getting out into the air, like Plato's hero who springs from the cave and lives a livelier life in the sun?

This spirit of renewal is as old as the land. It comes from the young, or the young at heart, and acting on it is wicked fun.

ON NOVEMBER 27, 1760, twenty-five-year-old John Adams walked into a bar. He was paunchy, tetchy, a wallflower by temperament. But this fine young Puritan was a red-blooded American, and he had an afternoon to kill. So he kicked back with a pipe, and a good sense of humor, and he watched our nation's great story get started.

# *Acknowledgments*

This book was written over many years, with a lot of trial and error and the help of countless people. It would never have been possible without the initial guidance of Sandra M. Gilbert, my dear friend, mentor, and dissertation adviser at the University of California, Davis, who urged me—with her own bottomless appetite for fun—to explore the rigors of this unlikely subject. Also indispensable at this early stage were the close readings and expert advice of Linda Morris, Georges Van Den Abbeele, Clarence Major, Michael Hoffman, and Riché Richardson. Many thanks, as well, to Sarah Boushey, Erika Kreger, Eric Smith, Rod Romesburg, Andrew Gross, Lisa Harper, Jennifer Hoofard, Carl Eby, Joe Aimone, and many others among our grad-student cohort for their generous advice, criticism, and support. Among my terrifically fun friends and colleagues at the Université de Bordeaux III, Jessie Magee, Michelle Church, Alexander Earl, Zoe Bond, Paul Egan, Federico Frédéric Aranzueque-Arrieta, John Jordan, Pauline Delpeche, Michael Moses, and Yves-Charles Grandjeat made an especially strong impact on this work. For a California education, from the Washoe Territory to Lake Anza and beyond, I warmly thank, among so many others: Melissa Stein, Mitchell Rose, Lucy Rose, Grey Wedeking, Maryam Eskandari, Shoshana Berger, and all my rocking friends in the Ashby Avenue Groop.

All of my friends and colleagues in the U.S. Naval Academy English Department have given incredible support during the writing of this book. My friends (and chairs) Anne Marie Drew, Allyson Booth, Tim

O'Brien, and Mark McWilliams have served as tireless advocates for travel, research, and promotion, in addition to being invaluable readers. I am deeply indebted to Charlie Nolan, Eileen Johnston, Bill Bushnell, Michael Parker, Michelle Allen-Emerson, and Temple Cone: thank you for your camaraderie and brilliant input. Many thanks to Reza Malek-Madani, the Faculty Development Center, and the Naval Academy Research Council for their constant advocacy and interest. Thanks to Christopher Simmons and the ripping music-night scene. Thanks to Hoss Mitchell and all the Galway Bay bon vivants and to Skipper Mark Elert and the Wind River crew.

Big chunks of this book were written in a cabin on breathtaking Norton Island, Maine. My unending gratitude goes to Steve Dunn and the Eastern Frontier Educational Foundation for providing this extraordinary opportunity. Among the many residents there who have touched this book with their stories, ideas, conversation, and cavorting, Brian Bouldrey, Camille Dungy, and Lesley Doyle must be singled out as paragons of American fun. Special thanks to Ammi Keller and Angela Woodward for regional anecdotes.

This book is deeply indebted to generations of historiographers and journalists whose investigations into all of these events and eras make it possible to tell fun's broader story. It is also indebted to the many libraries where I found these scholars' books as well as primary and unpublished materials. Many thanks to the circulation and special collections departments at Shields Library (UC Davis), Bancroft Library (UC Berkeley), Widener and Houghton libraries (Harvard), and the Beinecke Library (Yale). I am especially grateful to the generous and gifted Nimitz librarians at the U.S. Naval Academy who have supported this book's research at every stage: Katherine Lang, David Dudek, Nick Brown, Jack Martin, Jerry Alomar, Mary Danna, and Linda McLeod in Circulation; Michael Macan in Reference; Jennifer Bryan and David D'Onofrio in Special Collections; Florence Todd and Margaret Danchik in Interlibrary Loan. Diana Lachatanere, at the Schomburg Center for Research in Black Culture, provided indispensable help—as did Amber Paranick and Margaret Kiechefer (among many others) at the Library of Congress; Rick Watson at UT Austin's Harry Ransom Center; Christopher Geissler at Brown

University's John Hay Library; and Benjamin Gocker and Ivy Marvel at the Brooklyn Public Library. Many thanks to Ray Raphael for his invaluable insights and critique of my treatment of Samuel Adams, and to Andy Shernoff, the Christopher Columbus of Punk, for kindly fact-checking my account of the era that he made legend. Warm thanks to Adam Goodheart, Peter Manseau, and Washington College's C. V. Starr Center for the Study of the American Experience.

The two heroes of *American Fun* are Steve Wasserman, my inde-fatigable agent at Kneerim & Williams, who has shaped and champi-oned the manuscript for years, against all odds, and Keith Goldsmith, my ever-constant editor at Pantheon, who has encouraged and chal-lenged me through three full drafts, always applying the full force of his powerful intellect. My deepest gratitude to both of you for your faith, patience, generosity, and commitment. Many thanks to my agent Kathryn Beaumont, who has gallantly taken over the helm from Steve. Among the many people at Pantheon who have made this book, my spe-cial thanks to Nicholas Latimer, Andrew Miller, Susanna Sturgis for her gimlet-eyed copyediting, Cassandra Pappas for her elegant designing, Pablo Delcán for the stunning jacket, Michelle Somers for getting fun attention, and Roméo Enriquez, Ellen Feldman, and Andrew Dorko for managing production with such élan.

Among all the brilliant fellows and affiliates in my wife's Nieman year, particular thanks goes to Alysia Abbott and Jeff Howe, Ashwini Tambe and Shankar Vedantam, Alissa Quart and Peter Maass, and Beth Macy and Tom Landon for their unfailingly fun counsel and company. Among the beloved Americans, native and naturalized, who have supported and inspired me throughout this long project, I thank the following: Ed Carew has been my brother in crime since Catholic school, as have the Wahlert Golden Eagles Alan Hennagir and Thomas Lally. Bill Martin has seen me through it all. As have Gus "Gustavo" Rose and Nami "Naminko" Mun. Thomas Heise (who has too), Andrew Strombeck, and Robert Balog have guided/goaded me through bicoastal underworlds. Lev Grossman (who has too) and Sophie Gee are our model family. Jason Shaffer (who has too) is my early American maharishi. Mick Calhoun has been my brick. Tom Bissell, on this and other books, has been my godfather, and Julie Barer has been my rock. Tom De Haven and Steve Dunn are the sweetest men on earth. Glenn Keyser and Wendy Low ("Gwendy") have always indulged me. Gary ("Sir Novitz") Sernovitz cracks me up. Christy Stanlake and Judah Nyden have been no end of fun, as have Jeff Alexander and Amber Hoover, John and Barbara Hill, and Mick and Becky Loggins.

My parents, Ann and Jerry, and my brother, Tom, have been loving, lifelong champions of anything I pursue. My parents-in-law, Pedro and Cathy Valdes and Dan and Ximena Sessler, have been amazingly supportive.

My dearest Katy, you've taught me my finest lessons in life. My dearest Evita, now you're doing it too. My dearest Marcela, you're the heart and soul of everything I do.

IN FOND MEMORY OF GEORGE WHITMAN (1913–2011),
AMERICAN FUN'S AMBASSADOR TO PARIS

# *Notes*

### INTRODUCTION

xi    **"heroes and heroines"**: "East Defies West in Dance Marathon," *New York Times,* April 19, 1923, 22. See also Carol Martin, *Dance Marathons: Performing American Culture in the 1920s and 1930s* (Jackson: University Press of Mississippi, 1994), 14–15.

xii    **"the pioneer spirit of early America"**: Frederick Nelson, "The Child Stylites of Baltimore," *The New Republic,* August 28, 1929, 37.

xii    **"wandered aimlessly toward the door"**: "Tri-State Dance Marathon Ends in 69 Hours; Police Stop It After Woman Breaks Records," *New York Times,* April 18, 1923, 6.

xiii    **"I'm Irish; do you suppose"**: "East Defies West," 22.

xiv    **"sport, high merriment, and frolicsome delight"**: *Samuel Johnson's Dictionary: Selections from the 1755 Work That Defined the English Language,* ed. Jack Lynch (Delray Beach, FL: Levenger Press, 2002), 202.

xvii    **we haven't had a history of fun**: Or perhaps more precisely, we haven't had a history of the fun-as-radical-merriment that this book endeavors to present. At least three books, from three different eras, offer mighty precedents; they give essential histories of, respectively, humor, play, and commercial amusement. Constance Rourke's classic study, *American Humor: On the National Character* (1931), examines Jackson Age comic almanacs and other nineteenth-century sources and tracks several strong currents in performance and folk culture that helped to shape an American identity (New York: New York Review Books, 2004). In *America Learns to Play: A History of Popular Recreation, 1607–1940* (Gloucester, MA: Peter Smith, 1959), Foster Rhea Dulles provides a detailed and often witty history of American recreation and play. And most recently, in his exhaustive history *With Amusement for All: A History of Popular Culture Since 1830* (Lexington: University Press of Kentucky, 2006), LeRoy Ashby gives what he calls "an interpretive synthesis of almost two hundred years of American entertainment: the sale, and purchase, of fun." It makes good sense that Ashby's study begins in 1830, with the rise of P. T. Barnum and blackface minstrelsy, America's earliest innovations in the mass production of a certain kind of "fun"— amusements Ashby categorically (and rightly) divides "from the folk games, festivals, and celebrations that had marked societies around the globe for centuries" (vii–viii). To a large degree, *American Fun* is about the tenacity of such lingering folk fun, despite the entertainment industry's indomitable campaign.

xvii "civilizing function," "enjoyment," "play," "play-element": Johan Huizinga, *Homo Ludens: A Study of the Play-Element in Culture* (Boston: Beacon Press, 1950), 11.

xviii "creates order, *is* order": Ibid., 10.

xviii "the *fun* of playing": Ibid., 3.

xviii "in passing," "it is precisely": Ibid., 10.

xviii "merely" fun: Ibid., 33.

xviii "only for fun": Ibid., 8.

xviii "make believe": Ibid., 24.

xviii "no other modern language": Ibid., 3.

xviii "comes from doing": Anand Giridharadas, "America and the Fun Generation," *New York Times,* October 29, 2010.

xxi "pure democracy": James Madison, "No. 10," *The Federalist Papers: Hamilton, Madison, Jay* (New York: Penguin, 1961), 81. These ideas are nothing new. The notion that participatory democracy, active citizenship, and an engaged civil society all depend for their vitality on direct civic action and conflict derives from a long discursive tradition. On the short list of key texts informing this line of argument are, following the Students for a Democratic Society's "Port Huron Statement" (1962): Carole Pateman, *Participation and Democratic Theory* (New York: Cambridge University Press, 1976); C. Douglas Lummis, *Radical Democracy* (Ithaca, NY: Cornell University Press, 1997); Ernesto Laclau and Chantal Mouffe, *Hegemony and Socialist Strategy: Towards a Radical Democratic Politics,* 2nd ed. (New York: Verso, 2001); Benjamin R. Barber, *Strong Democracy: Participatory Politics for a New Age* (Berkeley: University of California Press, 1984).

xxiv "Peace, Love, Unity, and Having Fun": Jeff Chang and DJ Kool Herc, *Can't Stop, Won't Stop: A History of the Hip-Hop Generation* (New York: St. Martin's, 2005), 120.

xxiv "falling into fattened hands": Patti Smith, *Just Kids* (New York: HarperCollins, 2010), 245.

I ★ THE FOREFATHER OF AMERICAN FUN

3 "civill body politick," "most meete & convenient": William Bradford, *Of Plymouth Plantation,* ed. Harvey Wish (New York: Capricorn Books, 1962), 70.

4 those who trace America's democratic tradition: As Mark L. Sargent demonstrates, the Mayflower Compact, originally cited as a loyalist document, gradually was embraced as an original vestige of American democracy by nonpartisan framer James Wilson and presidents John and John Quincy Adams. In "The Conservative Covenant: The Rise of the Mayflower Compact in American Myth," *New England Quarterly* 61, no. 2 (June 1988): 233–51. Nathaniel Philbrick cites Pastor John Robinson's farewell letter to the Separatists, which advises them to "become a body politic, using amongst [themselves] civil government," as evidence that the compact was meant to lay "the basis for a secular government in America"—though of course Robinson wasn't along to frame said government or to see it through. *Mayflower: A Story of Courage, Community, and War* (New York: Viking, 2006), 41.

4 "discontented & mutinous speeches": Bradford, *Of Plymouth Plantation,* 69.

4 "to be as firme as any patent": Ibid.

4 "godly": Ibid., 70.

5 Bradford's childhood was filled with misery: Perry D. Westbrook, *William Bradford* (Boston: Twayne Publishers, 1978), 17–27; Bradford Smith, *Bradford of Plymouth* (New York: J. B. Lippincott, 1951), 70–71.

5 "grave & revered": Bradford, *Of Plymouth Plantation,* 27.

6  "**not out of any newfangledness**": Ibid., 38–39.

6  "**evill examples**": Ibid., 39. See also Wm. Elliot Griffis, *The Influence of the Nether-lands in the Making of the English Commonwealth and the American Republic* (Boston: DeWolfe Fiske & Co., 1891); Henry Martyn Dexter and Morton Dexter, *The England and Holland of the Pilgrims* (New York: Houghton Mifflin, 1905), 548–90.

6  "**those vast & unpeopled**": Bradford, *Of Plymouth Plantation,* 40.

6  "**lustie**," "**very profane younge**": Ibid., 57.

7  "**spared no pains**," "**had been boone companions**," "**but a small cann of beere**": Ibid., 71.

7  "**lusty yonge men**": Ibid., 80.

7  "**pitching the barr**," "**implements**," "**gameing and reveling**," "**mirth**," "**at least openly**": Ibid., 83.

7  "**buggery**," "**a mare, a cowe**," "**sadd accidente**," "**lesser catle**," "**Then he him selfe**," "**and no use made**": Ibid., 202. Detailed accounts of sexual surveillance and crimi-nalization in the New England colonies can be found in James Deetz and Patricia Scott Deetz's *The Times of Their Lives: Life, Love, and Death in Plymouth Plantation* (New York: W. H. Freeman, 2001), 131–70, and in Richard Godbeer's *Sexual Revolu-tion in Early America* (Baltimore: Johns Hopkins University Press, 2002), 84–116.

8  "**how one wicked person**," "**so many wicked persons**," "**mixe them selves amongst**," "**such wickedness**": Bradford, *Of Plymouth Plantation,* 203.

8  **Thomas Morton's "New English Canaan"**: Merry Mount received newfound atten-tion in the liberal academic climate of the 1960s and 1970s, its vogue reaching a climax in 1977, incidentally the peak of America's sexual revolution. That year at least four scholars gave Morton and his merrymakers their moment in the sun. Karen Ordahl Kupperman argued against the long-held but unproven assumption that Morton was ousted for selling firearms to the Indians, asserting, in his defense, that Native Amer-ican archery was known to be more effective than Pilgrim warcraft and that the latter more likely wanted to hoard the fur-trade market share. In "Thomas Morton, Histo-rian," *New England Quarterly* 50, no. 4 (December 1977): 660–64. Michael Zucker-man dismissed the Pilgrims' practical motives (apart from their abiding jealousy that Merry Mount ran a 700 percent profit while Plymouth Plantation operated at a loss), focusing instead on ample evidence that Morton "threatened what [the Pilgrims] lived for"—by celebrating the horrid wilderness; by eating, drinking, speaking, and "[keeping] sexual company" with the hated Indians; and especially for enjoying "car-nal pleasure" for reasons other than "procreation," "utility." "Pilgrims in the Wil-derness: Community, Modernity, and the Maypole at Merry Mount," *New England Quarterly* 50, no. 2 ( June 1977): 255–77. John Seelye, in his sparkling account, reads Morton as "an American version of Falstaff" and America itself as a "zone of plea-sure." *Prophetic Waters* (New York: Oxford University Press, 1977), 169, 166. John P. McWilliams Jr. argued that the chroniclers of Merry Mount's Maypole fracas histori-cally fall into two historical groups: "Post-Revolutionary Americans" who "saw in Merry Mount the opportunity for reflection on the origins of the national character" and "twentieth-century writers" who used the same story to "[trace] the beginnings of failure, decline, or betrayal." "Fictions of Merry Mount," *American Quarterly* 29, no. 1 (Spring 1977): 4. With one notable exception, Nathaniel Hawthorne, these two par-tisan groups are fundamentally opposed. The Post-Revolutionary Americans—who include Bradford himself, Catherine Sedgwick, Charles Francis Adams Jr., Whittier, and Longfellow—might be called, in the fight over fun, "Bradfordites": they dismiss Thomas Morton as the pettifogger, scofflaw, con man, and/or idiot who threatened our young nation's safety and integrity by selling firearms to savage terrorists. The

twentieth-century camp—including Morton himself, William Carlos Williams, Stephen Vincent Benét, Robert Lowell, and Richard Slotkin—could as easily be called "Mortonites." These writers tout Merry Mount as the first frontier, an amoral outpost a stone's throw from Plymouth, where sexual, political, and racial freedoms were squelched by mean-spirited philistines. But it is Nathaniel Hawthorne's version of events, "The May-Pole of Merry Mount" (1834)—a fanciful short story that historically belongs among the Post-Revolutionaries, while thematically anticipating Morton's modern champions—whose very popularity gives it the last word. This staple of college survey courses secures the incident in our national imagination as a missed opportunity for American democracy, which, alas, could have been such fun, had the majority not been too sober to pursue it.

8  **"hidious & desolate wilderness"**: Bradford, *Of Plymouth Plantation*, 60.

8  **"long[s] to be sped"**: Thomas Morton, *New English Canaan, or New Canaan* (Amsterdam: Jacob Frederick Stam, 1637), 10; facsimile edition (New York: Arno Press, 1972).

9  **"science," "Art of Revels"**: Sir George Buck, *The Thirde Universitie of London*, accessed August 13, 2012, from http://www.winerock.netau.net/sources/stow_third _universitie.html, where the transcription is explained as such: "from the NYPL Mid-Manhattan Research Library's copy of selected dance-relevant passages of Sir George Buck's *The Third Universitie of England*, an appendix to the 1615 edition of John Stow's *The Annales, Or Generall Chronicle of England* finished and edited by Edmond Howes. London: Thomas Adams, 1615, as well as a few passages from the main *Annales* text. The 1631 edition as viewed at the British Library also contains *The Third Universitie of England*, but while the main text differs, the 'Orchestice' and other *Third Universitie* passages are the same."

9  **"Master of Revels"**: Robert R. Pearce, *A history of the Inns of Court and Chancery: with notices of their ancient discipline, rules, orders, and customs, readings, moots, masques . . .* (London, 1848), 114–22.

9  **"did endeavour to take a survey"**: Morton, *New English Canaan*, 59–60.

10  **"Infidels"**: Ibid., 17.

10  **"the continuall danger of the salvage people"**: Bradford, *Of Plymouth Plantation*, 40–41. It was commonly held among early-modern Europeans that indigenous peoples needed to be "reduced to civility" from their current state of "barbarism" before they could receive Christianity. Until then, they were assumed to be lazy, disorderly, anarchic, unmannered, oversexed, and suspiciously itinerant. No moral creature would freely live in the wilderness without trying to bring its chaos to order. "The only acceptable notion of order," James Axtell writes of the Pilgrims, "was the order they had known at home, the all-encompassing order of institutions, written-law, and hierarchy." James Axtell, *The Invasion Within: The Contest of Cultures in Colonial North America* (New York: Oxford University Press, 1985), 137–38.

11  **"new creede"**: Morton, *New English Canaan*, 113.

11  **"modesty," "cumbered," "feate," "Diogenes hurle away his dishe"**: Ibid., 57.

11  **"without Religion, Law, and King"**: Ibid., 49.

11  **"uncivilized," "more just than the civilized"**: Ibid., 125.

11  **"poore wretches," "beggers"**: Ibid., 55.

11  **"feats and jugling tricks"**: Ibid., 34.

11  **"worshipped *Pan*"**: Ibid., 18.

12  **"According to human reason"**: Ibid., 57.

12  **"I, having a parte"**: Bradford, *Of Plymouth Plantation*, 140.

12  **"fell to great licentiousness," "gott much by trading with Indeans"**: Ibid., 140–41.

13 **protesting too much:** Anderson also suggests that Bradford's fanciful monologue may have been a poke at his contemporary Levellers, who "had come to represent an extreme expression of radical Protestant ideology." *William Bradford's Books:* Of Plimmoth Plantation *and the Printed Word* (Baltimore: Johns Hopkins University Press, 2003), 142.

13 **"worthy wights," "And pitty 't is I cannot call them Knights":** Morton, *New English Canaan*, 146. Michelle Burnham, reading *New English Canaan* "in the context of Morton's already intersecting regional and transcontinental economic relationships," makes a compelling point: that Morton "offers readers a kind of aristocratic colonial fantasy" by "promis[ing] would-be planter-gentlemen the pastoral possibilities of unlimited pleasure and leisure," but she reads the text quite narrowly to conclude that he dismisses Indians and bondservants alike as faceless economic resources. Despite Morton's obvious embrace of his contemporary culture and economics (the pastoral, Saturnalia, fur trading, tourism), what distinguishes his book (and colony) from those of his peers is both his explicit criticism of aristocratic "heraldry" and his deep and careful appreciation for these devalued groups' craftsmanship, intelligence, and human dignity. "Land, Labor, and Colonial Economics in Thomas Morton's *New English Canaan*," *Early American Literature* 41, no. 3 (November 2006): 405, 425.

14 **"Fouling peeces," "the hants of all sorts of game," "all the scume of the countrie":** Bradford, *Of Plymouth Plantation*, 142–43.

14 **the name's witty abominations:** Richard Slotkin, *Regeneration Through Violence: The Mythology of the American Frontier, 1600–1860* (Middletown, CT: Wesleyan University Press, 1973), 58–65.

14 **"memorial to after ages":** Morton, *New English Canaan*, 132.

14 **"they call it Merie-mounte":** Bradford, *Of Plymouth Plantation*, 141.

15 **"Jollity and gloom were contending":** Nathaniel Hawthorne, "The May-Pole of Merry Mount," in *Nathaniel Hawthorne's Tales*, ed. James McIntosh (New York: W. W. Norton, 1987), 88–93.

15 **"a barrel of excellent beare," "the olde English custome," "faire sea marke":** Morton, *New English Canaan*, 132.

15 **"wombe," "art & industry," "darck obscurity":** Ibid., 10.

15 **"a Satyrist":** Ibid., 9.

16 **making Merry Mount last:** Hawthorne's short story, written during the dreariest period in Native American history, seems to echo this poignant wish. It stages an actual wedding in the scene, but jollity's empire is nipped in the bud when the Lord and Lady of the May, "madly gay in the flush of youth," are dragged away in the end by the Pilgrims, those "most dismal wretches." Hawthorne, "The May-Pole of Merry Mount," 92–93.

16 **"and other fitting instruments":** Morton, *New English Canaan*, 132.

16 **"the good liquor":** Ibid., 134.

16 **"Make greene garlons," "Drinke and be merry":** Ibid.

17 **"drinking and dancing aboute it":** Bradford, *Of Plymouth Plantation*, 141.

17 **"Sport; high merriment; frolicksome delight":** *Samuel Johnson's Dictionary, Selections from the 1755 Work That Defined the English Language*, ed. Jack Lynch (Delray Beach, FL: Levenger Press, 2002), 202.

17 **competing social systems weren't held in check:** William Heath, who gives the liveliest and most detailed account of Merry Mount in recent years, reads Morton's colony as a rude intrusion of Renaissance England into a would-be Calvinist paradise: "As an Anglican cavalier with literary pretensions and a hedonistic bent, Morton epitomized the 'eat-drink-and-be-merry' England the Puritans hoped to leave

behind. His maypole festivities smacked of folk superstitions, pagan practices, Old Testament precedents, and King James I's *Book of Sports;* his consorting with Indian women violated their sexual and racial taboos" (153–54). The pleasure of this multiplex transgression, however, left England far behind; for all of its culturally British antecedents, the fun of Merry Mount crushed all the old aristocratic molds and experienced an audacious (if short-lived) civil society that was properly North American, a *New* English Canaan. "Thomas Morton: From Merry Old England to New England," *Journal of American Studies* 41, no. 1 (2007): 135–68.

18 "harmles mirth": Morton, *New English Canaan*, 135.

19 "over armed with drinke": Bradford, *Of Plymouth Plantation*, 144.

19 "the effusion of so much noble blood": Morton, *New English Canaan*, 142.

19 "We must be knit together": John Winthrop, "A Model of Christian Charity," in *The Norton Anthology of American Literature, Volume A*, ed. Nina Baym (New York: W. W. Norton, 2012), 176–77.

20 The American Self was menaced: Did the Puritans have fun? Bruce C. Daniel argues that they did. But what he spools out in a blurry list as their "quiet fun, spiritual fun, family fun, [and] civic fun" turns out to be, upon closer inspection, a catalogue of generally sanctioned activities that Puritans engaged in as a matter of course and therefore—according to an apparently Lockean idea of "pleasure" that arises merely from following laws—possibly enjoyed. Take, for instance, this business of "spiritual fun," much of which took place on the so-called Day of Joy, when "custom proscribed sexual intercourse, unnecessary traveling, and any type of frivolity." Even though the jacket copy on *Puritans at Play* promises a "reapprais[al]" of the old assumption that Puritans were "dour, joyless, and repressed," the author comes clean and lets us know that "brandings and mutilations for crimes committed on the Sabbath were not unusual, and a few ministers and civil leaders believed the death penalty appropriate for Sabbath breaking." If a Puritan could be mutilated or killed for frivolity on Sunday, what room was left for "spiritual fun"? The entire day was spent in church, in "rigid segregation by gender, class, age, and race characterized by physical arrangements." Daniels sets the stage with daring honesty:

> The proceedings were formal, the atmosphere somber, the audience passive, the message long and complex, the meetinghouse unpainted, undecorated, and unheated. Convention tolerated no instrumental music, no talking, no shuffling about, not even any daydreaming. And despite the fact that magistrates occasionally prosecuted people for "rude and indecent behavior" or for "laughing in the meetinghouse," the services usually lived up to the community's expectations for good conduct. We should not look for anachronistic Tom Sawyer behavior in Puritan boys or assume that the congregation secretly longed to be elsewhere.

So where was the fun? Even if we *were* to assume, along with Daniels, that Tom Sawyer–like fun was not only anachronistic but constitutionally undesirable for the Puritans—which is also to assume that the likes of Hawthorne's Edith and Edgar in "The May-Pole of Merry Mount" sowed no seeds of mirth at Plymouth—we would still have to distort "fun" beyond all recognition to agree with his claim, in the following paragraph, that "the entire milieu of the services" (drearily described above) "had entertainment value." A captive audience who is subjected to sermons that detailed the people's depravity and eternal perdition (per Calvinist doctrine) was neither having "fun" nor being "entertained." The sense one gets from *Puritans at Play*, as from most histories of early New England, is that what Daniels calls "boisterous" and "deviant fun" happened, like Thomas Morton's, in spite of Puritanism, and usually at a considerable remove. Bruce C. Daniels, *Puritans at Play: Leisure and Recreation in Colonial New England* (New York: St. Martin's Griffin, 1995), xiii, 77.

20 "**praying towns**": Alan Taylor, *American Colonies* (New York: Viking, 2001), 201.

20 "**sharply against Health-drinking**": Samuel Sewall, *The Diary of Samuel Sewall,* ed. Harvey Wish (New York: G. P. Putnam's Sons, 1967), 48–50.

## 2 ★ JACK TAR, UNBOUND

21 "**trifling, nasty vicious Crew**," "**to Prisons and the Gallows**": John Adams, *Diary and Autobiography of John Adams,* ed. L. H. Butterfield, 4 vols. (Cambridge, MA: Belknap Press of Harvard University Press, 1961), 1:129.

21 "**the nurseries of our legislators**": Ibid., 2:85.

21 **Adams had not been bred for taverns**: See ibid., 1:128, 257–69; 3:98–99, 257, 260, 261, 260.

22 "**Let no trifling diversion**": Ibid., 2:59.

22 "**fond**": Ibid., 2:47; dated July 22, 1771.

22 "**The Rabble**": All quotations in this and the following two paragraphs are from ibid., 1:172–73.

23 "**rhythmic crowd**": Elias Canetti, *Crowds and Power* (New York: Farrar, Straus and Giroux, 1960), 30.

23 "**Fiddling and dancing**": Adams, *Diary and Autobiography,* 1:172–73.

23 "**foolish enough to spend**": Ibid.

24 **a fast crowd collectively known as "Jack Tars"**: Paul A. Gilje, *Liberty on the Water-front: American Maritime Culture in the Age of Revolution* (Philadelphia: University of Pennsylvania Press, 2004), 3–129; Jesse Lemisch, *Jack Tar vs. John Bull: The Role of New York's Seamen in Precipitating the Revolution* (New York: Garland, 1997), 28, 150.

25 "**eighteenth century's most complex machine**": Daniel Vickers with Vince Walsh, *Young Men and the Sea: Yankee Seafarers in the Age of Sail* (New Haven, CT: Yale University Press, 2005), 88. Vickers spends little time recounting the "celebrations" in so-called "sailortowns"—the "drinking to excess, feasting on fresh victuals, regaling their friends and families with stories from abroad, and renewing their acquaintance-ships with women and girls" (133) that he says characterized the young mariner's shore leave—but presents a wonderfully detailed history of the young Jack Tar's work life and society.

25 "**the antics of a wild, harebrained sailor**": Samuel Leech, *Thirty Years from Home, or A Voice from the Main Deck* (Boston: Charles Tappan, 1844), 24–25. Recall, too, William Bradford's cautionary tale of the "proud & very profane younge . . . seaman" whom "it plased God . . . to smite with a greevous disease, of which he dyed in a desperate maner." Bradford, *Of Plymouth Plantation,* 57.

25 **The contagious fun**: In *Moby-Dick,* the *Pequod*'s variegated crew does a jig that would have boiled Cotton Mather's blood. The Icelandic, Maltese, and Sicilian sail-ors beg off for lack of female partners, to which the Long Island sailor chides these "sulkies" that "there's plenty more for the rest of us" and the all-male crowd lights up the deck. The Azores sailor beseeches Pip on the tambourine: "Bang it, bell-boy! Rig it, dig it, stig it, quig it, bell-boy! Make fire-flies! break the jinglers!" The Chinese sailor hollers: "Rattle thy teeth, then, and pound away; make a pagoda of thyself." The French sailor, beside himself in the frenzy, suggestively shouts: "Merry-mad! Hold up thy hoop, Pip, till I jump through it! Split jibs! tear yourselves!" All the while Tashtego, the "quietly smoking" Indian, watches over the ruckus in judgment:

"That's a white man; he calls that fun: humph! I save my sweat." Herman Melville, *Moby-Dick* (London: Everyman's Library, 1993), 146–47. This romp celebrates a seafaring camaraderie that predated the Revolution and would grew all the more diverse after 1776, when, as Gilje shows, Americans ignored Britain's Navigation Acts and welcomed crew members of all nationalities (25).

25 **"a Mob, or rather body of Men," "their Captivated Fr[ien]ds":** Dirk Hoerder, *Crowd Action in Revolutionary Massachusetts, 1765–1780* (New York: Academic Press, 1977), 62.

26 **"using Rigour instead of Mildness":** Cited in John Lax and William Pencak, "The Knowles Riot and the Crisis of the 1740s in Massachusetts," *Perspectives in American History* 19 (1976): 186.

26 **"rioting," "People can experience":** Gilje, *Liberty on the Waterfront,* 104.

27 **"such Illegal Criminal Proceedings":** Lax and Pencak, "Knowles Riot," 197.

28 **"who despises his Neighbor's Happiness":** Cited in John K. Alexander, *Samuel Adams: America's Revolutionary Politician* (New York: Rowman & Littlefield, 2002), 8. Alexander's indispensable book was among the first in a recent surge of Samuel Adams biographies; it also remains the most incisive account of his early political life. It has since been revised, expanded, and retitled: *Samuel Adams: The Life of an American Revolutionary* (2011). Pauline Maier's long biographical essay—in *The Old Revolutionaries: Political Lives in the Age of Samuel Adams* (1980; New York: W. W. Norton, 1990), 3–50—is also highly recommended. Other biographies consulted for this account are Benjamin H. Irvin, *Samuel Adams: Son of Liberty, Father of Revolution* (New York: Oxford University Press, 2002); Mark Puls, *Samuel Adams: Father of the American Revolution* (New York: Palgrave Macmillan, 2006); and Ira Stoll, *Samuel Adams: A Life* (New York: Free Press, 2008).

28 **"No man was more aware":** Maier, *Old Revolutionaries,* 40.

29 **"Folly," "Dissipation":** Ibid., 42.

29 **"Cause of Liberty and Virtue":** Ibid., 36.

29 **"zealous, ardent and keen in the Cause":** John Adams, *The Works of John Adams, Second President of the United States,* ed. Charles Francis Adams, 10 vols. (Ann Arbor: University of Michigan, 2010), 2:163.

29 **"Chief Incendiary":** Alexander, *Samuel Adams,* 103.

29 **"all serpentine cunning":** Peter Oliver, *Peter Oliver's Origin & Progress of the American Rebellion: A Tory View,* ed. Douglass Adair and John A. Schutz (San Marino, CA: Huntington Library, 1961), 39.

29 **"The true patriot":** Samuel Adams, *The Writings of Samuel Adams,* ed. Harry Alonzo Cushing, 24 vols. (McLean, VA: IndyPublish.com, n.d.), 2:106.

30 **"spent rather lavishly":** Clifford K. Shipton, *Sibley's Harvard Graduates,* vol. 10, 1736–1740 (Boston: Massachusetts Historical Society, 1958), 421–22. When he returned for his master's degree in 1743, Adams argued under his politically liberal father's influence "that it is lawful to resist the supreme magistrate if the commonwealth cannot be otherwise preserved."

30 **"No other caucus leader":** Alexander, *Samuel Adams,* 14.

30 **"difficulties":** Samuel Adams, *Writings,* 1:200.

30 **"a Master of Vocal Musick," "This genius he improved":** Oliver, *Peter Oliver's Origin,* 41.

30 **"had for years been complimented":** Shipton, *Sibley's Harvard Graduates,* 426.

30 **Boston's public houses, "slaves and servants":** David W. Conroy, *In Public Houses: Drink and the Revolution of Authority in Colonial Massachusetts* (Chapel Hill: University of North Carolina Press, 1995), 58, 59, 127.

31 **"many Americans":** Carl Bridenbaugh, *Cities in Revolt: Urban Life in America, 1743–1776* (New York: Alfred A. Knopf, 1955), 361; see 361–417.

31 **"distinct lower-class subculture"**: Eric Foner, *Tom Paine and Revolutionary America* (New York: Oxford University Press, 1976), 48, 50; see 45–56.

31 **"the traditional oral culture of taverns"**: Conroy, *In Public Houses*, 244, 180n, 254. See also Jürgen Habermas, *The Structural Transformation of the Public Sphere: An Inquiry into a Category of Bourgeois Society*, trans. Thomas Burger (Cambridge, MA: Harvard University Press, 1989).

31 **"were where republican concepts gripped"**: Conroy, *In Public Houses*, 254.

31 **it was Jack Tar who hoisted**: By tracing American seamen's crowd actions (from the Knowles riots forward) to a colorful array of boat burnings, slave revolts, and other violent uprisings in the larger eighteenth-century transatlantic context, Marcus Rediker's powerful article shows how and why Jack Tar's multiracial revolution "could not easily be contained" by the Sons of Liberty's conciliatory gestures. It was far more radical. After 1747, "Jack Tar took part in almost every port city conflict in England and America for the remainder of the century . . . [they] took to the streets in rowdy and rebellious protest on a variety of issues, seizing in practice what would later be defined as 'rights' by philosophers and legislators. Here, as elsewhere, rights were not granted from on high; they had to be fought for, won, and defended." "A Motley Crew of Rebels: Sailors, Slaves, and the Coming of the American Revolution," in *The Transforming Hand of Revolution: Reconsidering the American Revolution as a Social Movement*, ed. Ronald Hoffman and Peter J. Albert (Charlottesville: University Press of Virginia, 1995), 197, 168.

31 **"body of the people"**: John Locke, *The Second Treatise of Government*, in *The Selected Political Writings of John Locke*, ed. Paul E. Sigmund (New York: W. W. Norton, 2005), 116.

32 **"particularly strong collectivism"**: Benjamin L. Carp, *Rebels Rising: Cities and the American Revolution* (New York: Oxford University Press, 2007), 29. From the 1750s to the 1770s, new intellectual currents flowed into the colonies from Europe, loosening the Puritans' crumbling authoritarianism with Enlightenment ideas of liberty and equality—what John Adams loosely called "all the Nonsense of these last twenty Years" (*Autobiography and Diary*, 3:265). Bernard Bailyn, in his landmark history of the period, establishes how opposition writers who had been considered "Cassandras" in their luxurious, extravagant Georgian England—"doctrinaire libertarians, disaffected politicians, and religious dissenters"—"seemed particularly reasonable, particularly relevant, and . . . quickly became influential" in the disenfranchised colonies (*The Ideological Origins of the American Revolution* [Cambridge, MA: Harvard University Press, 1967], 92, 52–54). Jay Fliegelman demonstrates how the widespread rhetoric of independent children provided a rallying point for colonists who experienced, like kids, both exhilaration and fear in individuating themselves from England. "A call for filial autonomy and the unimpeded emergence from nonage" became "the quintessential motif. At every opportunity Revolutionary propagandists insisted that the new nation and its people had come of age, had achieved a collective maturity that necessitated them becoming in political fact an independent and self-governing nation" (*Prodigals and Pilgrims: The American Revolution and Patriarchal Authority, 1750–1800* [New York: Cambridge University Press, 1982], 3). Gordon S. Wood details the colonies' rapid upheaval from monarchical hierarchy to "enlightened paternalism" to an orderly form of autonomous democracy. Wood attributes this upheaval to, among other causes, an influx of new ideas: an increased interest in civilization and civility, an emphasis on benevolence and communal happiness, and an enlightened awareness of cosmopolitanism, as well as a lightening of punishments in general and vicious practices like public shaming (*The Radicalism of the American Revolution: How a Revolution Transformed a Monarchical Society into*

*a Democratic One Unlike Any That Had Ever Existed* [New York: Alfred A. Knopf, 1992]).

32 **The middle management:** Conroy, *In Public Houses,* 256.

32 **a deft little dance:** Pauline Maier, *From Resistance to Revolution: Colonial Radicals and the Development of American Opposition to Britain, 1765–1776* (New York: Alfred A. Knopf, 1972), 31–32.

33 **"A goodlier sight who e'er did see?":** Alexander, *Samuel Adams,* 32.

33 **"Many Gentlemen":** Francis Bernard, "The Stamp Act Riot, 1765," in *Documents to Accompany America's History, Sixth Edition,* ed. Melvin Yazawa (New York: Bedford/ St. Martin's, 2007), 107.

33 **"So much were they affected":** *Boston Newsletter,* August 22, 1765; Edmund S. and Helen M. Morgan, *The Stamp Act Crisis* (New York: Collier Books, 1963), 159–65; John Rowe, *Letters and Diary of John Rowe,* ed. Anne Rowe Cunningham (New York: New York Times and Arno Press, 1969), 88–89.

33 **"three huzzas":** Bernard, "The Stamp Act Riot," 107.

34 **"a Burnt-Offering":** Cited in Hoerder, *Crowd Action,* 98.

34 **"some bruises":** Bernard, "The Stamp Act Riot," 107.

34 **"gave universal Satisfaction":** Samuel Adams, *The Writings of Samuel Adams,* ed. Harry Alonzo Cushing, vol. 1, *1764–1769* (New York: G. P. Putnam's Sons, 1904), 59–60.

34 **"There is," he wrote:** John Adams, *Diary and Autobiography,* 1:39.

34 **"republican monarchist":** Richard Allen Ryerson, "John Adams, Republican Monarchist: An Inquiry into the Origins of His Constitutional Thought," in *Empire and Nation: The American Revolution and the Atlantic World,* ed. Eliga H. Gould and Peter S. Onuf (Baltimore: Johns Hopkins University Press, 2005), 72–92.

34 **"A Dissertation on the Canon and Feudal Law":** *Boston Gazette,* August 12, 1765, reprinted in John Adams, *The Political Writings of John Adams: Representative Selections* (New York: Liberal Arts Press, 1954), 18–21. Cited in David McCullough, *John Adams* (New York: Simon & Schuster, 2001), 61.

35 **"Head":** This and subsequent quotations in this and the following paragraph are from John Adams, *Diary and Autobiography,* 1:341–42.

36 **"parades, festivals, and shows of fireworks":** Shipton, *Sibley's Harvard Graduates,* 431.

36 **"Ears [were] ravished":** John Adams, "To William Crawford," *The Earliest Diary of John Adams,* ed. L. H. Butterfield (Cambridge, MA: Harvard University Press, 1966), 99.

36 **"higher object":** John Adams, *Diary and Autobiography,* 1:124.

37 **"body," "harangue," "constantly refused":** Ibid., 3:290–91.

37 **"No Mobs or Tumults":** *Boston Gazette,* quoted in Hoerder, *Crowd Action,* 151.

37 **"Where are the damned boogers":** All quotations in this paragraph are from *A Short Narrative of the Horrid Massacre in Boston, Perpetrated in the Evening of the Fifth Day of March, 1770, by Soldiers of the 29th Regiment, which with the 14th Regiment Were Then Quartered There; With Some Observations on the State of Things Prior to That Catastrophe* (1770; Williamstown, MA: Corner House Publishers, 1973), 50–63.

38 **"Council":** John Adams, *Diary and Autobiography,* 3:293.

38 **"by certain busy Characters":** Ibid., 3:292.

38 **"We have been entertained":** John Adams, *Legal Papers of John Adams, Ser. 3, General Correspondence and Other Papers of the Adams Statesmen* (Cambridge, MA: Harvard University Press, 1965), 266–69. Emphasis added to *"a motley rabble of saucy boys, negroes and mulattoes, Irish teagues and out landish jack tarrs."*

39 **"Mean and Vile Condition":** Lax and Pencak, "Knowles Riot," 197.

39　**"Not one extravagance"**: Cited in Conroy, *In Public Houses,* 247.

40　**"so very fat"**: Abigail Adams, quoted in McCullough, *John Adams,* 64.

40　**"Roxbury, I am told"**: Samuel Adams, *Writings,* 2:241.

40　**"Stop the Progress of Tyranny"**: Ibid., 2:238.

40　**"spirit"**: *Tea Leaves: Being a collection of letters and documents relating to the shipment of tea to the American colonies in the year 1773, by the East India Tea Company. Now first printed from the original manuscript. With an introduction, notes, and biographical notices of the Boston Tea Party,* by Francis S. Drake (Boston: A. O. Crane, 1884), xliv. Also consulted for this account were Wesley S. Griswold, *The Night the Revolution Began: The Boston Tea Party, 1773* (Brattleboro, VT: Stephen Greene Press, 1972); Benjamin Woods Larabee, *The Boston Tea Party* (New York: Oxford University Press, 1964); and Peter D. G. Thomas, *Tea Party to Independence: The Third Phase of the American Revolution, 1773–1776* (Oxford, UK: Clarendon Press, 1991).

41　**"the sharpest, the sharpest conflicts"**: *Tea Leaves,* lix.

42　**"he was willing to grant"**: Griswold, *The Night the Revolution Began,* 91.

42　**"Who knows how tea"**: *Tea Leaves,* lxiii.

42　**"A mob! A mob!," "This meeting can do nothing more,"**: Ibid., lxiv.

42　**"Mohawk"**: This and subsequent quotations in this paragraph and the next are from ibid., clxiii.

43　**"Sport; high merriment"**: *Samuel Johnson's Dictionary,* 202.

43　**"countryman"**: *Tea Leaves,* cxvi.

43　**"handled pretty roughly"**: Ibid., lxx.

43　**"speak[ing] to the British"**: Philip J. Deloria, *Playing Indian* (New Haven, CT: Yale University Press, 1998), 32.

44　playlike **"practice" for a possible republic**: William Pencak, "Play as Prelude to Revolution: Boston, 1765–1776," in *Riot and Revelry in Early America,* ed. Matthew Dennis et al. (University Park: Pennsylvania State University Press, 2002), 149.

44　**"mock ceremonies"**: Wood, *Radicalism of the American Revolution,* 90–91.

44　**"In 1765 the rioters had hung effigies"**: Ray Raphael, *A People's History of the American Revolution: How Common People Shaped the Fight for Independence* (New York: New Press, 2001), 46.

44　**"blackfaced defiance of the Tea Party"**: Deloria, *Playing Indian,* 32.

45　**"the suggestion of instinct"**: Adam Ferguson, *An Essay on the History of Civil Society* (1995; New York: Cambridge University Press, 2006), 85.

45　Such **"natural" citizens**: Ibid., 87, 86.

45　**"embrace the occasions of mutual opposition"**: Ibid., 25.

45　**"national or party spirit," "active and strenuous"**: Ibid., 29.

45　**"grimace of politeness"**: Ibid., 43.

46　**"happiness"**: Ibid., 46. How important was Ferguson's *Essay* to Thomas Jefferson's "pursuit of happiness"? Kevin J. Hayes recently states that Ferguson "would significantly shape Jefferson's ideas concerning man's responsibility to his fellow man," but in no way does he substantiate this claim in *The Road to Monticello: The Life and Mind of Thomas Jefferson* (New York: Oxford University Press, 2008), 113. Garry Wills goes so far as to promote Ferguson's *Essay* as one of the "obvious places" to look when parsing "the pursuit of happiness," but then he lets the subject drop. See Garry Wills, *Inventing America: Jefferson's Declaration of Independence* (Garden City, NY: Doubleday, 1978), 367–68. To overlook Ferguson's influence, as have all other of the Declaration's major interpreters, is to overlook a compelling explanation of how something so radical as the "pursuit of happiness" could ever become an inalienable right—and why this phrase would have motivated Patriots who had struggled, often felicitously, to obtain their *own* society: the right to pursue communal happiness would not be a guarantee of private property (as Lockeans have always had it) but instead every citizen's guarantee to enjoy the benefits of participatory democracy. For a strong argument for the materialist pursuits of individualist "happiness" to be found during the early revolutionary era, especially in the Chesapeake and Caribbean colonies, see Jack P. Greene, *Pursuits of Happiness: The Social Development of Early Modern British Colonies and the Formation of American Culture* (Chapel Hill: University of North Carolina Press, 1988).

46 **"If the individual owe every degree"**: Ferguson, *Essay,* 59.

46 **"the most magnificent Movement of all"**: John Adams, *Diary and Autobiography,* 2:85.

47 **"The people at the Cape," "You cannot imagine the height"**: Samuel Adams, *Writings,* 3:72.

47 **"were actually a great deal of fun"**: David Waldstreicher, *In the Midst of Perpetual Fêtes: The Making of American Nationalism, 1776–1820* (Chapel Hill: University of North Carolina Press, 1997), 51. See also Len Travers, *Celebrating the Fourth: Independence and the Rights of Nationalism in the Early Republic* (Amherst: University of Massachusetts Press, 1997).

47 **"public diversions as promote Superfluity"**: Samuel Adams to John Scollay, reprinted in Irvin, *Samuel Adams,* 151.

### 3 ★ TECHNOLOGIES OF FUN

49 **"Ours is a light-hearted race"**: Josiah Jenson, *Truth Stranger Than Fiction: Father Henson's Story of His Own Life. With an Introduction by Mrs. H. B. Stowe* (Boston: John P. Jewett and Company; Cleveland: Henry P. B. Jewett, 1858), 20–21. Important sources consulted for this chapter are Lawrence W. Levine, *Black Culture, Black Consciousness: Afro-American Folk Thought from Slavery to Freedom* (New York: Oxford University Press, 1977); Roger D. Abrahams, *Singing the Master: The Emergence of African American Culture in the Plantation South* (New York: Pantheon, 1992); Sterling Stuckey, *Slave Culture: Nationalist Theory and the Foundations of Black America* (New York: Oxford University Press, 1987); John W. Blassingame, *The Slave Community: Plantation Life in the Antebellum South* (New York: Oxford University Press, 1972); Eileen Southern, *The Music of Black Americans: A History* (New York: W. W. Norton, 1971); Jean Stearns and Marshall Stearns, *Jazz Dance: The Story of American Vernacular Dance* (New York: Da Capo, 1994); Larry Eugene Rivers, *Slavery in Florida: Territorial Days to Emancipation* (Gainesville: University Press of Florida, 2000), 162–209; Roderick A. McDonald, *The Economy and Material Culture of Slaves: Goods and Chattels on the Sugar Plantations of Jamaica and Louisiana* (Baton Rouge: Louisiana State University Press, 1993), 50–91, 129–66; Randolph B. Campbell, *An Empire for Slavery: The Peculiar Institution in Texas, 1821–1865* (Baton Rouge: Louisiana State University Press, 1989), 115–90; Leslie Howard Owens, *This Species of Property: Slave Life and Culture in the Old South* (New York: Oxford University Press, 1976); George P. Rawick, ed., *The American Slave: A Composite Biography,* vols. 1, 6, and 16 (Westport, CT: Greenwood, 1972); Julia Floyd Smith, *Slavery and Plantation Growth in Antebellum Florida, 1821–1860* (Gainesville: University Press of Florida, 1973); Lynn Fauley Emery, *Black Dance: From 1619 to Today* (Princeton, NJ: Princeton Book Company, 1989); Dena J. Epstein, *Sinful Tunes and Spirituals: Black Folk Music to the Civil War* (Urbana: University of Illinois Press, 1977); David Eltis, *The Rise of African Slavery in the Americas* (New York: Cambridge University Press, 2000); Eugene D. Genovese, *Roll, Jordan, Roll: The World the Slaves Made* (1972; New York: Pantheon, 1974).

49  **"slave in form"**: Frederick Douglass, *Narrative of the Life of Frederick Douglass, An American Slave, Written by Himself* (London: H. G. Collins, 1851), 68.

50  **"The staid, sober, thinking and industrious ones"**: Ibid., 68–70.

50  **"no moral religious instruction"**: Henry Bibb, *Narrative of the Life and Adventures of Henry Bibb, An American Slave, Written by Himself with An Introduction by Lucious C. Matlack* (New York: Published by the Author, 5 Spruce Street, 1849), 21–23.

50  **"buoyant, elastic"**: Solomon Northrup, *Twelve Years a Slave: Narrative of Solomon Northrup, a Citizen of New-York, Kidnapped in Washington City in 1841, and Rescued in 1853* (Auburn: Derby and Miller, 1853), 180–81, 218; electronic edition, http://doc south.unc.edu/fpn/northup/northup.html, accessed August 5, 2012.

51  **"slave minstrels"**: Leslie Howard Owens, *This Species of Property: Slave Life and Culture in the Old South* (New York: Oxford University Press, 1976), 169.

51  **"beloved violin"**: Northrup, *Twelve Years a Slave*, 180–81.

52  **"the moral, social, religious, and intellectual elevation"**: Frederick Douglass, *My Bondage and My Freedom* (1855; Urbana: University of Illinois Press, 1987), 248.

52  **"It was Christmas morning"**: Northrup, *Twelve Years a Slave*, 282.

54  **"To Federalists"**: Waldstreicher, *In the Midst of Perpetual Fêtes*, 230, 231n. Len Travers, in his version of the rise of partisan holidays, gives a sparkling account of Philadelphia's "Grand Federal Procession" on July 4th, 1788—a partisan take on Independence Day that was also "the largest, most lavish procession ever seen in the United States" (*Celebrating the Fourth*, 71).

54  **The earliest account of an African-American holiday**: All quotes in this paragraph are from "UTOPIA, April 10 _____" (letter), *The New-York Weekly Journal: Containing the Freshest Advices, Foreign, and Domestick*, March 7, 1736, 1, cited in Shlomo Pestcoe and Greg C. Adams, "Zenger's 'Banger': Contextualizing the Banjo in Early New York City, 1736," forthcoming in a yet-untitled collection of essays from the University of Illinois Press to be edited by Robert Winans.

55  **Joseph P. Reidy notes**: See Joseph P. Reidy, "'Negro Election Day' & Black Community Life in New England, 1750–1860," *Marxist Perspectives* (Fall 1978): 102–17.

56  **"Nine-tenths of the blacks"**: James Fenimore Cooper, *Works of J. Fenimore Cooper: Oak Openings. Satanstoe. Mercedes of Castile* (New York: P. F. Collier, Publisher, 1892), 277.

56  **"collected in thousands"**: Southern, *Music of Black Americans*, 53.

57  **"negroes patrol[led] the streets"**: "Pinkster," *Albany Centinel*, June 17, 1803, 3–4; emphases in original.

58  **"graceful mien"**: Absalom Aimwell, Esq., "A Pinkster Ode, for the year 1803, Most Respectfully dedicated to Carolus Africanus, Rex: Thus rendered in English; King Charles, Captain General and Commander in Chief of the Pinkster Boys" (Albany, NY: Printed Solely for the Purchasers and Others, 1803); Geraldine R. Pleat and Agnes N. Underwood, eds., "A Pinkster Ode, Albany, 1802," *New York Folklore Quarterly* 8 (Spring 1952): 31–45.

58  **"King Charley"**: James Eights, "Pinkster Festivals in Albany," in *Readings in Black American Music*, 2nd ed., ed. Eileen Southern (1971; New York: W. W. Norton, 1983), 42.

59  **"blacks and [a] certain class of whites," "biographer of devils"**: "Pinkster," *Albany Centinel*, June 17, 1803, 3–4.

59  **"still retained all the vigor"**: Eights, "Pinkster Festivals," 42–45.

59  **"most lewd and indecent gesticulations"**: "Pinkster," *Albany Centinel*, 3–4.

59  **"[T]here, enclosed within their midst"**: Eights, "Pinkster Festivals," 42–45.

60  **"cultural syncretization"**: See Melville J. Herskovitz, *The Myth of the Negro Past* (Boston: Beacon Press, 1990). More recently, Claire Sponsler makes this same critical

point and reads Pinkster, through Paul Gilroy's transatlantic theory, as the product of a "compound interculture . . . a transgeographical culture without national boundaries that thrives on syncretism and lateral networks." *Ritual Imports: Performing Medieval Drama in America* (Ithaca, NY: Cornell University Press, 2004), 49.

61 **"subversive music makers"**: To quote Gilroy's statement more fully: "I want to endorse the suggestion that these subversive music makers and users represent a different kind of intellectual not least because their self-identity and their practice of cultural politics remain outside the dialectic of pity and guilt which, especially among oppressed people, has so often governed the relationship between the writing elite and the masses of people who exist outside literacy." Then he goes on to dignify the content produced by these intellectuals—"the unrepresentable, the pre-rational, and the sublime"—while acknowledging the difficulty of reading such texts. Paul Gilroy, *The Black Atlantic: Modernity and Double Consciousness* (Cambridge, MA: Harvard University Press, 1993), 76–77.

61 **the fun expression of free-spirited community:** If collective fun, as suggested here, is the Pinkster Days' most legible text—how should it be read? How *can* it be read, as speech, in an objective way that doesn't once again project its reader's will? How can these "intellectuals," as Gilroy might call them, be understood? An intriguing solution comes from the philosopher Henri Lefebvre's book *Rhythmanalysis: Time, Space, and Everyday Life* (New York: Continuum, 2004), which sets out to establish a scientific "analysis of rhythms"—"repetitive time and space"—"with practical consequences." Several elements of Lefebvre's theory and method combine to make it relevant to Pinkster Days. The persistent dancing and drumming and singing, performed with variation in a single setting, presented an ever-changing dynamism that at the same time had unity and positivity. Hence, as musical events where "rhythm dominates" and "supplants melody and harmony (without suppressing them)," Pinkster had what Lefebvre calls "an ethical function," for intensely rhythmic music mirrors the body's internal functions and uses the body as its "resource." Lefebvre writes: "In its relation to the body, to time, to the work, [music] illustrates *real* (everyday) life. It *purifies* it in the acceptance of catharsis. Finally, and above all, it brings compensation for the miseries of everydayness, for its deficiencies and failures" (62; emphasis in original).

The dance on Pinkster Hill, to the extent that our meager evidence allows, presents a complex illustration of everyday life that stands in highest relief alongside the partisan celebrations taking place during the same era. If these contentious Fourth of July showdowns reflect a republic characterized by "arrhythmia"—what Lefebvre calls "disturbances" to rhythm "that sooner or later become pathology"—then Pinkster reflects "the eu-rhythmic body, composed of diverse rhythms, each organ, each function, having its own" and yet coexisting in harmony. As Claire Sponsler claims, the black participants' experience will never be known except as tendentiously reported by whites; put differently, the predominantly black revelers at the Albany Pinkster Days, like Gayatri Spivak's theorized subaltern, will never have the chance to "speak"—unless, perhaps, we broaden our sense of speech to include expressive bodily acts, much as Spivak does in interpreting Bhubaneswari Baduri's suicide for its political content. When we do, the clearest and most positive evidence of that experience, among all of the competing accounts of Pinkster, is in the participants' various displays of pleasure: bodily pleasure, ironic pleasure, rebellious pleasure, communal pleasure. See Gayatri Chakravorty Spivak, *A Critique of Postcolonial Reason: Toward a History of the Vanishing Present* (Cambridge, MA: Harvard University Press, 1999).

61 **Albany's Common Council passed:** See Shane White, "Pinkster: Afro-Dutch Syncretization in New York City and the Hudson Valley," *Journal of American Folklore* 102, no. 403 (January–March 1989): 68–75.

62 "The language of the slave's speech and song": Owens, *This Species of Property,* 175.

62 The storytellers themselves: Blassingame, *The Slave Community,* 57–59.

62 In a rustic opening in the Georgia pines: Fictional composite of a storytelling session drawn from a variety of works. The story itself was collected in Georgia by Emma Backus and cited in Levine, *Black Culture, Black Consciousness,* 110–11. Other sources include Joel Chandler Harris, *Uncle Remus: His Songs and His Sayings,* in *The Complete Tales of Uncle Remus,* compiled by Richard Chase (1955; Boston: Houghton Mifflin Company, 1983); Charles C. Jones Jr., *Negro Myths from the Georgia Coast, Told in the Vernacular* (Boston: Houghton, Mifflin and Company, 1888); J. Mason Brewer, *American Negro Folklore* (Chicago: Quadrangle Books, 1968).

63 "We started shuckin' corn": Roderick A. McDonald, *The Economy and Material Culture of Slaves: Goods and Chattels on the Sugar Plantations of Jamaica and Louisiana* (Baton Rouge: Louisiana State University, 1993), 112. Quilting parties had a similar appeal among plantation women, as did the "Coonjine" among river workers—the latter being "a combination of song and dance connected with freight handling on the steamboats" (Emery, *Black Dance,* 146). Deborah Gray White's landmark work on female slave culture emphasizes the relevance of work, fun, and community building in the "double duty" practices of laundry and quilting, arguing that a "saving grace . . . was that women got a chance to interact with each other": "On a Sedalia County, Missouri, plantation women looked forward to doing laundry on Saturday afternoons because, as Mary Frances Webb explained, they 'would get to talk and spend the day together.' Quiltings, referred to by former slaves as female 'frolics' and 'parties,' were especially convivial. South Carolinian Sallie Paul explained that 'when dey would get together den, dey would be glad to get together.'" *Ar'n't I a Woman?: Female Slaves in the Plantation South,* rev. ed. (New York: W. W. Norton, 1985), 122.

63 "extra swig of liquor": Emery, *Black Dance,* 112.

63 "usually the most original and amusing": Letitia Burwell, quoted in Abrahams, *Singing the Master,* the essential work on the culture of corn shuckings, 92.

64 "merciless," "meaningless etiquette," "rigid hierarchies," "slaves lied, cheated, stole": Levine, *Black Culture, Black Consciousness,* 122.

65 "music as a deceptive form": Campbell, *An Empire for Slavery,* 174.

65 "created for others": Rawick, *The American Slave,* 1:32.

65 "Negroes like to do everything at night": Rivers, *Slavery in Florida,* 167.

65 "by imitating the voices of slaveholders": James A. Colaiaco, *Frederick Douglass and the Fourth of July* (New York: Palgrave Macmillan, 2006), 24.

66 "underhanded, unsportsmanlike": Daryl Cumber Dance, *Shuckin' and Jivin': Folklore from Contemporary Black Americans* (Bloomington: Indiana University Press, 1978), 181.

66 "divine culture-hero": Paul Radin, *The Trickster: A Study in American Indian Mythology* (New York: Schocken Books, 1956), 125. Though Harris declares it "extremely doubtful" that any of "Uncle Remus's stories" (as he calls them) could have been "borrowed by the Negroes from the red men," Jay Hansford C. Vest has responded with a thorough and convincing study to the contrary, especially as it concerns the "aboriginal Rabbit-Trickster motif." Tracing Brer Rabbit tales to various stories in the Hare cycle as well as charting the countless sites and situations (not the least of them the institution of slavery) where African Americans and Native Americans commingled, Vest establishes the likelihood that more of these stories have North American than African origins. Harris, *Complete Tales,* xxii; Jay Hansford C. Vest, "From Bobtail to Brer Rabbit: Native American Influences on Uncle Remus," *American Indian Quarterly* 24, no. 1 (Winter 2000): 19–43.

66 And unlike the Trickster's morality tales: For a more optimistic response to Levine's

and others' arguments for Brer Rabbit's "amorality and brutality," which argues that his tales contain a deeper Christian morality, see William Courtland Johnson, "Trickster on Trial: The Morality of the Brer Rabbit Tales," in *Ain't Gonna Lay My 'Ligion Down: African American Religion in the South,* ed. Alonzo Johnson and Paul Jersild (Columbia: University of South Carolina Press, 1996), 52–71.

67  **"from round Yankees":** This and subsequent quotations in this and the following paragraph from Benjamin Henry Latrobe, *The Journal of Latrobe, Being the Notes and Sketches of an Architect, Naturalist and Traveler in the United States from 1769 to 1820* (New York: D. Appleton and Company, 1905), 161–63.

67  **general racial "blending":** Interview with Henry Kmen, quoted in Stearns and Stearns, *Jazz Dance,* 20.

68  **a pungent blend:** Ned Sublette, *The World That Made New Orleans: From Spanish Silver to Congo Square* (Chicago: Lawrence Hill Books, 2008), 274–81.

68  **"However much of the primitive":** Henry Kmen, *Music in New Orleans: The Formative Years, 1791–1841* (Baton Rouge: Louisiana State University Press, 1966), 229.

68  **"movements, gyrations, and attitudenizing exhibitions":** Creecy, quoted in Sublette, *World That Made New Orleans,* 282.

68  **While it is hard to say with precision:** See Southern, *Music of Black Americans,* 161–62.

68  **"a principal means by which":** Stuckey, *Slave Culture,* 24.

68  **" 'praise'-nights":** William Frances Allen, Charles Pickard Ware, and Lucy McKim Garrison, *Slave Songs of the United States* (New York: Peter Smith, 1951), xiii.

69  **"any assembly of [enslaved] Negroes or Negresses":** *Code Noir,* cited in Herbert Asbury, *The French Quarter: An Informal History of the New Orleans Underworld* (New York: Alfred A. Knopf, 1936), 239.

69  **"Oh, where are our select men":** Kmen, *Music in New Orleans,* 227.

69  **"a jerking, hitching motion":** Allen et al., *Slave Songs,* xiv.

69  **"unceasing, wave-like ripple":** T. Amaury Talbot, quoted in Stuckey, *Slave Culture,* 11.

69  **" 'danced' with the whole body":** Stuckey, *Slave Culture,* 362.

70  **"sensual, even blatantly erotic dances":** Crété quoted in Joseph Roach, *Cities of the Dead: Circum-Atlantic Performance* (New York: Columbia University Press, 1996), 65.

70  **"not altogether to understand":** Asbury, *The French Quarter,* 253.

70  **"rhythm and excitement":** Emery, *Black Dance,* 121.

70  **"turning around occasionally":** Ibid., 122.

70  **"Some gits so joyous":** Former Texan slaves Wes Beady and Richard Carruthers quoted in Rawick, *The American Slave,* 1:36, 37.

70  **"worship," "the sole object":** Schultz and Nuttall quoted in Sublette, *World That Made New Orleans,* 281–82.

71  **"the steps and figures of the court":** Stearns and Stearns, *Jazz Dance,* 28.

71  **"Long Dog Scratch":** Ibid., 29.

71  **"mass of nonsense and wild frolic":** Douglass, *My Bondage,* 155.

72  **"The Majesty of the People had disappeared":** Margaret Bayard Smith, *The First Forty Years of Washington Society: Portrayed by the Family Letters* (New York: Charles Scribner's Sons, 1906), 295.

72  **"Hangings and public executions":** Edward Pessen, *Jacksonian America: Society, Personality, and Politics,* rev. ed. (Urbana: University of Illinois Press, 1978), 12.

72  **"expressive," "recreational":** Michael Feldberg, *The Turbulent Era: Riot & Disorder in Jacksonian America* (New York: Oxford University Press, 1980), 55.

73  **"friendly rivalry":** Discussion following April Masten's presentation, "Shared Traditions: The Origins of Negro Jigging in Early America," at the conference Triumph in My Song: 18th & 19th Century African Atlantic Culture, History, & Performance,

University of Maryland, College Park, June 2, 2012. For Masten's groundbreaking analysis of the "friendly rivalry" between dancers and musicians during this period, see "Partners in Time: Dancers, Musicians, and Negro Jigs in Early America," *Common-Place* 13, no. 2 (Winter 2013), http://www.common-place.org/vol-13/no-02/masten/.

73 **White acknowledges that these fancy-dress balls:** The following quotations are from Shane White, *Stories of Freedom in Black New York* (Cambridge, MA: Harvard University Press, 2002), 49, 191–98.

74 **"at a signal":** Asbury, *The French Quarter*, 243.

74 **"abhor & detest the Sabbath-day":** Mark Twain, *Mark Twain–Howells Letters: The Correspondence of Samuel L. Clemens and William D. Howells, 1872–1910* (Cambridge, MA: Harvard University Press, 1960), 520.

74 **"frightful triumph of body over mind":** George Washington Cable, "The Dance in Place Congo," *The Century* 31, no. 51 (February 1886): 525.

74 **"what havoc":** Ibid., 522.

74 **"Now for the frantic leaps!":** Ibid., 525.

74 **"social death":** For a brilliant response to recent historical trends that argue for "social death" in slavery, see Vince Brown, "Social Death and Political Life in the Study of Slavery," *American Historical Review* 114, no. 5 (December 2009): 1231–49. See also Orlando Patterson, *Slavery and Social Death: A Comparative Study* (Cambridge, MA: Harvard University Press, 1982).

76 **"all this Congo Square business":** Cable, "Dance in Place Congo," 527.

76 **"No wonder the police stopped it":** Ibid., 525.

### 4 ⋆ A CALIFORNIA EDUCATION

77 **"quite dejected and sulky":** J. D. Borthwick, *Three Years in California* (London: William Blackwood and Sons, 1857), 10.

78 **"grumbled at everything":** Ibid., 150.

78 **were often ungoverned, ungodly fun:** Susan Lee Johnson, whose study of gold rush "leisure" includes church attendance, saloons, gambling, dancing, and popular blood sports like bull and bear baiting, makes the strong claim that "like domestic and personal service work, leisure was one of the key locations in which gendered and racialized meanings got made, unmade, and remade . . . When immigrant men laid down their picks and shovels, they found that the oppositions which created both social order and social relations—that is, society—back home were all out of kilter in California." Anglo-American men, in particular, used to enjoying positions of social domination, experienced what Johnson calls a "crisis of representation." *Roaring Camp: The Social World of the California Gold Rush* (New York: W. W. Norton, 2000), 144.

79 **"The streets were full of people":** Bayard Taylor, *El Dorado, or Adventures in the Path of Empire* (1850; Lincoln: University of Nebraska Press, 1988), 43.

79 **"Northern barbarians":** Ibid., 30.

80 **"for action":** This and subsequent quotations come from ibid., 44–46.

80 **"beggarly sum":** Ibid., 62.

80 **"disposition to maintain," "In the absence of all law," "thousands of ignorant adventurers":** Ibid., 77. Taylor also exposes self-government's dark side. He watches in Stockton as two defenseless blacks were apprehended, tried, accused, and sentenced for allegedly assaulting a Chilean woman in her tent—all in the course of one day. Their respective sentences of fifty and twenty lashes were administered on the

spot: "There was little of that order and respect shown which should accompany even the administration of impromptu law; the bystanders jeered, laughed, and accompanied every blow with coarse and unfeeling remarks" (ibid.).

81 **"They struggled to gain freedom"**: Sucheng Chan, "A People of Exceptional Character: Ethnic Diversity, Nativism, and Racism in the California Gold Rush," in *Rooted in Barbarous Soil: People, Culture, and Community in Gold Rush California*, ed. Kevin Starr and Richard J. Orsi (Berkeley: University of California Press, 2000), 69. For a penetrating study of African-American life in the diggings, see Rudolph M. Lapp, *Blacks in Gold Rush California* (New Haven, CT: Yale University Press, 1977).

82 **"ideological overtones"**: W. J. Rorabaugh, *The Alcoholic Republic: An American Tradition* (New York: Oxford University Press, 1981), 151. See pp. 149–83 for vivid examples of Americans' fidelity to alcohol—as a test of character, mark of freedom, and lubricant to community—in the early years of the republic.

82 **American Temperance Society (ATS)**: Thomas R. Pegram, *Battling Demon Rum: The Struggle for a Dry America* (Chicago: Ivan R. Dee, 1998), 3–42.

82 **Not content with just reforming hard drinkers**: Ian R. Tyrrell, *Sobering Up: From Temperance to Prohibition, 1800–1860* (Westport, CT: Greenwood Press, 1979), 77, 87, 159–60.

83 **"the natural bad passions of men"**: Borthwick, *Three Years in California,* 67.

83 **"sufficiency of schools and churches"**: Quotations in this and the following paragraph are from ibid., 68–69.

84 **the "disease" of "drunkenness"**: This and other quotations in this paragraph are from ibid., 71.

84 **"a farewell whiff of smoke"**: This and other quotations in this paragraph and the two following paragraphs are from ibid., 318–22.

85 **Such happenings were common**: Gary F. Kurutz, "Popular Culture on the Golden Shore," in *Rooted in Barbarous Soil*, 294–97.

85 **"cotillions upon the green prairie"**: Paula Mitchell Marks, *Precious Dust: The Saga of the Western Gold Rushes* (Lincoln: University of Nebraska Press, 1994), 77.

85 **"generous, hospitable, intelligent"**: Louise Amelia Knapp Smith Clappe, *The Shirley Letters from California Mines, 1851–52* (San Francisco: Thomas C. Russell, 1922), 165.

85 **"the 'ladies,' after their fatigues"**: Borthwick, *Three Years in California,* 321.

87 **"a very good move indeed"**: Alfred Doten, *The Journals of Alfred Doten,* ed. Walter Van Tilburg Clark, vol. 1, *1849–1903* (Reno: University of Nevada Press, 1973), 20.

87 **"slaves of King Alcohol"**: Ibid., 26.

87 **"several of the Americans drunk"**: Ibid., 37.

87 **"the most civil country"**: Ibid., 52.

87 **serious gold rush fun**: A small sample indicates Doten's daily frolics: "Harry sang her some of his naughty songs—We had the tallest kind of dancing and when we started for home again about one o'clock we were all more or less thick tongued and top heavy" (ibid., 144). "Ranch routine during the days, partying at night—Many snakes killed in the hayfields" (15). "The house was crowded—dancing, singing, and kicking up was the order of the night . . . waltzes and polkas . . . a most glorious *jollification* and we kept it up till daylight" (153). "We danced and kicked up to hearts' content till just before daybreak" (159). "We marched up and down the road and went through all the military maneuvers—We had a glorious time and kept it up till about two o'clock" (164). "Tom Locke, John Fernandez, Mike and a lot more of the boys came in and we had a most joyful jollification—We had plenty of the 'oh be joyful' and were very joyful and jolly—we had music and dancing and lots of songs" (165).

87 **"drinking and gambling"**: Ibid., 97.

87 "howling drunk": Ibid., 98, 117.

87 "a hell of a spree": Ibid., 125.

87 He "astonished" crowds: Ibid., 128–30.

87 "This is one of the best *'benders'*": Ibid., 141.

87 "jollification": Ibid., 137, 192, 779.

88 "plum cake": Ibid., 198.

88 "Mexicans are robbing and killing the Chinese": Ibid., 141.

88 "thieving Mexicans": Ibid., 107.

88 "it perfectly thunder beneath": Quotations in this and the next paragraph are from ibid., 168.

89 "little Spanish village": Ibid., 177.

89 "As usual in California": This and other quotations in this paragraph from ibid., 190.

90 "as fast as [they] could load": Quotations in this and the next paragraph are from ibid., 227–32.

91 "far famed," "No use for my pencil": Ibid., 716.

92 "considerable drunks & some fights": Ibid., 723.

92 "got on a big spree": Ibid., 727.

92 "skylarking": Ibid., 762.

92 "Evening stage brought a noted correspondent": Ibid., 763.

93 "Every feature of the spectacle": Mark Twain, *Roughing It* (Berkeley: University of California Press, 1993), 156; see also 1–284. Further, see Ron Powers, *Mark Twain: A Life* (New York: The Free Press, 2005), 110–30, and Paul Fatout, *Mark Twain in Virginia City* (Bloomington: Indiana University Press, 1964), 3–33.

93 "Oh, *don't* he buck": Twain, *Roughing It,* 161.

93 "Here was romance": Ibid., 67.

93 "It was dark as pitch": Ibid., 145.

94 "Unassailable certainty": Ibid., 274.

94 "could take [his] pen and murder": Ibid., 277.

94 Clemens's hoax of a "petrified man": Mark Twain, "Petrified Man," in *Early Tales & Sketches,* ed. Edgar Marquess Branch and Robert H. Hirst, vol. 1, *1851–1863* (Berkeley: University of California Press, 1979), 159.

95 But a medical journal: Kelly Driscoll, "The Fluid Identity of 'Petrified Man,'" *American Literary Realism* 41, no. 3 (Spring 2009): 214–31.

95 "Unreliable": Mark Twain, *Mark Twain of the* Enterprise: *Newspaper Articles & Other Documents, 1862–1864,* ed. Henry Nash Smith (Berkeley: University of California Press, 1957), 59.

95 "April Fool & Co.": Doten, *Journals,* 146.

95 "that most incorrigible of jokers": Dan De Quille [William Wright], *The History of the Big Bonanza: An Authentic Account of the Discovery, History, and Working of the World Renowned Comstock Silver Lode of Nevada* (Hartford, CT: American Publishing Company, 1877), 357.

95 "12 pound nugget": William P. Bennett, *The First Baby in Camp: A Full Account of the Scenes and Adventures During the Pioneer Days of '49* (Salt Lake City: Rancher Publishing Company, 1893), 6–7.

96 One famous prank: Twain, *Roughing It,* 221–27, 631–32n. For an earlier account of the landslide case, see also Mark Twain, "A Rich Decision," in *Early Tales & Sketches,* vol. 1, 280–81, 481–82n.

96 "to provoke cascades of inextinguishable merriment": Lucius Beebe, *Comstock Commotion: The Story of the Territorial Enterprise* (Stanford, CA: Stanford University Press, 1954), 40, 60.

96  **At a time when eastern culture:** Ann Douglas, *The Feminization of American Culture* (New York: Farrar, Straus and Giroux, 1977), especially 227–56.

97  **a rash of murders:** Mark Twain and Dan De Quille took a room in a house shared by the family of Tom Fitch, editor of their rival *Union,* and Twain managed to offend Fitch's hospitable wife, Anna, with the rumor that De Quille had hanged her cat. (He hadn't.) Making matters worse, Fitch had become the object of the *Enterprise*'s vicious ridicule for turning against the Union cause, a war of words that peaked, on September 27, in a Colt .44 duel between the two editors in chief. It was the season's best-attended social outing—numbering "gamblers, pimps, touts, bartenders, teamsters, newspaper reporters, con men, shills, spielers, gold-brick artists, and snake-oil venders" among the witnesses—and though it spared Fitch's life, it cost him a kneecap. Beebe, *Comstock Commotion,* 63–65.

97  **"great pine forest":** Mark Twain, "A Bloody Massacre near Carson," in *Early Tales & Sketches,* vol. 1, 324–26.

97  **"Presently his eyes spread wide open":** Mark Twain, *Mark Twain's Sketches New and Old* (Hartford, CT: American Publishing Company, 1882), 296.

97  **"as baseless as the fabric of a dream":** Richard G. Lillard, "Contemporary Reaction to 'The Empire City Massacre,'" *American Literature* 16, no. 3 (November 1944): 198–203.

98  **"fun," "gold as large as peas":** These quotes and the story of Tom and Pike are in De Quille, *History of the Big Bonanza,* 542–53.

100  **"Three Saints":** Nigey Lennon, *The Sagebrush Bohemian: Mark Twain in California; Samuel Clemens's Turbulent Years on the Barbary Coast* (New York: Paragon House, 1993), 30.

100  **"very wild":** Artemus Ward [Charles Farrar Browne], *(His Travels) Among the Mormons,* in *The Complete Works of Charles Farrar Browne* (London: Chatto and Windus, 1889), 204.

100  **"'opinions and reflections'":** Twain, *Mark Twain of the* Enterprise, 122–25.

101  **"composed of two desperadoes":** Twain, *Roughing It,* 321.

102  **"infinitely varied and copious":** Ibid., 309.

102  **"the wildest mob":** The story is told ibid., 293–98. See Lennon, *Sagebrush Bohemian,* 31–35.

103  **"All Politeness":** Anthony, Third Earl of Shaftesbury, *Characteristicks of Men, Manners, Opinions, Times,* vol. 1 (Indianapolis, IN: Liberty Fund, 2001), 42; emphasis added. Shaftesbury countered Hobbesian egotism with the idea that citizens don't strive just for their personal happiness, but also for their neighbors' happiness, and have what he called *sensus communis.* He argued that a sense for the "common good" is an instinct every bit as natural as hunger.

## 5 ★ SELLING IT BACK TO THE PEOPLE

106  **"Plenty, unless gorged to dyspepsia":** Samuel S. Cox, *Why We Laugh* (New York: Harper & Brothers, 1876), 38.

108  **"go farther, wait longer":** P. T. Barnum, *The Autobiography of P. T. Barnum, Clerk, Merchant, Editor, and Showman With His Rules for Business and Making a Fortune,* 2nd ed. (London: Ward and Lock, 1855), 3.

108  **"those dangerous things":** Ibid.

108  **"there could be found":** Ibid., 11.

108  **"organ of acquisitiveness":** Ibid., 5.

109  **"cheerful Christianity":** Philip B. Kunhardt Jr. et al., *P. T. Barnum: America's Greatest Showman* (New York: Alfred A. Knopf, 1995), 16.

109 "eternal hostility": P. T. Barnum and James W. Cook, *The Colossal P. T. Barnum Reader: Nothing Else Like It in the Universe* (Urbana: University of Illinois Press, 2005), 113.

109 "totally blind": Barnum, *Autobiography*, 49.

109 "curiously constructed automaton": Ibid., 54.

109 "began to take great delight": Quoted in Kunhardt et al., *P. T. Barnum*, 22.

110 "so perfectly ludicrous": Barnum, *Autobiography*, 253.

110 "as usual": P. T. Barnum, *Struggles and Triumphs, or Forty Years' Recollections of P. T. Barnum, Written by Himself* (Hartford, CT: J. B. Burr & Company, 1869), 81–82.

111 "Jollity and gloom": Nathaniel Hawthorne, "The May-Pole of Merry Mount," in *Nathaniel Hawthorne's Tales*, ed. James McIntosh (New York: W. W. Norton, 1987), 89.

111 "to arrest public attention": Barnum, *Struggles and Triumphs*, 67.

112 "Mr. Griffin, the proprietor of this curious animal": Notice in *New York Herald*, August 14, 1842, quoted in James W. Cook, *The Arts of Deception: Playing with Fraud in the Age of Barnum* (Cambridge, MA: Harvard University Press, 2001), 101.

112 "a new way of thinking": Cook, *Arts of Deception*, 29.

113 "Barnumization": Bluford Adams, *E Pluribus Barnum: The Great Showman & the Meaning of U.S. Popular Culture* (Minneapolis: University of Minnesota Press, 1997), 195.

113 Even Mark Twain: See, for example, Mark Twain, "Barnum's First Speech in Congress," in *Tales, Speeches, Essays, and Sketches*, ed. Tom Quirk (New York: Penguin, 1994), 24–27. Also, his protagonist Hank Morgan, a monster of humbugs, is a glorious send-up of this original Connecticut Yankee. Mark Twain, *A Connecticut Yankee in King Arthur's Court* (1889; Berkeley: University of California Press, 1979).

113 "business" as a breeding ground: P. T. Barnum, *The Humbugs of the World: An Account of Humbugs, Delusions, Impositions, Quackeries, Deceits and Deceivers Generally, in All Ages* (New York: Carleton, 1866), 13.

113 "greatest trick of all": Cook, *Arts of Deception*, 118.

113 "be systematic": P. T. Barnum, *Art of Money Getting, or, Golden Rules for Making Money* (1880; Bedford, MA: Applewood Books, 1999), 63, 83.

114 "Weel about and turn about and do jis so": T. D. Rice, "The Original Jim Crow," in W. T. Lhamon Jr., *Jump Jim Crow: Lost Plays, Lyrics and Street Prose of the First Atlantic Popular Culture* (Cambridge, MA: Harvard University Press, 2003), 96.

115 "that fascinating imaginary space": Eric Lott, *Love and Theft: Blackface Minstrelsy and the American Working Class* (New York: Oxford University Press, 1993), 51.

115 "Hottentot Venus": For an exceptional account, see Clifton Crais and Pamela Scully, *Sara Baartman and the Hottentot Venus: A Ghost Story and a Biography* (Princeton, NJ: Princeton University Press, 2009).

115 "improvised" "ecstatic," "demanded planned variety," "stress[ed] jolliness": Hans Nathan, *Dan Emmett and the Rise of Early Negro Minstrelsy* (Norman: University of Oklahoma Press, 1962), 71.

115 "de holy state of hemlock": Rice, "Original Jim Crow," 250.

116 "he should like to play Otello": Ibid., 293.

116 "Sambos": Lhamon, *Jump Jim Crow*, 36.

116 "overlapping publics": Ibid., 5.

116 "quick-quipping runaway," "pestered those who would enter": Ibid., 16.

116 "inspired the laughter of cruelty": Gary D. Engle, *This Grotesque Essence: Plays from the American Minstrel Stage* (Baton Rouge: Louisiana State University Press, 1976), xxvii.

116 "genuine negro": Thomas Low Nichols, quoted in Lott, *Love and Theft*, 112–13.

117 "Single shuffle, double shuffle": Charles Dickens, *American Notes for General Circulation* (Leipzig: Bernhard Tauchnitz, 1842), 107.

117 **Lane is believed to have been:** Nathan, *Dan Emmett and the Rise,* 71.

117 **He had learned to dance:** Eileen Southern, *The Music of Black Americans: A History* (New York: W. W. Norton, 1971), 121.

117 **"to give correct Imitation Dances":** Quoted in Lott, *Love and Theft,* 115. See also James W. Cook, "Dancing Across the Color Line," *Common-Place* 4, no. 1 (October 2003), section IV; http://www.common-place.org/vol-04/no-01/cook/cook-4.shtml.

118 **"rare boys":** Nathan, *Dan Emmett and the Rise,* 129.

118 **"the fun of these three nigger minstrels":** English actor H. P. Grattan quoted ibid., 145.

118 **This frantic endeavor to "reproduce" fun:** Ibid., 120.

118 **starting a trend that in decades to come:** Robert C. Toll, *Blacking Up: The Minstrel Show in Nineteenth-Century America* (New York: Oxford University Press, 1974), 31.

119 **"I have always strictly confined myself":** Emmett's introduction quoted in Nathan, *Dan Emmett and the Rise,* 232.

119 **urban riots:** At least fifty-three riots erupted in 1835 alone; Daniel Walker Howe notes that there probably were three times that many. *What Hath God Wrought: The Transformation of America, 1815–1848* (New York: Oxford University Press, 2007), 430–39. See also Feldberg, *The Turbulent Era,* 84–119.

120 **an efflorescence of political parties:** Sean Wilentz gives a lively account of the "radical democracies" during this period: *The Rise of American Democracy: Jefferson to Lincoln* (New York: W. W. Norton, 2005), 330–59. Ironically, however, beneath the blare of 1830s partisan conflict, there was a tepid turnout at the polls (a little more than 50 percent of eligible voters); this trend would hold steady until 1840, when—thanks to the same kinds of popular organization that fortified reform movements—there was what Altschuler and Blumin call "the *annus mirabilis* of American partisan democracy," when "fully eight of ten eligible voters cast ballots." Glenn C. Altschuler and Stuart M. Blumin, *Rude Republic: Americans and Their Politics in the Nineteenth Century* (Princeton, NJ: Princeton University Press, 2000), 14–18.

120 **"swing, which nobody but a Bowery Boy":** William M. Bobo, *Glimpses of New-York City* (1852), quoted in Tyler Anbinder, *Five Points: The 19th-Century New York City Neighborhood That Invented Tap Dance, Stole Elections, and Became the World's Most Notorious Slum* (New York: Free Press, 2001), 178. Also consulted: George G. Foster, *New York by Gas-Light and Other Urban Sketches,* ed. Stuart M. Blumin (Berkeley: University of California Press, 1990), 174–76; David S. Reynolds, *Walt Whitman's America: A Cultural Biography* (New York: Alfred A. Knopf, 1995), 102–5; David S. Reynolds, *Waking Giant: America in the Age of Jackson* (New York: HarperCollins, 2008), 303–7. Others have also followed Reynolds's lead in reading the b'hoys' influence on the slang, style, and attitudes of Walt Whitman's poetry and prose. See Robert M. Dowling, *Slumming in New York: From the Waterfront to Mythic Harlem* (Urbana: University of Illinois Press, 2007), 52–59.

120 **"with a perfect exuberance of flowers and feathers":** Foster, *New York by Gas-Light,* 176.

121 **"The gang had no regular organization":** John Riply quoted in Anbinder, *Five Points,* 181.

121 **"recreational":** Feldberg, *Turbulent Era,* 54–84.

121 **their bloody 1834 race riots:** Herbert Asbury, *The Gangs of New York* (New York: Alfred A. Knopf, 1927), 34–37.

121 **"Slamm Bang & Co.," "democratize":** Peter Adams, *Bowery Boys: Street Corner Radicals and the Politics of Rebellion* (Westport, CT: Greenwood Publishing Group, 2005), 63; Google eBook.

121  **"Thorough-going sporting-man"**: Anbinder, *Five Points,* 142–43.

121  **"shirtless democracy"**: See Sean Wilentz, *Chants Democratic: New York City & the Rise of the American Working Class, 1788–1850* (New York: Oxford University Press, 1984), 326–35. See also Adams, *Bowery Boys,* 107–8.

122  **Dorr Rebellion**: Adams, *Bowery Boys,* 47–60. Marvin E. Gettleman, *The Dorr Rebellion: A Study in American Radicalism, 1833–1949* (Huntington, NY: Robert E. Krieger, 1980), 135–36.

122  **"the first New Yorkers to leave for California"**: Anbinder, *Five Points,* 180.

122  **"dandies and dandizettes"**: Shane White and Graham White, *Stylin': African American Expressive Culture from Its Beginnings to the Zoot Suit* (Ithaca, NY: Cornell University Press, 1998), 85–119.

123  **So faithfully did he mimic their dress**: David Rinear, "F. S. Chanfrau's Mose: The Rise and Fall of an Urban Folk-Hero," *Theatre Journal* 33, no. 2 (May 1981): 199–212.

123  **"greenhorn"**: Benjamin Archibald Baker, *A Glance at New York* (Cambridge, MA: ProQuest Information and Learning Company, 2003), 4.

123  **"capital fun"**: This and subsequent quotations are from ibid., 11–14.

123  **"Waxhall," "Wawdeville," "first-rate shindig"**: Ibid., 21.

123  **"As may be supposed"**: *Albion* review quoted in Rinear, "F. S. Chanfrau's Mose," 202.

123  **"a pleasant place for family resort"**: *Herald* review quoted ibid., 204.

124  **"Onstage, the b'hoy gained superhuman powers"**: Reynolds, *Walt Whitman's America,* 104. Each of these folk heroes, in its era, captured a strain in American fun. The peddler was a rambling bricoleur who baffled yokels with pranks and stunts and quirkily practical contraptions. Trappers, woodsmen, and heel-cracking boatmen were monsters of risk and silly braggadocio who tackled the frontier's sublime opponents—great lakes, grand canyons, rocky mountains—and always with a bizarre sense of humor. Their citified Jackson Age cousins, moreover, updated the nation's puckish fury for Jacksonian democracy's social wilderness. Mose and Lize posted their brash white selves as America's cocky urban explorers. The classic treatment of these early American icons—Yankee peddlers and Kentucky woodsmen as well as blackface minstrels—is Constance Rourke's superlative 1931 *American Humor,* 15–91. Like these other icons and, say, Brother Rabbit, b'hoys and g'hals keep popping back up in the national consciousness—in Ned Buntline's dime novels and especially in Herbert Asbury's sometimes fanciful popular history, *The Gangs of New York,* which transcends his accounts of America's other skid rows (the Barbary Coast and Quartier Latin) to present a high-flying mythology of the b'hoys' gang wars and has inspired such titanic mythmakers as Jorge Luis Borges and Martin Scorsese. Kurt Andersen's 2007 historical novel *Heyday* also takes an admirable crack at the subject.

125  **It wouldn't have been the first time**: Nigel Cliff, *The Shakespeare Riots: Revenge, Drama, and Death in Nineteenth-Century America* (New York: Random House, 2007), xix.

126  **"carnival"**: Sante's claim that this rioting was "carnival" stands among the more convincing efforts to import this European concept stateside. Five Points rioters, like feudal peasants, saw no other way out, and they often acted with medieval naïveté in their attempts to upend society. But these efforts, like the "play" rebellions of traditional Saturnalia, did not strive for a permanent state of democracy. In their violent frustration and self-gratification, the b'hoys' riots strove for outright anarchy and thereby triggered even harsher measures of authoritarian rule and social inequality. Luc Sante, *Low Life: Lures and Snares of Old New York* (New York: Farrar, Straus and Giroux, 1991), 340.

127 **"an aristocracy of the dram shop"**: Quoted in Adams, *Bowery Boys,* 51.
127 **"the nightly revels at Dickens's Place"**: Quotations in this and the next paragraph are from Foster, *New York by Gas-Light,* 140–43.

### 6. ★ BARNUMIZING AMERICA

129 **Patriotic dramas**: Kunhardt et al., *P. T. Barnum,* 154.
129 **"ten times larger"**: Billboard reprinted ibid., 224.
131 **"new corporate context"**: Karen Halttunen, *Painted Ladies and Confidence Men: A Study of Middle-Class Culture in America, 1830–1870* (New Haven, CT: Yale University Press, 1982), 207.
131 **"humbug in the exhibition room"**: Barnum, *Humbugs of the World,* 13.
132 **athletics were largely primitive pastimes**: Puritans had long allowed certain games of skill—from footraces to combat sports—but as Eliot J. Gorn and Warren Goldstein put it, "when these very same activities became part of 'Romish' celebrations . . . then a line was crossed." Gorn and Goldstein, *A Brief History of American Sports* (New York: Hill & Wang, 1993), 33. Richard A. Swanson and Betty Spears, *History of Sport and Physical Education in the United States* (Dubuque, IA: WCB Brown & Benchmark, 1995), 32–144. See also Foster Rhea Dulles, *America Learns to Play: A History of Popular Recreation, 1607–1940* (Gloucester, MA: Peter Smith, 1959), 3–99.
133 **"exotic and frivolous indulgences"**: Stephen Hardy, "'Adopted by All the Clubs': Sporting Goods and the Shaping of Leisure, 1800–1900," in *For Fun and Profit,* ed. Richard Busch (Philadelphia: Temple University Press, 1990), 78.
133 **"chess, draughts, billiards, and bowling"**: William E. Dodge Jr. "The Young Men's Christian Association . . . Shall It Be a Club? About Amusements," *New York Times,* July 18, 1869, reprinted in George B. Kirsch, *Sports in North America: A Documentary History,* vol. 4, *Sports in War: Revival, and Expansion, 1860–1880* (Gulf Breeze, FL: Academic International Press, 1995), 3.
134 **"the growth of the professional spirit"**: Dudley Sargent, "The Evils of the Professional Tendency in Modern Athletics," *American Journal of Social Science* 20 (1884): 87–90, reprinted in Kirsch, *Sports in North America.*
134 **"the thing which produces most of the evils"**: E. L. Godwin, "The Athletic Craze," *Nation,* December 7, 1893, 422–23, reprinted in Kirsch, *Sports in North America.*
135 **"to embody his conception"**: John F. Kasson, *Amusing the Million: Coney Island at the Turn of the Century* (New York: Hill & Wang, 1978), 12–13.
135 **"transform[ed] public spaces"**: Lawrence W. Levine, *Highbrow/Lowbrow: The Emergence of Cultural Hierarchy in America* (Cambridge, MA: Harvard University Press, 1988), 177.
135 **"continuous performance"**: Quotations in this and the following paragraph are from Benjamin Franklin Keith, "The Vogue of Vaudeville," reprinted in *American Vaudeville as Seen by Its Contemporaries,* ed. Charles W. Stein (New York: Da Capo, 1991), 17.
136 **"The most dangerous acts of the trapeze"**: William Dean Howells, "On Vaudeville," in Stein, *American Vaudeville,* 76.
136 **the "Keith Circuit" commanded**: Edward F. Albee, "Twenty Years of Vaudeville," in Stein, *American Vaudeville,* 17.
136 **The Gilded Age population**: *The Statistical History of the United States from Colonial Times to the Present* (New York: Basic Books, 1976), 379.
136 **"country" newspapers**: George H. Douglas, *The Golden Age of the Newspaper* (Westport, CT: Greenwood Press, 1999), 83. See also Ted Curtis Smythe, *The Gilded Age Press, 1865–1900* (Westport, CT: Praeger, 2003), 33–44.

137 **the dramatic "facts" of modern life**: Joshua Brown, *Beyond the Lines: Pictorial Reporting, Everyday Life, and the Crisis of Gilded Age America* (Berkeley: University of California Press, 2002), 131–231.

137 **"very close to the untutored spirit"**: Review, *The Nation,* August 7, 1884, 116.

137 **"like Brer Rabbit"**: Julia Collier Harris, *The Life and Letters of Joel Chandler Harris* (Boston: Houghton Mifflin, 1918), 12; Walter M. Brasch, *Brer Rabbit, Uncle Remus, and the "Cornfield Journalist": The Tale of Joel Chandler Harris* (Macon, GA: Mercer University Press, 2000), 2–5; Michael Flusche, "Underlying Despair in the Fiction of Joel Chandler Harris," in *Critical Essays on Joel Chandler Harris,* ed. R. Bruce Bickley Jr. (Boston: G. K. Hall, 1981), 175. Wayne Mixon, "The Ultimate Irrelevance of Race: Joel Chandler Harris and Uncle Remus in Their Time," *Journal of Southern History* 56, no. 3 (August 1990): 458; R. Bruce Bickely Jr., "Joel Chandler Harris," in *Dictionary of Literary Biography,* ed. Stanley Trachtenberg, vol. 11, *American Humorists, 1800–1950* (Detroit: Gale Research, 1982), 191. Robert Cochran argues effectively that Harris, the author, was also more of a trickster than is commonly recognized: "It's high time," he writes, "to at least consider the possibility that Harris constructed his tales and their framing narratives with consummate skill and deliberate cunning, that multiple ironies were not only not lost upon him but were in fact something of his stock-in-trade, and that he was, in short, something of a Brer Rabbit among authors." "Black Father: The Subversive Achievement of Joel Chandler Harris," *African American Review* 38, no. 1 (Spring 2004): 24.

138 **"represent[ing] nothing on earth"**: Joel Chandler Harris, "Negro Customs," *The Youth's Companion,* June 11, 1885, 238, cited in Brasch, *Brer Rabbit, Uncle Remus,* 10.

138 **"From a nook in their chimney corners"**: Julia Collier Harris, *Life and Letters,* 34.

138 **"for a black world than a white one"**: Mixon, "The Ultimate Irrelevance of Race," 459.

138 **"their confidence and esteem"**: Joel Chandler Harris, "Introduction," from *Uncle Remus: His Songs and His Sayings,* in *The Complete Tales of Uncle Remus,* compiled by Richard Chase (1955; Boston: Houghton-Mifflin Company, 1983), xvi.

139 **"unfamiliar with the great body of their own folk-lore"**: Ibid., xiv.

139 **"Only in this shape"**: Ibid., xxvi–xxvii.

139 **"Uncle Remus Initiates the Little Boy"**: Harris, *Uncle Remus: His Songs,* 3.

140 **"de funniest creetur er de whole gang"**: Ibid., 124.

140 **"undersized, red-haired and somewhat freckled"**: Mark Twain, *Life on the Mississippi* (1883; New York: Harper & Brothers, 1901), 331.

140 **"Well, I tell you dis"**: Harris, *Nights with Uncle Remus,* in *Complete Tales,* 331.

141 **"No Tinsel," "Eight Thousand Attend"**: Billboard and headline quoted in Robert A. Carter, *Buffalo Bill Cody: The Man Behind the Legend* (New York: John Wiley & Sons, 2000), 248.

141 **"the belt full of murderous bowies and long pistols"**: William Frederick Cody, *Story of the Wild West and Campfire Chats by Buffalo Bill (Hon. W. F. Cody), A Full and Complete History of the Renowned Pioneer Quartette, Boone, Crockett, Carson and Buffalo Bill* (Freeport, NY: Books for Libraries Press, 1888), 405.

141 **"red devils"**: Ibid., 426–27. For differing analyses of this episode, see Carter, *Buffalo Bill Cody,* 31, and Don Russell, *The Lives and Legends of Buffalo Bill* (Norman: University of Oklahoma Press, 1960), 38.

142 **"was in school"**: Louis S. Warren, *Buffalo Bill's America: William Cody and the Wild West Show* (New York: Alfred A. Knopf, 2005), 20.

142 **"Mr. McCarthy"**: Cody, *Story of the Wild West,* 617–18.

142 **"Death to the Indians!"**: Sandra K. Sagala, *Buffalo Bill on Stage* (Albuquerque: University of New Mexico Press, 2008), 13, 7–41.

143 "jerking his war-bonnet off": Cody, *Story of the Wild West*, 675–77.

143 "hard work": Ibid., 691.

143 "broncho riding, roping, racing": John Bratt, *Trails of Yesterday* (Chicago: University Publishing Company, 1921), 279, 280.

144 Against popular fears: Warren, *Buffalo Bill's America*, 211–18.

144 "It brought vividly back": "[SLC to William F. Cody, 10 September 1884, Elmira, N.Y.], Elmira, NY (UCCL 12811)," catalogue entry, Mark Twain Project Online (Berkeley: University of California Press, 2007).

145 "America's National Entertainment": Warren, *Buffalo Bill's America*, 264.

145 "domesticate": Ibid., 250.

147 "Barnumism": David Burg, *Chicago's White City of 1893* (Lexington: University Press of Kentucky, 1976), 253. See also Reid Badger, *The Great American Fair: The World's Columbian Exposition & American Culture* (Chicago: Nelson Hall, 1979), 107–10; Stanley Applebaum, *The Chicago World's Fair of 1893* (New York: Dover, 1980), 75–102; Joe McKennon, *A Pictorial History of the American Carnival*, vol. 1 (Bowling Green, NY: Popular Press, 1972), 27–39.

148 "great democratic resort": *Appleton's* guidebook quoted in Michael Immerso, *Coney Island: The People's Playground* (New Brunswick, NJ: Rutgers University Press, 2002), 16.

148 "abandon all the restraint": Quoted in Jon Sterngass, *First Resorts: Pursuing Pleasure at Saratoga Springs, Newport, and Coney Island* (Baltimore: Johns Hopkins University Press, 2001), 110.

148 "The opposite gender rush together": Quoted in Gary S. Cross and John K. Walton, *The Playful Crowd: Pleasure Places in the Twentieth Century* (New York: Columbia University Press, 2005), 67.

149 "King of Coney Island," "Sodom by the Sea": Immerso, *Coney Island*, 48. For Tilyou's early biography, see also Edo McCullough, *Good Old Coney Island: A Sentimental Journey into the Past* (New York: Charles Scribner's Sons, 1957), 284–327.

150 "On This Site Will Be Erected": Kasson, *Amusing the Million*, 57.

150 "clean fun," "A ride on the horses": Promotional material quoted in Immerso, *Coney Island*, 57–58.

150 "We Americans want": Immerso, *Coney Island*, 78.

150 "caused laughter enough": Ibid., 57.

151 "sales people": Robert C. Ford and Ady Milman, "George C. Tilyou—Developer of the Contemporary Amusement Park," *Cornell Hotel & Restaurant Administrations Quarterly* 41 (August 2000): 2.

152 "flirtation, permissiveness, and sexual humor": Kathy Peiss, *Cheap Amusements: Working Women and Leisure in Turn-of-the-Century New York* (Philadelphia: Temple University Press, 1986), 136–37.

152 "Laughter": Immerso, *Coney Island*, 77.

152 "gigantic laboratory of human nature": Kasson, *Amusing the Million*, 59.

154 "What a sad people you must be!": H. A. Overstreet, *The Guide to Civilized Loafing* (New York: W. W. Norton, 1935), 17.

154 "a gigantic mistake": John Strasbaugh, "The Case of Sigmund F. and Coney I.," *New York Times*, July 22, 2009.

154 encourag[ing] positive citizenship": David Klaasen and Sally Ryan, "Historical Note," National Recreation Association records; http://special.lib.umn.edu/findaid/ead/swha/sw0074.xml. Accessed July 17, 2013.

154 multibillion-dollar international juggernaut: Disney's theme parks alone pulled in $3.4 billion in the third fiscal quarter of 2012, which ranks as the most profitable quarter in their history; http://www.themeparkpost.com/index/2012396-the-walt-disney-company-reports-largest-quarterly-earnings-in-its-history. Accessed August 14, 2012.

## 7 ★ MERRY MOUNT GOES MAINSTREAM

155 **According to legend:** Ted Gioia, *The History of Jazz* (New York: Oxford University Press, 1997), 29–34.

155 **"jes' grew":** James Weldon Johnson, *The Book of American Negro Poetry* (New York: Harcourt, Brace and Company, 1922), xi. To be precise, Johnson writes that "ragtime jes' grew."

156 **"kindly, rather simple, hard-luck personage":** Jessie Fauset, "The Gift of Laughter," in *The New Negro,* ed. Alain Locke (1925; New York: Touchstone, 1997), 162.

157 **"decide which of us":** James Weldon Johnson, *Black Manhattan* (New York: Da Capo, 1930), 105.

157 **"sex dance":** *Musical Courier* quoted in Stearns and Stearns, *Jazz Dance,* 122–23.

158 **"hummed, whistled, and played":** *San Francisco Call* and French newspapers quoted in Davinia Cady, "Parisian Cake Walks," *19th-Century Music* 30, no. 3 (Spring 2007): 288–317.

158 **Born Charles Joseph Bolden:** Donald M. Marquis, *In Search of Buddy Bolden, First Man of Jazz* (Baton Rouge: Louisiana State University Press, 1978), 36–37.

159 **"harem":** Ibid., 45.

159 **"keen rivalry":** Danny Barker and Alyn Shipton, *Buddy Bolden and the Last Days of Storyville* (New York: Continuum, 2001), 11.

159 **"best dancer":** Ibid., 18.

159 **"bosom buddies":** Ibid., 19. See also Marquis, *In Search of Buddy Bolden,* 60–61. As Marquis shows, police records are the best source for polling Bolden's fan base of rounders, pimps, prostitutes, drinkers, disturbers of the peace, and the occasional murderer. Morton himself was there one June night when Edward Ory shot Charles Montrell right above the eye. Montrell had rudely stepped on his foot. Morton recalls: "This big guy laid there on the floor, dead, and, my goodness, Buddy Bolden—he was up on the balcony with the band—started blazing away with his trumpet, trying to keep the crowd together." This night, however, even Bolden's galvanizing riffs couldn't prevent the mob from busting down the doors and fairly trampling the on-duty cop (Marquis, *In Search of Buddy Bolden,* 71). Also see Jelly Roll Morton, "In New Orleans, The Bolden Legend," in *The Saga of Mr. Jelly Lord,* vol. 11, pt. 1 and conclusion (Circle Records, Circle Sound).

159 **"keep it clean":** Barker and Shipton, *Buddy Bolden,* 21.

160 **"I thought I heard Buddy Bolden say," "on the spot," "You're nasty, you're dirty":** Marquis, *In Search of Buddy Bolden,* 110–11.

160 **"had the reputation":** Barker and Shipton, *Buddy Bolden,* 10.

160 **"Dusen and Bolden used to get," "I thought I heer'd Abe Lincoln shout":** Ibid., 23.

160 **"The police put you in jail":** Marquis, *In Search of Buddy Bolden,* 111.

161 **"hesitated and then explained":** Stearns and Stearns, *Jazz Dance,* 24.

161 **"dementia praecox, paranoid type":** Marquis, *In Search of Buddy Bolden,* 129.

161 **"leisure class":** Thorstein Veblen and Stuart Chase, *The Theory of the Leisure Class: An Economic Study of Institutions* (New York: Modern Library, 1934).

162 **"recreation centers," "nearer a frank and full enjoyment," "I do not maintain":** Robert L. Duffus, "The Age of Play," *The Independent,* December 20, 1924, 539.

162 **"the Golden Age of the roller coasters":** Todd H. Throgmorton, *Roller Coasters of America* (Osceola, WI: Motorbooks International, 1994), 25–26.

162 **"the spirit of play":** Duffus, "Age of Play," 539.

163 **the "Puritan," who was widely viewed:** Frederick J. Hoffman, *The Twenties: American Writing in the Postwar Decade* (New York: Viking Press, 1955), 314–15.

163 **"Victorian character":** See Stanley Coben, *Rebellion Against Victorianism: The Impe-*

*tus for Cultural Change in 1920s America* (New York: Oxford University Press, 1991), 3–35, 136–56.

164 **"stiffening, almost a deadening":** H. L. Mencken, "Maryland, Apex of Normalcy, May 3, 1922," in *These United States: Portraits of America from the 1920s,* ed. Daniel H. Borus (Ithaca, NY: Cornell University Press, 1992), 165. For a classic discussion of the twenties' cultural schizophrenia ("Of Bohemians and Consumers," "Of Coolidge and Hemingway," "Of Town and Country"), see Paul Carter, *The Twenties in America,* 2nd ed. (1968; Arlington Heights, IL: Harlan Davidson, 1975). For a marvelously schizoid account of the decade, see Frederick Lewis Allen's classic *Only Yesterday: An Informal History of the Nineteen-Twenties* (New York: Harper & Brothers, 1951).

165 **The U.S. population grew by 16 percent:** U.S. Bureau of the Census, *Historical Statistics of the United States: Colonial Times to 1957* (Washington, DC: U.S. Government Printing Office, 1960), 12, 401.

166 **"Each week about 100 million Americans":** Geoffrey Perrett, *America in the Twenties: A History* (New York: Simon & Schuster, 1982), 224.

167 **"gaping stupidly":** Mencken, "Maryland, Apex of Normalcy," 165.

167 **"My ears have run":** Stroheim quoted in *The Cinema Book,* ed. Pam Cook (London: British Film Institute, 1985), 7.

167 **"Billy Sunday of the Republican Party":** Francis J. Couvares, "Hollywood, Main Street, and the Church: Trying to Censor Movies Before the Production Code," in *Movie Censorship and American Culture,* 2nd ed., ed. Francis J. Couvares (Amherst: University of Massachusetts Press, 1996), 133.

167 **"decorated with bunting and flags":** Leonard J. Leff and Jerold L. Simmons, *The Dame in the Kimono: Hollywood, Censorship, and the Production Code from the 1920s to the 1960s* (New York: Grove Weidenfeld, 1990), 5–6.

168 **"Eleven Don'ts":** Motion Picture Producers and Distributors of America, "The Don'ts and Be Carefuls," in *The Movies in Our Midst: Documents in the Cultural History of Film in America,* ed. Gerald Mast (Chicago: University of Chicago Press, 1982), 213–14; emphasis added. For an excellent (and fun) treatment of Hollywood's censorship history, see also Jon Lewis, *Hollywood vs. Hard Core: How the Struggle over Censorship Created the Modern Film Industry* (New York: New York University Press, 2002).

168 **"Contrary to popular opinion":** F. Scott Fitzgerald, "Echoes of the Jazz Age," in *The Crack Up,* ed. Edmund Wilson (1931; New York: New Directions, 1945), 17.

169 **"Tragedy," he later wrote:** Charles Chaplin, *My Autobiography* (New York: Simon & Schuster, 1964), 303–4.

169 **"The very morons who worshipped":** Mencken's *Baltimore Sun* article cited in David Robinson, *Chaplin, the Mirror of Opinion* (Bloomington: Indiana University Press, 1983), 71. Also see Kenneth Anger's notorious *Hollywood Babylon* (San Francisco: Straight Arrow Books, 1975), 87–94.

170 **"I developed more stunt men":** Kevin Brownlow, *The Parade's Gone By* (Berkeley: University of California Press, 1968), 314.

171 **"I could lick any boy my size":** Clara Bow, "My Life Story, as Told to Adela Rogers St. Johns," *Photoplay,* part 1, February 1928. Transcribed by Jeffrey Ford. Http://the clarabowpage.tripod.com/clarabowlifestory/clarabowlifestory.html. Accessed August 1, 2012.

171 **"All I hadda do":** Clara Bow, "My Life Story, As Told to Adela Rogers St. Johns," *Photoplay,* part 2, March 1928. Transcribed by Jeffrey Ford. Http://theclarabowpage .tripod.com/clarabowlifestory/clarabowlifestory.html. Accessed August 1, 2012.

171 **"She is plastic, quick, alert":** David Stenn, *Clara Bow: Runnin' Wild* (1988; New York: Cooper Square Press, 2000), 27.

172  "In the picture I danced": Bow, "My Life Story," part 2, March 1928.

172  "Alverna channels all her vitality": Michael Sragow, *Victor Fleming: An American Movie Master* (New York: Pantheon, 2008), 115.

172  "running wild": Clara Bow, "My Life Story, as Told to Adela Rogers St. Johns," *Photoplay,* part 3, April 1928. Transcribed by Jeffrey Ford. Http://theclarabowpage .tripod.com/clarabowlifestory/clarabowlifestory.html. Accessed August 1, 2012.

173  "that shithead": Stenn, *Clara Bow: Runnin' Wild,* 79–86.

175  "I like young people and gaiety": Bow, "My Life Story," part 3, April 1928.

175  "democratic faith,": Paul A. Carter, *Another Part of the Twenties* (New York: Columbia University Press, 1977).

175  "Our national heritage of freedom": Quoted in Bruce Kellner, *Carl Van Vechten and the Irreverent Decades* (Norman: University of Oklahoma Press, 1968), 56–57. Whether indulging in it, reflecting on it, criticizing or regretting it, high-modernist writers were the first generation to take a long look at American fun. Their literary records of its delights and dangers are among their era's most vivid products. White male writers of this period showed an often-leering avidity for it: John Dos Passos, Warner Fabian, Ernest Hemingway, Joseph Hergesheimer, Thorne Smith, Carl Van Vechten, and Thomas Wolfe are just a short list of famous novelists who examined the 1920s wild party.

     Joseph Moncure March's long poem *The Wild Party,* written in the summer of 1926 after the author quit *The New Yorker*'s managing editorship, penetrated so deeply into fun's dark maw that it was banned in Boston and decades later became the septic source for an orgiastic film, a fiendishly smart Broadway musical, and a lavishly illustrated edition by Art Spiegelman. The wild party's hosts are Queenie and Burrs—a burlesque dancer and brutal vaudeville clown—and its sexually liberated guests pursue social mixing of an intimacy that is usually only hinted at in Jazz Age literature. Its lightly tapping verse makes all the danger fun. Even its peek into a multiracial orgy makes it sound like child's play (69):

>     The bed was a slowly moving tangle
>     Of legs and bodies at every angle.
>     Knees rose:
>     Legs in sheer stockings crossed,
>     Clung: shimmered: uncrossed: were lost.
>     Skirts were awry.
>     Black arms embraced
>     White legs naked from knee to waist.

     March's rhymes spread *The Wild Party*'s gospel of heedless drinking, sex, and hilarity. It all seems worth the costs, even reckless murder, right up to the concluding lines, when "The door sprang open / And the cops rushed in" (111). Its winsome attitude toward the kinky taboos aside, it leaves the reader with the puritanical assumption that the fun-loving people *should* be separated. When the modern crowd gets too hot, we need the cops to douse the flames. Joseph Moncure March, *The Wild Party* (New York: Pantheon, 1994).

176  "If the American people had had respect": William Randolph Hearst and Edmund D. Coblentz, *William Randolph Hearst: A Portrait in His Own Words* (New York: Simon & Schuster, 1952), 92.

176  "no scientific value": Daniel Okrent, *Last Call: The Rise and Fall of Prohibition* (New York: Scribner, 2010), 185–89.

176  "on the farm of Senator Morris Sheppard": Charles Merz, "The Crusade Starts," *Outlook and Independent,* October 15, 1930, 278.

176 **"the liberation of the individual"**: Harry S. Warner, *Prohibition, an Adventure in Freedom* (Westerhouse, OH: World League Against Alcoholism, 1928), reprinted in Carter, *Another Part of the Twenties,* 90.

177 **"Stills were everywhere"**: Herbert Asbury, "Where the Booze Came From," reprinted in *Ain't We Got Fun? Essays, Lyrics, and Stories of the Twenties,* ed. Barbara H. Solomon (New York: New American Library, 1980), 91.

177 **"Homosexuality, transvestitism, and interracial relationships"**: Michael A. Lerner, *Dry Manhattan: Prohibition in New York City* (Cambridge, MA: Harvard University Press, 2007), 178–79.

177 **"To it come all classes"**: George E. Worthington, "Night Clubs of New York," reprinted in George Edwin Mowry, *The Twenties: Fords, Flappers, and Fanatics* (New York: Prentice-Hall, 1963), 112.

177 **"Narcotics are said to be distributed"**: Ernest W. Mandeville, "Detroit Sets a Bad Example," reprinted in Mowry, *The Twenties,* 111. Singer Billy Daniels fondly recalled that "the Mob was always present" on the 1930s New York nightclub scene: "Some of Murder, Inc. . . . used to come in and have a good time, have a ball, a half-dozen of them that I got to know. They were always full of fun, usually on a kick or something." W. Royal Stokes, *The Jazz Scene: An Informal History from New Orleans to 1990* (New York: Oxford University Press, 1991), 53. While midwestern drinking and crime did decrease in the early years of Prohibition, "especially in towns and cities inhabited by Protestants of northern European extraction" (118), as Daniel Okrent specifies in *Last Call,* trangressions against the Volstead Act were hardly limited to the coasts. Chicago became an organized crime capital, and Detroit was considered "the liquor capital of the United States." Charles A. Selden calculated that "the manufacture and sale of automobiles in Detroit involves nearly $2,000,000,000 annually and the chemical industry about $90,000,000. Between the two stands Detroit's illegal liquor traffic, estimated at $215,000,000" ("Rum Row in the Middle West," *New York Times,* May 27, 1928, reprinted in Mowry, *The Twenties,* 105).

178 **"the matter of cocktail parties"**: Carl Van Vechten, *Parties* (1930; Los Angeles: Sun & Moon Press, 1993), 172.

178 **"Of the 113 establishments"**: Okrent, *Last Call,* 208.

178 **"in a decade that saw a declining interest in politics"**: David J. Goldberg, *Discontented America: The United States in the 1920s* (Baltimore: Johns Hopkins University Press, 1999), 56.

179 **"C'est lui Lindberg, LINDBERG!"**: Harry Crosby, *Shadows of the Sun,* ed. Edward Germain (Santa Barbara, CA: Black Sparrow Press, 1977), 146.

180 **"Only in America"**: Ann Douglas, *Terrible Honesty: Mongrel Manhattan in the 1920s* (New York: Farrar, Straus and Giroux, 1995), 456.

180 **"like[d] looping the loop"**: Crosby, *Shadows of the Sun,* 264.

180 **"his ambulance was vaporized"**: Geoffrey Wolff, *Black Sun: The Brief Transit and Violent Eclipse of Harry Crosby* (New York: Random House, 1976), 54.

180 **"Bodily he survived"**: Malcolm Cowley, *Exile's Return* (New York: Penguin, 1976), 250.

181 **"aristocrat"**: Crosby, *Shadows of the Sun,* 284.

181 **"a glamorous and charismatic man"**: Douglas, *Terrible Honesty,* 458. Full account of Julian from ibid., 457–61.

182 **"participatory" qualities**: Kathy J. Ogren, *The Jazz Revolution: Twenties America and the Meaning of Jazz* (New York: Oxford University Press, 1989), 8. Jazz dancers were inspired by both musicians and spectators. Zora Neale Hurston called dancing a chief form of "Negro Expression" and described how the dancer's "flex[ing]" knee, "thrust[ing]" chest, "clenched fists," and "elbows taut as in hard running or grasping

a thrusting blade" demand a response from the spectator, who "adds the picture of ferocious assault, hears the drums and finds himself keeping time with the music and tensing himself for the struggle."

182  **"dance-based music"**: Roger Pryor Dodge, "The Dance-Basis of Jazz," *Hot Jazz and Jazz Dance: Collected Writings 1929–1964,* ed. Roger Pryor Dodge (New York: Oxford University Press, 1995), 145. Article originally appeared in *The Record Changer,* March and April 1945.

182  **"Saxophone Supper[s]"**: Dicky Wells quoted in Ogren, *Jazz Revolution,* 82.

183  **"in control"**: Scott DeVeaux and Gary Giddins, *Jazz* (New York: W. W. Norton, 2009), 56.

183  **"compet[ing]"**: Gunther Schuller, *Early Jazz* (New York: Oxford University Press, 1968), 89.

184  *Let's Do the Black Bottom*: "Castle Novelty" instructional film, *Let's Do the Black Bottom,* 1924.

184  **"It was new to them"**: Stearns and Stearns, *Jazz Dance,* 315–16.

185  **"The Home of Happy Feet"**: Ibid., 324.

185  **Harlem's Savoy held special nights**: Ibid., 322.

185  **"segregated"**: Interview with Pearl and Ivy Fisher at 409 Edgecombe Ave., March 1975, p. 3. Schomburg Center for Research in Black Culture. David Levering Lewis, "Voices from the Renaissance Collection," MG 335, Box 1, Folder 1.

185  **"grab a cook or mechanic"**: "Savoy," Lucky Millinder, Warner Brothers Music Corp./ASCAP.

186  **"Cat's Corner"**: Stearns and Stearns, *Jazz Dance,* 327.

## 8 ★ "JOYOUS REVOLT": THE "NEW NEGRO" AND THE "NEW WOMAN"

187  **"the nobody's child of the levee"**: J. A. Rogers, "Jazz at Home," in *The New Negro,* ed. Alain Locke (1925; New York: Touchstone, 1997), 217, 223.

187  **"an average group of Negroes"**: Johnson, *Black Manhattan,* 162.

188  **"poison for the weak"**: Rogers, "Jazz at Home," 223. He writes:

> Joy, after all, has a physical basis. Those who laugh and dance and sing are better off even in their vices than those who do not. Moreover, jazz with its mocking disregard for formality is a leveler and makes for democracy. The jazz spirit, being primitive, demands more frankness and sincerity. Just as it already has done in art and music, so eventually in human relations and social manners, it will no doubt have the effect of putting more reality in life by taking some of the needless artificiality out.

188  **"This new spirit of joy and spontaneity"**: Ibid., 223.

188  **"the first influence of the Negro"**: W. E. B. DuBois, *The Gift of Black Folk* (1924; Millwood, NY: Kraus-Thomson Organization Limited, 1975), 146, 61.

189  **"gift of laughter"**: Fauset, "The Gift of Laughter," 165.

189  **some 555,000 in the 1910s alone**: Isabel Wilkerson, *The Warmth of Other Suns: The Epic Story of America's Great Migration* (New York: Random House, 2010), 161.

190  **"Red Summer"**: Cameron McWhirter, *Red Summer: The Summer of 1919 and the Awakening of Black America* (New York: Henry Holt, 2011), 13–17.

190  **"Long before the stock market crash"**: Jonathan Gill, *Harlem: The Four Hundred Year History from Dutch Village to Capital of Black America* (New York: Grove Press, 2011), 231, 227.

190 "white clients enthusiastically": David Levering Lewis, *When Harlem Was in Vogue* (New York: Penguin, 1979), 209.

190 "the more of a quiet reserved type": Alberta Hunter quoted in Ogren, *Jazz Revolution*, 77.

191 "The whole joint was rocking": Eddie Condon quoted in Ogren, *Jazz Revoution*, 77–78.

191 "transvestite floor shows, sex circuses": Lewis, *When Harlem Was in Vogue*, 209.

191 "catered to all varieties": Eric Garber, "A Spectacle in Color: The Lesbian and Gay Subculture of Jazz Age Harlem," in *Hidden from History: Reclaiming the Gay & Lesbian Past*, ed. Martin Duberman et al. (New York: Meridian, 1990), 323.

191 "ladies' maids and truck drivers": Langston Hughes, *The Big Sea* (1940; New York: Hill and Wang, 1964), 233.

192 "semi-illiterate night watchman": Chris Albertson, *Bessie*, rev. and expanded ed. (New Haven, CT: Yale University Press, 2005), 29.

192 "lighted cigarettes": Elaine Feinstein, *Bessie Smith: Empress of the Blues* (New York: Penguin, 1985), 61.

192 "Gimme a Pigfoot": Bessie Smith, "Gimme a Pigfoot," recorded November 24, 1933. Okeh 8949.

192 "fun to be a Negro": Lewis, *When Harlem Was in Vogue*, 103–4.

194 "violently interested in Negroes": Nathan Irvin Huggins, *Harlem Renaissance* (New York: Oxford University Press, 1973), 99–101.

194 "Coney Island": Carl Van Vechten, *Nigger Heaven* (New York: Alfred A. Knopf, 1926).

194 "the fat black bucks": Vachel Lindsay, "The Congo," in *The Poetry of Vachel Lindsay: Complete and with Lindsay's Drawings*, ed. Dennis Camp (Peoria, IL: Spoon River Press, 1984), 174.

194 "glistening African god of pleasure": Willa Cather, *My Ántonia* (New York: Virago, 1999), 191.

194 "a blow in the face": W. E. B. DuBois, "Books," *The Crisis*, December 1926, 81.

194 "caricature": Ibid., 82.

194 "there is laughter, color": Ibid., 81.

195 "race toward whiteness": Langston Hughes, "The Negro Artist and the Racial Mountain," in *The Norton Anthology of Theory and Criticism*, 2nd ed., ed. Vincent P. Leitch (New York: W. W. Norton, 2010), 1196. Originally appeared in *The Nation*, June 23, 1926.

195 "money to *spend*": Hughes, *The Big Sea*, 39.

195 "Fun!": Ibid., 62.

195 "Let the blare of Negro jazz bands": Hughes, "Negro Artist," 1196.

196 "Harlem Negroes, once their aversion": "Fire Burns: A Department of Comment," *Fire!!* 1, no 1 (November 1926): 47.

196 "debauched tenth": David Levering Lewis, *W. E. B. DuBois, 1919–1963: The Fight for Equality and the American Century* (New York: Henry Holt, 2001), 176. In 1928, Nella Larsen and Claude McKay released their debut novels, and DuBois yoked them together in a single review: he lauded Larsen's *Quicksand* as "the best piece of fiction that Negro America has produced since the heyday of Chesnutt" and said McKay's *Home to Harlem* "nauseate[d]" him and that "the dirtier parts of its filth" made him feel "distinctly like taking a bath" (W. E. B. DuBois, "Two Novels," *The Crisis*, June 1928). These novels, when juxtaposed, also illustrate Harlem's class-driven ambivalence over Jazz Age fun. DuBois admired Larsen's protagonist Helga Crane for her "whimsical, unsatisfied soul," the tragic feature that prevents this mixed-race nomad

from joining any of her possible communities, black, white, highbrow, lowbrow, or high-society Danish. Accordingly, in a key scene in a Harlem cabaret, she briefly joins the dancing throng and is "drugged, lifted, sustained by the extraordinary music, blown out, ripped out, beaten out, by the joyous, wild, murky orchestra" and is ultimately repulsed by what she considers the "fantastic motley of ugliness and beauty, semi-barbaric, sophisticated, exotic." She tries to reduce Harlem fun to primitivism, but what she describes is the welter of modern America, spun by the body-racking pleasures of jazz. DuBois accused McKay of "us[ing] every art and emphasis to paint drunkenness, fighting, lascivious sexual promiscuity and utter absence of restraint in as bold and as bright colors as he can." McKay's working-class protagonist, Jake, about whom even DuBois found "something appealing," is the portrait of a hedonist—he deserts the army (because he sees no action in the war) and returns home to "Good old Harlem! Chocolate Harlem! Sweet Harlem!" where he loses himself in its "sugared laughter" and "contagious fever"—but he is no flashy caricature like the Scarlet Creeper in *Nigger Heaven*. He brings a poet's light sensibility to Harlem's pool halls, brothels, and cabarets and is most at home in the Congo, "an amusement place entirely for the unwashed of the Black Belt," where "smells lingered telling the nature of their occupation. Pot-wrestlers, W.C. attendants, scrub maids, dish-washers, stevedores. . . . The Congo was African in spirit and in color. No white persons were admitted there." *Home to Harlem* (1928; Boston: Northeastern University Press, 1987), 7, 14, 15, 29–30. But McKay seems uninterested in offending readers like DuBois. He is showing Jake's intimacy with the fragrant crowd and his love of the dancers' sweaty "hot soup" (32). But of course such candor was in itself a kind of joyous revolt.

196 "adorable": "Mae Sullivan," interview with Mae Sullivan, at her home in Washington, D.C., April 19, 1977, page 3. Schomburg Center for Research in Black Culture, the New York Public Library. David Levering Lewis "Voices from the Renaissance Collection," MG 335, Box 1, Folder 2.

196 "miss something": Hughes, *The Big Sea*, 47.

196 "must be smelt": Ibid., 71.

196 "to shake hands": Ibid., 81.

197 "not fun": Ibid., 83.

197 "gaily mutinous state": Ibid., 111.

197 "hunched over": Ibid., 250.

197 "grandiloquently about democracy": Ibid., 255.

197 "Jim Crow policy": Ibid., 224–25.

198 "more amusing than any night club": Ibid., 229.

198 "the tom-tom of revolt": Hughes, "Negro Artist," 1195.

198 "marked the height": Arnold Rampersad, "Hughes's *Fine Clothes to the Jew*," in *Langston Hughes: Critical Perspectives Past and Present*, ed. Henry Louis Gates Jr. and K. A. Appiah (New York: Amistad Press, 1993), 53. Rampersad suggests that Van Vechten, who read through the volume before sending it on to Knopf, and to whom it is dedicated, may have suggested the title *Fine Clothes to the Jew*, with which Knopf (Jewish himself) took issue until persuaded by Van Vechten to keep it. As Rampersad also points out, Knopf did not take issue with Van Vechten's own controversial title, *Nigger Heaven*. The title comes from the poem *Hard Luck*: "When hard luck overtakes you / Nothin' for you to do. / Gather up yo' fine clothes / An' sell 'em to de Jew. // Jew takes yo' fine clothes, / Gives you a dollar an' a half. . . . Go to de bootleg's, / Git some gin to make you laugh" (*Collected Poems*, 82). In *The Big Sea* Hughes himself voices regret over it.

198 **"piffling trash"**: James A. Emanuel, *Langston Hughes* (New York: Twayne, 1967), 31–32.

199 **"Laughers"**: Langston Hughes, *The Collected Poems of Langston Hughes*, ed. Arnold Rampersad (New York: Vintage, 1995), 112, 114. "Laughers" shines in this somber volume. It parades Jessie Fauset's "gift of laughter" that "has its rise in the very woes that beset us." Its refrain—"Loud-mouthed laughers in the hands / Of Fate"— considers both the peoples' hazards and the gaiety with which they brave their dangers. And if its frowning question, "Laughers?," gives voice to Hughes's critics, then its exclamations ("What dancers!" "What singers!") put those critics in their place.

200 **"Jazz Band in a Parisian Cabaret"**: Ibid., 60.

201 **"Zelda just wasn't afraid of anything"**: Nancy Milford, *Zelda: A Biography* (New York: Harper & Row, 1970), 16–17.

202 **"ten boys"**: Ibid., 44.

202 **"gets stewed in public"**: Ibid., 60.

202 **That month they chaperoned a party**: Kendall Taylor, *Sometimes Madness Is Wisdom: Zelda and Scott Fitzgerald* (New York: Ballantine, 2001), 68.

202 **white-supremacist Scott**: "I believe at last in the white man's burden," he wrote to Edmund Wilson in 1921. "We are as far above the modern Frenchman as he is above the Negro." *The Letters of F. Scott Fitzgerald*, ed. Andrew Turnbull (New York: Charles Scribner's Sons, 1963), 326.

202 **"was nasty," "drunk," "was an original"**: Van Vechten as quoted in Milford, *Zelda*, 98–99.

203 **"The flapper springs full-grown"**: Zelda Sayre Fitzgerald, "What Became of the Flappers?" *McCall's*, October 1925, reprinted in *The Collected Writings of Zelda Fitzgerald*, ed. Matthew J. Bruccoli (Tuscaloosa: University of Alabama Press, 1991), 397–99.

203 **"Flapper Styles Will Prevail!"**: Cover text, *The Flapper*, October 1922. Fitzgerald calls 1922 "the peak of the younger generation" in "Echoes of the Jazz Age," 15.

203 **"Eulogy on the Flapper"**: Zelda Sayre Fitzgerald, "Eulogy on the Flapper," *Metropolitan Magazine*, June 1922, reprinted in *Collected Writings of Zelda Fitzgerald*, 391–93.

204 **"the quintessence of what the term"**: Stenn, *Clara Bow: Runnin' Wild*, 87.

205 **"the unrivaled embodiment of sex appeal"**: Elizabeth Atkins quoted in Sandra M. Gilbert and Susan Gubar, *Letters from the Front*, vol. 3, *No Man's Land: The Place of the Woman Writer in the Twentieth Century* (New Haven, CT: Yale University Press, 1994), 63.

205 **"liv[ing] in that gay poverty"**: Floyd Dell, *Love in Greenwich Village* (1926; North Stratford, NH: Ayer Publishing, 1970), 33.

205 **"jazzing music"**: Edna St. Vincent Millay, *Second April* (New York: Harper & Brothers, 1921), 88.

205 **"My candle burns at both ends"**: Edna St. Vincent Millay, *Collected Poems*, ed. Norma Millay (New York: Harper & Brothers, 1945), 127.

205 **"And if I loved you Wednesday"**: Ibid., 129.

205 **"I've been a wicked girl," "I see with single eye"**: Edna St. Vincent Millay, *The Harp-Weaver and Other Poems* (New York: Harper & Brothers, 1923), 55.

205 **"will never make you a hatband"**: "Flapping Not Repented Of," *New York Times*, July 16, 1922, reprinted in Mowry, *The Twenties*, 173.

206 **"The tittle-tattle of ingénues' luncheons"**: Warner Fabian, *Flaming Youth* (New York: Boni and Liveright, 1923), 129.

206  **racks her wanton frame:** At times her persona's wayward id rages like a house party:

> Heart, have no pity on this house of bone:
> Shake it with dancing, break it down with joy.

At others, she welcomes it like death:

> Sweet love, sweet thorn, when lightly to my heart
> I took your thrust, whereby since I am slain.

At others it jails her like a drug addiction:

> Shall I be prisoner till my pulses stop
> To hateful Love and drag his noisy chain.

Millay, *Collected Poems*, 658, 646, 647.

206  **"An American Art Student":** Quoted in Gilbert and Gubar, *Letters from the Front*, vol. 3, 76–78. Millay rewrote the romantic script to the female party's advantage. Gilbert and Gubar note her manipulation of the "femme fatale/flapper" persona, how she uses it "to expose the artifice and absurdity of romance" while at the same time flipping "conventional love scenes" to make them "fatal to male rather than female lovers."

206  **to *drink* as much:** For an excellent account of "New Women" and drink, see Lerner, *Dry Manhattan*, 171–98.

206  **were regularly tempered:** Paula S. Fass, *The Damned and the Beautiful: American Youth in the 1920s* (New York: Oxford University Press, 1977), 262–65.

207  **"Any girl I catch smoking anywhere":** Ibid., 299.

207  **"torches of freedom":** Burton St. John, *Press Professionalism and Propaganda: The Rise of Journalistic Double-Mindedness, 1917–1941* (Amherst, NY: Cambria Press, 2010), 30.

207  **"A Flapper's Dictionary":** *The Flapper,* July 1922, cited in Jim Lewin, *Book Flaps* (blog) at bookflaps.blogspot.com, April 10, 2011; accessed August 25, 2012.

208  **"Her girlish ways":** Dorothy Parker, *Not Much Fun: The Lost Poems of Dorothy Parker,* ed. Stuart Y. Silverstein (New York: Scribner, 1996), 105.

208  **"wholesome, engaging, uncorseted":** Stuart Y. Silverstein, "Introduction," in Parker, *Not Much Fun,* 35.

209  **"Not much fun":** Ibid., 23.

209  **she was the life of the party:** It seems Parker only had a taste for the wilder variety of party. As is evident from her "Hymn of Hate" called "Parties," her festive nature was hard to please, hating "clean, home games" like "guess[ing] the number of seeds in a cucumber," hating days in the country with their dozens of hard-boiled eggs, and above all hating the "informal little Dinner Party," which she considered "the lowest form of taking nourishment." Parker, *Not Much Fun,* 219–21.

209  **"You can lead a horticulture":** Silverstein, "Introduction," 27*n*.

209  **"There was a little girl":** Ibid., 14*n*.

210  **"all the earmarks of masterpiece":** W. Somerset Maugham, "Variations on a Theme," in Dorothy Parker, *The Portable Dorothy Parker* (New York: Viking, 1954), 601.

211  **"SEND ME A SAW":** Parker, *Not Much Fun,* 29.

211  **"the quick excitement":** Parker, *Portable Dorothy Parker,* 293.

211  **"by the time she was a teenager":** Lillian Schlissel, "Introduction," in *Three Plays by Mae West* (New York: Routledge, 1997), 3.

212  **"wildly uninhibited antics":** George Eels and Stanley Musgrove, *Mae West* (New York: William Morrow, 1982), 34.

212  **"make a better wife and mother":** Mae West, *Sex,* in *Three Plays,* 74.

212 **"shimmy shawabble"**: Schlissel, "Introduction," 10.

212 **"vulgar"**: Reviews cited ibid.

213 **"degenerate"**: Mae West, *The Drag,* in *Three Plays,* 107.

213 **"happier"**: Ibid., 102.

213 **"born homosexual"**: Ibid., 108.

213 **"people like that"**: Ibid., 107.

213 **"they like me"**: Ibid., 118.

213 **"It must be the wagon"**: Ibid., 133–34.

213 **"a restraining order"**: Schlissel, "Introduction," 15.

214 **"Let's see some other son of a bitch do that"**: Ibid., 23.


## 9 ★ ZOOT SUIT RIOTS

215 **"a whole race"**: This and subsequent quotations in this paragraph are from F. Scott Fitzgerald, "Echoes of the Jazz Age," in *The Crack Up,* ed. Edmund Wilson (1931; New York: New Directions, 1945), 15, 20, 19, 18. The *Complete Works* of Scott Fitzgerald (who said he coined the term "Jazz Age") reads like a saga of 1920s fun. The stories get woollier as they go: from the early stories and wisecracking first novel that taught young Americans how to read their own antics; to the glamorous recasting of his and Zelda's bad behavior in *The Beautiful and Damned;* to his 1925 masterpiece whose antihero observes his own wild parties with a forlorn sense of disengagement; to Fitzgerald's later period of failed recovery, when the zest of his youth has a foul aftertaste—the period of "Babylon Revisited" and *Tender Is the Night,* in which dashing Dick Diver, a figure of worldly merriment, fails three times at a waterskiing stunt and seals his fate as a post-fun grotesque. A master of self-aggrandizement, Fitzgerald projected his trials and triumphs onto an entire era. He had his fun—had it more glamorously and vigorously than most—and in the final analysis he didn't recommend it.

216 **"exciting story millions lost in an hour"**: Crosby, *Shadows of the Sun,* 284.

216 **"only one and a half million people"**: John Kenneth Galbraith, *The Great Crash, 1929* (Boston: Houghton Mifflin, 1954), 78.

216 **"decorated them with pretty girls"**: Fan-dancer Sally Rand quoted in Studs Terkel, *Hard Times: An Oral History of the Great Depression* (1970; New York: New Press, 2005), 170.

217 **"as hot an issue as Hitler"**: Cited in Marybeth Hamilton, "Goodness Had Nothing to Do with It: Censoring Mae West," in *Movie Censorship and American Culture,* 2nd ed., ed. Francis J. Couvares (Amherst: University of Massachusetts Press, 1996), 187.

217 **"West's acting style"**: Ibid., 193.

218 **"young Negro high-school girl"**: This and subsequent quotations from Henry James Forman, *Our Movie-Made Children* (New York: Macmillan, 1933), 141, 143–45, 147.

219 **"The very man who will guffaw"**: The Hays Office's Ray Norr quoted in Hamilton, "Goodness Had Nothing to Do with It," 202.

220 **"humanity crusading in the pursuit of happiness"**: *Modern Times,* dir. and prod. Charles Chaplin, Charles Chaplin Productions, USA, 1936.

220 **"the terrific kick"**: Zora Neale Hurston, "To Lawrence Jordan," February 18, 1927, The Zora Neale Hurston Collection, Schomburg Center for Research in Black Culture, New York Public Library, Zora Neale Hurston Collection, MG 130, Box 1, one of three unnumbered folders. Until they broke up over a plagiarism rhubarb, Hughes and Hurston were the life of a Harlem Renaissance party whose fun, as they knew, was based on conflict. As Wallace Thurman depicts them in his roman à clef, *Infants*

*of the Spring* (1932), Langston Hughes is the "mischievous boy" Tony Crews and Zora Neale Hurston is Sweetie May Carr, "noted for her ribald wit." When Dr. Parkes (Alain Locke) hosts a salon for Harlem's brightest writers, Tony and Sweetie May—unlike the morose DeWitt Clinton (Countee Cullen) and the testy Cedric Williams (Claude McKay)—contribute only winks and giggles. Sweetie interrupts a race debate to boast, "I can do the Charleston better than any white person." And when the evening bursts into an intellectual brawl over Marx, DuBois, and "the Negro Problem," Tony and Sweetie May trade "original verses to the St. James Infirmary." Wallace Thurman, *Infants of the Spring* (New York: Random House, 1999), 141–43, 149, 151.

220 **"Queen of the Niggerati"**: Robert F. Hemenway, *Zora Neale Hurston: A Literary Biography* (Urbana: University of Illinois Press, 1977), 44.

221 **"a city," as she characterized it**: Zora Neale Hurston, *Mules and Men* (New York: HarperPerennial, 1990), 20.

221 **"too much spirit," "jump at de sun," "God, Devil, Brer Rabbit"**: Zora Neale Hurston, *Dust Tracks on a Road: An Autobiography,* 2nd ed., ed. Robert E. Hemenway (1942; Urbana: University of Illinois Press, 1984), 63–64.

221 **"most amusing"**: Hughes, *The Big Sea,* 238–39.

222 **"feather-bed of resistance"**: Hurston, *Mules and Men,* 3.

222 **"carefully accented Barnardese"**: Hurston, *Dust Tracks,* 175.

222 **"poets of the swinging blade"**: Ibid., 179.

222 **"singing, laughing, cursing"**: Ibid., 180.

222 **"balling"**: Zora Neale Hurston, "Glossary of Harlem Slang," http://aalbc.com/authors/harlemslang.htm. Accessed July 17, 2013.

222 **"Dancing the square dance," "risky pleasure"**: Hurston, *Dust Tracks,* 182.

222 **"emotional strength"**: Clarence Major, *Juba to Jive: A Dictionary of African-American Slang* (New York: Viking, 1994), 138. In his superlative *The Signifying Monkey: A Theory of African-American Literary Criticism* (New York: Oxford University Press, 1988), Henry Louis Gates Jr. speculates that the word "dozens" "quite probably derives from an eighteenth-century meaning of the verb *dozen,* 'to stun, stupefy, daze,' in the black sense, through language" (71). It also belongs under the rubric of "Signifying," the variety of wordplay and verbal competition (a sort of "making fun"—though not fun *of*—through language [68]) that Gates believes should be part of standard home curriculum in the education of young African Americans—a social skill and rite of passage that children and adolescents learn from their parents: "Teaching one's children the fine art of Signifyin(g) is to teach them about this mode of linguistic circumnavigation, to teach them a second language they can share with other black people" (76).

223 **"If you have no faith"**: Hurston, *Dust Tracks,* 187.

223 **"contest[s] in hyperbole"**: Zora Neale Hurston, *Their Eyes Were Watching God* (New York: Perennial Library, 1990), 59.

223 **"the thing that Saul's daughter had done"**: Ibid., 75.

224 **"permanent transients with no attachments"**: Ibid., 125.

225 **"the Lindy off the ground"**: Stearns and Stearns, *Jazz Dance,* 324–27.

226 **"I just about went wild!"**: *The Autobiography of Malcolm X,* quoted in Luis Alvarez, *The Power of the Zoot: Youth Culture and Resistance During World War II* (Berkeley: University of California Press, 2008), 147.

226 **"Many zoot suiters"**: Ibid., 134; see also 142, 145.

227 **"every couple, almost"**: Dizzy Gillespie quoted in Alvarez, *Power of the Zoot,* 121.

227 **"juvenile delinquency," "revolt of callow youth"**: White and White, *Stylin',* 259–60.

227 "role in facilitating," "Mixed Dancing Closed Savoy Ballroom," "Christian youth center": The *Amsterdam News* and the *People's Voice* cited in Alvarez, *Power of the Zoot*, 120–24.

227 **Later that same month:** Alvarez, *Power of the Zoot*, 168–82.

### 10 ★ A CALIFORNIA EDUCATION, REDUX

230 "A Vote for Barry Is a Vote for Fun": *Magic Trip*, dir. Alison Ellwood and Alex Gibney, A&E Indie Films, 2011, 33:33.

231 "pudding": Tom Wolfe, *The Electric Kool-Aid Acid Test* (New York: Picador, 1968), 238.

232 "We don't propose to have": David Halberstam, *The Fifties* (New York: Random House, 1993), 417–78.

233 **Over the next five years:** Ibid., 134.

233 "one swimming pool was built": Ibid., 137.

233 **machine-made "freedom":** Herbert Marcuse, *One-Dimensional Man* (1964; London: Routledge & Kegan Paul, 1991), 6.

233 **women, now housebound:** Halberstam, *The Fifties*, 587–92.

234 "paranoia, delirium, frenzy, hysteria": Ellen Schrecker, *Many Are the Crimes: McCarthyism in America* (Boston: Little, Brown, 1998), 46.

234 **the languishing HUAC was energized:** Griffin Fariello, *Red Scare: Memories of the American Inquisition; An Oral History by Griffin Fariello* (New York: W. W. Norton, 1995), 255–314; *McCarthyism: The Great American Red Scare; A Documentary History*, ed. Albert Fried (New York: Oxford University Press, 1997), 1–47, 119–56.

235 "This was the great and final": Jack Kerouac, *On the Road* (New York: Viking Penguin, 1955), 248.

236 "cross-country truckers," black store on Beale Street: LeRoy Ashby, *With Amusement for All: A History of Popular Culture Since 1830* (Lexington: University Press of Kentucky, 2006), 340. See also Halberstam, *The Fifties*, 457.

236 "literary James Dean": "The Ganser Syndrome," *Time*, September 16, 1957.

236 "kicks," "fun": *Rebel Without a Cause*. Dir. Nicholas Ray, perf. James Dean, Natalie Wood, Sal Mineo, and Dennis Hopper, Warner, 1955.

236 **at Gregg's Drive-In:** Wolfe, *The Electric Kool-Aid Acid Test*, 38–39.

236 "participatory democracy": "Port Huron Statement," The Sixties Project, Institute of Advanced Technology in the Humanities, University of Virginia at Charlottesville; http://www2.iath.virginia.edu/sixties/HTML_docs/Resources/Primary/Manifestos/SDS_Port_Huron.html. Accessed July 17, 2013.

238 "Wilde West": Wolfe, *Electric Kool-Aid Acid Test*, 56.

238 "Funk Art": Charles Perry, *The Haight-Ashbury: A History* (New York: Wenner Books, 2005), 14.

238 "introduced the idea of *pranks*": Wolfe, *Electric Kool-Aid Acid Test*, 63.

238 "superprank": Ibid., 67.

239 "tootled": Ibid., 112.

239 *"go with the flow":* Ibid., 84; emphasis in original.

239 "doing rock dances and the dirty boogie": Ibid., 91.

239 "the first annual tour": Ibid., 106.

239 "I feel like we're a pastoral Indian village": Ken Babbs and Paul Perry, *On the Bus: The Complete Guide to the Legendary Trip of Ken Kesey and the Merry Pranksters and the Birth of the Counterculture* (New York: Thunder's Mouth Press, 1990), 96.

239 "out-front": Wolfe, *Electric Kool-Aid Acid Test*, 329.

240 "We're Clean, Willie!": Ibid., 150.

240 "It was fun": Ibid.

240 "hipster Christ": Ibid., 153.

240 "THE MERRY PRANKSTERS WELCOME": Ibid., 169.

241 "Oh, but it's great to be an Angel": Ibid., 173.

241 "the inordinate boredom of middle-class life": R. G. Davis, *The San Francisco Mime Troupe: The First Ten Years* (Palo Alto, CA: Ramparts Press, 1975), 13.

241 "pleased its audience": Ibid., 31.

241 "guinea pig": Ibid., 21.

241 "riff[s] of jazz," "participatory fun," "riffs or bits": Ibid., 20.

242 "indecent, obscene, and offensive": Susan Vaneta Mason, "Introduction," in *The San Francisco Mime Troupe Reader*, ed. Susan Vaneta Mason (Ann Arbor: University of Michigan Press, 2005), 11, 12.

243 "This is an Old Western town": Perry, *The Haight-Ashbury*, 10.

243 "an outlaw enclave": *The Life and Times of the Red Dog Saloon*, dir. Mary Works, 1996, 2:18–2:32.

243 "We knew we were American": Ibid., 20:00–20:72.

244 "The bottom line": Ibid., 48:00–50:00.

244 "a fireball": Ibid., 25:22.

244 But Virginia City was still the Old West: Perry, *The Haight-Ashbury*, 10–11.

245 "improvised lyrics": Ibid., 32.

245 "liquid": Bill Graham and Robert Greenfield, *Bill Graham Presents: My Life Inside Rock and Out* (New York: Da Capo, 2004), 120.

245 "people who'd never heard": Perry, *The Haight-Ashbury*, 31.

245 "the artistic community coming together": Graham and Greenfield, *Bill Graham Presents*, 120.

245 "*This* is the business of the future!": Ibid., 123.

245 "slightly hysterical": Ibid., 125.

246 "a more jubilant occasion": Trips Festival handbill, reproduced at http://www.flickr.com/photos/the_first_rays/5247960620/. Accessed August 25, 2012.

246 "non-drug recreation of a psychedelic experience": Perry, *The Haight-Ashbury*, 41.

246 "old home week": Graham and Greenfield, *Bill Graham Presents*, 140.

246 "a gold lamé space suit": Ibid., 138.

247 "'Goddamn son of a bitch'": Perry, *The Haight-Ashbury*, 46.

247 "It was one of those balanced-up helmets": Graham and Greenfield, *Bill Graham Presents*, 139.

248 "that minstrel shows were a part of our cultural heritage": Davis, *San Francisco Mime Troupe*, 49.

248 "We were not for the suppression of differences": Ibid., 63.

248 The show corked up both whites and blacks: Ibid., 50.

249 "wise conniver," "learned to respect him": These and the remaining quotations in this paragraph are from ibid., 52. See also R. G. Davis and Saul Landau, *A Minstrel Show, or Civil Rights in a Cracker Barrel*, in *The San Francisco Mime Troupe Reader*, ed. Susan Vaneta Mason (Ann Arbor: University of Michigan Press, 2005), 26–56.

249 "a courageous and creative act": Mason, "Introduction," 27.

250 "an empowering vision": Claudia Orenstein, *Festive Revolutions: The Politics of Popular Theater and the San Francisco Mime Troupe* (Jackson: University Press of Mississippi, 1998), 118.

250 "People thought we were on their side": Davis, *San Francisco Mime Troupe*, 63.

250 "[T]he hippies use black people": Nicholas von Hoffman, *We Are the People Our Parents Warned Us Against* (1968; Chicago: Elephant Paperbacks, 1989), 124, 123.

250 **"We don't want violence or trouble"**: Lewis Yablonsky, *The Hippie Trip* (New York: Pegasus, 1968), 218–19; emphasis in original. The black community wanted the hippies' "bread," but they didn't think much of their freely expressive dancing. Von Hoffman was at the Straight Theatre on Haight when "three hundred dopeheads" followed instructions "to find the moving, rhythmic spot inside [themselves]." As a result they "stamp[ed]" and "flutter[ed] their arms" to the Grateful Dead. A black girl watching them exclaimed, "They can't dance. They can't keep time, what *are* they doing, and they're so ugly!"(125).

251 **On September 27, 1966**: Walter C. Rucker and James N. Upton, *Encyclopedia of American Race Riots,* vol. 2 (Westport, CT: Greenwood Publishing Group, 2007), 584.

251 **"Psychedelic Community"**: Emmett Grogan, *Ringolevio: A Life Played for Keeps* (New York: Little, Brown, 1972), 238–39.

251 **"Go back to school"**: Ibid., 242.

252 **"Places of entertainment"**: "Take a Cop to Dinner Cop a Dinner to Take a Cop Dinner Cop a Take," *The Digger Papers* (August 1968), 14. The Digger Archives, http://www.diggers.org/digpaps68/takecop.html. Accessed August 11, 2012.

252 **"Regarding inquiries concerned with the identity"**: Grogan, *Ringolevio,* 239.

252 **Within a week the Diggers**: Ibid., 246–50.

253 **"Are you a digger?"**: George Metevsky [*sic*], "Delving the Diggers," *Berkeley Barb,* October 21, 1966, 3. The Digger Archives, http://www.diggers.org/digger_papers .htm. Accessed August 25, 2012.

253 **"charity"**: "The Diggers Mystique," *San Francisco Chronicle,* January 23, 1967, Digger Archives.

254 **"life acting"**: Peter Coyote, *Sleeping Where I Fall: A Chronicle* (Washington, D.C.: Counterpoint, 1998), 64–65.

254 **"the white kids are more advanced"**: Von Hoffman, *We Are the People,* 123.

254 **"tickled the people silly"**: Grogan, *Ringolevio,* 250–51.

254 **"Meatfest"**: Perry, *The Haight-Ashbury,* 104.

255 **"Oooo!," "A Munibus driver," "The streets belong to the people!"**: Grogan, *Ringolevio,* 259–60. See also Coyote, *Sleeping Where I Fall,* 96–97.

255 **"We want Hairy Henry!"**: Grogan, *Ringolevio,* 260.

255 **"The Digger Papers"**: Quoted in *"Takin' It to the Streets,"* ed. Alexander Bloom (New York: Oxford University Press, 1995), 321.

257 **"community switchboards"**: John McMillian, *Smoking Typewriters: The Sixties Underground Press and the Rise of Alternative Media in America* (New York: Oxford University Press, 2011), 32. Discussion of undergrounds sourced from McMillian, 140–72. A representative example of the *Realist*'s take-no-prisoners satire is Krassner's early 1960s piece on the women's gun craze in South Africa, titled "I Dreamed I Shot a Nigger in My Maidenform Bra." *Best of the Realist: The 60's Most Outrageously Irreverent Magazine* (Philadelphia: Running Press, 1984).

257 **"anarchistic organization," "Fuck Censorship press"**: McMillian, *Smoking Typewriters,* 73.

257 **"Electrical Banana"**: The story of the hoax is nicely detailed ibid., 66–71.

258 **"aborigines, Tonto, Inquisitor-General Torquemada"**: Coyote, *Sleeping Where I Fall,* 95.

259 **The first such party**: Helen Swick Perry, "The Human Be-In," in Bloom, *"Takin' It to the Streets,"* 313–16.

259 **"took drugs, danced, painted their faces"**: Coyote, *Sleeping Where I Fall,* 75.

259 **"the love shuck"**: Grogan, *Ringolevio,* 276.

259 **"San Francisco's diverse communities"**: The Glide website, http://www.glide.org/ page.aspx?pid=412#1960s. Accessed August 10, 2012.

259 **"improbable and outrageous"**: Coyote, *Sleeping Where I Fall,* 78.

259 **"love-making salons"**: Grogan, *Ringolevio,* 283.

260 **"Several couples"**: Ibid., 284.

260 **"surreal harmony"**: Ibid., 285.

260 **"Permission was the rule"**: Coyote, *Sleeping Where I Fall,* 79.

260 **"it was simply like letting steam out"**: Ibid.

261 **"disastrous Summer of Love"**: Alice Echols, *Shake Ground: The Sixties and Its After-shocks* (New York: Columbia University Press, 2002), 44, 45.

261 **"HOW MANY TIMES YOU BEEN RAPED"**: Quotations in this and the following paragraph are from Joan Didion, "Slouching Towards Bethlehem," in *Slouching Towards Bethlehem* (New York: Farrar, Straus and Giroux, 1990), 124–27. David Cavallo reads the Diggers' mid-sixties activities and "life-acts" as a riff on America's tradition of "self-reliant individualism" and the "malleable" sense of self that it often engenders. While Americans often exercise this individualism in " 'Free' enterprise—the 'performance' of buying and selling," as Cavallo puts it, "Grogan, Coyote, Berg, other Diggers and serious hippies did more than challenge this equation. They reversed it . . . They substituted a free life for free enterprise. Their versions of self-reliance and of becoming self-made had nothing to do with work, careers, economic competition, possessions or status-seeking." *A Fiction of the Past: The Sixties in American History* (New York: St. Martin's Press, 1999), 102, 144.

## I I ★ REVOLUTION FOR THE HELL OF IT

263 **"holy clown"**: Howard Zinn, "Remembering Abbie," afterword to Abbie Hoffman, *The Autobiography of Abbie Hoffman* (New York: Four Walls Eight Windows, 2000), 305.

263 **"a born rascal"**: Hoffman, *Autobiography,* 91.

264 **"waves of immigrants"**: Ibid., 87.

264 **"strait jackets"**: Ibid., 93.

264 **"Flatbush Conservative Club contingent"**: Free [Abbie Hoffman], *Revolution for the Hell of It* (1968; New York: Thunder's Mouth Press, 2005), 25.

264 **"money should be abolished"**: Jason Epstein, *The Great Conspiracy Trial* (New York: Random House, 1970), 335.

264 **"got the point"**: Free [Abbie Hoffman], *Revolution for the Hell of It,* 33.

265 **"the Wedge"**: For a detailed account, see Norman Mailer, *The Armies of the Night* (1968; New York: Penguin, 1994), 272–78.

265 **"We would *be* a party"**: Paul Krassner, *Confessions of a Raving, Unconfined Nut* (New York: Simon & Schuster, 1993), 157.

265 **"the kind of party you had fun at"**: Epstein, *Great Conspiracy Trial,* 338.

265 **"Yippies say if it's not fun"**: Jerry Rubin, *Do It!* (New York: Simon & Schuster, 1970), 85.

265 **"Energy—excitement—fun—fierceness—exclamation point!"**: Free [Abbie Hoffman], *Revolution for the Hell of It,* 81.

266 **"eternal bliss"**: Hoffman, *Autobiography,* 165.

266 **"naked swim-ins in the gym pool"**: Abbie Hoffman, *Woodstock Nation* (New York: Vintage, 1969), 34.

266 **"With Yippism"**: Hoffman, *Autobiography,* 165.

266 **"For Fun and Freedom"**: Epstein, *Great Conspiracy Trial,* 340.

267 **"If you gave good quote"**: Krassner, *Confessions,* 160–61.

267 **"a direct threat to our theater-in-the-streets"**: "The Yippies Are Going to Chicago," reprinted in Free [Abbie Hoffman], *Revolution for the Hell of It,* 104.

267 "a huge rock-folk festival": Ibid., 105–7.

268 "slow-motion car chase": Krassner, *Confessions,* 162–63.

268 "peace offerings of apple pies": Hoffman, *Autobiography,* 152.

269 his "wife," a sow named Piggy Wiggy: Ibid., 153.

269 "Perfect Mess": Free [Abbie Hoffman], *Revolution for the Hell of It,* 122.

269 "'greasers,' motorcycle toughs": Todd Gitlin, *The Sixties: Years of Hope, Days of Rage* (New York: Bantam, 1987), 329.

270 "They charged, clubbed, gassed, and mauled": Ibid., 327.

270 "right across the table": Hoffman, *Autobiography,* 159, 160.

271 "Conspire, hell": J. Anthony Lukas, *The Barnyard Epithet and Other Obscenities: Notes on the Chicago Conspiracy Trial* (New York: Harper & Row, 1970), 12.

271 "illegitimate father": Ibid., 16.

271 "the country's top Yippie": Epstein, *Great Conspiracy Trial,* 429.

271 "self-serving": Lukas, *Barnyard Epithet,* 73, 74. See also Schultz, *Motion Will Be Denied: A New Report on the Chicago Conspiracy Trial* (New York: William Morrow, 1972), 217.

271 "regarded himself as the embodiment": Lukas, *Barnyard Epithet,* 45.

271 "in a silent dare to the court": Ibid., 27. See also Schultz, *Motion Will Be Denied,* 128.

272 "allegiances": Schultz, *Motion Will Be Denied,* 14.

272 "Why don't we settle this right here and now": Lukas, *Barnyard Epithet,* 72; see also Epstein, *Great Conspiracy Trial,* 361.

272 When an undercover cop denied: Schultz, *Motion Will Be Denied,* 143.

272 "seriously Abbie and Jerry's statement": Ibid., 128–29.

273 "Fineglass," "Weintraub," "Weinrus," and "Weinrub": Ibid., 173.

273 "mirth": Ibid., 164.

273 "revolutionary discipline": Epstein, *Great Conspiracy Trial,* 256.

273 "constitutional rights": Ibid., 252.

274 "the kind of party you had fun at": Ibid., 338.

274 "I know those guys on the wall": Ibid., 428. See also Lukas, *Barnyard Epithet,* 78.

275 "to show that we were in the tradition": 445 F.2d 226: *Abbie Hoffman, Appellant, v. United States of America, Appellee,* United States Court of Appeals, District of Columbia Circuit. 445 F.2d 226. Argued December 18, 1970. Decided March 29, 1971. As Amended April 1, 1971. Paragraph IV.

275 "P. T. Barnum of the Revolution": Rubin, *Do It!,* unnumbered front matter.

276 "The recipe for revolution": Gerard J. DeGroot, *The Sixties Unplugged: A Kaleidoscopic History of a Disorderly Decade* (Cambridge, MA: Harvard University Press, 2008), 264.

## 12 ★ MUSTANGERS HAVE MORE FUN

278 "14 interlocking companies," "a leader of men": "The Entourage," *Wild in the Streets.* Dir. Barry Shearer. Perf. Shelly Winters, Christopher Jones. United States: American International Pictures, 1968.

279 "We're 52%": "Fourteen or Fight," *Wild in the Streets.*

279 "the biggest block party in history": "Heeding the Call," *Wild in the Streets.*

279 "the pursuit of happiness": "Victory," *Wild in the Streets.*

279 "America's greatest contribution": "Maiden Speech," *Wild in the Streets.*

280 "good old patriotic drunk": "High Crimes," *Wild in the Streets.*

280 "a happy trip, a *voting* trip," "They've been looking": "Switching Sides," *Wild in the Streets.*

280 **"retirement homes"**: "Golden Years," *Wild in the Streets*.

280 **"immense wealth," "We're going to put everyone"**: "Over 10," *Wild in the Streets*.

283 ***"So will you all do me a favor"***: Gerald Nachman, *Seriously Funny: The Rebel Comedians of the 1950s and 1960s* (New York: Pantheon, 2003), 487; italics in original.

283 **"things and attitudes"**: Quoted in William J. Stanton et al., *Fundamentals of Marketing* (New York: McGraw-Hill, 1994), 153. Circulation figure also on p. 153.

283 **"personal power"**: Stewart Brand, "Purpose," *Whole Earth Catalog*, Fall 1968, 2.

284 **"God is a verb"**: R. Buckminster Fuller, "God Is a Verb," *Whole Earth Catalog*, Fall 1968, 4.

284 **"act out our fantasies"**: Unattributed poem from the *Realist*, *Whole Earth Catalog*, Fall 1968, 44.

284 **"Come alive!"**: Pepsi Generation Advertisement, Description: Come Alive, You're the Pepsi Generation, Agency: Batton, Barton, Durstine & Osborn; National Museum of American History, Archives Center, Coll. 111, Box 1, Folder 13.

284 **"Un-Cola," "Dodge Rebellion," "Mustangers," "Today, millions"**: Advertisements cited in Thomas Frank, *The Conquest of Cool* (Chicago: University of Chicago Press, 1997), 82–87, 101–2.

284 **"Sugar swings"**: Sugar advertisement, *Time*, March 4, 1966, 3.

284 **"Happenings Are Happening"**: "Happenings Are Happening," *Time*, March 4, 1966, 76–77. Consistent with Bill Graham's commercial wishes for the Trips Festival, this article takes the form of an "entertainment" review.

285 **"a stripped-down, flexible, 'democratic' arrangement"**: Frank, *Conquest of Cool*, 101.

286 **"These hip outlaws"**: Gitlin, *The Sixties*, 386.

286 **"We Shall Overcome"**: David Carter, *Stonewall: The Riots That Sparked the Gay Revolution* (New York: St. Martin's Griffin, 2004), 150.

287 **"insane hippie drag queens"**: Http://www.cockettes.com/history1.html. Accessed August 27, 2012.

287 **"Yellow Submarine"**: Perry, *The Haight-Ashbury*, 106.

287 **"rock and roll music"**: John Sinclair, "Rock and Roll Is a Weapon of Cultural Revolution," in Bloom, *"Takin' It to the Streets,"* 301. David Cavallo writes of the era, "Relatively little of the music composed by the Grateful Dead, the Band, Zappa, Young, Hendrix or Dylan, in his post-folk music incarnation, contained explicit political 'messages.' In his autobiography, Levon Helm of the Band said, with some exaggeration, 'none of us ever thought to write a song about all the shit that was going on back then: war, revolution, civil war, turmoil' " (168).

288 **Yippies staged a mock police raid**: Hoffman, *Woodstock Nation*, 128–29.

288 **"the old America"**: "The days of audience died with the old America," in "The Yippies Are Going to Chicago," 106.

288 **"For the most part"**: Ellen Willis, "The Cultural Revolution Saved from Drowning," *The New Yorker* (September 1969), reprinted in *Out of the Vinyl Deeps: Ellen Willis on Rock Music*, ed. Nona Willis Aronowitz (Minneapolis: University of Minnesota Press, 2011), 184.

288 **"crumpl[ing]" to the stage**: Hoffman, *Woodstock Nation*, 143.

288 **"real leaders"**: Epstein, *Great Conspiracy Trial*, 350.

289 **"the za-za world"**: This and subsequent quotes in this paragraph are from Hoffman, *Woodstock Nation*, 5–7. In his recent memoir, *Who I Am* (New York: HarperCollins, 2012), Townshend himself takes a sober look at the episode, seems to regret his violent onstage reactions (both to Hoffman and to filmmaker Michael Wadleigh), and claims to share the Yippie! opinion of the za-za world the festival created: "Woodstock—a crock of shit in the estimation of at least two grouchy folk who had

taken the stage: Abbie Hoffman and me—came to represent a revolution for musicians and music lovers." Unlike Hoffman, however, this member of what he himself
calls rock's "aristocracy" refrains from saying *why* this seeming revolution may have
been a "crock of shit" (180–83).

290 **"Sly's ecstatic exuberance"**: Steve Lake's liner notes quoted in Rickey Vincent, *Funk:
The Music, the People, and the Rhythm of the One* (New York: St. Martin's, 1996), 94.

291 **"There were whites as well as blacks"**: Greil Marcus, *Mystery Train: Images of America in Rock 'n' Roll Music* (1975; New York: Penguin, 2008), 69.

291 **"Sly Stone *owned* pop music"**: Vincent, *Funk,* 90; emphasis in original.

292 **"Who needs the bullet when you've got the ballot?"**: "Chocolate City," George
Clinton, Bootsy Collins, Bernie Worrel. Parliament. Casablanca 831, May 1975. It
bears mentioning that George Clinton offered *himself* in 1992 as the alternative presidential candidate to George (H. W. Bush and Bill) Clinton.

## 13 ★ DOING IT YOURSELF, GETTING THE JOKE

293 **"Peace!"**: Jeff Chang and DJ Kool Herc, *Can't Stop, Won't Stop: A History of the
Hip-Hop Generation* (New York: St. Martin's, 2005), 76. Bronx history and episode
derived from ibid., 68–79.

294 **caught this new wave of urban creativity**: Story of Clive and Cindy Campbell
derived from ibid., 81–86.

294 **"Forget melody, chorus, songs"**: Ibid., 94.

295 **"broke daylight"**: Ibid., 92.

295 **"comic moves"**: Will Hermes, *Love Goes to Buildings on Fire: Five Years in New York
That Changed Music Forever* (New York: Faber & Faber, 2011), 257.

295 **"over a ritual of motion and fun"**: Chang and Herc, *Can't Stop,* 120.

295 **"Peace, Love, Unity, and Having Fun"**: Ibid., 105.

296 **"If you break on the cement"**: Joseph Schloss, *Foundation: B-Boys, B-Girls, and Hip-
Hop Culture in New York* (New York: Oxford University Press, 2009), 95.

296 **"how innocent and pure"**: Ibid., 96. For an excellent history and analysis of dynam-
ics "in the cypher," see ibid., chapter 5, as well as Jorge "Popmaster Fabel" Pabon,
"Physical Graffiti: The History of Hip-Hop Dance," in *That's the Joint! The Hip-Hop
Studies Reader,* ed. Murray Forman and Mark Anthony Neal (New York: Routledge,
2012), 57–61.

296 **"four elements"**: Chang and Herc, *Can't Stop,* 90, 110.

296 **"'Cause it was a whole gig, y'know?"**: Ibid., 130.

297 **crafted new tools**: To be sure, it was in 1975 and 1976 that two college dropouts,
Bill Gates and Steve Jobs, emerged from their respective garages and founded their
revolutionary microcomputer companies.

297 **Historically, DIY is the American way**: The American magazine *Do It Yourself*
emerged in the 1950s to empower homeowners in the costly world of commercial
contractors. *Readymade* magazine appeared half a century later and updated this
domestic ethic for millennial hipsters.

298 **"Death to Invaders," "You could get impaled"**: "Pacific Ocean Park," "The Cove,"
*Dogtown and Z-Boys,* Orsi, A., Peralta, S., Stecyk, C., Penn, S., Kubo, S., Biniak, B.,
Sony Pictures Classics, Vans "Off the Wall" Productions, ADP Productions, &
Columbia TriStar Home Entertainment (2002).

299 **"clubhouse," "pirates"**: "Capt. Hook & the Pirates," *Dogtown.*

299 **"Part of the thrill was knowing"**: "Riding Swimming Pools," *Dogtown.*

300 **"Skaters," Stecyk wrote that year**: *Skateboarder* article quoted in "The Dogtown
Articles," *Dogtown.*

300 **"Bet you can't ride it, pig!":** April 1977 *Skateboarder* article reprinted in C. R. Stecyk III and Glen E. Friedman, *DogTown: The Legend of the Z-Boys* (New York: Burning Flags Press, 2000), 56.

300 **In the fall of 1977:** "The Birth of Vertical," *Dogtown.*

301 **"guys didn't seem like they were having":** "Jay Adams," *Dogtown.*

302 **"crazed quaking uncertainty," "a strong element of cure":** Lester Bangs, "Of Pop and Pies and Fun: A Program for Mass Liberation in the Form of a Stooges Review, or, Who's the Fool?," reprinted in *Psychotic Reactions and Carburetor Dung: The Work of a Legendary Critic: Rock 'n' Roll as Literature and Literature as Rock 'n' Roll*, ed. Greil Marcus (New York: Vintage, 1987), 32.

302 **"in the faces of performers":** Ibid., 36.

303 **"a jock strap with red lipstick swastikas":** Meltzer article cited in Steve Waksman, *This Ain't the Summer of Love: Conflict and Crossover in Heavy Metal and Punk* (Berkeley: University of California Press, 2010), 115.

303 **"funniest":** Andy Shernoff, interview by Jason Gross, Perfect Sound Forever, May 1996, http://www.furious.com/perfect/dictators.html. Accessed September 1, 2012.

303 **"We knocked 'em dead in Dallas":** "The Next Big Thing," the Dictators, *Go Girl Crazy!* KE 33348, Epic Records, USA, 1975.

303 **"Hippies," "We tell jokes to make you laugh":** "Master Race Rock," the Dictators.

304 **"Ooooo-wheee-aaah-ooooo":** "(I Live for) Cars and Girls," the Dictators.

305 **"Now I'm a guide for the CIA":** "Havana Affair," The Ramones, *The Ramones*, Sire Records, 1976.

305 **"that there was a line between":** Tricia Henry, *Break All Rules!: Punk Rock and the Making of a Style* (Ann Arbor: University of Michigan Press, 1989), 108.

306 **"Rock 'n' roll is supposed to be fun":** Johnny Rotten quoted in Virginia Boston, *Punk Rock* (New York: Penguin, 1978), 108.

306 **"one of the first punk bands":** Nicholas Rombes, *A Cultural Dictionary of Punk: 1974–1982* (New York: Continuum, 2009), 61.

308 **To listen to their scorching diatribes:** Hardcore historian Steven Blush writes: "Punk gave lip service to 'Do It Yourself' (D.I.Y.) and democratization of the Rock scene, but Hardcore transcended all commercial and corporate concerns. . . . If you played Hardcore, you couldn't possibly have been in it for the money, although you might've gone for the glory. . . . Hardcore established a new definition of musical success: in non-economic terms. Sociologists might see this as an example of 'tribal syndicalism': unlike money-oriented economies, Hardcore was an objective-oriented, community-based culture—like a commune or an armed fortress." *American Hardcore* (New York: Feral House, 2001), 275.

308 **"I did my usual swan dive":** Interview with Jello Biafra in Vivian Vale, *Pranks! Devious Deeds and Mischievous Mirth* (San Francisco: RE/Search Publications, 1987), 61.

308 **"exclamation point":** Ryan Moore, *Sells Like Teen Spirit: Music, Youth Culture, and Social Crisis* (New York: New York University Press, 2010), 37.

309 **"shrewd youth":** This quotation and those in the following two paragraphs are from Nathaniel Hawthorne, "My Kinsman, Major Molineux," in *Nathaniel Hawthorne's Tales*, ed. James McIntosh (New York: W. W. Norton, 1987), 14–17.

312 **a nation's "consciousness":** See Frantz Fanon, *The Wretched of the Earth*, trans. Richard Philcox (1961; New York: Grove, 2004), 170–80.

315 **cleverly precede our 3-D reality:** Apologies, of course, to Jean Baudrillard, *The Precession of Simulacra* (Ann Arbor: University of Michigan Press, 1994).

315 **The video-game proponent Jane McGonigal:** Jane McGonigal, *Reality Is Broken: Why Games Make Us Better and How They Can Change the World* (New York: Penguin, 2011), 32–33.

316 **"dance more"**: Ibid., 347.

316 **"reward circuitry of the brain"**: Ibid., 33.

317 **Tom Bissell tells a harrowing tale**: Bissell writes, "Video games and cocaine feed on my impulsiveness, reinforce my love of solitude, and make me feel good and bad in equal measure. The crucial difference is that I believe in what video games want to give me, while the bequest of cocaine is one I loathe and distrust. As for GTA IV, there is surely a reason it is the game I most enjoyed playing on coke, constantly promising myself 'Just one more mission' after a few fat lines." A video-game critic and designer (in addition to being one of his generation's most deeply thoughtful writers), Bissell is genuine in trusting what certain games "want to give him" (the book performs a trenchant reading of *Grand Theft Auto*'s narratology), but the compulsive, reactive, and chemically charged gaming habit he describes better resembles the mind-blowing *fiero* that the gaming industry and Jane McGonigal prize. Which is to say, the compulsion itself is nothing to trust. *Extra Lives: Why Video Games Matter* (New York: Vintage, 2011), 181.

317 **A recent Google search**: September 10, 2012.

317 **The American Psychiatric Association has the condition slated**: A study of 3,034 Singaporean schoolchildren recently published in the journal *Pediatrics* concluded that socially at-risk children were drawn to gaming, which in turn exacerbated social pathologies: "Greater amounts of gaming, lower social competence, and greater impulsivity seemed to act as risk factors for becoming pathological gamers, whereas depression, anxiety, social phobias, and lower school performance seemed to act as outcomes of pathological gaming." Douglas A. Gentile, Ph.D., Hyekyung Choo, Ph.D., Albert Liau, Ph.D., Timothy Sim, Ph.D., Dongdong Li, M.A., Daniel Fung, M.D., and Angeline Khoo, Ph.D., "Pathological Video Game Use Among Youths: A Two-Year Longitudinal Study," *Pediatrics* 127, no. 2 (2011), e319–e329; published ahead of print January 17, 2011.

317 **"go beyond flow and *fiero*"**: McGonigal, *Reality Is Broken,* 43.

317 **"very big games represent the future"**: Ibid., 348.

317 **"We did not owe any"**: David Kocieniewski, "GE's Strategies Let It Avoid Taxes Altogether," *New York Times,* March 24, 2011. See also Megan McCardle, "Did GE Really Pay No Taxes in 2010?" *TheAtlantic.com,* March 29, 2011.

318 **It was the latest coup**: "Yes Men Claim Hoax GE Tax Press Release," MSNBC, March 13, 2011.

318 **His advice for activating the citizens' bodies**: Saul Alinsky, *Rules for Radicals* (1971; New York: Vintage, 1989), 138–39; emphasis added.

320 **"the queen and high priestess"**: Marcyliena Morgan, *The Real Hiphop: Battling for Knowledge, Power, and Respect in the LA Underground* (Durham, NC: Duke University Press, 2009), 134.

320 **"crowd-pleasing anthem," "us[ing] gangsta, a hiphop term"**: Ibid., 156–57. Project Blowed account drawn from ibid., 130–59. For an incisive history of early hip-hop's gender politics and feminist wave, see Jeffrey O. G. Ogbar, *Hip-Hop Revolution: The Culture and Politics of Rap* (Lawrence: University Press of Kansas, 2007), 72–104.

321 **"beergutboyrock"**: "Riot Girl Manifesto," *Bikini Kill Zine* 2, 1991.

321 **"rock 'n' roll fun"**: Sleater-Kinney, "You're No Rock N' Roll Fun," *All Hands on the Bad One,* Kill Rock Stars, 2000.

321 **new wave of fire-breathing zines**: Sarah and Jen Wolfe Collection of Riot Grrrl and Underground Music Zines, MsC 878, Special Collections and Archives, University of Iowa Libraries; http://www.lib.uiowa.edu/spec-coll/msc/ToMsC900/MsC878/wolfesarahandjenzines.html. Sample zine titles accessed September 1, 2012.

321 **"When was the last time"**: Katha Pollitt, "Talk the Talk, Walk the SlutWalk," *The Nation,* July 18/25, 2011, 9.

321 **"Volunteers" staged disruptive pranks:** Didi Kirsten Tatlow, "A Merry Band of Rights Pranksters," *New York Times,* December 4, 2012.

323 **"really diverse group of agents":** Charlie Todd, *Causing a Scene* (New York: Harper-Collins, 2009), 695 of 3253 in Google eBook.

323 **"clueless," "misinformed":** Ibid., 1198 of 3253.

323 **"The golden rule of pranks":** Interview with Charlie Todd by Shelley DuBois, "How to Get 4,000 People to Take Off Their Pants," *CNNMoney,* April 20, 2012, http://management.fortune.cnn.com/2012/04/20/improv-everywhere-charlie-todd/. Accessed September 9, 2012. Todd's golden rule is no joke: pranks pulled with vicious intent or with no forethought to the consequences—like the pot brownies two University of Colorado students served their classmates and professor on "bring food day," resulting in several trips to the hospital and multiple felony charges to the pranksters—are in fact a threat to civil society: they cause mayhem, anger, and physical harm. They make citizens retreat in fear and resentment. But pranks in the tradition of American fun nimbly follow this golden rule; their collective fun sustains itself on the widespread pleasure of getting the joke. Sometimes a killjoy is the butt of the joke, sometimes society itself is the butt, but the punch line is illuminating, not hurtful. "Police: 2 University of Colorado Students Arrested for Feeding Pot Brownies to Classmates, Professor." U.S. News on NBC.News.com, December 10, 2012, http://usnews.nbcnews.com/_news/2012/12/09/15797353-police-2-university -of-colorado-students-arrested-for-feeding-pot-brownies-to-classmates-professor?lite.

323 **Improv Everywhere is radically civil:** In his interview with Shelley DuBois, Charlie Todd makes it plain: "I think a big appeal of our projects is that there is no agenda behind them—it's comedy for comedy's sake." They may not be driving an agenda (even when disrupting Best Buy's commerce), but their fun breaks the fourth wall of civil society: between the ostensible performers and observers of everyday social inter-action. Which is to say, even with "comedy for comedy's sake," they call out citizens to react and participate in what wouldn't otherwise be a public forum.

325 **some of the nation's most authoritarian citizens:** In 2008, former U.S. senator and Republican presidential hopeful Rick Santorum associated the Democratic Party with Woodstock, sexual freedom, and what he believed to be their misappropriation of the Founding Fathers' ideas of liberty. Channeling the spirit of William Brad-ford describing Merry Mount, Santorum said, "Woodstock is the great American orgy. This is who the Democratic Party has become. They have become the party of Woodstock. They prey upon our most basic primal lusts, and that's sex. And the whole abortion culture, it's not about life. It's about sexual freedom. That's what it's about. Homosexuality. It's about sexual freedom. All of the things are about sexual freedom, and they hate to be called on them. They try to somehow or other tie this to the founding fathers' vision of liberty, which is bizarre. It's ridiculous." Charles M. Blow, "Santorum and the Sexual Revolution," *New York Times,* March 2, 2012.

325 **an academic cottage industry:** Among the recent scholarly books on the subject (not to mention countless scholarly articles) are Rachel Bowditch, *On the Edge of Utopia: Performance and Ritual at Burning Man* (Chicago: University of Chicago Press, 2010); Katherine K. Chen, *Enabling Creative Chaos: The Organization Behind the Burning Man Event* (Chicago: University of Chicago Press, 2009); *Theatre in a Crowded Fire: Ritual and Spirituality at Burning Man,* ed. L. Gilmore. and M. Van Proyen (Berkeley: University of California Press, 2010).

326 **three hundred thousand ravers:** Isaac Brekken, "The New Stars in Vegas: D.J.'s and Dance Music," *New York Times,* June 11, 2012.

# *Index*

## ABOUT THE AUTHOR

JOHN BECKMAN is a professor of English at the U.S. Naval Academy. His writing has appeared in *The Washington Post, Granta, Book, McSweeney's, Arizona Quarterly,* and elsewhere. His novel, *The Winter Zoo,* was named a *New York Times* Notable Book of Year. He lives in Annapolis, Maryland, with his wife, the writer and critic Marcela Valdes, and their baby daughter.

A NOTE ON THE TYPE

This book was set in Adobe Garamond. Designed for the Adobe Corporation by Robert Slimbach, the fonts are based on types first cut by Claude Garamond (c. 1480–1561). Garamond was a pupil of Geoffroy Tory and is believed to have followed the Venetian models, although he introduced a number of important differences, and it is to him that we owe the letter we now know as "old style."

Composed by North Market Street Graphics,
Lancaster, Pennsylvania

Printed and bound by Berryville Graphics,
Berryville, Virginia

Designed by Cassandra J. Pappas